Food, Texts, and Cultures in
Latin America and Spain

Food, Texts, and Cultures in Latin America and Spain

*Rafael Climent-Espino and
Ana M. Gómez-Bravo, editors*

VANDERBILT UNIVERSITY PRESS
Nashville, Tennessee

© 2020 by Vanderbilt University Press
Nashville, Tennessee 37235
All rights reserved
First printing 2020

Library of Congress Cataloging-in-Publication Data

Names: Climent-Espino, Rafael, 1977- editor. | Gómez-Bravo, Ana M. (Ana María), editor.
Title: Food, texts, and cultures in Latin America and Spain / Rafael Climent-Espino and Ana M. Gómez-Bravo, eds.
Description: Nashville : Vanderbilt University Press, [2019] | Includes bibliographical references and index. | Summary: "Approaches Hispanic and Latin American food from the perspective of literary and cultural studies. Fourteen essays apply a food lens to colonial studies, ethnic and racial studies, gender and sexuality studies, and studies of power dynamics, nationalisms and nation building, theories of embodiment, and identity"— Provided by publisher.
Identifiers: LCCN 2019031046 (print) | LCCN 2019031047 (ebook) | ISBN 9780826522818 (hardcover) | ISBN 9780826522825 (paperback) | ISBN 9780826522832 (ebook)
Subjects: LCSH: Food in literature. | Cooking in literature. | Latin American literature—History and criticism. | Spanish literature—History and criticism. | Food habits—Latin America. | Food habits—Spain. | Cookbooks—Latin America—History. | Cookbooks—Spain—History.
Classification: LCC PN56.F59 F685 20194 (print) | LCC PN56.F59 (ebook) | DDC 641.30098—dc23
LC record available at https://lccn.loc.gov/2019031046
LC ebook record available at https://lccn.loc.gov/2019031047

This study was supported in part by funds from the Vice Provost for Research at Baylor University.

CONTENTS

Introduction: Food Studies in Latin American and Spanish Contexts 1

1. Food, Blood, and a Jewish *Raza* in Fifteenth-Century Spain   39
   ANA M. GÓMEZ-BRAVO
2. Taste and Taxonomy of Native Food in Hispanic America: 1492–1640   76
   GREGORIO SALDARRIAGA ESCOBAR
3. Still Life, Food, and Fiction: Diversions from the Colonial Baroque   99
   RODRIGO LABRIOLA
4. Furniture and Equipment in the Royal Kitchens of Early Modern Spain   115
   CAROLYN A. NADEAU
5. Enlightened Meals: Literary Perspectives on Food in Eighteenth-Century Spain   150
   MARÍA ÁNGELES PÉREZ SAMPER
6. Madrid: Cuisine as Cultural Melting Pot   178
   MARÍA DEL CARMEN SIMÓN PALMER
7. Beyond the Recipes: Authorship, Text, and Context in Canonical Spanish Cookbooks   201
   MARÍA PAZ MORENO
8. Cooks and Ladies: The Writing of Culinary Knowledge in Argentina in the Late Nineteenth and Early Twentieth Centuries   220
   PAULA CALDO

9. The Evolution of Mexican Cuisine: Five Gastronomical Seasons, *Mole*, *Pozole*, *Tamal*, *Tortilla*, and *Chile Relleno* 238
   ADOLFO CASTAÑÓN

10. What the Palate Knows: Nicaragua's Culinary Cultures 272
    SERGIO RAMÍREZ

11. A Gastrocritical Reading of Miguel Ángel Asturias's Early Narrative: *Legends of Guatemala*, *The President*, and *Men of Maize* 295
    RAFAEL CLIMENT-ESPINO

12. On Hunger and Brazilian Literature 318
    SABRINA SEDLMAYER

13. Food in Recent Cuban Literature (1990–2016): From Hero in the Special Period Fiction to Almost Zero in the Generation Zero 340
    RITA DE MAESENEER

Index 365

INTRODUCTION

Food Studies in Latin American and Spanish Contexts

Ana M. Gómez-Bravo
and Rafael Climent-Espino

A GROWING INTEREST IN food studies, particularly in relation to economic, environmental, political, and cultural issues, has translated into a large number of publications across a wide range of venues. From books such as Marion Nestle's *Food Politics* or Michael Pollan's *The Omnivore's Dilemma* to the Slow Food movement, popular academic journals such as *Gastronomica, Food and Foodways,* and *Food, Culture, and Society,* and city-specific periodicals such as *Edible Communities,* food consumption choices are understood to have enormous impact on the environment, the socioeconomics of food access, and health and disease prevention. New scientific research on metabolic diseases (including state-of-the-art "omics" disciplines such as genomics, proteomics, and metabolomics) and other types of medical research in key areas such as nutrient needs and deficiencies or eating disorders have helped bring food studies to the fore. At the same time, fiction, mass media, and social media have increasingly been preoccupied with what people eat, along with the social, political, and environmental context of food. The consistent popularity over the last twenty years of films such as *What's Cooking* (2000) and *Fuera de carta* (*Chef's Special*; 2008), documentaries like *King Corn* (2007) and *The Meaning of Food* (2004), and fiction like Josep Pla's *Lo que hemos comido* (2013) and Cristina Campos's *Pan de limón con semillas de amapola* (2018) shows that the centrality of food remains inescapable.[1] Food's strong presence in social and visual media—for example, in the numerous iterations of Masterchef; food blogs like *Gastro Andalusí* (Jiménez), *El Comidista-El País* (López Iturriaga), and *México en mi cocina* (Martínez); and Instagram posts—brings attention to the visual components of food commercialization, consumption, and sociability, prompting new concepts and terms like "foodography" or "food porn," coined by Rosalind Coward. The need to combine cultural studies with those based on the biological sciences has been underscored in several collective volumes in the field of food studies, most recently from a historical approach by Jennifer J. Wallach and Michael Wise, from a literary standpoint by Rita De Maeseneer,[2] and from an interdisciplinary perspective in the studies collected by Montserrat Piera and Ángeles Mateo del Pino and María N. Pascual Soler, all of which correctly warn against trivializing a focus on food in academic humanities research.

From a curricular perspective, the rise of food studies programs in university structures and curricula clearly shows that food is a junction where diverse disciplines in the humanities, social and natural sciences, health and nutrition, and medicine can meet and begin productive dialogues and collaborations. The critical paths that lead from such intersections point to an exciting role for the humanities by creating a widening interest in interdisciplinary research and collaboration, for which scholars such as Warren Belasco have made a compelling case. As Lorna Piatti-Farnell and Donna L. Brien point out in the introduction to *The Routledge Companion to Literature and Food*, university courses on food fill up quickly, posing a strong pedagogical platform from which to engage students across disciplines, as well as presenting the humanities in a synergistic way with other fields. The role of the humanities in food studies goes beyond the analysis of mimetic representation to become a critical player in the disciplinary intersectionality at the core of food studies. At a time when the disconnect between people and the soil has grown to reportedly unprecedented levels, the study of food, texts, and cultures can contribute valuable insights to food studies, and the humanities can make a significant impact, adding meaning, creating content, and engaging powerful analytical lenses. An exciting related development is the incorporation of food topics into the Spanish curriculum, an increasingly popular addition to Spanish courses made easier by the recent publication of textbooks on Hispanic food and culture geared toward students enrolled in secondary and higher-education Spanish classes (Gómez-Bravo, *Comida*).

Anthropological approaches were among the first to produce important studies on food and culture and food history. Susan Bordo, Mary Douglas, Margaret Mead, Paul Rozin, and others opened exciting new vistas that placed food at the center of social, religious, ethnic, and literary practices. In *The Raw and the Cooked*, structural anthropologist Lévi-Strauss used binary oppositions in sociocultural analysis, later drawing a culinary triangle that presented cooking as a language based on unconscious structures, borrowing elements of language analysis: "Thus we can hope to discover for each specific case how the cooking of a society is a language in which it unconsciously translates its structure—or else resigns itself, still unconsciously, to revealing its contradictions" ("The Culinary Triangle" 595). Social anthropologist Mary Douglas highlighted the symbolic power of food prohibitions and their role in the creation of boundaries. From the standpoint of cultural materialism, Marvin Harris pinpointed the adaptive needs that weigh into food choice and religious food prohibitions. He viewed culture as influenced by the material conditions from which it arises and put forth a functionalist explanation for food-centered religious laws. In her chapter included in this volume, Ana M. Gómez-Bravo analyzes the combined efforts of medical theory, religious belief, and Church doctrine in channeling an understanding of food as racialized marker. In *Distinction*, Pierre Bourdieu approached food from the standpoint of class and developed the concepts of *habitus*, or acquired dispositions, and cultural capital, exploring their role in the formation of taste in reference to art, music, and gastronomy. Bourdieu's sociological emphasis, as well as the important issues raised by anthropologists, would resonate with many scholars working from a variety of fields and looking to examine the implications of combined biological and cultural approaches to food studies.

Other critics such as Michel de Certeau pointed to the limits of a purely sociological study that leaves out the individual practices and appropriations that take place in the everyday. In a related development, the study of the everyday and the material, which had thus far seemed to fall outside the study of culture, received a boost from social historians linked to the Annales School. A prominent such historian, Fernand Braudel exemplified the productive results of a combined study of components of daily life, such as food, with social and economic considerations. In a similar vein, through a miller's particular cosmovision of a universe constituted by cheese and worms, Carlo Ginzburg presented a way to look at history through a microhistorical lens that emphasizes culture and a study of mentalities and subaltern cultures. Also using a historical outlook, Massimo Montanari illustrated the cultural nature of all food-related actions. Jack Goody similarly emphasized the intertwining of culture and the material world, particularly in relation to the shaping action of technologies. Following in Goody's footsteps and using a historical scope, Sidney W. Mintz showed how the study of one food commodity, sugar, could help explain major changes in industrial and capitalist systems. In *Contrapunteo Cubano* (*Cuban Counterpoint*), Fernando Ortiz developed the concept of transculturation through a cultural and biological analysis of sugar and tobacco as crops, commodities, and food in order to examine cultural exchange in Cuba. Similarly, in *La isla que se repite* (*The Repeating Island*), Antonio Benítez Rojo used the Caribbean's biological and cultural diversity, with particular attention to sugar as food and commodity, to study the region's complexities, fragmentation, dispersion, and instability. Carole Counihan has highlighted the importance of examining the intersections of food, gender, and power from a feminist and anthropological perspective, while Eduardo Viveiros de Castro and Peter Skafish have argued for a decolonization of thought, proposing a metaphysics that cannibalistic practices of the Amazon basin help conceptualize.

Gastrocriticism, a term coined by Ronald Tobin, attempts to harness the multidisciplinary endeavor that a focus on food elicits. The emphasis of gastrocriticism on personal, political, gendered, and national identities, as well as aesthetic and social movements, has been highlighted by De Maeseneer in contemporary Caribbean literature and by Maria Christou, who has successfully applied it to the study of twentieth-century modernist and postmodernist literature. A similar approach has also proven successful when examining contemporary women's fiction, as evidenced in Sarah Sceats's study. The chapters by Rafael Climent-Espino and Rita De Maeseneer in this volume showcase productive applications of gastrocritical approaches. Placing food at the center of his analysis, and using Arjun Appadurai's concept of gastro-politics, Climent-Espino studies the varying attitudes toward food and nature in two different ethnic groups—Mayas and Ladinos—as presented in Asturias's fiction. De Maeseneer also uses a gastrocritical approach to show the contrasting attitudes toward food in the writing of two different Cuban generations, the one marked by the Special Period and Generation Zero.

From a humanities standpoint, the study of literary texts can enrich a multidisciplinary perspective by suggesting new theoretical and analytical paths or by entering into existing ones. An example may be seen in the study of food commodities such as sugar, coffee, and chocolate. A discussion of the novel *Sab* by Gertrudis Gómez de

Avellaneda, for instance, could include the combined roles of sugar, slavery, and African diaspora, all of which can help us better understand the story's context and content, which in turn provides a powerful narrative of such associations. The established link between the consumption of sugar and that of coffee can lead to a consideration of not only the botanical and commercial spread of coffee but also the culture surrounding cafés. The link between coffee and literary culture is evident in works as different as Leandro Fernández de Moratín's *La comedia nueva o El café*, Benito Pérez Galdós's *La Fontana de Oro*, or Max Aub's *La verdadera historia de la muerte de Francisco Franco*. The café as the locus for the exchange of literary and political ideas can similarly be examined in contrast to alternate establishments and the foods served there. Much like coffee competed with alcohol, and cafés vied with taverns for customers, the emerging cultubar presents a viable alternative as a locus for dialogue and sociability as the café rapidly loses its role in the exchange of ideas and shifts toward an isolationism that relies on Internet access and the use of personal computers (Stabiner). Literary works such as Mario Vargas Llosa's *Conversación en La Catedral*, Pérez Galdós's *Montes de Oca*, and popular television series like *Los ladrones van a la oficina* can be examined for the contrasting role that traditional bars and taverns have had on sociability and group solidarities, whether political or social. Similarly, chocolate can be placed at the center of a discussion on transculturation of both food commodities and attendant cultural practices in its passage from liquid to solid food, from male drink to femminized edible, and from Native American privileged commodity to European bastion of political and social conservatism, linking the study of such works as Juan de Cárdenas's *Primera parte de los problemas y secretos maravillosos de las Indias*, Antonio de Ulloa's *Viaje al Reino del Perú*, Gaspar Betancourt Cisneros's *Escenas cotidianas*, and Laura Esquivel's *Como agua para chocolate*. The cultivation and harvest of the cacao crop is the main axis of Jorge Amado's "cocoa cycle," which is comprised of five novels, the first of which, *Cacau* (*Cocoa*; 1933), must be highlighted for its central importance in Amado's work.

Productive disciplinary intersectionality involving the humanities can engage neurogastronomy's interest in perception, memory, and cognition (Shepherd), which can enrich analyses of food memoirs or food nostalgia in literary and historical accounts of food's role in the colonizing experience (e.g., Fray Bernardino de Sahagún's *Historia general de las cosas de la Nueva España*) or within diasporic communities. Examples include Francisco Delicado's *La lozana andaluza* for the Sephardic community in Rome, Ana Miranda's *Amrik* for the Lebanese community in Brazil, and Oscar Nakasato's *Nihonjin* for the Japanese community in Brazil. At the same time, the study of food narratives in situations of trauma or religious persecution, such as Inquisition or Holocaust records (De Silva; Gitlitz and Davidson), can provide illuminating case studies to use as a backdrop for biocultural research.

The study of literary, technical, and other texts promises to yield exciting results in collaborative efforts within the field of gastroarcheology (Hastorf), with which it shares a focus on textual artifacts. These artifacts are made relevant not only through their own referentiality but also through shared (hermeneutical) efforts to discern the meaning of material objects and the tangible aspects of the experience of those living before us. Literary scholars feature in productive collaborations with journalists and archives in order to engage a centuries-old food heritage that is proving to be extremely meaningful to a contemporary public. Along these lines, a public effort on the part of local governments is similarly generating joined projects among journalists, local chefs, and scholars looking to recover local culinary and ethnic heritage through the combined use of archival research, visual and written adaptations of old recipes, as well as finished dishes. A case in point is the Chef BNE initiative of Madrid's National Library (*Chef BNE*; Minder). In clear alignment with responses to globalization, recent efforts to capitalize on national cuisines, resulting in such brands as Marca España, Marca Perú, and Hecho en México, have been interrogated for the potentially problematic uses of culture and artistic expression at the service of a centralized state power (Martínez-Expósito).

Conversely, meaningful synergies can also be created with other cross-disciplinary approaches such as ecocriticism: current discussions on the status of food in the Anthropocene, for example, in this new age of human-caused climate and environmental change (Menely and Taylor; Trexler). Alexandre Nodari has underscored the role of literature as a speculative anthropology that enables the narration of a contingent ecology. Literary works such as Emilia Pardo Bazán's naturalist *La madre naturaleza,* José María Pereda's panegyric *Peñas arriba,* Juan Rulfo's disenfranchised narrative "Nos han dado la tierra," and Ricardo Güiraldes's elegiac *Don Segundo Sombra,* alongside *La vorágine* by José Eustasio Rivera and *Doña Bárbara* by Rómulo Gallegos, can be examined through this perspective and help shed light on the shifting relationship between humans and their environment. Along a parallel line of inquiry, food studies also encourages an in-depth analysis of their role in globalization studies, following recent approaches such as those found in Bethany Aram, Bartolomé Yun-Casalilla, and James Farrer, including current trends in gastrotourism and traveling cuisines. In a similar vein, Gregorio Saldarriaga's study on the *scala naturae* (Great Chain of Being) included in this volume explains the terms by which colonialism affected the understanding of ecosystems and how the food chain was conceptualized in terms of value differentials assigned to New World food. As an important step toward globalization, the so-called Columbian exchange also helped relate food to nation-building.

Collaboration between the humanities and medical sciences includes inquiries into other areas, such as eating disorders, as framed by Susan Bordo and studied in different periods (e.g., Bell), from medieval and early modern narratives (Bynum; Mazzoni) to such contemporary works as Cielo Latini's *Abzurdah* and Carlos Cuauhtémoc Sánchez's *Los fantasmas del espejo.* In a compelling approach that combines the health and social sciences with literary analysis, Nieves Pascual Soler has studied self-starvation and hunger as a symbolic language and as an emotion of a culturally constructed body. Conversely, the complex relationship among body, perception, and society is at the core of fat studies, which is explored in such venues as the journal *Fat Studies: An Interdiciplinary Journal of Body Weight and Society* and Esther Rothblum and Sondra Solovay's *The Fat Studies Reader*. The mentions of different periods and literary movements invite a similar consideration of food-theory developments in the history of science, as well as their cultural and social impact. Psychological considerations of food choice found in medical texts over a wide time span predate current discussions on food and mental health and should be analyzed alongside other texts for both their social and medical impact. In the sixteenth century, Huarte de San Juan, following Galenic ideas in his *Examen de ingenios para las ciencias*, formulated a theory of the mind that was directly dependent on the food that fed the body and that ultimately dictated mental functions. In spite of being censored by the Inquisition, the book was widely read in Spanish and in translation into several other languages for centuries. Huarte de San Juan's psychobiological and neuropsychological theses are touted as forerunners of current debates on the modularity of the mind within cognitive sciences (García García) and psycholinguistics (Martín-Araguz and Bustamante-Martínez; Virués Ortega). *Examen de ingenios para las ciencias* may also be studied alongside Cervantes's *Don Quijote de la Mancha* and the work of Francisco de Quevedo as prime examples of the productive intersectionality among literature, medicine, and food studies (Nadeau).

The heated debates in such areas as pleasure studies, including neuroaesthetics, present another promising disciplinary junction. Current evidence shows that the pleasure derived from the contemplation of a work of art is no different from that experienced while eating (Christensen; Pearce et al.). As a way to further that debate in literature, one need look no further than Neruda's "Oda al caldillo de congrio" ("Ode to Conger Eel Broth"; where, "through the essences of Chile" the poet promises "you may know heaven"), Laura Esquivel's *Íntimas suculencias*, or Isabel Allende's *Afrodita*. Considering the link between gustatory and aesthetic *taste* can lead to exploring of the manifold ways in which the body and the mind are inescapably intertwined in physical and cultural processes in both literature and material culture (Korsmeyer). In a similar vein, there is a clear conjunction between food studies and sensory studies that can be analyzed in relation to food preparation, ingestion, and food representations (Howes; *Journal of Sensory Studies*). Rodrigo Labriola's contribution to this volume similarly highlights the central role of food aesthetics in seventeenth-century and neo-baroque art in Spain and Latin America. Labriola's analysis of the still life as a foremost pictorial genre helps him bring baroque visual arts to neo-baroque literary rhetoric in a persuasive and innovative move. These connections are relevant before and beyond what have been identified as key moments in Romanticism and Modernity (as studied by Gigante; Lara Nieto).

Menéndez Pidal's oft-quoted attribution of the coining of the expression "buen gusto" to Queen Isabel, alongside late medieval sources that trace the term and concept to a particularly Spanish turn of mind and language, suggest the complex ways in which food, sensory evaluation, and stylized discourse can combine in the context of nation-building narratives. Food's role in creating personal or collective memories is central to the writings of authors such as Alfonso Reyes in *Memorias de cocina y bodega*, while Miguel Ángel Asturias and Pablo Neruda combine memory with the pleasures of gastronomy and commensality in *Comiendo en Hungría*. Food and the gastronomic experience are featured in their own right in the works of such authors as Ramón Rocha Monroy (*Crítica de la sazón pura* and *Todos los cominos conducen aroma*), while others have delved into culinary history (Cunqueiro's *La cocina gallega* and *La cocina cristiana de Occidente*) or cookbook writing (Pardo Bazán's *La cocina española antigua* and *La cocina española moderna*; Carmen de (Colombine) Burgos's *¿Quiere usted comer bien?*). Such a focus on food and the gastronomic pleasures it affords is featured unapologetically in the fiction of such authors as Vázquez Montalbán's *Contra los gourmets*, *Recetas inmorales*, and *Mis almuerzos con gente inquietante*, an interest perhaps most emblematically embodied in the character of Pepe Carvalho, the famous gastronome detective. Along similar lines, Héctor Abad Faciolince's *Tratado de culinaria para mujeres tristes* and Mayra Santos-

Febres's *Tratado de medicina natural para hombres melancólicos* offer compelling examples of fictionalized treatises that engage prescriptive traditions and place the narrative of material practices at the center of fiction writing while exploring gender differentials.

Food-related topics may be perceived as deceptively trivial if approached as superficial elements of life at its more material and ephemeral, consumed without a trace and without a thought. However, food can provide a privileged vantage point that enables a disciplinary paradigm shift, a change in analytic angle that allows for a richer scope engaging multiple perspectives. Rebecca Earle has shown how food study can provide meaningful insight into colonial processes, their environmental impact, and the development of medical theory and practice. Similarly, Ferguson's study documenting the rise of the gastronomic field and locating it within a model of cultural ascendancy in France is one of many that can be deployed as background for exploring gastronomy's use in creating culture differentials. Food can be a powerful tool, helping ground pervasive dichotomies of high and low cuisines and cultures as well as cultural-dominance narratives and imperialism practices. For example, the study of literary texts such as Pablo Neruda's "Oda a la papa" can help explain the central symbolic position of the potato in the Chilean imaginary as both an expression of its ethnic identity ("eres oscura / como nuestra piel, / somos Americanos, / papa, / somos indios") ("you are dark / like our skin, / we are Americans, / potato, / we are Indians"), its geography ("Chiloé marino"), and its gustatory and culinary profile in ways that help set it apart from Inquisitorial, Imperial Spain ("España / inquisidora / negra como águila de sepultura") ("Spain / inquisitorial / black like the eagle over a grave"). Gastronomic borders that both separate and unite communities in situations of contiguity can be explored through the concept of *isogastrias*, a term coined by Emilio Alarcos Llorach (9) and further developed by Rafael Climent-Espino ("Miragens do Japão" 60–70). *Isogastrias* are imagined lines that delimitate ethnic communities according to their particular gastroculinary practices. Similarly, food and cooking helped Fernando Ortiz examine issues of nationhood and ethnicity, Cuban culture, and *mestizaje* (miscegenation). For Ortiz, Cuban identity is an *ajiaco*, a stew pot that is made up of all the peoples that populate Cuba and the ingredients they contributed to its agriculture and cuisine:

> Cuba is an ajiaco, above all an open cooking pot. That is Cuba, the Island, the pot set to the fire of the tropics. [. . .] Singular casserole, that of our land, with our ajiaco, that needs to be made of clay and be very open. [. . .] The image of the creole ajiaco is a good symbol of the constitution of the Cuban people. [. . .] The Indians gave us corn, potato, taro, sweet potato, yucca, chili pepper [. . .] with the meat from hutias, iguanas, crocodiles, boas, turtles. [. . .] The Castilians cast aside those Indian meats and replaced them with their own. With their pumpkins and turnips, they brought their fresh beef, cured, salted, and smoked meats, their pork. And all that went to give substance to the new ajiaco in Cuba. With the whites from Europe came the blacks from Africa, and these contributed bananas, plantains, yams, and their cooking techniques. Then came the Asians with their mysterious spices from the Orient; and the French with their balanced flavors that softened the causticity of the wild peppers; and the Anglo-Americans came with their electrical appliances that simplified kitchen work, though looking to turn into metal and cooking pot of their own the clay pot that nature gave us, along with the heat of the tropics to warm it up, the water from its skies for its broth, and the sea water for the sprinkling of salt. With all of it our national ajiaco has been constituted.[3]

The ajiaco represents a vivid materialization of the process of transculturation, by which cultures in contact have a lasting transformative effect on one another. The ajiaco, then, is not a metaphorical "melting pot" but rather a material manifestation of a cultural convergence that results in the very expression of Cuban identity (*cubanidad*). Ortiz's work highlights the roles of colonialism, racial and ethnic identities, and conflict as they appear in both the cooking pot and the nation. The imprint of biocultural developments on language is readily acknowledged by Ortiz, who explains that the word *ajiaco* is made up of morphological and lexical components of Spanish, pre-Columbian, and African origin, with a native Cuban plant at its core. Thus, language bears the imprint of the biological world and the merging of cultures in the cooking pot. Ortiz's positioning of food at the core of such diverse disciplines as ethnography, anthropology, history, politics, lexicography, and semantics points to the productive cross-disciplinary conversations that the study of food can facilitate. It seems no coincidence that Alejo Carpentier used the ajiaco when trying to underscore the centrality of food in the making of textual culture and illustrate the importance of the "culinary context" for an author (34). The chapters in this volume by Adolfo Castañón and Sergio Ramírez follow in the same footsteps by presenting food as central to the processes of national identity formation in Mexico and Nicaragua, respectively. Their comprehensive outlook encompasses the Native American, Spanish, African, and other contributions to food and national identity as an ongoing process many centuries in the making.

Food, place, and identity weigh heavily in diasporic situations, where geographic dislocation can be examined through a food lens to help explain national and citizen positions, what Anita Mannur has termed "culinary citizenship." The notion of a nation that imagines, narrates, and enacts itself around a common cuisine can be productively applied to many other communities, the Sephardim being a clear example. The study of literary and historical texts has been successful in recovering biological and gastronomic traditions that are as important to literary scholars as they are to culinary researchers or to ethnic communities looking to rediscover lesser-known aspects of their collective past. In *A Drizzle of Honey: The Lives and Recipes of Spain's Secret Jews*, Gitlitz and Davidson perfectly exemplify the dynamic dialogue that the study of food can help establish using texts ranging from inquisitorial records to medieval poetry, chronicles, and prose fiction.[4] Temporary dislocation and the issues of colonialism, politics, and hegemonic cultural positions are explored in travel narratives, where a food-studies outlook can also yield illuminating examples of acculturation, casting cultural encounters in a new light. In *Life in Mexico*, the Scottish-born Frances Calderón de la Barca, *née* Erskine Inglis, author of one of the most compelling accounts of women's life in nineteenth-century Mexico, tells of her first reaching Veracruz and her rejection of the new tastes, cooking techniques, and foods: "We had a plentiful supper—fish, meat, wine, and chocolate, fruit and sweetmeats; the cookery, Spanish *Vera-Cruzified*. A taste of the style was enough for me, garlic and oil enveloping meat, fish, and fowl, with pimentos and plantains, and all kinds of curious fruit, which I cannot yet endure" (fourth letter, 33). Her letters are peppered with references to food, which acquires multiple meanings in the wide range of situations she describes, from war, conflict, and hunger to social and gender roles. At the end of her stay, the acculturation process has taken place through her relationship with Mexican food, as she explains in her fifty-second letter:

> I find, personally, one important change in taste if not in opinion. Vera Cruz cookery, which two years ago I thought detestable, now appears to me delicious! What excellent fish! and what incomparable frijoles! Well, this is a trifle; but after all, in trifles as in matters of moment, how necessary for a traveler to compare his judgments at different periods, and to correct them! First impressions are of great importance, if given only as such; but if laid down as decided opinions, how apt they are to be erroneous! It is like judging of individuals by their physiognomy and manners, without having had time to study their character. We all do so more or less, but how frequently we find ourselves deceived! (397–98)

The processes of gustatory and cultural acculturation described in *Life in Mexico* show the central role of food in cross-cultural communication. Roland Barthes and others pointed to the differential uses of food and their meaning, thus underscoring the role that food plays in the semiotics of communication and, perhaps just as importantly, arguing against the dismissal of food as lacking meaning or relevance in cultural analysis. Food's semiotic and communicative role in conflict creation and resolution in Hindu South Asia, explored in Arjun Appadurai's *gastro-politics*, can offer some thinking points for other geographic areas. Appadurai's analysis can be combined with that of colonial stratification of agricultural societies and land access to study food production and consumption narratives in such works as Rigoberta Menchú's account of Mayan K'iche' practices (in E. Burgos). A similar approach can be used to study Esteban Echeverría's *El matadero*, in which the author presents issues of animal treatment and food access (most notably meat) as both metaphors and material manifestations of sociopolitical injustice in Argentina during the turbulent Rosas regime.

On the topic of geographic dislocations, food can be similarly studied in relation to migration and migrant cultures, including food memories and nostalgia, identity and terroir, as well as migrant communities in the postnational outlook proposed by Chicana/o perspectives that complement those found in Gloria Anzaldúa, Chela Sandoval, and Emma Pérez. Ana Castillo's *So Far from God*, Sandra Cisneros's *Caramelo*, and works by the Taco Shop Poets can all be analyzed from this perspective (e.g., studies in Pascual Soler and Abarca). The same perspective can be equally applied to films related to Chicana/o issues, as for example in *El bracero del año*'s portrayal of early *bracero* culture.[5] A postnational outlook combining the analysis of food and migration can be equally productive in films involving different countries and economic politics such as *Una gallega en México*, *Cándida*, and *El Norte*. The consideration of migration and displacement also invites that of globalized food trends. The reevaluation of national cuisines may look at past and current efforts to examine disjunctions between center and periphery in nation-building narratives like that of Francoist Spain after the Spanish Civil War, as studied by Lara Anderson. Two of the chapters in this volume present compelling arguments for the relevance of *culinary capital*: María Paz Moreno and María del Carmen Simón Palmer view cities as loci where local and migrant cultures meet while being subject to political, social, economic, and culinary forces.

The use of food narratives in constructing competing national identities alongside hegemonic imbalances helps create what Graham Huggan has termed a "postcolonial exotic" that is marketed for consumption. In a provocative subversion of colonial narratives, Oswald de Andrade upends the savage/civilized hierarchy present in cultural and sociopolitical analysis in his *Cannibalist Manifesto* (or *Anthropophagic Manifesto*) in order to proclaim cannibalism as cultural affirmation and resistance against European colonizers. This view is explored by other scholars such as Carlos Jáuregui and in a variety of artistic explorations on the topic, as in the film *Como era gostoso o meu francês*. In a related but contrasting approach, Cristina Peri Rossi presents cannibalism as eroticism in "Rabelesiana." Glauber Rocha sees a very different postcolonial narrative involving Latin America, one driven by an "aesthetics of hunger" that helps place Latin America as a perpetual colony, subject to never-ending colonialism and underlying violence (see also De Maeseneer). The aesthetics of hunger can be applied to other periods and geographic areas, as it is eminently relevant for the study of whole literary genres such as the Golden Age picaresque novel. Hunger and the need to secure daily sustenance are powerful forces that shape the narratives of *Lazarillo de Tormes*, Mateo Alemán's *Guzmán de Alfarache*, and much later, Manuel Mujica Láinez's "El hambre," among others. Graciliano Ramos's *Vidas secas* depicts hunger in its dehumanizing cyclicity as experienced in rural Brazil. Conflict, scarcity, and hunger appear in other narratives with a social message such as Miguel Delibes's *Las ratas*, in which hunting rats for food enables the author to address issues of food access in relation to land ownership and human nature. Lastly, following Rocha's and others' emphasis on food's usefulness in film studies (see also Bower; Padrón Nodarse), movies such as *El hambre nuestra de cada día*, *En la cuerda del hambre*, *Los últimos*, and even *También la lluvia* provide illustrative examples of a rich cinematic corpus that can be productively engaged through a food-studies lens in order to examine issues of food consumption, hunger, and the politics of (post)colonial access to natural resources. Two of the chapters included in this volume study hunger as a key motif in literature as distant in time and geography as eighteenth-century Spain and present-day Brazil. María Ángeles Pérez Samper discusses the impact on food accessibility that socioeconomic differences had in eighteenth-century Spain. Pérez Samper shows how hunger, excess, the commodification of foodstuffs, and the social value ascribed to them played a central role in enlightened literature and thought. Sabrina Sedlmayer shows hunger as a continuous theme in Brazil, from the first colonial chronicles to contemporary Brazilian writers such as Graciliano Ramos, Guimarães Rosa, Clarice Lispector, and Raduan Nassar. Conversely, several chapters in this book highlight the cultural significance that primordial staples like corn masa (Climent-Espino) and wheat bread (Gómez-Bravo and Pérez Samper) have as life-giving, identity-forming foods.

The use of food in creating powerful visual and textual narratives suggests strong links between food and text, pointing to a key role for literary scholars and encouraging textuality interrogation in food studies. At a very basic level, food as textual medium, as well as the long-standing tradition of inscribing eating and drinking vessels, may be seen in a continuum with current practices of food labeling. In this context, texts assume a mediating role that, while clearly commercial, helps place food in a textually coded signifying and signifier universe. While very little supermarket food is currently sold without text accompaniment, the strong link between food and text invites, among other considerations, the mirror link between book jackets and the text they envelop and market. From the standpoint of textual studies, a focus on food helps bring into relief the relationship between texts and material culture, as well as the text's own materiality. Access to food, then, often involves acts of reading as a necessary preliminary to eating, the inscribed food having been imbued with meaning and contained in a textualized vessel before becoming solely material again on the plate or in the mouth. This practice is in direct relation to many others, such as that of using newspaper to wrap food for sale or parchment manuscript pages to cook and wrap food. As related practices, traditional writing materials such as parchment and paper were substituted with food surfaces such as avocado pits or pear skins when people's need for written communication overwhelmed their lack of traditional materials in such sequestered places as sixteenth-century jails on both sides of the Atlantic (Castillo Gómez, "El aguacate y los plátanos"). In those same jails, meaningful written messages could be inscribed on the precious paper that wrapped food gifts of raisins, or sent via bananas or melons that had been partially carved in order to accommodate writing (Castillo Gómez, *Entre la pluma y la pared* 115–16). Texts function as a food to fill an emotional void in Diego de San Pedro's novel *Cárcel de amor*, where Leriano, its protagonist, commits suicide through self-starvation. As a final act, Leriano tears his beloved Laureola's letters into a cup filled with water and consumes them before dying. The study of food and writing raises the issue of corporeality, the body, through the mouth and hands, significantly functioning as a common locus for eating, speaking, and writing, all physical activities tied to the intellect. The intimate link between language and the body, which emphasizes the physical dimension of textuality, is mirrored by that of food and the body and is acknowledged through expressions related to food consumption, including the medieval concept of text "rumination" as a form of learning and understanding. In a similar vein, texts can be "eaten," "vomited," "regurgitated," "spit out," and "cooked," while they can also be "digested," "swallowed," and "ingested" as forms of reading. These actions are more than images or metaphors, as there exist numerous instances of texts being actually eaten for reasons religious or magical (charms and amulets), political (compromising messages), or romantic and self-effacing (e.g., Laureola's letters in *Cárcel de amor*), in a practice that Cardona has termed *graphophagy* (145–48; see also Climent-Espino, "Al margen del códice" 101–4; Goody, *La lógica de la escritura* 21–68).

The study of corporeality from the standpoint of feminist studies as applied to food can be combined with a focus on literacy and textuality. Authors such as Gabriel García Márquez and Rosario Ferré have pointed to the similarities between writing and cooking: their understanding of writing is as a cooking process, which shares techniques that in fact constitute cognitive associations. For this reason, Rosario Ferré has referred to a "cuisine of writing," or *cocina de la escritura*, and García Márquez to "cooking" and "seasoning" texts with salt and pepper (in Guibert 326). Cookbooks' narrative nature is often underscored by their very users, who affirm that cookbooks can be read in a continuous act, "as novels" with a particular purpose and common thread. Cookbooks can also be viewed as a collection of shorter stories, as an assemblage of units or "discourse colonies," in the term coined by Michael Hoey, disjoined from one another and standing on their own. As a child, Amado Nervo purportedly learned how to read using his mother's cookbook, *La cocinera poblana*, with his mother's kitchen acting as his first classroom and her cookbook as his primer. Nervo's experience brings up the ties between early literacy and cooking, as well as the feeding of the intellect and the body, as being within the purview of women's work.

However, conceptualizing body and intellect as two sides of a dichotomic humanity would obscure the intellectual nature of food acts. Cookbooks also pose compelling questions on the relation between material culture and writing, providing narratives on the cultural and social meaning of food. The last decades have directed keen attention to cookbooks as historical and cultural artifacts brimming with information that is relevant to many of the issues analyzed in a variety of disciplines from various theoretical perspectives (see for example Claflin). The study of the cookbook as a textual artifact sheds light on its connections to the manuscript and printed book as it encourages the exploration of the related issues of authorship, readership, or social networks (Moreno). The need to study the intertextual connections between culinary books and other texts is obvious in the cases of such multifaceted authors as Pardo Bazán or Enrique de Villena, but also in the food writing that flourished among journalists in the first half of the twentieth century. Lastly, cookbooks may be seen as interdisciplinary loci, textual matrices where biology, medicine, history, literacy, gender, economy, and other fields can intersect. When they call attention to form, cookbooks can help explore the relation between materiality and aesthetics. Marinetti's *Futurist Cookbook* and Dali's surrealist cookbook, *Les dîners de Gala*, can be studied from this perspective alongside their artwork (e.g., Dali's clocks in *La persistencia de la memoria* inspired by melting cheeses), as well as illustrations of cookbooks as art. Marinetti's cookbook may thus be examined in relation to modernist illustrations in such books as Colombine's *¿Quiere usted comer bien?*

More recently, the transfer of modernist aesthetics to food has been most famously undertaken in the so-called *modernist cuisine* (or *molecular gastronomy*) shaped by Ferrán Adriá (Myhrvold et al.). His novel application of laboratory equipment to cooking has allowed him to present ontological and aesthetic challenges and to persuasively argue that eating is fundamentally an intellectual act. The high costs of cooking and eating modernist food have drawn criticism, making obvious the persistence of dichotomous formulations of high and low, learned and popular, cuisine and cooking. Such conceptualization of elitist food practices can also be examined in contrast to the work of artists and authors who present a contrasting perspective on daily life, poverty, and politics, as in Miguel Hernández's "Nanas de la cebolla."

Three of the chapters included in this volume explore the central importance of cookbooks as texts, artifacts, and extant witnesses to a material culture enmeshed in contemporaneous social and textual transactions. Paula Caldo examines the power differentials involved in a food writing that is enmeshed in a complex negotiation between the power elite and the subaltern. Paula Caldo and María Paz Moreno focus on issues of textuality, society, and authorship, thus helping highlight the relevance of textual agency vis-à-vis food production. The narrative that revolves around food as an element of material culture in direct relationship to other objects and to cookbooks and other texts helps Nadeau similarly highlight the importance of taking into account the very materiality of objects and the need to visualize and factor them into any food-culture study.

The considerations presented here may lead to a conceptualization of food as the ultimate disciplinary medium. In its organic materiality, food is rehumanizing and may provide the best cure for post-humanist blues. The studies included in this volume showcase the advantages of the critical use of a food lens within colonial studies, ethnic and racial studies, gender and sexuality studies, as well as power dynamics, nationalism and nation-building, and theories of embodiment and identity. These chapters contain important synergies that point toward continuities and lines of inquiry that go beyond a strict compartmentalizing periodization. Food hierarchies and their relation to New World and Old World taxonomies are discussed in Chapters 2, 3, 4, 9, and 10. The relevance of a transatlantic outlook when studying the Hispanic world is made evident in Chapters 2, 3, 9, and 10. The cultural, symbolic, and economic significance of key foodstuffs like maize is dicussed in Chapters 2, 9, and 11. Textuality and cookbook writing is explored in Chapters 4, 7, and 8, with Chapters 4 and 7 examining the key work of Martínez Montiño. Chapter 12, which emphasizes the importance of studying hunger, can be read alongside Chapter 5 for the contrasts it highlights between hunger and excess, and alongside Chapter 13, which points out how food scarcity and food access can shape a generation. Chapters 1, 10, and 11 point out how food can be used as an important factor in nation-building while emphasizing the positive or negative valuation of foods associated with racialized minorities, while Chapter 5 examines the combined factors of immigration and nationhood in the construction of a culinary capital.

In Chapter 1, "Food, Blood, and a Jewish *Raza* in Fifteenth-Century Spain," Ana Gómez-Bravo examines the role food played in late-medieval medical theories of the body's constitution. The chapter examines a variety of sources, ranging from slanderous poetry and *El libro del Alborayque*, a libelous pamphlet, to historical accounts, legal texts, and medical writing. Gómez-Bravo's essay examines the development of racialized ideas of difference in the late-medieval and early-modern periods from the standpoint of historical semantics as well as ethnic, religious, medical, and social controversies, particularly as they apply to Jewish *conversos* and are later developed in theories of blood purity. Focusing on the role of food in the emerging conceptualization of race, Gómez-Bravo contends that legal and medical writings helped conceptualize an idea of difference that lay in the blood and was shaped through food.

In Chapter 2, "Taste and Taxonomy of Native Food in Hispanic America: 1492–1640," Gregorio Saldarriaga analyzes a number of important Spanish documents that provide accounts of the foods found in the New World, paying close attention to the input of authors who were also merchants, courtiers, sailors, and soldiers. The document authors' diverse educational backgrounds played a key role in the innovation they brought to their botanical and food observations, which have thus far received little attention. Using such varied sources as letters, conquest reports, chronicles, medical treatises, and *relaciones geográficas* of the Indies, Saldarriaga analyzes the ideological, cultural, and social elements that helped create new taxonomies of food during the colonial period.

In Chapter 3, "Still Life, Food, and Fiction: Diversions from Colonial Baroque," Rodrigo Labriola shows how food featured as a key component of the neo-baroque imaginary through its depiction in *bodegones*, or still lives. In seventeenth-century Spanish art, peninsular and transatlantic, the pictorial genre of the still life as something "still alive" displayed people's fascination with "inanimate objects" that helped shape their food aesthetic. In this vein, Labriola argues that artistic innovation at this time emerged from a vital, indispensable, and animalistic need: the "desire" to eat that was inscribed in art as well as written works. The writing of the "new" by Spanish chroniclers from the sixteenth century through the colonial baroque can be thus thought of as experimental, turning the *imaginable* (what can be painted and eaten) into something *plausible*, thereby creating modern fiction by means of travel literature and with the help of a rhetoric of irony about food.

In Chapter 4, "Furniture and Equipment in the Royal Kitchens of Early Modern Spain," Carolyn Nadeau examines the work of Francisco Martínez Montiño, head of the kitchens for both Philip III and Philip IV of Spain, who published what would become the most recognized Spanish cookbook before the twentieth century, his 1611 *Arte de cocina, pastelería, vizcochería y conservería* (*The Art of Cooking, Piemaking, Pastrymaking, and Preserving*). In this work, Martínez Montiño includes 508 recipes and close to 5,000 ingredients. But, how does he write about preparing these very dishes, and more specifically, what are the necessary kitchen spaces, appliances, and utensils used to create them? The chapter begins by signaling the priorities Martínez Montiño establishes in the cooking spaces of the royal kitchens, including access to water. It then turns to essential kitchen furnishing and heat sources and explains how cooking temperatures were identified without the use of thermometers. Moving from big kitchen items to medium and then small, the last two sections provide an account of prepware, serveware, and hand-held utensils that facilitate for readers today an understanding of the evolution of kitchen apparatuses. By sharing data analysis of the hundreds of material objects described by the master cook in charge of the royal kitchen, the aim of the chapter is to provide scholars and gastronomes today with an increased understanding of kitchen technology in early-modern Spain and to contribute to an understanding of the standardization of the material culture of early-modern royal kitchens.

In Chapter 5, "Enlightened Meals: Literary Perspectives on Food in Eighteenth-Century Spain," María Ángeles Pérez Samper examines issues of social justice, hunger, and national identity in the works of Feijoo, Ramón de la Cruz, Clavijo y Fajardo, Meléndez Valdés, and Gregorio de Salas. Pérez Samper examines food as social paradox in eighteenth-century Spain and the many texts that underscore the sharp contrast between the daily hunger that is the way of life of many in the lower social scale and the excess and overabundance of food in the houses of the rich. This chapter further shows how food served as a display of taste and distinction for the upper classes, while new foods such as coffee were coded as markers of modernity. The discussion of Ramón de la Cruz and other authors leads to the examination of another binary opposition in eighteenth-century Spain, that of French and Spanish cuisines, with their high and low, international and local, vain and honest disjunctions. In contrast with the French fashions of city and court and the consumeristic positions of urban populations, Juan Meléndez Valdés and Francisco Gregorio de Salas praised the joy of honest Spanish peasant food, which, as Pérez Samper points out, was marked by its reassuring cyclical nature and its connection to the soil, the nation, and productive agriculture.

In Chapter 6, "Madrid: Cuisine as Cultural Melting Pot," María del Carmen Simón Palmer analyzes the combined importance of cuisine, politics, and literature. This chapter shows how a focus on the changing gastronomic cityscape of a single city can help explore the relation of food, literature, and politics. From the beginning of its time as Spain's capital, Madrid welcomed cooks from different countries into its royal kitchens and later into its city streets in order to attend to the monarchs and the moneyed, as well as the working classes. Simón Palmer relates the success stories of Italian immigrant entrepreneurs who managed to run some of the city's most emblematic establishments, combining innovative ideas and dishes with traditional Spanish food. Simón Palmer analyzes the literary work of such authors as Benito Pérez Galdós, Clarín, and Rubén Darío in order to provide a rich portrayal of the culture of eating establishments in nineteenth-century Madrid, examining the role these establishments served in the political developments of the period. Significantly, the alternating French and Italian food influences mirrored the fluctuations in royal power and government that were located in Madrid as the nation's capital.

In Chapter 7, "Beyond the Recipes: Authorship, Text, and Context in Canonical Spanish Cookbooks," María Paz Moreno examines four canonical cookbooks from Spain, dating from the seventeenth to the twentieth centuries, focusing on issues of authorship and culinary capital, analyzing specific textual elements, and placing them within the historical context in which they were produced. Building upon Susan Leonardi's idea that a recipe is a form of text and should be studied in context, and informed by Naccarato and LeBesco's concept of *culinary capital*, the chapter looks at several Spanish landmark cookbooks as examples of a genre that presents a unique authorship style while serving very specific purposes. The cookbooks examined are Francisco Martínez Montiño's *Arte de cocina, pastelería, vizcochería y conservería* (1611), Juan de Altamiras's *Nuevo arte de cocina* (1745), María Mestayer de Echagüe's *La cocina completa* (1940), and Ignacio Doménech's *Cocina de recursos. Deseo mi comida* (1941).

In Chapter 8, "Cooks and Ladies: The Writing of Culinary Knowledge in Argentina in the Late Nineteenth and Early Twentieth Centuries," Paula Caldo studies cookbook publishing as a way to explore issues of authorship, textual access, taste, and the transmission of knowledge in late nineteenth- and early twentieth-century Argentina. Focusing on two highly influential cookbooks, *La perfecta cocinera argentina* and *La cocinera criolla y recetario curativo doméstico*, Caldo analyzes the sociocultural forces behind the books as collaborative compilations and astounding editorial successes. The study argues that women were able to enter the publishing market by leveraging their socioeconomic standing as members of the upper classes. However, their editorial success rested on the thorough culinary knowledge their books displayed and which was acquired directly from the working-class cooks of different ethnicities that the authors employed in their households. As the books grew in popularity and became available in ever-expanding editions, the single authorship model that the published books conveyed was overrun by internal textual evidence of multiple and collaborative authorships. The chapter emphasizes the social aspects of writing in female circles and the sexual politics of publishing as a public act in Argentina at the turn of the twentieth century.

In Chapter 9, "The Evolution of Mexican Cuisine: Five Gastronomical Seasons, *Mole, Pozole, Tamal, Tortilla, and Chile Relleno*," Adolfo Castañón presents an overview of Mexican gastronomy from pre-Columbian times to the twentieth century using a wide variety of historical, anthropological, and literary sources that also includes cookbooks. The impressive process of hybridization that resulted from the cultural encounters of different groups on Mexican soil gave way to what Castañón portrays as the five seasons of Mexican gastronomy, each centered around a different food: *mole, pozole, tamal, tortilla,* and *chile relleno*. The result of the hybridization process is a rich and original cuisine in constant evolution. The chapter presents food as central to cultural and textual analysis while highlighting the interrelated issues of nation-building, material culture, hybridity, and textuality.

In Chapter 10, "What the Palate Knows," Sergio Ramírez offers a detailed panorama of Nicaraguan cuisine and, by extension, Central American food. Because of Nicaragua's geographical location, Ramírez understands Nicaraguan cuisine as a hybrid of incessant fusions that have been operating since pre-Columbian times. Ramírez presents Nicaragua as a meeting place of many cultures, with its cuisine having been influenced by, among other groups, Aztecs, Mayas, Arawaks, Caribs, Chorotegas, and Nahuatls. The mixing process continued after the conquest and colonial periods, and aboriginal cuisine mixed with Spanish and African dishes to make new combinations. All the new African and Spanish elements entered the Pacific coast through the Caribbean, bringing with them Taino culinary culture. Ramírez points out the importance of African touches to understanding Nicaraguan cuisine, mainly along the Caribbean coast. Nicaraguan cuisine of the Atlantic coast is marked by the contributions from Native American groups such as Miskitos, Sumos, and Ramas, as well as Africans, insular Afro-Caribbeans such as the Garifuna and Jamaicans, Creoles, and Europeans, especially Britons. Ramírez examines the influences brought to Nicaraguan cuisine by different ethnic groups: indigenous peoples, Spaniards, and descendants of African slaves.

In Chapter 11, "A Gastrocritical Reading of Miguel Ángel Asturias's Early Narrative: *Legends of Guatemala*, *The President*, and *Men of Maize*," Rafael Climent-Espino combines his interest in objects, texts, and the everyday life, analyzing food representations in the early work of Miguel Ángel Asturias. According to Climent-Espino, food symbolism in *Hombres de maíz* must be understood in the same mythical context as in *Leyendas de Guatemala*. In *Hombres de maíz*, the clash of two different understandings of nature give shape to the narrative's main conflict. The Mayans' mythical perspective is essentially one of respect toward their ancestral thoughts on nature and its cycles of productivity. They believe nature is a superior spiritual provider that should be respected at all cost. The partially assimilated Ladino people hold the opposing view that nature is a space that must be subordinated, a resource of material and economic profit

Introduction   27

that can be exploited as much as possible. The control of food production means controlling both satiation and scarcity, and such control can be used to defy or consolidate a status quo. Using mainly gastrocriticism and Arjun Appadurai's gastro-politics as theoretical approaches, Climent-Espino aims to analyze how food interacts with ethnicity, gender, and social class in Asturias's work.

In Chapter 12, "On Hunger and Brazilian Literature," Sabrina Sedlmayer uses the concept of an "aesthetic of hunger" created by the Brazilian filmmaker Glauber Rocha in order to propose that hunger is not only a theme but also an important element that engenders its own enunciation. In order to illustrate this point, Sedlmayer analyzes five novels written by twentieth-century Brazilian writers: *Vidas secas* by Graciliano Ramos, *Grande Sertão: Veredas* by João Guimarães Rosa, *A hora da estrela* by Clarice Lispector, *Um copo de Cólera* by Raduan Nassar, and *O peixe e o pássaro* by Bartolomeu Campos de Queirós. These works clearly propose a polarized relationship between hunger and language. The novels are studied in contrast to other Brazilian writers' proposals in relation to hunger, as they emphasize the use of dichotomies and the presentation of characters who are experiencing famine or malnourishment and live in the margins of urban areas.

In Chapter 13, "Food in Recent Cuban Literature (1990–2016): From Hero in the Special Period Fiction to almost Zero in the Generation Zero," Rita De Maeseneer analyzes food representations in Cuban novels, paying special attention to those texts that deal with the so-called Special Period, which started in 1990 and was characterized by severe austerity and even hunger. Using gastrocriticism as theoretical framework, De Maeseneer examines food as a referential topic within Cuban letters and relates food and the absence of food to national identity and the socio-political system. However, recent Cuban texts (2006–2016) move away from this topic, and the most current writers seldom mention food. As De Maeseneer points out, these mentions are non-identitarian, delocalized, and mainly used for metaliterary and metaphorical purposes, which suggests a change of paradigm in food representation within Cuban literature. As an example, De Maeseneer illustrates the obsessive longing for meat, one of the most identitarian products that expresses Cubanness in many Special Period narratives. De Maeseneer focuses on food references in the work of the three most internationally established Cuban writers today: Zoé Valdés, Pedro Juan Gutiérrez, and Leonardo Padura Fuentes, while also discussing the Generation Zero, the last generation of Cuban writers.

NOTES

We would like to thank Katherine Carriveau, Jorge González Casanova, Sam Jaffe, Alicia Raftery, Clara Raftery, Aedan Roberts, and Sheehan Trippel for their help in editing and proofreading different parts of this book.

1. Other literary works include Javier Guzmán's *El cocinero del papa* (2012), Gustavo Rodríguez's *Cocinero en su tinta* (2012), Lina Meruane's *Fruta podrida* (2007), Raphael Montes's *Jantar secreto* (2016), Jorge Amado's *Doña Flor y sus dos maridos* (2016), Lola Piera Lozano's *Gran soufflé* (2013), Yanet Acosta's *El chef ha muerto* (2011), and Manuel Vázquez Montalbán's *La soledad del manager* (1995).
2. In her introduction to De Maeseneer and Collard.
3. "Cuban ajiaco [. . .] La imagen del ajiaco criollo nos simboliza bien la formación del pueblo cubano. [. . .] Ante todo una cazuela abierta. Eso es Cuba, la isla, la olla puesta al fuego de los trópicos. [. . .] Cazuela singular la de nuestra tierra, como la de nuestro ajiaco, que ha de ser de barro y muy abierta. [. . .] La indiada nos dio el maíz, la papa, la malanga, el boniato, la yuca, el ají [. . .] con carnes de jutía, de iguanas, de cocodrilos, de majás, de tortugas. [. . .] Los castellanos desecharon esas carnes indias y pusieron las suyas. Ellos trajeron con sus calabazas y nabos, las carnes frescas de res, los tasajos, las cecinas, el lacón. Y todo ello fue a dar sustancias al nuevo ajiaco de Cuba. Con los blancos de Europa llegaron los negros de África y estos nos aportaron guineas, plátanos, ñames y su técnica cocinera. Y luego los asiáticos con sus misteriosas especias de Oriente; y los franceses con su ponderación de sabores que amortiguó la causticidad del pimiento salvaje; y los angloamericanos con sus mecánicas domésticas que simplificaron la cocina y quieren metalizar y convertir en caldera de su estándar el cacharro de tierra que nos fue dado por la naturaleza, junto con el fogaje del trópico para calentarlo, el agua de sus cielos para el caldo y el agua de sus mares para las salpicaduras del salero. Con todo ello se ha hecho nuestro nacional ajiaco." ("Factores humanos de la cubanidad" 80; My translation)

4. See also Gómez-Bravo, "Gastronomía."
5. Through the bracero program, millions of guest laborers from Mexico went to work in the United States between 1942 and 1964.

WORKS CITED

Abad Faciolince, Héctor. *Tratado de culinaria para mujeres tristes.* Alfaguara, 1997.
Acosta, Yanet. *El chef ha muerto.* Amargord, 2011.
Alarcos Llorach, Emilio. "Entrada." *Comer y contar: Un viaje colectivo por la cocina asturiana.* Maguncia, 1992, pp. 7–9.
Alemán, Mateo. *Guzmán de Alfarache,* edited by Luis María Gómez Canseco, Real Academia Española, 2012.
Allende, Isabel. *Afrodita.* Debolsillo, 2010.
Amado, Jorge. *Doña Flor y sus dos maridos.* Alianza, 2016.
———. *Cacau.* 1933. Record, 1996.
Anderson, Lara. *Cooking up the Nation: Spanish Culinary Texts and Culinary Nationalization in the Late Nineteenth and Early Twentieth Century.* Tamesis, 2013.
Andrade, Oswald de. "Cannibalist Manifesto." Introduction by Leslie Bary, *Latin American Literary Review,* vol. 19, no. 38, 1991, pp. 38–47.
Appadurai, Arjun. "Gastro-politics in Hindu South Asia." *American Ethnologist,* vol. 8, no. 3, 1981, pp. 494–511.
Aram, Bethany, and Bartolomé Yun-Casalilla, editors. *Global Goods and the Spanish Empire, 1492–1824: Circulation, Resistance and Diversity.* Palgrave Macmillan, 2014.
Asturias, Miguel Ángel, and Pablo Neruda. *Comiendo en Hungría.* Lumen, 1969.
Aub, Max. *La verdadera historia de la muerte de Francisco Franco.* Cuadernos del Vigía, 2014.
Barthes, Roland. "Toward a Psychosociology of Contemporary Food Consumption." *Food and Culture,* edited by Carole Counihan and Penny Van Esterik, Routledge, 2013, pp. 23–30.
Belasco, Warren. *Food: The Key Concepts.* Berg, 2008.
Bell, Rudolph M. *Holy Anorexia.* U of Chicago P, 1987.
Benítez Rojo, Antonio. *La isla que se repite: El Caribe y la perspectiva posmoderna.* Editorial Plaza Mayor, 2010.
———. *The Repeating Island: The Caribbean and the Postmodern Perspective.* Duke UP, 1996.
Betancourt Cisneros, Gaspar. *Escenas cotidianas.* Ministerio de Educación de la República de Cuba, Dirección de Cultura, 1950.
Bordo, Susan. *Unbearable Weight: Feminism, Western Culture, and the Body.* U of California P, 1993.

Bourdieu, Pierre. *Distinction: A Social Critique of the Judgement of Taste.* Translated by Richard Nice, Harvard UP, 1996.

Bower, Anne L., editor. *Reel Food: Essays on Food and Film.* Routledge, 2004.

El Bracero del año. Directed by Rafael Baledón, México, Churubusco Azteca, 1964.

Braudel, Fernand. *The Structures of Everyday Life: The Limits of the Possible.* Harper and Row, 1981.

Burgos, Carmen de (Colombine). *¿Quiere usted comer bien?* Ramón Sopena, 1949.

Burgos, Elizabeth. *Me llamo Rigoberta Menchú y así me nació la conciencia.* Siglo Veintiuno, 2005.

Bynum, Caroline Walker. *Holy Feast and Holy Fast: The Religious Significance of Food to Medieval Women.* U of California P, 1987.

Calderón de la Barca, Frances Erskine Inglis. *Life in Mexico.* U of California P, 1982.

Campos, Cristina. *Pan de limón con semillas de amapola.* Planeta, 2018.

Cándida. Directed by Luis Bayón Herrera. Establecimientos Filmadores Argentinos, 1939.

Cárdenas, Juan de. *Primera parte de los problemas y secretos maravillosos de las Indias.* Academia Nacional de Medicina de México, 1980.

Cardona, Giorgio Raimondo. *Antropologia della scrittura.* UTET, 2009.

Carpentier, Alejo. "Problemática de la actual novela latinoamericana." *Obras completas*, vol. 13: *Ensayos*, México D. F., Siglo Veintiuno Editores, 1990, pp. 11–44.

Castillo, Ana. *So Far from God.* Norton, 1993.

Castillo Gómez, Antonio. "El aguacate y los plátanos. Cárcel y comunicación escrita en ambas orillas del Atlántico (siglo XVI y XVII)." *Grafías del imaginario. Representaciones culturales en España y América (siglos XVI-XVIII)*, edited by Carlos A. González Sánchez and Enriqueta Vila Vilar, Fondo de Cultura Económica de México, 2003, pp. 72–95.

———. *Entre la pluma y la pared: una historia social de la escritura en los Siglos de Oro.* Ediciones Akal, 2006.

Certeau, Michel de. *The Practice of Everyday Life.* U of California P, 1984.

Cervantes, Miguel de. *Don Quijote de la Mancha.* Real Academia Española y Asociación de Academias de la Lengua Española, 2015.

Chef BNE. Biblioteca Nacional de España, Madrid, 2016. chefbne.bne.es. Accessed 3 Sept 2019.

Christensen, Julia F. "Pleasure Junkies All Around! Why It Matters and Why 'the Arts' Might Be the Answer: a Biopsychological Perspective." *Proceedings of the Royal Society B: Biological Sciences.* Published 3 May 2017. royalsocietypublishing.org/doi/10.1098/rspb.2016.2837.

Christou, Maria. *Eating Otherwise: The Philosophy of Food in Twentieth-Century Literature.* Cambridge UP, 2017.

Cisneros, Sandra. *Caramelo*. Vintage Books, 2002.
Claflin, Kyri W. "Representations of Food Production and Consumption: Cookbooks as Historical Sources." *The Handbook of Food Research*, edited by Anne Murcott, Warren Belasco, and Peter Jackson, Bloomsbury Academic, 2013, pp. 109–27.
Climent-Espino, Rafael. "Al margen del códice: Análisis de tres ejemplos recientes de objetos-libro en España." *Arizona Journal of Hispanic Cultural Studies*, vol. 22, 2018, pp. 89–109.
———. "Miragens do Japão: Nostalgia, comida e isogastrias em *Nihonjin* de Oscar Nakasato." Monographic Issue on Taste, Memory, and Writing. *O Eixo e a Roda: Revista de Literatura Brasileira*, vol. 28, no. 2, 2019, pp. 49–74.
La Cocinera poblana y el libro de las familias: Novísimo manual práctico de cocina española, francesa, inglesa y mexicana, higiene y economía doméstica. Herrero Hermanos, 1890.
Como era gostoso o meu francês. Directed by Nelson Pereira dos Santos, Brasil, Condor Films, 1971.
Counihan, Carole. *The Anthropology of Food and Body: Gender, Meaning and Power*. Routledge, 1999.
Coward, Rosalind. *Female Desire: How they are Sought, Bought and Packaged*. Grove, 1985.
Cuauhtémoc Sánchez, Carlos. *Los fantasmas del espejo*. Editorial Diamante, 2008.
Cunqueiro, Álvaro. *La cocina cristiana de occidente*. Austral, 2015.
———. *La cocina gallega*. Edicións do Cumio, 2013.
Dali, Salvador. *Les dîners de Gala*. Translated by John Peter Moore, Taschen, 2016.
De Maeseneer, Rita. "The Aesthetics of Hunger and the Special Period in Cuba." *Caribbean Food Cultures: Culinary Practices and Consumption in the Caribbean and Its Diasporas*, edited by Wiebke Beushausen, Transcript, 2014, pp. 27–48.
De Maeseneer, Rita, and Patrick Collard, editors. *Saberes y sabores en México y el Caribe*. Editions Rodopi, 2010.
De Silva, Cara, editor. *In Memory's Kitchen: A Legacy from the Women of Terezín*. Translated by Bianca Steiner Brown, Rowman and Littlefield, 2006.
Delibes, Miguel. *Las ratas*. Ediciones Destino, 1983.
Delicado, Francisco. *Retrato de la lozana andaluza*, edited by Rosa Navarro Durán, Fundación José Antonio de Castro, 2017.
Douglas, Mary, editor. *Constructive Drinking: Perspectives on Drink from Anthropology*. Cambridge UP, 1991.
Earle, Rebecca. *The Body of the Conquistador: Food, Race and the Colonial Experience in Spanish America, 1492–1700*. Cambridge UP, 2012.
Echeverría, Esteban. *El matadero; La cautiva*, edited by Leonor Fleming, Cátedra, 1996.

Edible Communities Publications. 2019. www.ediblesubscriptions.com. Accessed 6 Nov 2019.

En la cuerda del hambre. Directed by Gustavo Alatriste, México, Producciones Alatriste, 1979.

Esquivel, Laura. *Como agua para chocolate*. Debolsillo, 2017.

———. *Íntimas suculencias: Tratado filosófico de cocina*. Debolsillo, 2015.

Farrer, James. *The Globalization of Asian Cuisines: Transnational Networks and Culinary Contact Zones*. Palgrave MacMillan, 2015.

Fat Studies: An Interdisciplinary Journal of Body Weight and Society. Taylor and Francis Online, Informa UK Limited, 2018, www.tandfonline.com/loi/ufts20.

Ferguson, Priscilla Parkhurst. *Accounting for Taste: The Triumph of French Cuisine*. U of Chicago P, 2004.

Fernández de Moratín, Leandro. *La comedia nueva: El sí de las niñas*, edited by Jesús Pérez Magallón and Fernando Lázaro Carreter, Crítica, 1994.

Ferré, Rosario. "La cocina de la escritura." *Teoría del cuento*, vol. 2, UNAM, 1995, pp. 213–24.

Food, Culture and Society. Taylor and Francis Online, Informa UK Limited, 2018, www.tandfonline.com/loi/rffc20.

Food and Foodways. Taylor and Francis Online, Informa UK Limited, 2018, www.tandfonline.com/loi/gfof20.

Fuera de carta [*Chef's Special*]. Directed by Nacho García Velilla, Spain, Ensueño Films / Antena 3 Films / Canguro Producciones, 2008.

Una Gallega en México. Directed by Julián Soler, México, Cinematográfica Filmex, 1949.

Gallegos, Rómulo. *Doña Bárbara*. Edición de Domingo Miliani, Cátedra, 2008.

García García, Emilio. "Huarte de San Juan. Un adelantado a la teoría modular de la mente." *Revista de Historia de la Psicología*, vol. 24, 2003, pp. 9–25.

Gastronomica: The Journal of Critical Food Studies, edited by Daniel E. Bender, U of California P, 2017. gastronomica.org.

Gigante, Denise. *Taste: A Literary History*. Yale UP, 2005.

Ginzburg, Carlo. *The Cheese and the Worms: The Cosmos of a Sixteenth-Century Miller*. The Johns Hopkins UP, 2013.

Gitlitz, David M., and Linda K. Davidson. *A Drizzle of Honey: The Lives and Recipes of Spain's Secret Jews*. St. Martin's P, 1999.

Gómez-Bravo, Ana M. *Comida y cultura en el mundo hispánico*. Equinox, 2017.

———. "Gastronomía y memoria histórica. El papel de lo culinario en la construcción de identidades nacionales en la cultura española y la tradición sefardí." *Cultura Gastronómica: Representaciones Identitarias en España*, special issue of *La Nueva Literatura Hispánica*, vol. 23, 2019, pp. 157–77.

Gómez de Avellaneda, Gertrudis. *Sab*. Anaya, 1970.
Goody, Jack. *Cooking, Cuisine, and Class: A Study in Comparative Sociology*. Cambridge UP, 1982.
———. *La lógica de la escritura y la organización de la sociedad*. Alianza Editorial, 1990.
Guibert, Rita. *Seven Voices: Seven Latin American Writers talk to Rita Guibert*. Vintage Books, 1973.
Güiraldes, Ricardo. *Don Segundo Sombra*. Altaya, 1995.
Guzmán, Javier. *El cocinero del papa*. La Discreta, 2012.
El Hambre nuestra de cada día. Directed by Rogelio A. González, México, Alfa Film, 1952.
Harris, Marvin. *Good to Eat: Riddles of Food and Culture*. Waveland P, 1998.
Hastorf, Christine Ann. *The Social Archaeology of Food: Thinking about Eating from Prehistory to the Present*. Cambridge UP, 2017.
Hernández, Miguel. "Nanas de la cebolla." *Cancionero y romancero de ausencias: El hombre acecha. Últimos Poemas*. Editorial Losada, 1975, pp. 118–20.
Hoey, Michael. *Textual Interaction: An Introduction to Written Discourse Analysis*. Routledge, 2001.
Howes, David, editor. *Empire of the Senses: The Sensual Culture Reader*. Berg, 2005.
Huarte de San Juan, Juan. *Examen de ingenios para las ciencias*. Cátedra, 2005.
Huggan, Graham. *The Postcolonial Exotic: Marketing the Margins*. Routledge, 2001.
Jáuregui, Carlos A. *Canibalia: Canibalismo, calibanismo, antropofagia cultural y consumo en América Latina*. Iberoamericana/Vervuert, 2008.
Jiménez, Conxy. *Gastro Andalusí: Illustrated Generational Recipes*. 2009–2018, www.gastroandalusi.com.
Journal of Sensory Studies. Edited by MaryAnne Drake, 1999–2019, John Wiley and Sons, onlinelibrary.wiley.com/journal/1745459x.
King Corn. Directed by Aaron Wolf, Balcony Releasing, 2007.
Korsmeyer, Carolyn. *Making Sense of Taste: Food and Philosophy*. Cornell UP, 1999.
———. *Savoring Disgust: The Foul and the Fair in Aesthetics*. Oxford UP, 2011.
Los Ladrones van a la oficina. Directed by Tito Fernández and Miguel Ángel Díez, Spain, Aurum Producciones, 1993.
Lara Nieto, María del Carmen. "El buen gusto en la educación estética: Baltasar Gracián y Joseph Addison." *Revista de educación de la Universidad de Granada*, vol. 15, 2002, pp. 155–74.
Latini, Cielo. *Abzurdah*. Planeta, 2016.
Lazarillo de Tomes. Edición de Francisco Rico, Real Academia Española, 2011.

Lévi-Strauss, Claude. "The Culinary Triangle." *Partisan Review*, vol. 33, 1966, pp. 586–96.

———. *The Raw and the Cooked*. Harper and Row, 1969.

López Iturriaga, Mikel. *El comidista*. El País, elcomidista.elpais.com. Accessed 7 Nov 2019.

Mannur, Anita. *Culinary Fictions: Food in South Asian Diasporic Culture*. Temple UP, 2010.

Marinetti, Filippo Tommaso. *The Futurist Cookbook*. Translated by Suzanne Brill, edited by Lesley Chamberlain, Penguin Classics, 2013.

Martín-Araguz, A., and C. Bustamante-Martínez. "*The Examination of Men's Wits* by Juan Huarte de San Juan, and the Dawn of the Neurobiology of Intelligence in the Spanish Renaissance." *Revista de Neurología*, vol. 38, no. 12, 2004, pp. 1176–85.

Martínez, Mely. *México en mi cocina*. 2008–2018, www.mexicoenmicocina.com.

Martínez-Expósito, Alfredo. "Tapas, dietas y chefs: La Marca España en el nuevo cine gastronómico español." *Encrucijadas Globales: Redefinir España en el siglo XXI*, edited by José F. Colmeiro, Iberoamericana / Vervuert, 2015, pp. 285–309.

Mateo del Pino, Ángeles, and María Nieves Pascual Soler, editors. *Comidas Bastardas: Gastronomía, tradición e identidad en América Latina*, Editorial Cuarto Propio, 2013.

Mazzoni, Cristina. *The Women in God's Kitchen: Cooking, Eating and Spiritual Writing*. Continuum, 2005.

Mead, Margaret. "The Factor of Food Habits." *The Annals of the American Academy of Political and Social Science*, vol. 225, 1943, pp. 136–41.

The Meaning of Food. Created and produced by Sue McLaughlin et al., PBS Home Video, 2005.

Menely, Tobias, and Jesse Oak Taylor. *Anthropocene Reading: Literary History in Geologic Times*. Penn State UP, 2017.

Meruane, Lina. *Fruta podrida*. Fondo de Cultura Económica, 2007.

Minder, Raphael. "Old Recipes, New Format: Spain Puts Historic Dishes on Video." *The New York Times*, 12 July 2018.

Mintz, Sidney W. *Sweetness and Power: The Place of Sugar in Modern History*. Penguin, 1986.

Miranda, Ana. *Amrik*. Translated by Rafael Climent-Espino, Fondo Editorial Casa de Las Américas, 2016.

Montanari, Massimo. *Food is Culture*. Columbia UP, 2006.

Montes, Raphael. *Jantar secreto*. Companhia das Letras, 2016.

Moreno, María Paz. *De la página al plato: El libro de cocina en España*. Ediciones Trea, 2012.

Mujica Láinez, Manuel. *Misteriosa Buenos Aires*. Debolsillo, 2012.

———. "El hambre," *Cuentos completos I*. Alfaguara, 1999, pp. 213–17.

Myhrvold, Nathan, Chris Young, Maxime Bilet, Ryan Matthew Smith, and Cooking Lab. *Modernist Cuisine: The Art and Science of Cooking*. The Cooking Lab, 2011. 6 vols.

Nadeau, Carolyn A. *Food Matters: Alonso Quijano's Diet and the Discourse of Food in Early Modern Spain*. U of Toronto P, 2016.

Nakasato, Oscar. *Nihonjin*. Benvirá, 2011.

Neruda, Pablo. "Oda al caldillo de congrio." *Odas elementales*, Seix Barral, 1980.

———. "Oda a la papa." *Nuevas odas elementales*, Losada, 1977, pp. 109–12.

Nestle, Marion. *Food Politics: How the Food Industry Influences Nutrition and Health*. U of California P, 2013.

Nodari, Alexandre. "A literatura como antropologia especulativa." *Revista da Anpoll*, vol. 38, 2015, pp. 75–85.

El Norte. Directed by Gregory Nava, Americana Playhouse, 1983.

Ortiz, Fernando. *Contrapunteo cubano del tabaco y el azúcar*. Cátedra, 2002.

———. *Cuban Counterpoint: Tobacco and Sugar*. Duke UP, 1995.

———. "Los factores humanos de la cubanidad." *Ensayo cubano del siglo XX*, edited by Rafael Hernández and Rafael Rojas, Fondo de Cultura Económica, 2002, pp. 74–99.

Padrón Nodarse, Frank. *Co-cine: El discurso culinario en la pantalla grande*. La Habana, ICAIC, 2011.

Pardo Bazán, Emilia. *La cocina española antigua*. Academia Galega de Gastronomia, 2005.

———. *La cocina española moderna*. Academia Galega de Gastronomia, 1999.

———. *La madre naturaleza*. Cátedra, 1999.

Pascual Soler, Nieves. *Hungering as Symbolic Language: What Are We Saying When We Starve Ourselves?* Edwin Mellen P, 2011.

Pascual Soler, Nieves, and Meredith E. Abarca, editors. *Rethinking Chicana/o Literature through Food: Postnational Appetites*. Palgrave Macmillan, 2013.

Pearce, Marcus, Dahlia W. Zaidel, Oshin Vartanian, Martin Skov, Helmut Leder, Chatterjee Anjan, and Marcos Nadal. "Neuroaesthetics: The Cognitive Neuroscience of Aesthetic Experience." *Perspectives on Psychological Science*, vol. 11, 2016, pp. 265–79.

Pereda, José María. *Peñas arriba*. Espasa-Calpe, 1999.

Pérez Galdós, Benito. *La Fontana de Oro*. Aguilar, 1961.

———. *Montes de Oca*. Historia 16, 1994.

Peri Rossi, Cristina. "Rabelesiana." *Otra vez Eros*. Lumen, 1994.

Piatti-Farnell, Lorna, and Donna Lee Brien. *The Routledge Companion to Literature and Food*. Routledge, 2018.

Piera Lozano, Lola. *Gran soufflé*. Sepha, 2013.

Piera, Montserrat, editor. *Forging Communities: Food and Representation in Medieval and Early Modern Southwestern Europe*, U of Arkansas P, 2018.

Pla, Josep. *Lo que hemos comido*. Destino, 2013.

Pollan, Michael. *The Omnivore's Dilemma: A Natural History of Four Meals*. Penguin, 2006.

Quevedo Villegas, Francisco de. *Obras completas. Obra en prosa*. Aguilar, 1986.

Ramos, Graciliano. *Vidas secas*. Editora Record, 1991.

Reyes, Alfonso. *Memorias de cocina y bodega*. Comba, 2015.

Rivera, José Eustasio. *La vorágine*. Edited by Monserrat Ordóñez, Cátedra, 1990.

Rocha, Glauber. "The Aesthetics of Hunger." Translated by Randal Johnson, *New Latin American Cinema*, vol. 1: *Theories, Practices, and Transcontinental Articulations*, edited by Michael T. Martin, Wayne State UP, 1997, pp. 59–61.

Rocha Monroy, Ramón. *Crítica de la sazón pura*. El País, 2004.

———. *Todos los cominos conducen aroma*. El País, 2007.

Rodríguez, Gustavo. *Cocinero en su tinta*. Planeta, 2012.

Rothblum, Esther, and Sondra Solovay, editors. *The Fat Studies Reader*. New York UP, 2009.

Rozin, Paul, et al. "Attitudes to Food and the Role of Food in Life: Comparisons of Flemish Belgium, France, Japan and the United States." *Appetite*, vol. 33, 1999, pp. 163–80.

Rulfo, Juan. "Nos han dado la tierra." *Relatos*, Alianza Editorial, 1994.

Sahagún, Fray Bernardino de. *Historia general de las cosas de la Nueva España*. Porrúa, 1992.

San Pedro, Diego de. *Cárcel de amor*, edited by Carmen Parrilla, Editorial Crítica, 1995.

Santos-Febres, Mayra. *Tratado de medicina natural para hombres melancólicos*. Agentes Catalíticos, 2011.

Sceats, Sarah. *Food, Consumption and the Body in Contemporary Women's Fiction*. Cambridge UP, 2000.

Shepherd, Gordon. *Neurogastronomy: How the Brain Creates Flavor and Why It Matters*. Columbia UP, 2012.

Stabiner, Karen. "What to Do When Laptops and Silence Take Over Your Cafe?" *New York Times*, 13 February 2018, www.nytimes.com/2018/02/13/dining/cafe-wifi-remote-workers.html.

También la lluvia. Directed by Icíar Bollaín, Spain, Morena Films, 2010.

Tobin, Ronald W. "Qu'est-ce que la gastrocritique?" *Dix-septième siècle*, vol. 217, no. 4, 2002, pp. 621–30.

Trexler, Adam. *Anthropocene Fictions: The Novel in a Time of Climate Change*. U of Virginia P, 2015.

Ulloa, Antonio de. *Viaje al Reino del Perú*. 1748. Real Academia Española, Banco de datos (CORDE), Corpus diacrónico del español, www.rae.es. Accessed 1 Sept. 2018.

Los Últimos. Directed by Nicolás Puenzo, Argentina, Historias Cinematográficas, 2017.

Vargas Llosa, Mario. *Conversación en La Catedral*. Alfaguara, 2016.

Vázquez Montalbán, Manuel. *Contra los gourmets*. Mondadori, 2001.

———. *Mis almuerzos con gente inquietante*. Debolsillo, 2004.

———. *Recetas inmorales*. Afanias, 1996.

———. *La soledad del manager*. Planeta, 1995.

Virués Ortega, Javier. "Huarte de San Juan in Cartesian and Modern Psycholinguistics: An Encounter with Noam Chomsky." *Psicothema*, vol. 17, 2005, pp. 436–40.

Viveiros de Castro, Eduardo, and Peter Skafish. *Cannibal Metaphysics*. U of Minnesota P, 2017.

Wallach, Jennifer Jensen, and Michael D. Wise. *The Routledge History of American Foodways*. Routledge, 2016.

What's Cooking? Directed by Gurinder Chadha, Lions Gate Home Entertainment, 2000.

CHAPTER I

Food, Blood, and a Jewish *Raza* in Fifteenth-Century Spain

Ana M. Gómez-Bravo, *University of Washington*

THE PEACEFUL COEXISTENCE of the "three cultures" in medieval Iberia—Christian, Jewish, and Muslim—known as "convivencia" had quickly begun deteriorating toward the later Middle Ages, most notably after the 1391 pogroms that raided the Peninsula and resulted in the destruction of whole Jewish communities. The growing and often forceful pressure on Jewish communities to assimilate that came from the Church, the Christian population, and, increasingly, the state resulted in the rapid growth of a new social group, the *conversos*, or converts from Judaism to Christianity.[1] From the standpoint of religion, the body politic and the social order, the conversos were hard to fit into existing taxonomies and challenged notions of individual and group identities. Exactly who these conversos were, how Christian they were, and what role they played in the social body were highly contested questions. It was widely agreed that the converso was a hybrid that needed to be closely examined in order to determine the degree of underlying Jewishness. The conversos had their advocates who, citing such authorities as Paul, argued that baptism was the great equalizer and that all Christians, both old and new, were on par with each other and should be treated equally by the Church (and supposedly the Crown and municipalities).[2] However, many considered conversos as second-class Christians and citizens, seeing them as monstrous hybrids that remained partly or entirely Jewish. Hence, the difference between "new" and "old" Christians was in some cases more biological than religious, and the difference was drawn between new Christians and "Christians by nature" ("de natura").[3] The animosity against the conversos precipitated the institution of the purity of blood statutes, laid out in Pedro Sarmiento's 1449 *Sentencia-Estatuto* (in Benito Ruano, *Los orígenes* 39–92) and the 1478 papal bull (*Exigit sincerae devotionis*; in Beltrán de Heredia) authorizing the creation of the Spanish Inquisition. The purity of blood statutes sought to legally discriminate against anyone of Jewish or Muslim ancestry by preventing them from holding office in the Church and in government institutions, schools, universities, and guilds, while the Inquisition attempted to eradicate heresy and heretics, which in its early years included mostly Jewish conversos.[4] However, as scholars have noted, the issues involved in both the purity of blood statutes and the work of the Inquisition are hardly the sole domain of religion (Cuart Moner; García Cárcel; Kamen). Rather, they also involve contemporary ideas on blood and lineage and psychobiological theories (based on humoral theory).[5] In a departure from current scholarship on early racism, this study contends that the early articulation of difference did not rest on the strength of genealogical considerations but rather on the conceptualization of inborn qualities that resided in the blood and were acquired in the process of generation and through food intake.

Several scholars have highlighted the medieval period's central importance in any study on race. Heng has made a powerful argument for the invention of race in the European Middle Ages, and scholars such as Hering Torres and María Elena Martínez have pointed to the key importance that medieval developments had on the birth of racism(s) in the modern period, a line of inquiry that has been further bolstered by the evidence presented by the uses of the word *raza* (race) beginning in late-medieval texts. The importance of understanding the semantic field(s) of *raza* is underscored, among other considerations, by the presence of the term in the formulae used in purity of blood documents, where an individual must be shown to be "without *raza* of Jews, Muslims, or anyone condemned by the Inquisition" in order to be proven as an old Christian and accepted into the institutions requiring such proof. In order to better understand some of the complexities of all the forces at play, it is important to look at late-medieval ideas on generation and bodily constitution and, in particular, the role that religious and medical practices assign to food as well as the ways these theories are mirrored in literature and culture. As the texts examined here show, food played a central role in the attempts to justify ethnoracial difference by helping to root it in the biological, within the body. The popularity of these ideas is evident in broadly circulated texts, as well as in more specialized treatises.

The Converso Mark

A growing body of slanderous texts sought to denounce the true nature of the conversos, claiming to bring into the light their covert practices. A poem by Comendador Román written in the last decades of the fifteenth century and directed to Antón de Montoro, a converso tailor and poet living in Córdoba, attempted to expose Montoro in that fashion. The long poem "Antón parias sin arrisco" (199–205), morphs into a long list of topics suitable for Montoro's pen, which include foods within the dietary laws of kashrut. It states that Montoro's poetry should deal with the observation of the Sabbath (*sabadear*), the eating of *ollas* without eel, hare, or pork (*tocino*), which are all forbidden, but with the addition of mutton slaughtered according to the laws of kashrut, as well as cilantro, eggplant, roasted eggs, and acorns. All this needs to be slow-cooked overnight (*trasnochado*). Montoro should also drink kosher wine and eat unleavened bread and kosher meat. He should be attired in Jewish garb, pray and study Jewish texts (*meldar*), and hold stereotypical Jewish professions.[6] While some of these admonishments regarding diet are intended as satirical and seek to uncover Montoro's Jewish practices by following the laws of kashrut, many of the foods mentioned, chickpeas and spinach for example, do not have assigned kosher values, but they are marked Jewish and understood to be recognized as such by the readers. In one important poem written toward the end of his life, Montoro complained in turn that, in spite of his behaving like a Christian and eating like a Christian, he could never pray long or hard enough because his Jewish identity was indelibly marked in him:

> Oh bitter, sad tailor
> don't you feel your pain!
> Born seventy years ago
> you always recited
> your Marian hymns
> and never swore against God!
>
> I said the Creed and adored
> pots filled with fatty pork,
> and half-cooked rashers;
> I listened to Mass and prayed
> making the sign of the Cross
> and I could never kill
> this converso mark.[7]

The problematic "mark" of the converso to which Montoro refers in such bitter terms was the subject of most legal, medical, and religious writings attempting to elucidate the nature of the conversos.

Marked by an Indelible Character: Food and Baptism

Andrés Bernáldez, chaplain to Diego de Deza, who became inquisitor general of Castile, was a self-appointed chronicler of his time. An important topic in his chronicle, or as he termed it, "memory book," of the reign of Catholic monarchs Isabel and Fernando was the so-called "converso problem." His work, which was widely copied through later centuries, exposes the terms of animosity against the conversos, which include to a large degree the foods that the conversos (and Jews) ate as the source of their despicable nature:

> You should know that the customs of the common people among [the conversos] before the Inquisition were no more and no less than those of the foul-smelling Jews themselves, and the cause of this was the continuous contact that they had with them. [The conversos] were so greedy and such gluttons that they never stopped eating according to Jewish custom dishes and pots of *adefinas* [Sabbath stew], dishes of onions and garlic fried in oil; and they cooked the meat with oil, which they used instead of salt pork and fat so as to avoid using pork; and the meat cooked with oil and all the other things that they cook cause terrible breath, and likewise from their homes and doors emanated a horrible stench because of those dishes; and they themselves smelled like Jews because of all these foods and because they were not baptized. And even assuming that some were baptized, since nullity and judaizing deadened the character of baptism in them, they reeked like the Jews. They did not eat pork unless they were forced to do it; they ate meat during Lent, vigils, and in the four periods of mandated abstinence in secret; they observed their holidays and Sabbaths as best they could; they sent oil for the lamps to the synagogues; they had Jews who would preach to them in

their homes in secret, particularly the women. They had rabbi Jews that slit the throats of cattle and birds for them; they ate unleavened bread when it was mandated for the Jews and clean meat, performing all the Jewish ceremonies in secret, whenever they could, men as well as women.[8]

It is telling that Bernáldez mentions adherence to kosher laws only after establishing that the Jewish and converso body is abominable due to the *adafinas* (Sabbath stew or one-pot dish) and other specific foods that feed it, as well as the cooking techniques that are presented to be quintessentially Jewish.[9] The negative aspects of Jewish (and converso) food consumption are not based merely on the ritual adherence to kosher laws but also on the inherent loathsomeness of the food cooked and consumed by them, with its manifestation on a particular odor, the *foetor Judaicus* that also characterizes Jewish depictions during the period.[10] Such mentions of Jewish odor appear in other late medieval texts, like the poem "A mí grave me sería" by Pero González de Mendoza, where this old Christian noble compares his own food choices with those of the inhabitants of the Jewish Quarter, or *Judería*:

> It would be a grave thing for me
> to leave the meadows with flowers,
> in May, the cold fountain,
> lush gardens with nightingales,
> to go to the Jewish quarter
> to live among tanners,
> where there are such smells,
> where good smell has no place.
>
> How will I leave the mountains,
> where there is fine air and fine trout,
> to go and dwell in the place
> where there are melons and mushrooms,[11]
> where people shut themselves

within thick curtains,
celebrations and the smell of adefinas,
which I do not feel whom it will not kill? . . .

How will I leave partridges
in winter, when they are wholesome,
in summer, quail
to hunt in the morning,
to go with such noses
where the attractive women live,
who with their great pride
make a mockery out of every man?[12]

The main force of Bernáldez's argument rests on the weight he gives to food consumption, which marks the body with traits that are put on par with baptism, a sacrament that, according to Church doctrine, imprints indelible character. According to Bernáldez, both Jewish food and lack of baptism bear the same physical imprint, and both result in a detectable (sensorial) Jewishness. However, Jewishness had become by Bernáldez's time very hard to detect visually, which presented a problem for the state and resulted in the repeated (and largely unsuccessful) attempts to impose visual markers by way of regulations on hair, clothing, headdress, and (for the men) beard styles, as well as external markings on the clothes such as the red circle (*rodela roja*), as is evident for example in the 1412 *Pragmática* given by Queen Catalina de Lancaster (Suárez Bilbao 425–30).[13] Stereotypical representations of Jews in visual art stress a difference in the Jewish body that was not empirically proven (Resnick 268–319). These representations are telling in scenes depicting the baptism of Jews, as they highlight the physically transformative power of the sacrament. In the miniatures in Alfonso X's *Cantigas de Santa María*, the Jews, depicted with the stereotypical features of the time, including a malevolent gaze, closely set almond-shaped eyes, a hook nose and conical hat, emerge from the baptismal waters looking like the figures depicted as Christians in the miniatures and completely devoid of their previous "Jewish" physical traits (e.g., "Dereit' é de s' end' achar," *CSM* 108).[14] The transformative power attributed to both food and baptism points to an internal conceptualization of difference.

Bernáldez's mention of baptism is highly significant, as the nature and power of this sacrament was at the very core of the heated disputes over religious conversion. The claim that the conversos could never really stop being Jewish supported, even in Church circles where this idea was strongly opposed, the differentiation between Christians and "baptized and non-baptized Jews," or between "new Christians" and "Christians by nature." The grave schismatic danger that this differentiation posed for the Church was promptly acknowledged by important Church authors such as Alonso de Oropesa and Alonso de Cartagena and led to the 1449 bull *Humani generis inimicus* issued by Pope Nicholas V against those who negated the power of baptism in the context of conversion and in particular in the case of Jewish converts. However, the view that conversos could not immediately acquire the same status as "old Christians" in Church and other offices was accepted as a matter of course even by authors defending the equalizing and regenerative power of baptism. The papal bull recognized the variance of the new Christians by assigning them the same status as old Christian apostates if they were found to persevere in their Jewish beliefs after baptism (Benito Ruano, *Toledo en el siglo XV* 199–200). At the core of the matter was the recognition that mass conversions, and conversos, from the seventh-century reign of Visigothic King Sisebuto to the fifteenth century, had not been the result of free choice but had arisen from coercive measures by a state that aimed to unite nation and religion.[15] The recognition that some, many, or most of these Jews had converted "insincerely" and that they had lapsed into their old religion soon after being baptized led to questions of whether they could really become *fully* Christian. The questions raised were not only religious but also ontological and social, leading to such objections that someone who was yesterday studying and praying in the synagogue should not today really be praying in church or holding a key office in city council and exercising authority over old Christians, who had thus far been their superiors. As the testimony of Andrés Bernáldez demonstrates, religious and legal matters ultimately rested on the body of the converso, a body fed by the specific foods that constituted it and gave it a character as indelible as baptism.

Monstrous Hybridity: Food, Covert Identity, and Blood Libel

The nature of the converso body was the subject of many widely disseminated texts. Viewed as neither Jewish nor Christian *and* both Jewish and Christian, the converso body revealed that religious belief could no longer serve as a clear marker of identity. The monstrous hybridity of the converso was explained using an assemblage of biological metaphors in the libelous book of the *Alborayque*, which lists the twenty identifying marks of the converso based on the peculiar characteristics of the *alborayque*, the steed that in the Quranic legend took Muhammad to heaven. The conversos, the work states, are nominally Christian but their nature is that of Jews, much like bats are more land animals than birds because of the foods they consume: "el nombre de christianos, las condiciones de judíos. En la verdad de las conversaciones e condiciones, el morciélago es más animalia que ave, segúnd los manjares que come e sus propiedades" ("the name of Christians, the characteristics of Jews. In the true [evidence] of its interactions and characteristics, the bat is rather a [land] animal than a bird, judging from the foods it eats and its properties"; 93). The book takes each of the twenty characteristics as a metaphor to help explain the true nature of the converso. Of particular importance for this study are number one, which deals with the hypocritical, covert nature of the converso; number two, which involves the blood libel; and number fifteen, which identifies the converso with the specific diet that serves to establish his or her hybrid nature. The converso is first likened to the *alborayque* in that he has the mouth of a wolf, because the converso is a lying hypocrite and a false prophet that will at times appear in a sheep's skin to deceive and feign being a good Christian. This point is meant to frame the rest of the metaphors by showing that the conversos are in fact practicing Judaism and disregarding their Christian duties. The conversos keep the Sabbath and Jewish holidays, eat meat during Lent, pray and study Jewish texts like the Jews, and observe Jewish fasts and Passover; they never go to Confession, nor do they take Communion; they do not observe Sunday precepts; they do not attend Mass; they do not praise Mary or Jesus Christ, nor do they read the Gospels.

The second characteristic is that the converso, like the *alborayque*, has the face of a horse and, much like the horse during war, hastens to spill the blood of Christians, as well as the blood of the Prophets (Isaiah, Zechariah), the Apostles, the martyrs, and Christ. The importance of this point cannot be overemphasized, for it shows the breadth and central importance of blood in the construction of an abominable Jewish/converso identity. The establishment of hierarchies based on blood quality had been furthered by the pervasiveness of the blood libel in much of medieval Europe. The blood libel accused Jews of deicide and of a hatred of Christian blood, giving way to the many accusations of ritual blood sacrifices involving Christian children and the desecration of the blood and body of Christ in the form of the Host.

The book next lists human eyes, dog's ears, a nag's neck with a mane, an ox's body, a snake's tail with a crane's head and a peacock's body at its tip, an elegantly dressed man's leg and a horse's leg with a horseshoe for its front legs, an eagle's leg with its talons and a lion's leg without its claws for its hind legs, and a multicolored coat. These are intended to present the conversos as deceitful, cruel, rabid, unproductive, greedy, venomous, pompous, vain, arrogant, oppressive, rapacious, and overall evil. Conversos are also likened to dogs because, as characteristic number four intends to show, they go back to Judaism and to the Jewish practices of consuming adafinas and *cazuelas*, or casseroles, like dogs return to their vomit (77–78).

The material aspects of converso identity are further explored in characteristic number fifteen, which exposes the foods they eat. Alboraycos or conversos show their hybrid nature by eating all manners of food, including animals such as rabbits, partridges killed by Christians or Muslims, fish, hares, and fowl, but they eat little salt pork and, like Jews, they habitually eat the quintessential Sabbath dish, adafina. These three factors—covert nature, blood, and food intake— would combine to mark the true nature of the converso.[16]

Humoral Theory and Diet: Blood as the Repository of Inherent Qualities That Mark the Individual

The creation of a physiological hierarchy, based on the inherent qualities of the blood and the food that formed it, was of central interest to contemporary discussions on the nature of nobility. As Quintanilla Raso has pointed out, the preeminence of blood as the repository of identity characterizes fifteenth-century discussions on nobility. The renewal of the nobility starting in the fourteenth century had emphasized the importance of lineage. But this lineage was supported on something deeper than a genealogical tree, as its value rested on an individual's alleged innate qualities, which justified his or her rise from relative obscurity to the noble state. The shift to blood as the repository of nobility during this century was in many ways an attempt to essentialize a status that in all evidence had been acquired as a result of outside forces.[17] At the same time, it was also an attempt to elevate old over new nobles. The biological underpinnings that appeared as philosophical disquisitions in some texts on the relative values of deeds versus birth and the ways in which either correlated (or not) with nobility (e.g., in Diego de Valera)[18] found a biological justification in diet and humoral theory, particularly because the allusions to blood were made quite literally as pertaining to the biological qualities of the specific blood of groups and individuals. Contemporary (and later) medical theory helped explain such understanding of the blood as difference and of its relation to the foods that constituted it.

As seen in Bernáldez's testimony as well as in the legislation limiting Jews' physical contact with foodstuffs in the market and in heterosocial relations (detailed in Gómez-Bravo, "El judaísmo"), food had a role as an internal marker beyond that assigned by religious laws. Food's constitutive role in the individual's very physical makeup was supported by humoral medical theory, which held that through digestion food became transformed into a substance similar to the one who ate it. A look at medical treatises such as the influential late fourteenth-century *Sevillana medicina* by Juan de Aviñón can help us better comprehend how medicine provided physiological explanations for the relation between food and body generation:

> The nutritive function is the one that changes the food in a substance similar to the one that is fed; and the growing ability is what makes the different parts of the body grow in length, width, and height, and all this is due to the natural faculties administered; and the natural administrative functions are four: attractive, retentive, [digestive], and expulsive; the attractive one is hot and dry; the second, the retentive, cold and dry; the digestive, hot and moist; the expulsive, cold and moist. These four functions serve the nutritive function, and the nutritive function serves the growth function, and the growth function serves the begetting function, and the begetting function has four other functions that serve it: the first is the capacity that transforms the semen with respect to the form it had before; the second changes it into another form similar to that of the one that provided the semen; the third creates the body parts in form and shape; the fourth makes them resemble their procreator in their qualities and in the natural substance.[19]

Juan de Aviñón also explains the current understanding of conception and semen, whose matter originates from the various parts of the father's and mother's bodies (both men and women produced semen during coitus, though men's provided the form, while women's provided the matter), as an excess stemming from the fourth digestion, with the brain playing the crucial role in directing reproduction: "Semen is superfluity of the fourth digestion, which takes place in all parts of the body. The matter of semen comes from all parts. And, for this reason, the creature resembles the father and the mother in all of them, but most of it comes from the brain."²⁰ Once conceived, the fetus is surrounded by blood, which is fed by the food the mother eats and which in turn feeds the fetus (Aviñón 418). After birth, food continued to play a formative role in the constitution of the body, which would acquire its characteristics following humoral theory. Thus, discussion on the properties of food and their effect on the human body was given a central role in medical treatises (e.g., Aviñón 125–307). The conceptualization that the body was constituted by the specific foods that generate it had a strong staying power through later centuries, as witnessed by the fact that Juan de Aviñón's work was disseminated in the sixteenth century through Nicolás Monardes's 1545 edition. Other testimonies such as Juan Pablo Mártir Rizo's *Historia de Cuenca*, published in 1629, make clear the endurance of such a belief in food's effect on the differential constitution of bodies:

> [This chapter] deals with nobility, and it is proven that nobility resides in old roots and that the only noble is he who descends from an old lineage . . . this same difference is found between the noble of old and clear lineage and the new noble: as the latter has been raised rustically and the grossness of his nourishment has made his matter gross from the gross foods that engender similar humors, as is obvious in men of obscure lineage. For a shepherd hinders nature through rustic foods and grows of gross complexion, and he is made of that same matter and engenders dull virtues of the soul and understanding. On the contrary, he who descends from an old and clear lineage is fed under a different rule and order, with moderate abstinence or temperance, with delicate and fine foods, and for this reason he has naturally and hereditarily finer humors, which refine the intellect, elevate the understanding, purify and engender blood that is cleaner and purer, which results in a greater perfection.²¹

Mártir Rizo was in fact repeating ideas, at times verbatim, of earlier authors such as Fernando Mexía, whose 1479 *Nobiliario vero* locates nobility in the blood and clearly explains the crucial importance of food. After explaining that subtle substances are nobler because they rise through evaporation and come down in a thickened form, Mexía applies such properties to nobles, aligning the differential qualities of coarse and delicate foods with the humors they engender:

> So it must be necessarily the same with the new noble or with the one who is noble and descends from an old lineage, because the new noble is raised grossly, and the coarseness of his nutritive ability has made his matter coarse due to the coarse foods that engender thick humors, as it appears in everyone who is of obscure lineage, because a laborer has coarse nature and rustic complexion and is turned to a rude disposition due to coarse foods. And such coarse matter makes or engenders the virtues of the soul and of understanding coarse, as is naturally seen in barbarians, peasants, shepherds, savages, and others of such condition. For as the one who descends from lofty and clear and old lineage is nourished and raised very differently and in another orderly or arranged rule, in moderate abstinence or temperance, and also with delicate, subtle, and digestible foods, he naturally and even hereditarily has more subtle humors, which causes to refine the intellect, to elevate understanding, and to purify and generate cleaner and purer blood.[22]

The value of food in the constitutive processes of the body mentioned in these and other texts was firmly rooted in the theory of the humors, which had originated from Hippocrates and been further developed by Galen. Humoral theory identified four main humors in the body: blood, choler, phlegm, and melancholy. In order to understand the central importance of food, it is necessary to look at contemporaneous ideas on the relation of food's properties vis-à-vis the body's properties and the digestion process. In relation to nourishment, digestion was understood as a process by which food is cooked in the stomach and then passed in the form of a refined "extract/juice" or "chyle" to the liver. The liver sanguifies the chyle, turning it into blood, which is then distributed throughout the body by means of a process known as "assimilation," which transforms nutrients into flesh. Once it leaves the liver, blood also needs to be further refined in the brain (producing phlegm), the gallbladder (producing choler), and the spleen (producing melancholy). Afterward, the blood can be further refined into humors by the organs as it carries nutrients to all parts of the body. In this way, the properties of food affect all four humors. After leaving the liver, blood was thought to follow a third path into the heart. From the heart, blood proceeds to the lungs, where harmful vapors are expelled. In the heart (left ventricle), the blood comes into contact with outside air, which revitalizes the blood. This blood enters the arteries, which distribute the resulting spirit or *pneuma* (breath of life). The arteries also carry the vitalized blood to the brain, where the blood comes into contact with a cooling net called *rete mirabile* (literally "wondrous net"), through which the "animal spirits," or *animus*, one's rational soul, is distilled. This animus is then carried to the whole body through the nervous system, putting into effect the commands issued by the brain.[23] Any problem or fault introduced in the diet or in the digestive process has therefore a direct impact on the brain, on thoughts and behavior, and on the rational soul or spirit.

Aviñón also expressed the common undersanding of wheat's ideal nature as the "seed" most like the human body: "El trigo es la mas ygual simiente que sea en el mundo para el cuerpo del ome" ("Wheat is the most similar seed in the world for the human body"; 149). In medical writings, the direct relationship between wheat and the generation of the human body was made evident not only through wheat's stated beneficial properties but also in the fact that both seed and semen were termed *simiente* in Spanish, thus clearly marking the link between wheat grain and the human seed or semen that generated the human body. Important medical writings such as Huarte de San Juan's 1575 *Examen de ingenios para las ciencias* (*Examination of Intellects for the Sciences*) followed earlier medical theories on wheat bread like Aviñón's (149–57) and explained how humoral theory, when combined with theories of generation, made food, and in particular wheat, a central constitutive principle of the self from the moment of conception, giving it precedence over two of the other factors, air and water quality, that were considered essential for good health at the time. Huarte de San Juan conceptualized bread as a particularly character-forming foodstuff:[24]

Although it is true that it is very important to breathe delicate, tempered air and to drink water with similar qualities, but it is much more important to eat fine foods that have the balance that best suits the intellect, for food engenders blood, and blood engenders the seed, and the seed engenders the fetus. If the foods are delicate and tempered, so will be the blood, from which the seed stems, from which the brain stems. If the brain is tempered and composed of fine and delicate substances, Galen states that the intellect will follow suit, because our rational soul, though it is incorruptible, is always attached to the brain's disposition, which, if it is not what it needs to be in order to properly think and reason, says and does much nonsense. The foods, then, that the parents must eat in order to produce children of great understanding (which is the most common in Spain) are, first, white bread, made from finely-ground flour kneaded with salt: this is cold and dry food, and of subtle and very delicate parts. Another is made (says Galen) of golden wheat, which, although it is very nourishing and makes the men robust and full of many bodily strengths, it spoils the understanding because it is also humid and thick. I said the bread needs to be kneaded with salt because no other of the foods eaten by men produces such a good understanding as this mineral. [This mineral] is cold and of the greatest dryness among all things; and let us remember the judgment of Heraclitus, who said: *splendor siccus, animus sapientissimus*; by which he wanted to make us understand that the dryness of the body makes the soul very wise.[25]

Thus, food intake had a direct correlation with identity, which had a psychobiological basis established during the process of generation and was supported by diet throughout an individual's lifetime. Such a conceptualization of the link between food and blood placed a heavier weight on blood by emphasizing not solely its being inherited through family lineage but also its role in establishing an individual identity through a localized and contextualized process of generation as well as through sustained practices of individual food intake.

Making It Legal: Food, Blood, and Abomination

The clearly materialist implications that such understandings of identity had on the nature of the soul certainly had detractors and could not but alarm the Church (García García). However, this view of identity formation endured, and it helped form the basis for a racialized understanding of blood that enabled the establishment of the purity of blood statutes and helped institutionalize the abomination of ethnic and religious minorities. As Freidenreich has convincingly shown, the rejection of Jewish food (considered impure, like the Jews and their celebrations) and the consequent prohibitions regarding the exchange of food gifts and commensality between Christians and Jews had become an integral component of Christianity very early on. The processes by which Christianity was repeatedly formulated as a religion opposed to Judaism can be seen in conciliar Church documents (Freidenreich, esp. 110–28).

The prohibitions for Christians against commensality with Jews and against contact with Jewish foods appear in many medieval texts, including the *Confessional* by Martín Pérez, who prohibits various forms of contact between Christians and both Jews and Muslims, including "eating with them or eating their unleavened bread or their viands, or taking medicine from them" (468). Similarly, legislation spanning several centuries regulated the contact between Jews and Christians in such areas as the purchase and sale of food, the preparation and administration of medicines, commensality, and physical contact with food.[26] However, these prohibitions were not only aimed at limiting sociability between Christians and Jews (and Muslims), but they also reveal a conceptualization of Jews and Jewish foods as contaminants that justified the prohibitions against physical contact with food. This included, for example, legislation prohibiting Jews from touching any type of food in the market and mandating the use of a rod, as seen in the texts published by Sabaté, as well as Sanahuja: "Further, the said councilmen resolved that their first decision would be made into an ordinance that no Jew or Jewess could go shopping with naked hands or be able to otherwise touch bread, fruit, or anything else that is for sale in the city, but rather use a rod that they should carry in their hand."[27] Legislative measures thus show that the regulations regarding commensality and Jewish food did not rest on objections against sociability or religious dietary laws alone but went deeper by helping conceptualize the abominable nature of all physical aspects of the Jewish body and the polluting effect of the food that fed it.

The conceptualization of a faulty Jewish blood intrinsically tied to the foods that constituted it formed the basis for further discriminatory legislation. At its most evident, the legislation forbade conversos from holding food-related jobs. One example may be seen in such rulings as that regarding Benito García, a converso described as being "naturalmente judío" ("Jewish by nature") before his baptism (Horozco, *Relaciones Históricas Toledanas* 40), who was burned at the stake in 1491 as a result of the blood libel trial known as "Santo Niño de La Guardia" ("Holy Child of La Guardia"), in which García and others were accused for the ritual murder of a Christian child. The accused were tried and burned at the stake.[28] Benito García's descendants were forbidden from operating any shop where spices, food, or drink were sold because they had the *damaged and infected* blood of their father and grandfather: "And [we pronounce that] they may not be spicers, innkeepers, tavern keepers, or hostellers, because *the damaged and infected blood* of the said Benito Garçia, their father, their grandfather accompanies them from infancy" (emphasis added).[29]

The idea of a tainted blood and body similarly explains the fear and prohibitions against using Jewish physicians and pharmacists. These professionals had the power to take life as much as to give it through malpractice and poisoning, *and*, as Jews, they were considered dirty and highly contagious.[30] The resulting prohibitions, identical to ones installed in Visigothic times and later during King Alfonso X's reign in the thirteenth century, forbade the use of non-Christian wet nurses (human milk was thought to be refined blood, or "white blood")[31] and attempted to diminish the power of Jewish doctors and apothecaries or pharmacists to prescribe any remedies for Christians.[32]

The disablement that the conversos' tainted blood was said to elicit was also applied to positions of political power in city and state offices. Converso and royal chronicler Fernando de Pulgar commented emphatically and critically on the negative conceptualization of converso blood and the social and political practices associated with it. In his letter to "a friend of his in Toledo" (Toledo being an important city for the Crown and one with a large converso population), Pulgar put the critical comments in the mouth of an old noble and chief magistrate of Toledo, Gómez Manrique: "In this noble city, it is hardly suffered that some, whom you judge not to be 'of lineage' have honors and posts in government, because you understand that the defect in their blood takes away their ability to govern."[33] As Pulgar explains, such blood prejudice is built on the concepts of low blood (*la baxa sangre*), lineage (*linaje*), and numberless variations on the "vileness" of the blood (*vileza de la sangre*) of the conversos (67–71). Many of the characteristics associated with Jewish blood, food, and disease appear clearly combined in the anti-Semitic mock "Letter of privilege that King Don Juan II gave a nobleman" ("Traslado"). In it, the King grants the "nobleman," who is actually a converso, privileges to act destructively in ways that mirror the stereotyped actions of conversos:

> And we also give you and your descendants said license so that you can be apothecaries, physicians, and surgeons and, under the cover of curing and looking to heal the diseases of the body of any old Christian, labor and seek, as all of the generation of the marranos do, to kill and humiliate the old Christians because of the hatred and enmity they have toward them, as well as to marry the women of those old Christians whom they kill, to swallow their property and belongings, and to dirty and sully clean blood. And I also grant that you may try to take over the posts of those who will pass from this life through your good diligence, all in order that one of the line and generation of the said Hebrew marranos or of another such stock may attain it.[34]

The success of radicating Jewish identity in the blood and thus turning it into a biological rather than a religious trait also rested on the general familiarity and use of medical discourse and on the dissemination of relevant ideas in popular literature.

Defective Blood as Contagious Disease

The polluting, transformative touch of the converso was clearly aligned with their faulty blood. This polluting touch was not only the subject of astringent legislation but also very much present in popular culture. In the poem "Juan Poeta en vos venir" (text in *Electronic corpus*) written by Fadrique Manrique, count of Paredes, various religious objects, people, and places become unhappily transformed by mere physical contact with the converso Juan Poeta. The paten becomes a dish of eggplant (*caçuela con berengena*) when Juan Poeta takes it to his mouth, the consecrated altar becomes the Sabbath stew (adafina) when Poeta touches it (lines 31–40), and even the Body of Christ becomes a calf upon contact with the converso (lines 16–20). As quintessential Jewish foods, eggplant and adafina mark Poeta as converso in the poem, while the sacrificial calf into which the body of Christ is transformed points to animal sacrifices identified in the text with the Jewish tradition.[35]

Such texts mirror the marked and diseased conceptualization of Jewish blood in religious texts. In his sermon against the Jews, Frei João de Ceita emphasized that Jewish blood was bad blood that needed to be purged of the viper's venom it contained (Glaser 173). Inquisitorial records from the onset of the tribunal to the time of King Fernando's death and beyond published in *Bulario de la Inquisición española* repeatedly refer to the conversos as tainted by a "stain" ("macula," "maculados"), "infected" ("infisionadas") by a "heretical, depraved pestilence" ("peste de la pravedad heretica") that is a "cancer," spreading venom (80–82, 92–93).[36] There exist obvious ties between the language and pathology surrounding the "grave illness" of Judaism, which is coded as a "contagious pestilence" ("contagio de tal peste"; 108–9, 118–19, 139), which used to refer, among other diseases, to the Black Death (*peste, pestilencia*).[37] In the texts produced by the Inquisition examining the legal and religious status of the conversos, published in *Bulario de la Inquisición española*, the ties between conversos and Jews are not presented as those who have only common beliefs, however "wrong" they may be, but as those who are consanguineous and share a common stock and blood ("origene," "de eo genere," "consanguinitate"; 128–29; "de genere iudaeorum prouenientibus"; 142). Those found to possess such "stain" ("macula") or "infection" in their blood need to be physically marked through a "stain or note of disablement" ("mancha o nota de inhabilitacion"; 242–43), thus making the internal "converso mark" explicit.

The legal and religious texts cited here state that the blood bond between Jews and conversos conveys its character from parents to their offspring, who inherit their "bad blood." The genealogy of tainted blood was woven into biblical narratives like the one developed in Alfonso X's *General Estoria*, where the daughters of Cain ("del linage de Caím") are depicted as being beautiful but of "bad blood" and thus inherently evil (45–46). In a similar vein, Sebastián de Horozco advised that for a clean and happy life, a Christian should marry a Christian, while a *marrano* (converso) should marry a *marrana* (conversa). Horozco warned the Christian not to fall into avarice and marry for money and thus "change his skin," making "stained children." Further, Horozco warns about the consequences of marrying a converso/a, as such a stain spreads rapidly and taints the family for generations to come until the end of time, never disappearing.[38]

The circle closed when religious texts leveraged medical theory and dictated that religious and ethnic identity was physically transmitted. For instance, the 1494 manual for inquisitors would further support this understanding of a physiological basis of religious difference as something transmittable to offspring through the blood: "For not only are the Jews passing from father to son the perfidy of the old law through the blood, but at home the sons remain for the most part in the same state as their parents" (Sala-Molins 78). Authors such as Lope de Barrientos wrote extensive treatises attempting to argue against such formulations, quoting Gratian when explaining, for instance, that the reproduction of Jewish evil seed (*semen*) took place according to sin and not the flesh: "Sicut enim qui filii promissionis sunt, existimantur in semen bonum, ita etiam qui erroris sunt, existimantur in semen malum; nam et Iudaei ex patre diabolo sunt, intelligas non utique carnis successione, sed criminis" (Martínez Casado 44); translated from Latin into Spanish by Barrientos himself as: "Just as those who are children of promise are reputed to be good seed, so those who are children of error are considered as bad seed, because the father of the Jews is the devil, but this is not according to the succession of the flesh, but according to the succession of sin" (my translation from the Spanish text).[39] Radicating difference in the blood would be at the core of purity of blood statutes and of the notion of a Jewish and Muslim *raza*.

Raza as Defect: *Raza* and the Diseased Body

The use of the word *raza* (race), when used in the context of a discussion on human character during the fifteenth century, is always a negative term most often used as a synonym for "defect" or "stain."[40] In his famous dictionary published in 1611, Sebastián de Covarrubias explains in very clear terms the different meanings of the word: *raza* can mean "stock," the lineage of pure-bred horses that are marked with an incandescent iron so that they may be clearly identifiable. *Raza* is also a technical term for weavers and tailors, as it refers very specifically to a defect in the weave (*diferencia*). This defect creates a separation of the threads so that the cloth becomes sparse. Similarly, *raza* is a crack or defect that develops in the hooves of equines. Lastly, Covarrubias gives the meaning of *raza* in relation to human genealogy: "when in reference to lineages, race is taken as a negative term, as in having a *raza* of Moor or Jew."[41] Although scholars have used Covarrubias's definition to associate *raza* with the first meaning he lists, as part of the vocabulary of animal husbandry understood to refer to stock or lineage, it must be noted that the term is clearly documented as implying "fault," "stain," or "defect" starting in the fourteenth century. The semantic fields of *raza* include not only "breed" or "stock" as used in some administrative texts but, most often, "mark," "stain," "crack," and "defect" as it appears in the language of gemology, veterinary, and textiles referenced in Covarrubias and in earlier dictionaries like Alonso de Palencia's and Antonio de Nebrija's, both published in or around 1490.[42] Since the fourteenth century, the semantic field of *raza* has included such metaphorical uses in reference to internal personal characteristics. An early attestation of the use is found in 1350, when Pedro de Veragüe advised in his *Doctrina* against recurring to slander in order to cover one's own faults: "If to cover your faults (*raças*) / you condemn another's error / when you see what you get / you will cry."[43] The metaphorical transfer of textile lexicon to human traits is amply documented beginning in the fourteenth century in the various versions of the widely quoted proverb "En el mejor paño cae la raza" ("The stain can fall on the best cloth") or "No hay paño sin raza" ("There is no cloth without defect").[44]

The uses of *raza* / *raça* seem to be the result of an evolution of *radius>*radia>raça*,[45] and it is clear that during the last decades of the fifteenth century it always carried a negative connotation when it referred to Jews or Muslims, as well as to those who carried their blood, even if it was only in a minimal proportion. The extension of the semantic field of *raza* as internal defect, both physical and behavioral, is amply documented in the fifteenth and early sixteenth centuries. In his 1473 will, Fernan García Barba de Figueroa stipulated that his sons and grandsons must marry "senpre con cristianas vellas e non de pouco convertidas nin infeitas da mala raça de mouros ou judios ou de outra mala sangre" ("always with old Christian women and not recently converted nor infected with bad *raza* of Moors or Jews or any other bad blood"; "Testamento" 32). If they did, they would lose their inheritance rights. The early sixteenth-century *Corónica de Adramón* presents a similar formula in a chivalric context, where the knight utters the oath that "he is engendered from legitimate marriage and that he merits [the order of chivalry] on account of both his parents and his four grandparents, and that he would deserve it even if it were far greater, for there was not in him or in his predecessors *raza* or mixture of bad blood" ("que es engendrado de legytymo matrymonyo, y por entranbos padres y sus IIII auelos la mereçe, y sy muy mayor fuese, la mereçya, no avyendo en él ny en sus anteçesores rraça ny mescla de mala sangre"; 397), thus pointing to the same association of blood and *raza* as defect that would be institutionalized in the statutes of blood purity. The phrase "sin raza" appears in the middle of the fifteenth century in reference to the "flawless" or "defectless" *hidalgo* (noble) nature of magistrate and poet Gómez Manrique in his slanderous address to converso poet Juan Poeta.[46] Manrique, old Christian and noble, "hidalgo syn raça" ("Poeta de la nobleza" 332; v. 6) was obviously threatened by the hybridity of not a Jew, not a Christian, but a *marrano* ("no judío ni christiano / mas exçelente marrano"; vv. 53–54). The poem clearly contrasts the *raza* or defect of the converso author, which marks his body and his writing, with the "raceless" nature of the Christian noble, who is free from such defects and can thus produce a superior "unmarked" poetry. With such negative understanding of the Jewish and converso bodies, and building on medical treatises and religious polemic, the purity of blood statutes would help coin the term *raça/raza* as a negative trait (*tener raça de*) that was radicated in the body. Thus, the formula did not refer to a Jewish or Muslim "lineage" but to a Jewish or Muslim *defect* that lay in one's blood. The statutes would place Jews, Muslims, heretics, and their descendants at a disadvantage in the social, political, religious, and economic spheres and would help justify a long-standing prejudice against religious and "racial" minorities.

Such negative conceptualization of difference needs to be further considered alongside that of the discourse of infection discussed above and the effect of diseased foods, which for centuries people believed had a crucial impact on the body and the soul. The fifteenth-century Spanish translation of the work of Johannes de Ketham explained that infected foods engender infected semen, which the soul abhors for it cannot allow the noble human form to be instilled in it: "Why do pregnant women who eat infected foods soon abort? Answer: because the infected seed is generated out of such foods, which the soul very much abhors and throws out of the field of nature, which is like its dwelling; because it is not willing for such matter to be infused with human form, which is most noble."[47] In the case of Jews, medical authors considered the additional factors that they live in rottenness and putridness, for Jews are evil and afflicted by illness,[48] and the streets of the Jewish quarter are "dirty and tainted to the fourth degree."[49] Personal food habits were also viewed as being lethal to others upon contact. Aviñón states that those raised with poisonous foods will be able to thrive on them out of habit, but those same foods will act as a poison to others upon contact (Aviñón 305–7), laying the foundation for legislation limiting the physical contact of religious and ethnic minorities with food that was intended for Christian consumption. The Jewish (and converso) diet inevitably fed an inferior, tainted body, marked by the stereotyped consumption of foods like the eggplant that medical theory problematized and presented as less desirable and noxious to health (e.g., Aviñón 144, 196). Further, Jews (and conversos), as well as Muslims, abstained from eating pork, the animal that was most like the human body,[50] a problematic issue given that, as medical texts pointed out, "The material cause of eating is the need for food, which is defined as a substance that has the ability to transform itself in the likeness of the body, as well as bread, wine, meat, and the like."[51] Refraining from eating the flesh of the animal that was most human-like could potentially prevent racialized minorities from acquiring healthy human properties. Thus, food consumption practices and the legislation and medical theories that aimed at regulating them would encourage a biological understanding of that which made those minorities "faulty" or "defective."

The study of the making of *raza*, the development of its semantic field, is particularly illuminating when undertaken alongside that of notions of a "defect" that is physically generated from the moment of conception and radicated in the blood with the help of key material factors such as food intake. In light of the evidence presented here, a strong argument emerges for the consideration of the key roles that food and the body, along with relevant practices in medieval Spain, play in the manifold and shifting notion of race until the present day. The push to make difference internal and locate it in the body encouraged giving food considerations central importance in the articulation of identity and difference, particularly since food was understood to be a key factor in the generation of the human body and its preservation through continued acts of individual food choices. The development of a concept of *raza* inevitably points to that of racism, "The belief that all members of each race possess characteristics, abilities, or qualities specific to that race, especially so as to distinguish it as inferior or superior to another race or races," as defined by the *Oxford English Dictionary*. As this chapter has shown, medieval evidence points to an early association of "defect" and "stain" to *raza*, and of such *raza* as residing in a blood fed by specific foods. The texts show the makings of an internal conceptualization of difference that supported itself in medical theories of bodily constitution, in which both food and the blood that it helped produce were key in the establishment of a physical and biological basis for the racialization of religious difference.

NOTES

1. On the medieval theory of state, see Bertelloni; Gordillo Pérez; Pérez Johnston.
2. On the status of the conversos, see for example Benito Ruano 2001; Domínguez Ortiz; Netanyahu.
3. An example from the documents published in Madurell Marimón (60, 72–74).
4. There is ample bibliography on these statutes. See for example Sicroff; Hernández Franco.
5. See García García for the debate on the organicist body-soul relationship. On the centrality of blood for Christianity, see Anidjar. Nirenberg has highlighted the role of lineage and the emphasis on genealogy.
6. I have analyzed Román's poem as well as Montoro's in detail in two forthcoming articles ("Antón de Montoro" and "Comendador Román").
7. "¡O Ropero amargo, triste, / que no sientes tu dolor! / ¡Setenta años que naçiste / y en todos siempre dixiste / *ynviolata permansiste* / y nunca juré al Criador! // Hize el *Credo* y adorar / ollas de toçino grueso, / torreznos a medio asar, / oyr misas y rezar, / santiguar y persignar / y nunca pude matar / este rastro de confeso" (75, lines 1–13). All translations in this chapter are my own.

8. "Aveis de saber que las costunbres de la gente común de ellos antes de la Inquisición, ni más ni menos eran que de los proprios hediondos judíos; e esto causava la continua conversación que con ellos tenían. Así eran tragones y comilitones, que nunca dexaron el comer a costunbre judaica de manjarejos e olletas de adefinas e manjarejos de cebollas e ajos refritos con aceite, e la carne guisavan con aceite, e lo echavan en lugar de tocino e de grosura, por escusar el tocino; e el aceite con la carne e cosas que guisan hace muy mal oler el resuello, e así sus casas e puertas hedían muy mal a aquellos manjarejos; e ellos eso mismo tenían el olor de los judíos, por causa de los manjares e de no ser baptizados. E puesto caso que algunos fueran baptizados, mortificado el carácter del baptismo en ellos por la nulidad e por judaizar, hedían como judíos. No comían puerco sino en lugar forçoso; comían carne en las cuaresmas e vigilias e cuatro ténporas, en secreto; guardavan las pascuas e sábados como mejor podian; enbiavan aceite a las sinagogas para las lánparas; tenían judios que les predicasen en sus casas de secreto, especialmente a las mugeres. Tenían judíos rabíes que les degollavan las reses e aves para sus negocios; comían pan cenceño al tienpo de los judios carnes tajeles, haciendo todas las ceremonias judaicas de secreto, en cuanto podían, así los honbres como las mujeres" (96–97). On the evolution of baptism in the early Church see for example García de Cortázar (17, 41, 46–47, 87, 90, 160, 194, 201–2, 373, 463).

9. On the adafinas, see Gómez-Bravo, "Adafina."

10. On the *foetor Judaicus*, see Resnick (232–43).

11. The meaning of "porçinas" is unclear. The *Cancionero de Juan Alfonso de Baena* editors propose "mushrooms."

12. "A mí grave me sería / dexar los prados con flores, / en mayo la fuente fría, / vergeles con ruiseñores, / por ir a la judería / bevir entre cortidores, / a do ay tales olores / donde buen olor no ha parte. // ¿Cómo dexaré la sierra, / do ay aire y truchas finas, / por ir morar a la tierra / do ay badehas y porçinas, / a do la gente se ençierra / con las espesas cortinas, / fiesta e olor de adefinas, / que non siento a quien non mate? . . . // ¿Cómo dexaré perdizes / en ivierno, que son sanas, / en verano codornizes / de caçar por las mañanas, / por ir con tales narizes / a do biven las loçanas, / que con sus grandes ufanas / a todo hombre dan su mate?" (*Cancionero de Juan Alfonso de Baena* 322, lines 5–20, 29–36). Similarly, the long poem *Coplas del Provincial* makes a slanderous reference to a peculiar Jewish odor: "My lady doña María, / don't remain in my dwelling any longer, for you very much reek like a Jew, / even if you are wearing perfume" ("Señora doña María, / no estéis más en mi posada, / que hedéis mucho a judía, / aunque vengáis perfumada"; in Rodríguez Puértolas 256).

13. A full account of laws regulating Jewish life in Christian Spain is given in Suárez Bilbao. For internal regulations or Taqqanot of Jewish communities, see for example Moreno Koch.

14. Patton has studied the physically transformative power of the Eucharist on the Jewish physique as depicted in visual art ("Constructing"; see also *Art of Estrangement*).
15. For the relationship between the purity of blood statutes and earlier law, see for example Kaplan.
16. "La xv condición del Alborayque es que come de todos manjares. Assí, los alboraycos comen conejos, perdizes muertas de manos de christianos e de moros, e pescado (que ellos comen poco tozino), liebres e otros animales e aves, adafina como judíos. E cómenlo en todo tiempo, y en la Quaresma de los christianos: y en el ayuno de los judíos y en el ayuno de los moros, los más dellos, que pocos guardan las cerimonias de los otros" (94).
17. For my study of issues associated with notions of nobility see Gómez-Bravo (*Textual Agency* 15–32).
18. On Diego de Valera's position on nobility and the conversos, see Accorsi.
19. "La virtud nutritiua es la que torna el gouierno en semejança del gouernado; y la virtud crecedera es la que faze crecer los miembros en luengo y en ancho y en alto, y todo esto viene de las virtudes naturales administradas; pero las virtudes naturales administraderas son quatro: atratiua, retentiua, [digistiua], espulsiua; la atratiua es callente y seca; la .ij., fria, seca; la digistiua, callente y humida; la espulsiua, fria y humida. Y estas quatro virtudes siruen a la virtud nutritiua, y la virtud nutritiua sirue a la crecedera, y la crecedera a la virtud engendradera, y la virtud engendradera tiene otras virtudes, que la siruen y son quatro: la .j. es la virtud que trasmuda la simiente de su forma que tenia ante: la segunda, la que le faze tornar en otra forma semejante del que la echa; la .iij., la virtud que forma los miembros en forma y en figura; la quarta, la que las faze semejar en las qualidades y en la sustancia natural del fazedor" (414–15). On some of the aspects of the impact of Aviñón's *Sevillana medicina*, see Amasuno Sárraga (esp. 101–31); Carmona García (174–83); and the introductory study in Mondéjar's edition.
20. "Y la simiente es superfluydad de la quarta digistion, que es en los miembros. Y la materia de la simiente viene de todos los miembros del cuerpo; y, por esta razon, parece la criatura al padre y a la madre en todos los miembros, pero la mayor parte viene del meollo" (429–30).
21. "[Este capítulo] trata de la nobleza y se prueua como en la antiguedad consiste la nobleza y que solamente es noble el que deciende de antiguo linage . . . esta (misma) diferencia se halla entre el noble de antiguo y claro linage, y del que es noble nueuo: porque assi como este se ha criado rusticamente, y de la grossedad de su nutrimiento ha hecho su materia gruessa, respeto de los manjares gruessos, que engendran semejantes humores, como parece en los hombres de oscuro linage, pues vn pastor respeto de los rusticos manjares entorpeze la naturaleza, y se haze de complesion grossera, y esta misma materia trae, y engendra torpes las virtudes del anima, y entendimiento. Y por el contrario, el que deciende de

antiguo y claro linage está alimentado de otra forma con diferente regla, y orden, con moderada abstinencia ó templança, con delicados, y sutiles manjares, y por esto trae natural, y hereditariamente mas sutiles humores, lo qual es causa de sutilizar el ingenio, eleuar el entendimiento, purificar, y engendrar mas limpia sangre, y mas pura, de lo qual resulta mayor perfeccion" (208). Here as in Mexía's text, the terms "grueso" and "grosedad" mean both "thick" or "thickness" and "coarse/ness" or "rude/ness," following the meanings of the terms during the period. On the medieval theory of humors, see for example Siraisi (101–6).

22. "Otrosy es de notar que toda cosa sotyl es mas digna e mas noble que lo grueso, e lo ralo mas que lo espeso. Esto paresçe asy que lo sotyl sube al çielo vaporysando e del çielo desçiende e cae espesado, bien asi pues es nesçesaryo açerca del nueuo noble o de aquel que noble es e de antigo lynaje desçiende. Ca el nuevo es cryado gruesamente e la grosedat de su nutrityva ha fecho su materya gruesa por rrespecto delos manjares gruesos que engendran gruesos vmores commo paresçe en todo aquel que es de obscuro linaje. Ca vn gañan por rrespecto de los gruesos manjares es en gruesa natura e conplisyon rrustica e grosera dispusiçion convertido. E la tal gruesa materya trae o engendra gruesas las virtudes del anima e del entendimiento. Como naturalmente es visto açerca de los barvaros, de los labradores, de los pastores, de los syluestres e delos otros de la tal condiçion, pues commo el que es desçendido de alto e claro e antigo linaje sea nudrydo e cryado por el contraryo e en otra ordenada o arreglada obseruançia, açerca de moderada abstynençia o tenprança, asy mismo delicados sotyles e dyrygibles manjares trae natural e avn heredytarya mente mas sotyles vmores lo qual es cabsa de a sotilizar el yngenio a eleuar el entendimiento e a puryfycar e a generar mas linpia e mas pura sangre" (Fernando de Mexia, *Nobiliario vero.* Biblioteca Nacional, Madrid, Ms. 3311, fol. 97v–98r).

23. For a detailed description of the process of digestion, see Albala (54–66). See also the explanation in Aviñón (357–60), who also provides the typical period depiction of digestion as cooking process (357–59).

24. On the importance of bread according to Juan de Aviñón, see Mondéjar; Solomon.

25. "Pero, aunque es verdad que importa mucho respirar aires muy delicados y de buen temperamento, y beber aguas tales, pero mucho más hace al caso usar de manjares sutiles y de la temperatura que requiere el ingenio; porque destos se engendra la sangre, y de la sangre la simiente, y de la simiente la criatura. Y si los alimentos son delicados y de buen temperamento, tal se hace la sangre, y de tal sangre, tal simiente, y de tal simiente, tal celebro. Y siendo este miembro templado y compuesto de sustancia sutil y delicada, el ingenio dice Galeno que será tal; porque nuestra ánima racional, aunque es incorruptible, anda siempre asida de las disposiciones del celebro, las cuales, si no son tales cuales son menester para discurrir y filosofar, dice y hace mil disparates. Los

manjares, pues, que los padres han de comer para engendrar hijos de grande entendimiento (que es el ingenio más ordinario en España) son, lo primero, el pan candial, hecho de la flor de la harina y masado con sal: éste es frío y seco, y de partes sutiles y muy delicadas. Otro se hace (dice Galeno) de trigo rubial o trujillo, el cual, aunque mantiene mucho y hace a los hombres membrudos y de muchas fuerzas corporales, pero por ser húmido y de partes muy gruesas echa a perder el entendimiento. Dije masado con sal, porque ningún alimento de cuantos usan los hombres hace tan buen entendimiento como este mineral. Él es frío y con la mayor sequedad que hay en las cosas; y si nos acordamos de la sentencia de Heráclito, dijo de esta manera: splendor siccus, animus sapientissimus; por la cual nos quiso dar a entender que la sequedad del cuerpo hace al ánima sapientísima" (647–48).

26. Laws and regulations published in Suárez Bilbao 165, 169, 181, 189, 198, 265, 298–300, 307, 308, 312–13, 324, 373, 396, 398, 426, 428, 432, 434, 439, 445, and 448.

27. "Item los dits Conseyllers acordaren quel primer Conseyll general fos feyt ordenament que nengun jueu ni juyia no gos mercadeiar ab la má nua ni en altra manera tochar ab la má negun pan, fruyta ni altres coses ques venen en la Ciutat, sino ab una vergueta que porten en la má" (Sanahuja 43n5).

28. See Perceval; J. Pérez 185–86. Weissberger's study shows the persistence of the topic in Spanish literature and its continued use in discrimination against conversos.

29. "Y que no puedan ser espeçieros, mesoneros, venteros, taverneros, pues que *la sangre dañada infiçionada* de la infancia del dicho Benito García, su padre, su agüelo los acompaña" (in Horozco, *Relaciones Históricas Toledanas* 45).

30. For the position of Jews in medical practice, see Shatzmiller. For the work of Jewish physicians in the Spanish kingdoms, see García Ballester.

31. See for example Vicente de Burgos (1494): "ca la materia de la leche es la sangre muy coçida en las tetas" ("for the matter of milk is blood cooked in the breasts") (folio 43v).

32. In Alfonso X's *Fuero Real* (1255), also in Cortes and Church councils. On Jewish practices, see Baumgarten (122–53); for laws, see Suárez Bilbao (300, 312, 324, 426, 428, 431, 432).

33. "En esa noble cibdad no se puede buenamente sofrir que algunos que iuzgais no ser de linaje tengan honras e oficios de gouernación, porque entendeis que el defecto de la sangre les quita la habilidad del gouernar" (67).

34. "E asímismo damos licencia a vos e a los dichos vuestros descendientes para que podáis ser boticarios, físicos y zurujanos e so color de curar e procurar por la salud de las enfermedades del cuerpo de qualquier christiano viejo trabajéis e procuréis como trabajan e procuran todos los de la dicha generación de los maranos de matar e apocar a los christianos viejos, así por el odio y enemistad que les

tienen como por casar con las mugeres de aquellos christianos viejos que matan, por tragar sus bienes e faciendas y ensuciar y mancillar la sangre limpia; e de aquéllos que por vuestra buena diligencia pasaren de esta vida podades procurar de aver los oficios de los tales defunctos, todo a fin que lo aya y alcanza otro de la línea y generación de los dichos maranos hebreos o de otra semejante stirpe o ralea" ("Traslado" 385).

35. The more common sacrificial animal associated in Christian sources with Judaism was the lamb (Resnick). However, the use of the "lamb of God" in the Mass and other liturgical texts may have made it harder to present the animal as a Jewish sacrifice in this poem, while the calf clearly refers to the gentile sacrifices into which the Jews fell in the Old Testament.

36. For the conceptualization of Judaism as disease, see Gómez-Bravo ("El judaísmo").

37. This connection needs to be explored in further detail in relation to the widespread and well-known accusations that the Jews were responsible for the spread of the Black Death.

38. "Y así es consejo sano / para contentos vivir, / que xpiana con xpiano / y marrana con marrano / procuren de se enxerir. / Y quien es xpiano viejo, / por codiçia de ducados / no tome tan mal consejo / de querer mudar pellejo / haziendo hijos manchados. // Y es mancha que tanto cunde, / que donde una vez entrare / todo lo limpio confunde, / y es imposible se munde / mientras el mundo durare. / Cada uno tenga aviso / en se saber conservar, / que el que otra cosa quiso / vivirá siempre arrepiso" (*Cancionero* 767 lines 11–30).

39. "Ansy commo aquellos que son fijos de promissión son reputados por symiente buena, ansy los que son fijos de error son avidos por simiente mala, ca el padre de los judíos el diablo es, pero non es esto segund la sucçesión de la carne, mas segund la sucçesión del pecado" (Martínez Casado 45). Gratian's text in Richter and Friedberg, vol. 1, col. 362.

40. A full study on the use of the term is in Gómez-Bravo ("*Raza*: A Word at Fault").

41. "Raza: la casta de caballos castizos, a los cuales señalan con hierro para que sean conocidos. Raza en el paño, la hilaza que diferencia de los demás hilos de la trama. Parece haberse dicho quasi reaza, porque 'aza' en lengua toscana vale hilo, y la raza en el paño sobrepuesto desigual. Raza en los linages se toma en mala parte, como tener alguna raza de Moro, o Judio" (896–97).

42. The first dictionary definition of *raça* appears in Alfonso de Palencia's 1490 *Universal Vocabulario*, which, in the entry for *Ignia*, states that *raça* is a crack that may appear in a piece of clay pottery. Nebrija's *Vocabulario español-latino* (circa 1495) gives two different entries and meanings: "sun ray" and "a sparse line in the thread of a piece of cloth."

43. "Sy por encobryr tus raças / yerro de otro profaças, / quando vieres lo que caças, / llorarás" (5).
44. For example in Juan Ruiz, Archpriest of Hita, *Libro de buen amor* (Book of Good Love): "Diz la dueña, sañuda: "Non ay paño sin raça / nin el leal amigo non es en toda plaça" (34).
45. Menéndez Pidal (363) and García de Diego (904). Corominas and Pascual (entry *Raza*) are partially in line with Menéndez Pidal and García de Diego.
46. On Montoro as *mediano* converso and some of his exchanges with Gómez Manrique and other poets, see Gómez-Bravo ("Ser social y poética material"; "Slander").
47. "Porque las mujeres preñadas que comen manjares infeccionados luego abortan? Responde: porque de aquellos tales manjares se engendra la simiente infecta, lo qual el alma mucho aborrece e echa del campo de natura, que es la madriguera; porque no es dispuesta para que enella se jnfunda forma humana, que es nobilissima" (159).
48. "por el pudrimiento y por la corrupcion que sale de la juderia, que son malos, enconados y condenados de muchas dolencias, segun dixo Dauid: 'E firio Dios sus enemigos en el trasero;' verguença para siempre jamas les ha dado" (Aviñón 91).
49. "son suzias y corruptas en quarto grado" (Aviñón 104).
50. "non ay carne en el mundo que tan semejante sea del cuerpo del ome como es el puerco" (Aviñón 220).
51. "La causa material del comer es gouierno, la qual definicion dello es sustancia que a natura de conuertirse y semejança del gouernado, assi como el pan y el vino y la carne y sus semejantes" (Aviñón 125).

WORKS CITED

Accorsi, Federica. "El *Espejo de verdadera nobleza* y la cuestión de los conversos." *Mosén Diego de Valera: Entre las armas y las letras*, edited by Cristina Moya García, Tamesis, 2014, pp. 21–52.

Albala, Ken. *Eating Right in the Renaissance*. U of California P, 2002.

Alborayque. Edited by Dwayne E. Carpenter, vol. 1, Editora Regional de Extremadura, 2005.

Alfonso X, King of Castile and Leon. *Cantigas de Santa María*, edited by Walter Mettmann, vol. 2, Castalia, 1986–1989.

———. *Fuero Real*, edited by Azucena Palacios Alcaine, PPU, 1991.

———. *General Estoria: Primera Parte*, edited by Pedro Sánchez Prieto-Borja, vol. 1: *Génesis*, Fundación José Antonio de Castro, 2001.

Amasuno Sárraga, Marcelino V. *La peste en la corona de Castilla durante la segunda mitad del siglo XIV*. Consejería de Educación y Cultura de la Junta de Castilla y León, 1996.

Anidjar, Gil. *Blood: A Critique of Christianity*. Columbia UP, 2014.

Aviñón, Juan de. *Sevillana medicina*, edited by José Mondéjar, Arco Libros, 2000.

Baumgarten, Elisheva. *Mothers and Children: Jewish Family Life in Medieval Europe*. Princeton UP, 2004.

Beltrán de Heredia, Vicente. "Las bulas de Nicolás V acerca de los conversos de Castilla." *Sefarad*, vol. 21, 1961, pp. 22–47.

Benito Ruano, Eloy. *Los orígenes del problema converso*. Real Academia de la Historia, 2001.

———. *Toledo en el siglo XV: Vida política*. CSIC, 1961.

Bernáldez, Andrés. *Memorias del Reinado de los Reyes Catolicos*, edited by Juan Mata Carriazo and Manuel Gómez-Moreno, Real Academia de la Historia, 1962.

Bertelloni, Francisco. "La teoría política medieval entre la tradición clásica y la modernidad." *El pensamiento politico en la Edad Media*, edited by Pedro Roche Arnas, Fundación Ramón Areces, 2010, pp. 17–40.

Bulario de la Inquisición española (hasta la muerte de Fernando el Católico), edited by Gonzalo Martínez Díez, Editorial Complutense, 1998.

Burgos, Vicente de, Fray. *Traducción de El Libro de Propietatibus Rerum de Bartolomé Anglicus*, edited by María Teresa Herrera and María Nieves Sánchez, Universidad de Salamanca, 1999. Real Academia Española. Banco de datos (CORDE), Corpus diacrónico del español, www.rae.es. Accessed 20 June 2019.

Cancionero de Juan Alfonso de Baena, edited by Brian Dutton and Joaquín González Cuenca, Visor, 1993.

Carmona García, Juan Ignacio. *Enfermedad y sociedad en los primeros tiempos modernos*. Secretariado de Publicaciones de la U de Sevilla, 2005.

Corominas, Joan, and José A. Pascual. *Diccionario Crítico Etimológico Castellano e Hispánico*, vol. 4, Gredos, 1980.

La Corónica de Adramón, edited by Gunnar Anderson, Juan de la Cuesta, 1992.

Covarrubias, Sebastián de. *Tesoro de la lengua castellana o española*, edited by Martín de Riquer, facsimile edition, Alta Fulla, 1998.

Cuart Moner, Baltasar. *Colegiales mayores y limpieza de sangre durante la Edad Moderna: El estatuto de San Clemente de Bolonia (ss. XV-XIX)*. U de Salamanca, 1991.

Domínguez Ortiz, Antonio. *Los judeoconversos en España y América*. Istmo, 1971.

Electronic Corpus of 15th Century Castilian Cancionero Manuscripts. Compiled and edited by Elena Carrillo, María Jesús Díez Garretas, Fiona Maguire, Manuel Moreno, Dorothy S. Severin, and Andrea Zinato, cancionerovirtual.liv.ac.uk. Accessed 15 October 2018.

Freidenreich, David. *Foreigners and Their Food: Constructing Otherness in Jewish, Christian, and Islamic Law.* U of California P, 2011.
García Ballester, Luis. *Medicine in a Multicultural Society: Christian, Jewish, and Muslim Practitioners in the Spanish Kingdoms, 1220–1610.* Ashgate, 2001.
García Cárcel, Ricardo. *Inquisición: Historia crítica.* Temas de hoy, 2000.
García de Cortázar, José Ángel. *Historia religiosa del Occidente medieval (1313–1464).* Akal, 2012.
García de Diego, Vicente, and Carmen García de Diego. *Diccionario etimólogico español e hispánico.* Espasa-Calpe, 1985.
García García, Emilio. "Huarte de San Juan: Una adelantado a la teoría modular de la mente." *Revista de Historia de la Psicología*, vol. 24, 2003, pp. 9–25.
Glaser, Edward. "*Convertentur ad Vesperam*: On a Rare Spanish Translation of an Inquisitorial Sermon by Frei João de Ceita." *Collected Studies in Honour of Américo Castro's 80th Year*, edited by M. P. Hornik, Oxford UP, 1965, pp. 137–74.
Gómez-Bravo, Ana M. "Adafina." *Converso Cookbook.* jewishstudies.washington.edu/converso-cookbook-home. Republished in MyJewishLearning.com.
———. "Antón de Montoro's 'Oh Ropero, amargo, triste' and the Converso Voice." *Open Iberia/América Teaching Anthology: Open Access Pedagogical Editions of Premodern Iberian and Latin American sources*, edited by David Wacks, openiberiaamerica.hcommons.org. Forthcoming in 2020.
———. "Comendador Román's *Antón, parias sin arrisco* and the Poetics of Converso Slander." *Open Iberia/América Teaching Anthology*, openiberiaamerica.hcommons.org/. Forthcoming in 2020.
———. "El judaísmo como enfermedad en el discurso médico y literario del siglo XV." *eHumanista: Journal of Iberian Studies*, vol. 39, 2018, pp. 12–24.
———. "*Raza*: A Word at Fault." In Preparation.
———. "Ser social y poética material en la obra de Antón de Montoro, mediano converso." *Hispanic Review*, vol. 78, 2010, pp. 145–67.
———. "Slander and the Right to Be an Author in Fifteenth-Century Spain." *Journal of Spanish Cultural Studies*, vol. 16, 2015, pp. 239–53.
———. *Textual Agency: Writing Culture and Social Networks in Fifteenth-Century Spain.* U of Toronto P, 2013.
Gordillo Pérez, Luis Ignacio. "¿Por qué surge el Estado? Una metodología holística para entender el origen, la función y los retos del poder público." *Pensamiento: Revista de Investigación e Información Filosófica*, vol. 72, 2016, pp. 563–91.
Heng, Geraldine. *The Invention of Race in the European Middle Ages.* Cambridge UP, 2018.
Hering Torres, Max Sebastián. "'Limpieza de sangre' ¿Racismo en la edad

moderna?" *Tiempos Modernos: Revista Electrónica de Historia Moderna*, vol. 9, 2003–2004, pp. 1–16.
Hernández Franco, Juan. *Sangre limpia, sangre española: El debate sobre los estatutos de limpieza (siglos XV-XVII)*. Cátedra, 2011.
Horozco, Sebastián de. *Cancionero*, edited by José J. Labrador Herraiz, Ralph A. Di Franco, and Pérez R. Morillo-Velarde, Consejería de Educación, Ciencia y Cultura de Castilla-La Mancha, 2010.
——. *Relaciones Históricas Toledanas*, edited by Jack Weiner, I.P.I.E.T., 1981.
Huarte de San Juan, Juan. *Examen de ingenios para las ciencias*, edited by Guillermo Serés, Cátedra, 1989.
Kamen, Henry. *The Spanish Inquisition: A Historical Revision*. Yale UP, 2014.
Kaplan, Gregory B. "The Inception of *Limpieza de Sangre* (Purity of Blood) and Its Impact in Medieval and Golden Age Spain." *Marginal Voices: Studies in Converso Literature of Medieval and Golden Age Spain*, edited by Amy I. Aronson-Friedman and Gregory B. Kaplan, Brill, 2012.
Ketham, Johannes de. *Compendio de la humana salud*, edited by María Teresa Herrera, Arco Libros, 1990.
Madurell Marimón, José M. "La cofradía de la Santa Trinidad de los conversos de Barcelona." *Sefarad*, vol. 18, 1958, pp. 60–82.
Manrique, Gómez. *Cancionero*, edited by Francisco Vidal González, Cátedra, 2003.
Martínez, María Elena. *Genealogical Fictions: Limpieza de Sangre, Religion, and Gender in Colonial Mexico*. Stanford UP, 2008.
Martínez Casado, Ángel. "La situación jurídica de los conversos según Lope de Barrientos." *Archivo Dominicano: Anuario*, vol. 17, 1996, pp. 25–64.
Mártir Rizo, Juan Pablo. *Historia de la muy noble y leal ciudad de Cuenca*, facsimile edition, Extramuros Edición, 2009.
Menéndez Pidal. Ramón. "Etimologías españolas." *Romania*, vol. 29, 1900, pp. 334–79.
Mexia, Fernando de. *Nobiliario vero*. Biblioteca Nacional, Madrid, Ms. 3311, fol. 97v–98r.
Mondéjar, José. "Del pan y del vino en un texto médico del siglo XIV." *Revista de Dialectología y Tradiciones Populares*, vol. 62, 2002, 167–88.
Montoro, Antón de. *Cancionero*, edited by Marcella Ciceri and Julio Rodríguez-Puértolas, U de Salamanca, 1990.
Moreno Koch, Yolanda. *Fontes Iudaeorum Regni Castellae*, vol. 5: *De Iure Hispano-Hebraico: Las Taqqanot de Valladolid de 1432: Un estatuto comunal renovador*, U Pontificia de Salamanca, 1987.
Nebrija, Antonio de. *Vocabulario español-latino*, facsimile edition, Real Academia Española, 1951.

Netanyahu, Benzion. *The Marranos of Spain: From the Late 14th to the Early 16th Century, According to Contemporary Hebrew Sources.* Cornell UP, 1999.

Nirenberg, David. "Mass Conversion and Genealogical Mentalities: Jews and Christians in Fifteenth-Century Spain." *Past and Present*, vol. 174, 2002, pp. 3–41.

Oxford English Dictionary. Oxford UP, 2000.

Palencia, Alfonso de. *Universal vocabulario en latín y en romance*, facsimile edition, Comisión Permanente de la Asociación de Academias de la Lengua Española, 1967.

Patton, Pamela A. *Art of Estrangement: Redefining Jews in Reconquest Spain.* Pennsylvania State UP, 2012.

———. "Constructing the Inimical Jew in the Cantigas de Santa María: Theophilus's Magician in Text and Image." *Beyond the Yellow Badge: Anti-Judaism and Antisemitism in Medieval and Early Modern Visual Culture*, edited by Mitchell B. Merback, Brill, 2008, pp. 233–56.

Perceval, José María. "Un crimen sin cadáver: El Santo Niño de la Guardia." *Historia*, vol. 16, no. 202, 1993, pp. 44–58

Pérez, Joseph. *Los judíos en España.* Marcial Pons Historia, 2005.

Pérez, Martín. *Libro de las confesiones: Una radiografía de la sociedad medieval española*, edited by Antonio García y García, Bernardo Alonso Rodríguez, and Francisco Cantelar Rodríguez, Biblioteca de Autores Cristianos, 2002.

Pérez Johnston, Raúl. "Los aportes del derecho público medieval a la teoría del Estado y de la Constitución. (Diálogo con Paolo Grossi)." *Historia Constitucional*, vol. 5, 2004, pp. 275–307.

Pulgar, Fernando [de]. *Letras*, edited by Paola Elia, Giardini editori e stampatori, 1982.

Quintanilla Raso, María Concepción. "'Nobilitas virtutis causa': De la virtud al pecado en la nobleza." *Pecar en la Edad Media*, edited by Ana I. Carrasco Manchado and María del Pilar Rábade Obradó, Sílex, 2008, pp. 149–84.

Resnick, Irven M. *Marks of Distinction: Christian Perceptions of Jews in the High Middle Ages.* Catholic U of America P, 2012.

Richter, Aemilius Ludwig, and Emil Friedberg. *Corpus Juris Canonici.* Akademische Druck- U. Verlagsanstalt, 1959.

Rodríguez Puértolas, Julio, editor. *Poesía crítica y satírica del siglo XV.* Castalia, 1989.

Ruiz, Juan (Arcipreste de Hita). *Libro de buen amor*, edited by Alberto Blecua, Cátedra, 1992.

Sabaté, Flocel. "L'ordenament municipal de la relació amb els jueus a la Catalunya baixmedieval." *Cristianos y judíos en contacto en la Edad Media: Polémica, conversión, dinero y convivencia*, edited by Flocel Sabaté and Claude Denjean, Editorial Milenio, 2009, pp. 733–804.

Sala-Molins, Louis. *Le dictionnaire des inquisiteurs: Valence, 1494.* Galilée, 1981.
Sanahuja, Pedro. *Lérida en sus luchas por la fe (judíos, moros, conversos, Inquisición y moriscos).* Publicaciones del Instituto de Estudios Ilerdenses, 1946.
Shatzmiller, Joseph. *Jews, Medicine, and Medieval Society.* U of California P, 1994.
Sicroff, Albert A. *Los estatutos de limpieza de sangre: Controversias entre los siglos XV y XVII.* Juan de la Cuesta, 2010.
Siraisi, Nancy G. *Medieval and Early Renaissance Medicine: An Introduction to Knowledge and Practice.* U of Chicago P, 1990.
Solomon, Michael. "Breaking Nonnatural Bread: Alimentary Hygiene and Radical Individualism in Juan de Aviñon's Medicina sevillana." *Forging Communities: Food and Representation in Medieval and Early Modern Southwestern Europe*, edited by Montserrat Piera, U of Arkansas, 2018, pp. 147–58.
Suárez Bilbao, Fernando. *El fuero judiego en la España cristiana: Las fuentes jurídicas, siglos V-XV.* Dykinson, 2000.
"Testamento de Fernan García Barba de Figueroa." *Colección diplomática de Galicia histórica*, edited by Antonio López Ferreiro, vol. 1, Tipografía Galaica, 1901, pp. 27–34.
"Traslado de una carta de privilegio que el rey don Juan II dio a un hijo dalgo." *Los judaizantes castellanos y la Inquisición en tiempo de Isabel la Católica*, edited by Nicolás López Martínez, Seminario Metropolitano de Burgos, 1954.
Veragüe, Pedro de. *Doctrina de la discripción o Tractado de la doctrina*, edited by Raúl A. del Piero, Real Academia Española, 1971.
Weissberger, Barbara F. "Motherhood and Ritual Murder in Medieval Spain and England." *Journal of Medieval and Early Modern Studies*, vol. 39, 2009, pp. 7–30.

CHAPTER 2

Taste and Taxonomy of Native Food in Hispanic America, 1492–1640

Gregorio Saldarriaga, *University of Antioquia, Colombia*

THIS CHAPTER AIMS to explain how the classification of American food worked in Hispanic America following the ideas found in almost all descriptions of nature written between 1492 and 1640. In spite of the "academic" context of such descriptions, their authors had varying degrees of education. Although there were some highly educated authors like Tomás López Medel and José de Acosta, many of the authors included in this study had only basic training as merchants, courtiers, sailors, and soldiers. For these reasons, the documentary sources studied include accounts by illiterate people as transcribed by scribes.

Although the focus of this article is food, it is important to understand that the model it follows classifies both human consumers and the objects of consumption. The working taxonomies of the period under study were based upon European ideologies of class differentiation and upon the new connotations they acquired in Spanish America. In order to explain the changes that took place on American soil over time, I will consider ideological, cultural, and social elements that forced these models to adapt to the challenges of the New World.

The source materials used in this study include letters about America, conquest reports, chronicles, historical accounts, medical treatises, and *relaciones geográficas* of the Indies. The variety of sources makes it possible to address the wide and diverse social and cultural background of the people who produced them: from royal officials and physicians to surgeons, friars, merchants, and private citizens. The corpus and sources analyzed account for the Antilles, New Spain, New Kingdom of Granada, Peru, and Quito. However, as a model of thought it was applicable to the entire American continent, as that was what Gonzalo Fernández de Oviedo and José de Acosta intended in their texts.

Within the history of food, the clash of America and Europe is a subject that has valuable research from different perspectives. These works have allowed us to understand the complexity of the food exchange process. Among them, *Ecological Imperialism* by Alfred W. Crosby and *A Plague of Sheep* by Elinor Melville have revealed the profound impact that the introduction of European species produced on Native Americans and on the geographical environment. In the same vein, *Sweetness and Power* by Sidney Mintz and *Political Gastronomy* by Michael LaCombe have shown how food, prestige, and power intersect in areas of cultural contact. Finally, from a strictly culinary perspective, I would like to mention Sophie Coe's *America's First Cuisines*, Jeffrey Pilcher's *Five Hundred Years of Fusion*, and Rachel Laudan's *Cuisine and Empire*, as they offer a global vision on how kitchens in America were configured and mixed from the conquest. No doubt, the complexity of these texts and their contributions are of capital importance to understanding the food transformation process of America after 1492.

The Great Chain of Being

A preeminent model used in the classification of Hispanic American food is one known as *scala naturae*, or the Great Chain of Being, understood to have been the worldview during the period between 1492 and 1640 (Lovejoy; Bouza Álvarez 219–22; Hespanha 49). This model was based upon the idea that there existed a God-given natural order that established a chain from Sun to Earth that went from warmth to coldness, and in which every element occupied a specific place. The most elaborate treatises show a model that divided nature by elements, establishing a clear hierarchy that went from the perfect to the imperfect: first was air, then water, and finally, earth. Fire only figured at a theoretical level in reference to food, since no animal or vegetable products are made out of this element. The intent was not only to classify the world according to the elements but also to organize food in a hierarchical way within each element, which had important taxonomical implications. Using this double organization, authors developed a kind of ladder that went from warm (perfect) to cold (imperfect) or vice versa.

It should be noted that this was not simply an analytical methodology. Rather, it was understood to be the order in which God had created the world, making it necessary to respect it when analyzing and describing it. Thus, for instance, Tomás López Medel, in *Tratado de los tres elementos* (*Treatise of the Three Elements*), pointed out explicitly that "we will keep the order that Nature itself usually has and keeps in producing and perfecting natural things, proceeding from the least to the most and from the lowest to the highest" (135).[1] The Jesuit José de Acosta also divided his *Historia natural y moral de las Indias* (*Natural and Moral History of the Indies*) according to the elements, going from the lowest to the highest, adding an explanation on the ways one was subjected to the other (194). Fernández de Oviedo followed the same principle of the Great Chain of Being throughout all his *Sumario de la natural historia* (*Summary of Natural History*; 1526), although sometimes inaccurately. His lack of rigor may be partially explained because the author had to improvise based on memory and the notes he was using to write a larger work (Sánchez 263–64), his great and systematizing *Historia general y natural de las Indias* (*General and Natural History of the Indies*), in which he clearly followed the Great Chain of Being, in part because he was using Pliny as his model (2: 197).

A Detour

Curiously enough, *Historia Natural de la Nueva España* (*Natural History of New Spain*), the most systematic sixteenth-century work on Hispanic American nature, did not follow the model of the Great Chain of Being. King Felipe II of Spain named its author, Doctor Francisco Hernández, protophysician of the Indies so he could undertake the study, which lasted nearly seven years.[2] During that period, Hernández was in New Spain not only observing nature but also receiving information from the indigenous people and experimenting with the possible remedies that plants and animals provided. According to José Pardo Tomás, his extensive work was not organized by classical criteria but kept organizational principles based on the Nahuatl language (159). Hernández did not explain why he had organized the information in such a way, which was an ostensible innovation with regards to the classical model. The fact that the most important and official work on American nature did not follow the classical and omnipresent pattern represents an obvious contradiction to leading trends during the period.

Rather than attempting to explain this deviation from the classic model, the pages that follow will focus on the reception of Hernández's work, as it shows the strength of the Great Chain of Being model during the period. Despite the monumentality of Hernández's work, it was not accepted by the Council of Indies or by King Felipe II, possibly because Hernández was not present to explain and defend it, and, above all, because his innovative system was unconvincing. Neapolitan doctor Nardo Antonio Recchi was tasked with taking over Hernández's work in order to "arrange it and put it in order, so we can continue to use it and profit from it" (Pardo Tomás

158).³ As the order makes obvious, the quality of the information that Hernández had gathered was not questioned. Rather, it was his organizational system that was problematic, as it did not allow the king to benefit from Hernández's work.

The first change implemented by Recchi was that of narrowing his scope to one area and trying to choose what he considered to be the most important. He did not mean to produce a full natural history but to focus on medicinal products, thus the title of his work, *De materia medica Novae Hispanie*, which Recchi clearly structured according to the Great Chain of Being. This is evidenced in the section on animals, which he divided by element and level of perfection. In turn, following Dioscorides to a large extent, he classified vegetables into aromatic plants, trees, bushes, and herbs. Recchi followed the principle of perfection, going from the highest to the lowest. He even divided herbs into categories: acrid and bitter, sweet and salty, and astringent and sour. This distribution in pairs of categories corresponds, following the same order, to the way tastes were organized according to a scale, whether they were warm, temperate, or cold. Recchi placed the warmest tastes first, while the last were the coldest; thus, he structured them according to the hierarchical principle of the Great Chain of Being (Recchi 163; Grieco, "Medieval" 28; Flandrin 500).

Meanwhile, when Friar Francisco Ximénez freely translated Nardo Antonio Recchi's text into Spanish in New Spain, he followed the same organizational model generally. One exception was the classification of herbs, which he ordered by "acute and bitter taste, saline and sweet, and of other flavors and the tasteless and with no noticeable flavor or none" (f. 178r).⁴ It appears obvious that some of the tastes coincide. It should be recalled that the Early Modern Period recognized nine different tastes, of which Recchi omitted three and Ximénez four. However, Ximénez organized tastes in descending order, with the warmest being first, then the less warm, and so on. The most notable difference between Recchi and Ximénez is that Ximénez's organization of taste ended with a temperate taste such as insipid, without reaching the truly cold, a temperature he does include when describing plants.

Both Recchi and Ximénez acknowledge Hernández's work in an explicit or tacit way, as many other naturalists did in the sixteenth and seventeenth centuries. For that reason, a significant part of the description of fruits, trees, plants, and herbs mostly follows Hernández's work. Nevertheless, both authors altered the order to adapt it to a comprehensive principle, a structure loaded with meaning that explained how the world was organized. For this reason, both worried about clearly establishing a hierarchy of foods and even of flavors.

The World Order According to the Laymen

Understandably, the texts written by doctors or people with a strong scholastic education followed the Great Chain of Being, because it corresponded with the academic principles of the period, in which natural philosophy, medicine, and taxonomy concurred. Moreover, it was a complex model in which living things were organized hierarchically according to their humoral condition. Despite these complexities, it is clear that it was not a pattern followed exclusively by those with university-level education but by others as well. For example, the model is followed in an implicit and simplified way in *Viaggio e Relazione delle Indie* (*Travel and Report from the Indies*), written by the merchant Galeotto Cei, and more specifically in his description of the tropical flora, where he followed the model that Albertus Magnus had taken in a simplified manner from Theophrastus, who had divided the vegetal world into trees, bushes, herbs, and roots (Cei 100). Although Cei's diverges in several places from his model, as he mixes natural history with social history and with the chronicle of his journey from the Antilles to the mainland, the model's organizational structure is clear.

The worldview resulting from this model had an impact beyond the production of a purely descriptive taxonomy, as it affected daily life and helped European appropriation of Spanish American foods and peoples. As Allen Grieco has shown, the quality of food became directly linked to the quality of the people who could consume it, according to the model that was operative in Europe at the time. Some food was apt for Spaniards due to its location in the Great Chain of Being, while other foods were only appropriate for indigenous and black people. Usually, fruit that grew on trees and bushes were suitable for Spaniards, while the ones that grew at ground level or underneath it were appropriate for indigenous or black people (Grieco, "Alimentation" 484–87; Saldarriaga 67–68). As Grieco has pointed out, differential uses of food helped evince that there was a natural order in society and a social order in nature ("The Social Order" 905).

In the early period of discovery, explorers, travelers, and chroniclers of Spanish America sent news of the New World, placing great emphasis on the indigenous diet. From a contemporary point of view, they can be considered neutral descriptions. However, there was nothing neutral about them at the time, as they were openly pejorative, strongly conditioned by the idea of the Great Chain of Being, which helped place Native Americans in a subaltern position within creation. It is important to consider the accounts of witnesses who travelled to the New World, as well as the information provided by those who were never in America but served as transmitters of ideas. In spite of their lack of direct knowledge, these transmitters served to synthetize news and place it in a comprehensive frame of reference. In so doing, they infused this new information with European meaning in an effort to help their readers understand the unknown world. A case in point is that of Giambattista Strozzi, who was in Cádiz when the first ships from the Antilles arrived. On March 19, 1494, he forwarded a letter stating, "In the said islands there are no four-footed animals, nor grains, nor wine, and they live from the ears of grass and fruits and human flesh" (43). Other Italian commentators made similar points: that Antilles natives lacked or did not use agriculture and were fed with roots or foods that were similar to turnips or acorns (Cei 101; Cuneo 55). Those were deformed echoes of the Antillean communities' lifestyle, where vegeculture, fruit harvesting, and fishing were the main source of daily sustenance. Emphasis was placed on a productive model that was not based on cultivation, where people consumed roots and wild fruit, apt only for the lowest levels of society or for those who were marginalized from it, like hermits (Grieco, "Les plantes" 11–29).

In his 1495 letter to Girolamo Annari, Michele da Cuneo—who traveled with Christopher Colombus on his second voyage—dedicates a whole section to describing nature. Unlike Acosta and others, da Cuneo did not follow the classical division of the Great Chain of Being. Instead, he went from trees to pineapples, which he described as stems, then moved again to a description of trees and roots and some other large trees. This means that he did not follow the set order, from highest to lowest, or vice versa. Far from being arbitrary, da Cuneo's organization simply followed a principle of acceptability that went from what he had found acceptable to what he had not, a principle only applicable to indigenous people and animals. Da Cuneo himself emphasized how indigenous people ate inadequate and poisonous animals, while using turnips and other similar roots as bread. This description could be taken as a distortion of the Antillean diet, in which the author simply compared yucca roots to turnip roots and assumed that the animals they ate were dangerous to their health. Nevertheless, it was not a simple distortion but a reflection of the period's principles and values. Thus, da Cuneo added, "to my mind they [the Indians] are cold people, not very lustful, which is perhaps a result of their poor diet" (58).

As part of the humoral theory and the idea of the Great Chain of Being, it was thought that people had specific temperaments, conditioned by both innate group features, the class to which they belonged, and the type of diet they followed (Earle; Saldarriaga). In general terms, it was thought that the people who were at the highest level of the social hierarchy were warmer than the people placed at the lowest echelons of society. It was an ideology of social differentiation that identified some groups as more perfect, due to their warm quality, and deemed others imperfect because of their cold nature. Da Cuneo shows that this model was applied to American taxonomies as early as Columbus's first travels, and he placed the indigenous people in the lowest level of the social ladder due to both their nature and their diet. The many references to turnips and acorns being suitable foods for the indigenous peoples is in line with similar statements about the food that was considered apt for the European peasantry, which was also associated with coldness and a poor diet.

Classifying Foods

With the model of ideological differentiation described above in mind, it is worth returning to the way Europeans classified and valued American food. In order to do that, it is important to understand the values assigned to each of the four elements: fire, air, water, and earth.

American birds and fish were appreciated for their taste and considered suitable for European consumption, especially those who had similarities in appearance or taste with what were considered to be their Old World counterparts. The most valued American bird was the turkey, but native varieties of what were termed quails, partridges, and hens were also appreciated. For this reason, they figured in the taxation of some communities before the Crown systematically imposed the breeding of hens as tribute, as part of a priest's wages or *congrua*,[5] and for sale to the Hispanic population. Although it is true that some American birds were not valued for their taste, the same can be said about some European birds. As for fish, they were appreciated according to the quantity of their flesh and fat. In general, sea and river fish were valued over pond fish, but there were some local fish that were appreciated regardless of their origin. Turtle and iguana eggs—which would correspond to the element of water, although they were sometimes qualified as belonging to neutral animals—were deemed appropriate for indigenous and black people, even though they were also considered suitable for Spaniards in periods of crisis ("Descripción de la villa de Tenerife" 345). Although the chewy consistency of these eggs could have been a factor, it is possible that their negative consideration was linked to the way they were harvested by digging them out of the sand at riverbanks. In order to better understand how the harvesting method influenced categorization, the next element, earth, needs to be considered.

Earth as an element allowed for greater food discrimination, both in plants and animals, and the possibility of assigning to each group of people (Spaniards, Native Americans, and Africans) the ones that were best suited for consumption. In regards to animals, the situation was more or less clear: in general, game animals were good to eat if they were quadrupeds of a certain size, like, for example, tapirs and collared peccary. But as their size decreased, as in the case of native dogs or moles, they were thought to be closer to the vermin category, and therefore only apt for indigenous and black people (Acuña, *Nueva Galicia* 40, 73–74; *México* 2: 87, 193, 199, 200, 237; "Descripción de la villa de Tenerife" 311).

As previously mentioned, among plant products, fruit was for the highest levels of society; legumes, grains, and cereals were more or less suitable for everyone; while herbs and roots were only for peasants, much like the practice in Europe (Grieco, "Alimentation" 488–89; "The Social Politics" 135). In Spanish America, the Spanish, mostly *encomenderos* (holders of *encomienda*, labor grants given by the Spanish Crown) and royal officials, constituted the highest levels of society, while indigenous people and, to a lesser extent, black people formed the peasant estate. Many descriptions of indigenous people explicitly equate them with the European peasants, or *serranos*, due to their condition as much as their diet (Acuña, *México* 2: 84).

Early descriptions of America in the chronicles of the second half of the sixteenth century and in seventeenth-century reports state that the native diet was composed of herbs, roots, and low fruit, which were usually described as having little substance or flavor. These were considered the distinct foods of the indigenous people, just as yam and squash were the stereotypical foods of black people. To state this association in the terms used during the period, they were herbs "suited to their complexion."

In animals, vegetables, and turtle and iguana eggs, their proximity to the earth served to mark them with a stigma, because, in general terms, it was assumed that such proximity to the earth/soil gave them qualities and flavors that made them only appropriate for the lower classes. Vegetables were understood to be insipid and acrid.

Even if their place in the Great Chain of Being was an influential factor in determining the value and quality of food, it was not the only classificatory system used. Another factor that helped determine the quality of a food was taste, which was a more effective mode of assessing food quality (Manfredi f.196v; Montanari, *Il riposso de la polpetta* 97–98). In this manner, many fruits that may have been suitable for higher classes based on their distance from the soil ended up being considered food for indigenous peoples or for animals, as was the case of the American carob (*Hymenaea courbaril*) ("Relación de Chilapan" 115–16; "Descripción de la ciudad de Guayaquil" 29). Likewise, some roots or herbs were appreciated for their pleasant taste and, therefore, considered apt for Spaniards. As an example, the sweet potato (*Ipomea batata*) was considered a proper food for indigenous people because it is a tuber. Nevertheless, Europeans appreciated its sweetness early on and deemed it suitable for their consumption. Its sweet taste made it classifiable as warm in spite of its growing beneath the soil, which would have made it taxonomically cold (Fragoso 631; Sardela 266). Another similar example was that of the pineapple (*Ananas comosus*), considered an herb and, therefore, cold. Yet, due to its sweetness, the pineapple was classified as warm and appropriate for consumption by Spaniards (Fernández de Oviedo, *Sumario* 80; Cei 30; Gage 61). A last example, taken from the animal world, is that of the armadillo (*Dasypodidae*), which from the beginning had attracted the attention of Europeans because of its appearance as well as its habits and habitat (Acuña, *México* 2: 150). Spaniards considered the armadillo a type of "wild vermin" ("Descripción de la villa de Tenerife" 341), but because of its taste and the recognizable features of its meat, from a European perspective, as "white and fatty as bacon" ("blanca e gruesa como tocino") ("Relación de Anzerma" 354), it received a more positive categorization and was more valued as a food, though it did not become a mass-consumed animal ("Descripción de Guayaquil" 30; Cei 114).

Another factor that was thought to affect the quality of all foods, and in particular that of plants, was whether they were wild or cultivated. The chronicles of the period clearly link difficult times during conquering campaigns with the Spaniards' need to eat mostly wild fruit, roots, and herbs (Benzoni f.85v). Vegetables growing in the wild were understood to pose a danger for health and, to a lesser extent, a setback for palates, since their taste was less pleasant than those that were cultivated (Fernández de Oviedo, *Historia general* 2: 192, 220, 229; "Relación de la conquista de los carare" 439; Acosta 254, 258; Cárdenas 38). In Fernández de Oviedo's tree classification, there is a special section on "wild trees," "those that do not bear fruit that may be eaten, nor are they cultivated by the industry of men" (*Historia general* 2: 269).[6] Fernández de Oviedo's tree descriptions make it clear that his references to "fruit that may be eaten" allude to Spanish perceptions, as these fruits were part of the regular diet of indigenous peoples but were consumed by Spanish conquerors only in times of need. The logic that wild foods were exclusively for indigenous people was only broken when those wild foods were very sweet or when the Europeans thought they resembled civilized fruit such as grapes (Ximénez f.68r). With only a few exceptions, it is clear that, for Europeans, wild foods were for indigenous people and animals.[7]

Chroniclers were not the only ones contrasting cultivated plant foods with wild ones. This division can also be found in the *relaciones geográficas* of New Spain, the New Kingdom of Granada, and Quito, which similarly show that only cultivated foods were adequate for the Spaniards, while wild foods were for indigenous people, black people, and animals ("Descripción de Guayaquil" 13, 29). In some of New Spain's *relaciones geográficas*, this reasoning was taken a step further by almost automatically assuming that any wild food was American, while any cultivated plant had been brought by Europeans to each region with varying degrees of success (Acuña, *Méx-*

ico 2: 88, 171, 195). Although this point of view was widespread, it did not necessarily imply that American foods were inadequate for Spanish consumption but that, in many ways, they were inferior to European foods.

The Florentine Galeotto Cei best exemplified this point of view, although with a particular angle in his analysis and reach. After spending fourteen years in the Antilles, Venezuela, and the New Kingdom of Granada, he stated that: "All of the fruits of the Indies, even if they are sweet, are also somewhat sour" (26).[8] He also adds that by his time (the 1540s) there were already many types of European fruit growing in America and, as he says, "They make copious amounts of compotes and jams with the fruit, but these are not as perfect as they would be in Spain and in Portugal because the sweet fruit does not taste as sweet, and the sour fruit is more tart" (27).[9] Not only did he point out that American fruit always had a little bit of *agro*, or sour, but also that European fruits cultivated in America acquired the same taste. How are we to understand these statements? A possible interpretation is that Cei was looking to show that fruit grown locally was not as perfect as that grown on the Iberian Peninsula, a perfection being measured by the degree of sweetness. This was a significant point because sweetness played an important role in Renaissance cookery and dietary traditions, as it was thought to translate a humoral "temperate" quality that was especially appropriate for humans. Cei conveyed the idea that all American food had wild qualities when compared to European foods, adding that, in America, European foods lost their cultivated qualities.

Cei was not the only one who thought in those terms. The Spanish physician Juan de Cárdenas shared the same idea in his *Problemas secretos maravillosos de las Indias* (*Wonderful Secret Problems of the Indies*). For Cárdenas, the different qualities of food grown in Europe and in the inter-tropical area of America were explained by the heat and humidity of the tropical region. According to Cárdenas, the absence of substantial weather changes during the course of the year caused the plant roots to not penetrate properly into the earth, while preventing the branches from rising high enough, both characteristics bearing a negative effect on the quality of the fruit (ff.35v–36r). Cárdenas's statements were in line with period ideas that "[t]he taller the plant, the longer the digestion process, and the longer the digestion, the more the inferior earthbound sources were transformed into some kind of superior, more ethereal food" (Grieco, "Social Politics" 148–49). Hence, the problem in America, at least in the inter-tropical zone, resided in intrinsic and non-modifiable characteristics of the land that substantially altered the condition and quality of the fruit. Ultimately, it was a reasoned metaphor of the dangerous power of the New World: America turned cultivated foods into wild ones, returning to nature what was a product of culture.

Diet Adaptation and Feature Transformation

Succinctly stated, the main classificatory model divided human beings and food into low and high, of good or bad taste, and cultivated or wild. This was an ideological as well as cosmological conceptualization of the world that had implications for daily life. It was not an absolute rule but rather a frame of reference with a certain elasticity. Within such a frame it was possible that: 1) the value and perception of foods could vary significantly depending on the region, and 2) food consumption rules could be altered so the Spaniards could consume products classified as "indigenous."[10] It might be assumed that Spaniards ended up eating local foods due to an inverse acculturation process, which did in fact take place. However, it is important to understand how Spaniards understood this process and how they justified it, and, perhaps more importantly, what cultural patterns were put in place during the process of appropriation and consumption of indigenous foods and how those patterns helped justify the class and group divisions that existed between Spaniards and other groups.

First of all, it is clear that need was a powerful motivator. Spaniards consumed wild foods, indigenous herbs, and roots in desperate times, as a substitute for basic foods like bread (Cei 31–32, 51, 107–

108; Fernández de Oviedo, *Historia general* 2: 261, 277). Second, the consumption of indigenous foods was identified with only certain groups within Hispanic society (e.g., women and Creoles) at various points (Fernández de Oviedo, *Historia general* 2: 271–75; Ximénez f.135). Third, the consumption of indigenous foods was viewed as a marginal practice by isolated individuals with unbridled appetites. For friar Francisco Ximénez de Cisneros, those individuals were dominated by gluttony, a capital sin that went against accepted Christian behavior, pushing people away from God, as they worshipped the gut and moved closer to animality (ff.45v–46r). From the perspective of an ideology of differentiation, these three modes of classification had one thing in common: they were viewed as anomalies and only adopted by people whose behavior was inconsistent with that of the group to which they belonged.

The aforementioned examples show different paths in the process of assimilation of consumption patterns, yet there is a faster and more important path due to its social impact: that of identity, which is situation-specific and changeable. The contextualization of subjects as studied by the social sciences (Burke 36) may also be applied to foods. The description and valuation of foods could similarly change depending on conditions that were organized using the same logic as ideological differentiation, which also happened at three levels: 1) cultivation of wild foods to improve them and make them edible, if they were seen as having the potential for improvement; 2) the context of food consumption; and 3) cooking.

In the first case, Spaniards selected and cultivated American foods that had some noteworthy virtue due to their taste—for instance, the avocado, the pineapple, and the guava (Fernández de Oviedo, *Historia general* 2: 192, 229; Cei 28; "Relación de Loja" 127; Acuña, *Nueva Galicia* 287)—or because they were found to possess medical properties—for example, the icaco (*Chrysobalanus icaco*) (Fernández de Oviedo, *Historia general* 2: 220). Thus, some foods could be placed on the side of "culture," the term for "cultivation" at the time, and deemed more suitable for consumption.

The food consumption context mentioned above refers to the ways of ingesting food, particularly its accompaniments, and to the role it played within the diet. For instance, the sweet potato could be a good food for Spaniards, not only because of its sweetness, but because it was not an everyday food, as it was for black people and indigenous people, but a complement to the diet. The same can be said of the chile, which, according to friar Francisco Ximénez de Cisneros, was sustenance for indigenous people but only a condiment and sauce for Spaniards. Likewise, some wild products could be eaten if they were accompanied by bread or by *casabe*, the yucca flatbread. After all, bread was the cultural and civilizing food par excellence in the Hispanic perspective. To use Montanari's expression, we must pay attention to "the grammar of food," to the role different foods play and the relations among them (*Gusti del Medioevo* 23–42). All social groups can eat the chile pepper, but not all eat it in the same way. A useful example is that of the "American fig" or prickly pear cactus fruit (*Opuntia ficus-indica*). Although it was one of the most appreciated fruits, it is also clear that for many indigenous people, for example the Chichimecas, it was one of the main sustenance foods. By contrast, the Spaniards ate it as fruit, because, according to the medical logic of the time, it was a body disruptor since it had cool properties. For Spaniards, it could also cause constipation, making it advisable to eat only in small amounts, as with all other fruit, and to eat it with bread (Acuña, *México* 3: 23). For the Chichimecas, the prickly pear cactus fruit did not have that effect because, among other reasons, they ate it with its skin but not with bread, which was thought suitable for the indigenous peoples but unsuitable for the Spaniards (Cárdenas 119). As this example shows, bread continued to be the central axis of the Spanish diet and, for this reason, subsistence foods or American foods were thought to only function as accompaniments and were domesticated when eaten with bread.

These were not mere rhetorical turns of phrase employed by authors in their writing. Rather, these were matters of great import where health and life could be placed at risk. This is the reason, in fact, that *Problemas y secretos maravillosos de las Indias* may be considered a medical treatise. We can examine yet another example told by Cieza de León about food consumption in San Sebastián Buenavista, a village located on the Eastern strip of the Gulf of Darién, where in around 1535 the Spaniards' main sustenance was heart of palm, which they harvested with difficulty in the outskirts of the city. As Cieza de León recounts, "they ate without bread, and drank much water, so that many Spaniards died" (16).[11] According to Cieza de León, this was not an isolated case, but a problem found in other places and dependent on three factors: the consumption of wild foods, the lack of bread to accompany them, and the excessive drinking of water, which was not found advisable during the time period (Montanari, *Gusti del Medioevo* 144; Gentilcore 159–62).

Culinary transformation was seen as a cultural process that could alter the nature of foods and make them suitable for consumption. In the Middle Ages and the Modern Age, cooking was understood to provide the means to correct the nature of foods and to ensure that, while nourishing, they would not alter the condition of the people who ate them (Flandrin 491–506; Montanari, *La comida como cultura* 50). For this reason, different cooking techniques were applied to American foods that were not deemed suitable for Spaniards. A case in point is that of the sweet potato, both a sweet and a root, discussed above. Europeans found sweet potatoes were good because, when cooked, they could be transformed into various delicacies, depending on their mode of preparation: grilled, cooked with meat, bathed with almond milk, cured, or preserved (Álvarez 173–75; Coma 189; Fernández de Oviedo, *Historia general* 2: 175). Another example is yucca, which was eaten as bread and also appreciated because its flour was used to make delicious fritters (Ximénez ff.67r, v). Thus, acceptance of an American food was dependent on the way it was integrated in a consumption model that the Spaniards considered civilized.

Conclusion

In summary, it became acceptable for Spaniards to consume foods that were only taxonomically suitable for the indigenous peoples when those foods were framed within a consumption structure that made them acceptable, whether through cultivation, their relation to other foods, the marginal or supplementary role they could play in the diet, or their transformation into a recognizable food through cooking. The Spanish could eat native foods as long as they did not eat them the way the indigenous peoples did. All social groups could eat the same foods, but there were small differences that could create a class abyss. Such differences were established for both political and health reasons, since each person had to eat according to his or her natural condition. It should be pointed out that this model of status preservation and the idea of health at first brought by the Spaniards also became popular among the indigenous populations, at least in some cases. I will only mention two examples: sugar and poultry. Sugar became a favored ingredient, as may be seen in the proliferation of sweet fruit preserves and milk-caramel sweets. It also featured as an ingredient in *chicha* (a fermented beverage, made, in this case, from corn), most likely beginning at the turn of the seventeenth century. In these cases, sugar functioned as a quality-correcting agent, intended to make foods more temperate and suited to the Spaniards' health patterns. Similarly, chicken was increasingly added to the indigenous slow-cooked soupy stews like *sancochos, locros,* and *ajiacos* in order to balance its warm properties with colder ingredients like, for instance, yuccas or potatoes. Overall, in the midst of the obsessive hierarchies imposed on American foods and people, there were elements that allowed certain mobility. Slowly, symbols of distinction became generalized life models.

NOTES

Chapter translated by Ana M. Gómez-Bravo. This study was made in the frame of a research leave granted by the University of Antioquia to be in residence Villa I Tatti, The Harvard Center for Italian Renaissance Studies.

1. "Guardaremos el orden que la mesma Naturaleza suele tener y guardar en el producir y perficionar (sic) las cosas naturales, procediendo de lo menos a lo más y de lo ínfimo a lo superior."
2. A *protomédico*, or protophysician, was a leading physician who was in charge of passing those who sought to practice medicine. For Hernández's complete work online, see *Obras completas de Francisco Hernández*.
3. "Concertarlo y ponerlo en orden, para que se siga utilidad y provecho de ello."
4. "Sabor agudo y amargo, salinoso y dulce, y de los otros sabores y de las insípidas y que no tienen sabor notable o ninguno."
5. A canonical term that designates the lowest sum appropriate for the yearly income of a cleric.
6. "Los que no son de fructa para se poder comer, ni son cultivados por la industria de los hombres."
7. Perhaps the most notable exception is that of the Port of Veracruz, where the local wild fruits seemed to satisfy the cravings for European fruit ("Relación de la ciudad de Veracruz y su comarca" 321).
8. "Tutte le frutte, ancora che dolce, hanno un poco di agro in tutta l'India."
9. "Ve ne fanno copia di composte et confetture, ma non sono in quella perfectione che sariano in Ispagna et Portogallo, perché le dolce hanno le dolce minore et l'agre l'agro più acuto."
10. Maybe the best example is the Port of Veracruz, where maize was seen as food for indigenous people, even though by 1580 it was accepted as both Indian food and food for Spaniards in the rest of America. In the same port, it was argued that wild fruit placated the desire for Spanish fruit, while in the rest of the Spanish possessions, American fruit was viewed with suspicion ("Relación de la ciudad de Veracruz y su comarca" 321).
11. The Spanish version is more eloquent: "y como los comían [los palmitos] sin pan y bebían mucha agua, muchos españoles se hinchaban y morían."

WORKS CITED

Acosta, José de. *Historia natural y moral de las Indias*. Jaime Cendrat, 1591.
Acuña, René, editor. *Relaciones geográficas del siglo XVI: México*, vols. 2 and 3, UNAM, 1986.
———. *Relaciones geográficas del siglo XVI: Nueva Galicia*. UNAM, 1988.
Álvarez Chanca, Diego. "Carta del doctor Diego Álvarez Chanca al Cabildo de Sevilla." *Cartas de particulares a Colón y relaciones coetáneas*, edited by Juan Gil and Consuelo Varela, Alianza, 1984, pp. 152–76.
Benzoni, Girolamo. *La historia del mondo nuovo di M. Girolamo Benzoni milanese: La qual trata delle isole & mari nuevamente ritrovati, et delle nuove città da lui proprio vedute, per acqua, e per terra in quattordeci anni*. Venetia, Pietro and Francesco Piti, 1572.
Bouza Álvarez, Fernando. "La cosmovisión del Siglo de Oro. Ideas y supersticiones." *La vida cotidiana en la época de Velázquez*, edited by José N. Alcalá-Zamora, Temas Hoy, 1999, pp. 217–34.
Burke, Peter. "Performing History: The Importance of Occasions" *Rethinking History*, vol. 9, no. 1, 2005, pp. 35–52.
Cárdenas, Juan de. *Problemas y secretos maravillosos de las Indias compuesta por el doctor Juan de Cárdenas, médico*. Museo Nacional de Arqueología, Historia y Etnología (México), 1913.
Cei, Galeotto. *Viaggio e Relazione delle Indie (1539–1553)*. Bulzoni Editore, 1992.
Cieza de León, Pedro de, and Clements R. Markham. *The Travels of Pedro De Cieza De León, A.D. 1532–50, Contained in the First Part of His Chronicle of Peru*. B. Franklin, 1964.
Coe, Sophie. *America's First Cuisines*. Texas UP, 1994.
Coma, Guillermo. "Relación de Guillermo Coma, traducida por Nicolás Esquilache." *Cartas de particulares a Colón y relaciones coetáneas*, edited by Juan Gil and Consuelo Varela, Alianza, 1984, pp. 177–203.
Crosby, Alfred W. *Ecological Imperialism: The Biological Expansion of Europe, 900–1900*. Cambridge UP, 1986.
Cuneo, Michele da. "Letter to Gerolamo Annari, 15 october 1495." *Repertorium Columbianum*, edited by Geoffrey Symcox, vol. 12: *Italian Reports on America: 1493–1522*, Brepols, 2002.
"Descripción de la ciudad de Guayaquil." *Relaciones histórico geográficas de la Audiencia de Quito: Siglo XVI–XIX*, edited by Pilar Ponce Leiva, vol. 2: *Siglo XVII–XIX*, Marka/Abya-Yala, 1994, pp. 10–48.
"Descripción de la villa de Tenerife de las cosas de la tierra que mandó azer el muy ilustre señor don Lope de Orozco, G(obernador) perpetuo y capitán general de la ciudad de Santa Marta y sus provincias por su majestad (19 de

mayo de 1580)." *Relaciones y visitas a los Andes: Siglo XVI*, edited by Hermes Tovar Pinzón, vol. 2: *Región del Caribe*, Colcultura/Instituto Colombiano de Cultura Hispánica, SF, 1993, pp. 309–54.

Earle, Rebecca. *The Body of the Conquistador: Food, Race, and the Colonial Experience in Spanish America, 1492–1700*. Cambridge UP, 2012.

Fernández de Oviedo, Gonzalo. *Historia general y natural de las Indias, islas y Tierra-Firme del mar océano*. Guarania, 1944–1945. 14 vols.

———. *Sumario de la natural y general historia de las Indias*. 1526. Espasa Calpe, 1978.

Flandrin, Jean-Louis. "Assaisonnement, cuisine et diététique aux xive, xve et xvie siècles." *Histoire de l'alimentation*, edited by Jean-Louis Flandrin and Massimo Montanari, Fayard, 1996, pp. 491–509.

Fragoso, Juan. *Cirugia universal, ahora nuevamente añadida, con todas las dificultades, y questiones, pertenecientes a las materias de que se trata*. Madrid, Viuda de Alonso Martín, 1627.

Gage, Thomas. *A New Survey of the West-Indies, or, The English American His Travel by Sea and Land*. London, A. Clark, 1677.

Gentilcore, David. *Food and Health in Early Modern Europe: Diet, Medicine, and Society, 1450–1800*. Bloomsbury, 2016.

Grieco, Allen J. "Alimentation et clases sociales à la fin du Moyen Âge et à la Renaissance." *Histoire de l'alimentation*, edited by Jean-Louis Flandrin and Massimo Montanari, Fayard, 1996, pp. 479–90.

———. "Medieval and Renaissance Wines: Taste, Dietary Theory, and How to Choose the 'Right' Wine (14th–16th centuries)." *Mediaevalia*, vol. 30, 2009, pp. 15–42.

———. "Les plantes, les régimes végétariens et la mélancolie à la fin du Moyen Age et au début de la Renaissance italienne." *Le monde végétal (XII-XVII siècles): Savoirs et usages sociaux*, edited by A. J. Grieco, O. Redon, and L. Tongiorgi Tomasi, PU de Vincennes, 1993, pp. 11–29.

———. "The Social Order of Nature and the Natural Order of Society in Late 13th–Early 14th Century Italy." *Miscellanea Mediaevalia*, vol. 21, no. 2, 1992, pp. 898–907.

———. "The Social Politics of Pre-Linnaean Botanical Clasification." *I Tatti Studies: Essays in the Renaissance*, vol. 4, 1991, pp. 131–49.

Hernández, Francisco, and German Somolinos. *Obras Completas*. UNAM, 1959.

Hespanha, António M. *Imbecillitas: As bem-aventuranças da inferioridade nas sociedades do Antigo Regime*. Annablume, 2010.

LaCombe, Michael A. *Political Gastronomy: Food and Authority in the English Atlantic World*. U of Pennsylvania P, 2012.

Laudan, Rachel. *Cuisine and Empire: Cooking in World History*. U of California P, 2013.

López Medel, Tomás. *De los tres elementos: Tratado sobre la naturaleza y el hombre del nuevo mundo*. edited by de Berta Ares Queija, Alianza, 1990.

Lovejoy, Arthur. *The Great Chain of Being: A Study of the History of an Idea*. Harvard UP, 1936.

[Manfredi, Girolamo]. *Libro llamado El porque, provechosissimo para la conservación de la salud, y para conocer la phisonomia, y las virtudes de las yerbas. Traduzido de Toscano en lengua Castellana*. Alcalá, Juan Iñiguez de Lequerica, 1587.

Melville, Elinor G. K. *A Plague of Sheep: Environmental Consequences of the Conquest of Mexico*. Cambridge UP, 1994.

Mintz, Sidney. *Sweetness and Power: The Place of Sugar in Modern History*. Viking, 1985.

Montanari, Massimo. *Gusti del Medioevo: I prodotti, la cucina, la tavola*. Laterza, 2014.

———. *Il riposso della polpetta e altre storie intorno al cibo*. Laterza, 2010.

———. *La comida como cultura*. Trea, 2006.

Obras completas de Francisco Hernández. 2015. Universidad Nacional Autónoma de México. www.franciscohernandez.unam.mx/home.html.

Pardo Tomás, José. *El tesoro natural de América: Colonialismo y ciencia en el siglo XVI*. Nivola, 2002.

Pilcher, Jeffrey. "Five Hundred Years of Fusion: Histories of Food in the Iberian World." *Writing Food History: A Global Perspective*, edited by Kyri W. Claflin and Peter Scholliers, Berg, 2012, pp. 87–104.

Recchi, Nardo Antonio. *De materia medica Novae Hispaniae. Libri Quatuor. Cuatro libros sobre la materia médica de Nueva España*, edited by Raquel Álvarez Peláez and Florentino Fernández González, Doce calles/Junta de Castilla y León, 1988.

"Relación de Anzerma." *Relaciones y visitas a los Andes: Siglo XVI*, edited by Hermes Tovar Pinzón, vol. 1, Colcultura/Instituto Colombiano de Cultura Hispánica, 1993, pp. 335–61.

"Relación de Chilapan." *Relaciones geográficas del siglo XVI: Tlaxcala*, edited by René Acuña, vol. 2, UNAM, 1985, pp. 109–19.

"Relación de la ciudad de Veracruz y su comarca." *Relaciones geográficas del siglo XVI: Tlaxcala*, edited by René Acuña, vol. 2, UNAM, 1985, pp. 301–6.

"Relación de la conquista de los carare [9 de mayo de 1601]." *Relaciones y visitas a los Andes. Siglo XVI: Región Centro-Oriental*, edited by Hermes Tovar Pinzón, Colcultura/Instituto Colombiano de Cultura Hispánica, SF, vol. 3, 1993, pp. 427–82.

"Relación de Loja." *Relaciones histórico-geográficas de la Audiencia de Quito: Siglo XVI-XIX*, edited by Pilar Ponce Leiva, vol. 1, Marka/Abya-Yala, 1992, pp. 122–43.

Saldarriaga, Gregorio. "Comer y ser: La alimentación como política de la diferenciación social en la América española, siglos XVI y XVII." *Varia Historia*, vol. 32, no. 58, 2016, pp. 53–77.

Sánchez Jiménez, Antonio. "Memoria y utilidad en el *Sumario de la natural historia de las Indias* de Gonzalo Fernández de Oviedo." *Colonial Latin American Review*, vol. 13, no. 2, 2004, pp. 263–73.

Sardela, Juan Bautista. "Relación de lo que subcedio al magnifico señor capitán Jorge Robledo." *Relaciones y visitas a los Andes: Siglo XVI*, edited by Hermes Tovar Pinzón, vol. 1, Colcultura/Instituto Colombiano de Cultura Hispánica, 1993, pp. 263–331.

Strozzi, Giambattista. "Cadiz, 19 March 1494." *Repertorium Columbianum*, vol. 10: *Italian Reports on America. 1493–1522. Letters, Dispatches, and Papal Bulls*, edited by Geoffrey Symcox, Brepols, 2001.

Ximénez de Cisneros, Francisco. *Cuatro libros de la naturaleza y virtudes de las plantas, y animales*. México, Viuda de Diego López, 1615.

CHAPTER 3

Still Life, Food, and Fiction
Diversions from the Colonial Baroque

Rodrigo Labriola, *Federal University of Rio de Janeiro*

> Aquí tengo destas costas
> por cuantas desiertas playas
> descubren las atalayas
> con sus fuegos y sus postas
> las centollas y langostas
> sabogas, ostias, tortugas,
> verderoles y lampugas
> que comerás con toronjas
> apretando como a esponjas
> sus mal formadas verrugas.[1]
>
> LOPE DE VEGA, "Bodegón"
> *El peregrino en su patria (The Pilgrim in His Homeland)*

FOOD IS ONE of the most prominent neo-baroque imaginaries. The aesthetic representations of food characterize seventeenth-century Spanish art, peninsular or transatlantic, with the pictorial genre of still life seen as something "still alive," or rather as a fascination with inanimate objects. In this essay, I argue that the desire to eat is a feeling reflected in art that comes from a vital, indispensable, and animalistic need that becomes inscribed in various styles of literary writing. The *memento mori* topos usually connected to still lifes reaches its limit—its anti-theological though historical character—and its wondrous but nonetheless material representation in the descriptive writing of several of the chroniclers of the Indies, whose artistic relevance is unquestionable.[2] The writing of the "new" in the chronicles, starting in the sixteenth century and continuing through the colonial baroque period, can thus be understood as experimentation with written forms that turned the imaginable—what can be painted and eaten—into something plausible. Creating modern fiction involved engaging travel literature, as well as a rhetoric of irony about food.

Undoubtedly influenced by *Contrapunteo cubano del tabaco y el azúcar* (*Cuban Counterpoint: Tobacco and Sugar*; 1940), written by Cuban anthropologist Fernando Ortiz, literary representations of food are an ongoing focus in analyses of Latin American culture starting in the second half of the twentieth century. Ortiz was the first to draw attention to the link between food and literature, a true Gordian knot that tightly links the past of the white colonial baroque to multiple cultural identities, and to the art of the still life.

In "Problemática de la actual novela latinoamericana" ("Problems of the Current Latin American Novel"; 1967), Alejo Carpentier points out the importance of culinary contexts. When expounding his theory of the novel, Carpentier explains:

> [Culinary contexts] have their importance in terms of their particular historical contexts. The Cuban *ajiaco*, for example, a national dish of Creole cuisine, gathers, in the same casserole, elements of Spanish cuisine —the one that Columbus brought in his caravels—with products (the "viands") from the first land sighted by the discoverers. Later, Spanish cuisine was called *bucán* because of the influence of some French adventurers, duly called buccaneers, and began to systematize in Cuba an elementary industry consisting of sunbaking, smoking, and salting venison and wild swine meat. [. . .] The kitchen responds to a philosophy, to a system, to a discourse of the method, of the treatment of delicacies. (23)

Carpentier subordinated the subject of food to its historical-political context perhaps in an excessively rigid way. In fact, in Carpentier's work, food's cultural force extends beyond theory, driving the copious *representations* of food in his fiction in such a way that food appears as an integral part of the structure that sustains textual composition. From the first pages of *El reino de este mundo* (*The Kingdom of this World*; 1940), the slave Ti Noel, who works as the nexus between all the chapters, observes the wigged heads of the white masters in the hair salon:

> By a funny coincidence, the next grocery exhibited heads of calves, skinned, with a little piece of parsley on the tongue, which had the same waxy quality, as if numbed among scarlet tails, jelly legs, and pots containing stewed guts cooked in the fashion of Caen. Only a wooden partition separated the two counters, and Ti Noel amused himself by thinking that, next to the discolored heads of the calves, heads of white gentlemen were served on the tablecloth of the same table. Thus, as the birds were ornamented with their feathers to be presented to the guests of a banquet, an expert and quite ogre cook would have dressed the foreheads with their best wigs. They lacked only a border of lettuce leaves or radishes carved in fleur-de-lis patterns. Furthermore, the Arabian foam pots, the lavender water bottles, and the rice powder boxes, next to the tripe pots and the trays with kidney, completed, with singular coincidences of bottles and containers, that portrait of an abominable treat. (61)

An anthropophagic banquet of white heads, prepared by a cook who was "expert and quite ogre," as in fairy tales, is the imaginary fantasy of a black slave.[3] Here, the text introduces the common plentiful abundance of food that the slave will never enjoy. The banquet of heads is a banquet within a banquet, a metonymic transposition from the heads that eat to the heads to be eaten. In addition, the loss of the head, or the guillotine as allegory and political object, as a loss of a primordial subject in political science will return indirectly throughout the novel by way of Paulina Bonaparte's character. However, Ti Noel's imaginary feast is rhetorically enveloped as a "funny coincidence," but it is in fact represented as the "portrait" (*cuadro*) of an abominable invitation.[4]

Carpentier will use a similar artifice years later in *Concierto Barroco* (*Baroque Concert*; 1974).[5] A dazzling description of the still-virgin banquet's table, as in a decorative art display, leads the reader through intricate silverware and utensils, trailing to the silver chamber pot where the Master urinates and says: "Here is what remains, here is what leaves" (15–16). The ellipse goes from the inside out, in mirror image with the digestive tract, whose continuity goes from the top to the bottom. This process is not reversible: the final image is a portrait of the Master, his face reflected in the mirror soaked in his own urine.

Carpentier delved deeper into these representations in two other highly commented-upon episodes. The first one takes place in *El siglo de las luces* (*Explosion in a Cathedral*; 1962) with the preparation of a "Bucán de bucanes."[6] The second appears in *El recurso del método* (*Reasons of State*; 1974) with the preparation of a *bodegón tropical* (tropical still life) or banquet that the forewoman serves for the first magistrate, exiled in Paris, and which fuels the French cook's anger and Ophelia's Proustian memory. Few critics have analyzed these fragments in the interpretive key of the feast, a key that leads, in all cases, to the topics of abundance, transgression, and authorized excess (chaos in order, or controlled chaos), of the collective act as an expression of identity, belonging, liberation, and regeneration, and of suspension of time in the present as a feature of completeness.[7] Finally, it leads to a kind of reading that, at its core, posits America and Europe as opposites, looking to determine a Latin American identity, engaging a nineteenth-century hermeneutics that is related to the teleological matrix of Romantic historiography. Impregnated by a sociological apparatus, such a line of interpretation inevitably ends by erasing the aesthetic conflicts of South America's cultural heterogeneity, as Antonio Cornejo Polar believes, plunging them into an amalgam of politically innocuous miscegenation and transculturation, to follow Fernando Ortiz and Ángel Rama.

However, it is often unnoticed that the beginnings of *El reino de este mundo* and *Concierto barroco* are qualitatively different from the narratives of long banquets that appear later in each of the novels and that have been the object of much critical attention. There are three reasons for this: first, the banquet narratives are synthetic, and their position in the texts works as a veil but not as the climax of the plot; second, they describe fixed images, without elaborating on them and without temporality, whether in Ti-Noel's imagination or in the specular reflection of the Master; third, they avoid any sacralization of sense, and from a hierarchy of objects they present a perspective that is clearly plebeian and profane, either through Ti-Noel's gaze or in the portrayal of the Master that links urine and silver. Carpentier constructs these "pictures" not only with the help of the subjects—inanimate objects—but, above all, through modes of representation. Carpentier's depictions recover the *ut pictura poesis*, the key baroque precept that formally links poetry and painting, bringing rhetoric closer to the visual art used in still lifes in general.

The choice of rhetoric and its conditions of fictional possibility serve to present the subject of food in culinary or political terms, as in hermeneutical readings. However, Roberto González Echevarría proposes that intertextuality and parody are the formal resources in Carpentier's late fiction. Hence, for González Echevarría the hermeneutics of the feast appear later than the rhetoric: "The author of the latest Carpentierian fiction mocks himself and undermines his own authority by proclaiming the absence of originality of his texts on which it was supposedly based. Now intertextuality and parody govern the discourse, and the twists and turns of chronology, instead of being hidden, are displayed. It is, in short, a freedom like that of the slaves as revelers on the Feast of the Epiphany" (136). Indeed, the reiterated mention of the still life pictorial genre in Carpentier's essays and novels generates a rhetoricity (Wellbery) that links food and speech, a visual reference and a form of fictional representation in both literature and art.

In "Problems of the Current Latin American Novel," Carpentier discusses style after writing about cultural contexts, emphasizing that the baroque style is the quintessential form of American expression. Significantly, a reference to the kitchen of Combernon in the first act of *L'Annonce faite à Marie* (*The Tidings Brought to Mary*; 1912) by Paul Claudel heads his comments on style. Carpentier adds that a detailed description of the kitchen would be unnecessary, as it can easily be imagined by the reader, for Claudel explains that it resembles a painting by Brueghel. Carpentier states that humble Latin American kitchens were never depicted in art, though they may have been set in "baroque style." Carpentier underscores the differences between Spanish and indigenous kitchens: "While kitchens of olive and wheat were elegantly painted, the kitchens of corn were marginalized, anonymous" (25). Culinary hermeneutics depends on the prior evaluation of the history of still life as a manner of modern painting. *Ut pictura poesis*, metaphysical and aesthetic, combines a proper naturalism with modern rationality stimulated by light and matter, by sensuality.

Although diverging from several aspects of Carpentier's understanding of the neo-baroque, José Lezama Lima holds views on still lifes that are similar to Carpentier's. Representations of food in Lezama Lima's work are condensed in chapter 7 of *Paradiso* (1966). In the midst of the narrative, the dinner prepared by Mrs. Augusta, the grandmother, seems to want to exhaust with insatiable voracity all the symbolic possibilities surrounding food, becoming funereal as we learn that Augusta will not be the one to die, but rather her son, Alberto. Critics have commented on the parallelisms between this and the banquets in *El reino de este mundo* and *Concierto barroco*. However, as Severo Sarduy noted, in Lezama Lima's *Paradiso*, the banquet is constructed as a series of successive portraits and still lifes throughout the chapter. Sarduy reorients the reading of Lezama Lima by noting that "more than in the literary [models], we should look for the illustration of the magnificent Lezamian treat, of his polished cornucopia, in those painted banquets —imbrications, collage—, anthropomorphized, which are Archimboldo's portraits" (289). Sarduy reviews the history of European art and, by revaluing Giuseppe Archimboldo (1530–1593), usually considered merely an eccentric artist in the Renaissance and baroque universe, he redoubles his bet by appealing to the rhetorical form. Sarduy differentiates between European and Creole baroque following Lezama's characterization of the baroque as the art of the counterconquest, or *contraconquista*.

The "fixed, precise laws" that govern baroque art also operate in culinary culture, and both are combined and transformed through fictional narratives. The axis that joins food and baroque is painting, especially the still life:

> Of all baroque themes, the one that best suits to American open gnostic space is food, with its European "overloaded" still lifes, its frozen forms [...]; none of these abandons their humanist heritage to become an elegant, yet wasteful fabric. Lezama's table matches the wedding banquet of Góngora's in its "delicacies," but surpasses it in the convoluted parts of his inventions [...]. Creole cuisine is not a variegated cuisine, or the inconsequential improvisation of dishes, of vanity, but rather a knowledge of precise, fixed laws. (288–89)

The terms for the still life pictorial genre appear for the first time in painting inventories in the Netherlands around the year 1650: in Dutch, *stilleven* meant "inert model" and coexisted with other no-less descriptive terms like *fruytagie* (painting with fruits) and *bancket* or *ontbitj* (paintings representing banquets or snack-type meals). The painter Joachim von Sandrart had already spoken of "things at rest" in 1675 (Schneider). The word passed into English with the same meaning as *still life*. The name *nature morte* appeared in the Renaissance as a term borrowed from French. The term went through semantic mutations, which the baroque world transferred to the aesthetic field and which were contemporaneous with the semantic transfer. Du Pont de Nemours understood it to be a new word and found it necessary to explain the term *nature morte*, writing that it meant "objets immobiles" ("inanimate things") in a letter addressed to Carolina-Louise de Baden in 1779. Shortly after, in 1780, Jean-Baptiste Descamps defined the concept of *nature morte* as a representation of "immobile objects." This rationalization of pictorial objects is symptomatic of the abandonment of the baroque landscape, reflected in the images of gardens and the privileged theater of feasts, as well as the transformation of wild nature into an *artificiosa natura* as its signifying nucleus (Checa and Morán).

Thus, perhaps the paintings of objects represented the most decorative part of those gardens of the baroque feast. The American still life was a *memento mori*: a remembrance of death that made all *vanitas* futile. In this modest but effective way, art contributed to a larger religious project served by the pedagogical intention of images. In seventeenth-century perspective, artifice opposed life, while during the eighteenth century the progressive appreciation of nature under the rationalistic lens of science deprived the genre of its baroque allegorical component, making it dead, free from the vitality that characterized the new illuminist nature, "naturalism." It is important to consider that while during the baroque period the superlative genre displays were religious representations, they became replaced in the following century by state ceremonies, which would feature at the top of a public-art hierarchy. As Walter Benjamin notes, the "naturalization" of these acts in the baroque period would mean the naturalization of history. However, from the end of the seventeenth century, when the term *nature morte* arose, history gained independence from Nature and was constituted as a criterion of hierarchical legitimacy among the different artistic genres.

Leaving aside the theoretical threads linked to the rediscovery of Aristotle's *Poetics* and its reception in the sixteenth century, baroque experimentation with still life works in two ways that are related to the construction of fictional representations:[8] 1) imitation due to resemblance, where the observer casts an embracing gaze toward the object so that he is not struck by referential illusion, and 2) the *trompe d'oeil*, where the observer is engaged in representation by means of deception. In the first, the look is presented as subjective, while in the second referentiality is an illusion that points to an empty referent. There is no other painting under Parrásio's painting. The *trompe d'oeil* acts like a palimpsest by turning the gaze illusory and, with it, turning the subject illusory. This form of fictionalization reaches its peak with Archimboldo's portraits, in which *imitatio* and *trompe d'oeil* are positioned in a hierarchical parity, a balance that materializes the illusion and makes the representation problematic, so it is difficult to decide, as the eye sees two equally mimetic and indeterminable referents. The reality of the referent does not lie in either object or subject but in the distance between both: from close up, it portrays an American still life, but from a distance it appears as a portrait.

Golden Age Spain and Spanish viceroys did not know *nature morte*, but did enjoy *bodegones*. In fact, the Spanish term *naturaleza muerta* (still life) comes from late French, when the descriptive tradition of the name *bodegones*, in its meaning as decorative representations of food, was already well established within the space frame of a kitchen or a room linked to meal service. Golden Age *bodegones* show wild game, fruit, flowers, kitchen utensils, tableware, household items, etc. The Spanish Juan van der Hamen y León (1596–1631), whose surname testifies to the political and cultural interdependence between Spain and Holland during the sixteenth and seventeenth centuries, was a recognized *bodegón* artist. Some historians believe that his fame was eclipsed by the work of contemporaries Diego de Velázquez (1599–1660) and Fernando de Zurbarán (1598–1664). The nexus of *bodegón* with the kitchen was so strong in Spain that, even when painting represented inert objects that did not necessarily belong in the kitchen, the term was still used, as in the case of the subgenre dedicated exclusively to flowers called *bodegón floral* (flowery still life), of which those by Juan de Arellano (1614–1676) were considered some of the best.

For Peter Cheney, the rediscovery of seventeenth-century *bodegón* painting in Spain is a twentieth-century phenomenon (27). Academic interest in elucidating its origins and its role in Golden Age literature is certainly a subject of the twenty-first century. As Julio Ortega states:

> The Spanish *bodegón* [. . .] is a genre that arises as a cultural response to the material crisis of the early seventeenth century. It responds to want and caducity as empirical forms of a language of the natural world, which recovers its common and modest fruits as a typically baroque allegory according to which the image re-appropriates the object it depicts in order to occupy the empty space with new material and terrestrial versions. [. . .] This tasty re-appropriation was a cultural lesson forged in the chronicles of the Indies. ("O bodegón e a mescla" 105)

Taking Ortega's ideas as a starting point, I undertook a similar survey of the Mesoamerican region in 2002.[9] However, the subject of food representation is made more complex because of the influence of medieval rhetoric on the texts of the Conquest. Hans Ulrich Gumbrecht has considered the possibility of linking cultural studies to epistemological theories of literature and has proposed "to find a complementary relationship still to be undertaken in charting a discursive archeology" (513). Thus, a discursive archeology of food and its cultural derivations may point to the appearance of a new "discourse" (a term understood in line with Foucault's theories) on food in the sixteenth century. Such discourse found ways to reproduce itself in the chronicles in a remarkable number of textual iterations.

Complex representations of food were made possible thanks, on one hand, to an unprecedented cultural contact: the arrival of the Europeans in America; and, on the other hand, the process of acculturation of native peoples through evangelization, particularly as carried out by Franciscans in New Spain. A new discourse on food as a privileged material place of cultural confrontation—a discourse that permeates the texts of conquerors, evangelizers, and travelers—reveals a rupture of the medieval *episteme*, a rupture that will also lay the foundations of Spanish literature in the Golden Age.

The imagery of American historiography at first revolved around gold (*where is the gold?*), which was set within a larger imagery of "American abundance": a new land previously unknown but now linked to the needs and wants of European culture and, in all cases, characterized by excess. However, something was lacking in the early dialogues between Europeans and Native Americans. The chronicles of the Indies show a hidden and implicit dialogue about hunger and a search for food after the Europeans' terrible sea voyages or after endless land marches, an imagery *stuffed* with scarcity and misery. This unwanted part of the conquest, this first contact with others in a climate of amazement and extreme material need, emerged only furtively in the dialogues of the sublime encounters between both worlds written for historical or political reasons and relayed by such authors as Pero Vaz de Caminha (1450–1500) and Hernán Cortés (1485–1547). Supported by the myth of continental geography's generous abundance, the image of American bountifulness appeared in letters to the king and queen, in official histories commissioned by the Crowns, and even, almost as a paradox, in modern Latin American historiography. Although such hidden dialogue is irreproducible, it exists in the absence and voids that can be read obliquely in the chronicles of the Indies.[10]

At the core of the new and complex discourse on food is an inseparable problematic of otherness, in the three categories proposed by Tzvetan Todorov—conquering, loving, and knowing—and in the dual view of the chronicler as a conqueror and an evangelizer. At the crossroads of these two sides of otherness lies a tension involving discursive representations of food. A discourse on food was shaped after that about gold.

At the beginning of the sixteenth century, gold was conceptualized in highly symbolic terms. Gold was dematerialized because, in addition to being an exchange value, a means to value other things, it was also a coveted symbolic reservoir of what was most pure and beautiful in the world. However, a shift toward a more materialized representation of gold took place in the sixteenth century. The gold found in the Indies, in Mexico and Peru, was no longer of purely symbolic value but a commodity that could be carried—extracted, melted into coins, and stolen as treasure. The gradual change in the meanings assigned to gold had resulted in a record number of variations in the early seventeenth century. Gold had been transformed into three things: a *symbol* of what was highest and purest; a privileged commodity of commercial exchange, a *coin*; and a heavily material object that could be stolen, a *treasure*.

This path that leads from gold being understood in symbolic terms to gold being presented in material terms is exactly the opposite of the path taken in the discursive conceptualization of food. The representations of food by the chroniclers of the Indies were at first of pragmatic and material significance. They then moved to a commercial discourse, which involved the exchange of commodities such as potatoes, corn, and peppers. The discourse on food ended with an extremely symbolic form: the anthropophagic rite as the ultimate symbolization of otherness. The representations of food were being abstracted; food was becoming more and more complex within discourse. Thus, in the writings of the chroniclers, gold, which was considered an important symbolic element for rhetorical purposes, became a concrete thing with economic value. Meanwhile, food (maximum estrangement of others), which early on had been regarded in such concrete terms that rhetoric could not digest it, would be appropriated by the new *bodegones*, elevating its symbolic value with the aura of art.

Julio Ortega has established a theoretical link between writing, in the representations of food in the chronicles, and the aesthetic form of *bodegones*: "Unfolded through a baroque syntax capable of incorporating, adding, and opening a space to overseas foods, both in the image of the traditionally woven basket as in the public kitchen, the representation of food poses [. . .] the materiality of baroque culture. My hypothesis is that accumulation and blending, those cultural forms in which the New and Old World meet and intertwine, are mechanisms of representation and appropriation underlying the allegories of *bodegones*" ("O bodegón e a mescla" 105).

Although his ideas seem close to Romantic sociological readings, Ortega introduces the general problem of "blending," not miscegenation, facilitated by "baroque syntax." It is a formal rather than an ideological rooting of *bodegones* or still lifes, and thus a typically modernistic materialist and sensualist reading:

> In the Spanish *bodegón* and in its American versions, the subject of *bodegón* is more present for its lack of representation. We see the scene with baroque eyes, the intensity of its representation, as the action of the individual that includes us in the narrative of his vision [. . .] the communication that gets established in front of *bodegón* is a dialogical drama of the senses, allegorized in that figure of speech, in that communicative action. [. . .] For that reason, the *bodegón* seems to assume the lessons of a Chronicle of the Indies: what we see is what we do not possess, and we can only possess through the art of

nature and the artifice of painting. The foods of the Spanish *bodegón*, it could be said, represent the vehemence of a desire: its presence is sensorial and at the same time epiphanic. [. . .] A display begins by revealing the opposite: the world is more complete in its absence. Hence, the *bodegón* is a story about the place of a subject in a problematic modernity. (106–7)

Thus, unlike the rest of European *nature mortes* (dead natures), linked to the absolute religious or moral *memento mori*, the Spanish *bodegón* would necessitate a subjective, temporal, and localized reading. As Ortega asserts, "the subject is no more Iberian or Inca: he is a transatlantic subject, convened by the cultural syntax of blending, in the scene of the page, in the works of reading, in the new geotextuality of modern Spanish language" (107).

E. M. Forster stated that food in fiction has, above all, a social function, since the characters rarely experience hunger or particularly enjoy the taste of food, an idea that minimizes the importance of the subject. If Forster's observation is undoubtedly admissible in reference to psychological literature starting in the nineteenth century, it contributes little to the understanding of the irony of feeding that structured some of the works by Cervantes, Rabelais, or Swift in the baroque period. Similarly, the study of avant-garde fascination with the bodily and fluid hospitality of the mouth and tongue may not be considered to provide a complete understanding of food's cultural centrality. The honorable aversions of the Protestant bourgeoisie, as in Marcel Proust, the Mann brothers, or Italo Svevo, all of them stylized and coherently perverse, might similarly prove to be of limited help. In his "Sociologia da refeição" ("Sociology of Meal"), published almost at the end of his life, Georg Simmel stated that: "The immeasurable sociological meaning of the meal is contained in the possibility that people who do not share specific interests meet for a common meal, a possibility based on primitivism and, therefore, on the triviality of material interest" (2). It was Guy Daveport in *Objects on a Table* who brought our attention again to the magical value of food representation in seventeenth-century *bode-*

gones. Following a similar impetus, a key work by Xavier Domingo, *De la olla al mole* (*From Stew to Mole*; 1984), recovers the playful character of food representations in the Hispanic world.

Sociological and aesthetic approaches are the two main theoretical lines engaged in the study of still lifes and *bodegones*, following cues from literary studies. However, while the first line of inquiry has been abundantly developed since Fernando Ortiz's *Cuban Counterpoint: Tobacco and Sugar*, the second remains almost unexplored in spite of invaluable resources such as Alfonso Reyes's *Memorias de cocina y bodega* (*Memoires of Kitchen and Cellar*; 1953). As this essay has attempted to show, a productive theoretical path would balance the contributions by Ortiz and Reyes in order to provide a more comprehensive overview of the complexities of still lifes and their central importance to both baroque and post-colonial aesthetics.

NOTES

Chapter translated by Ana M. Gómez-Bravo.

1. Here I have from these coasts, / going through as many deserted beaches / as the watchtowers discover / with their fires and their posts, / the crabs and the lobsters / shads, turtles, oysters / dolphinfish, and cockles / that you will eat with grapefruits / squeezing like sponges / their badly formed warts.
2. *Memento mori*, meaning "remember that you will die," is a medieval concept that reflects on mortality, the vanity of earthly life, and the transient nature of all earthly goods.
3. According to European mythologies, ogres were giants who fed on human flesh.
4. The word "cuadro" in Spanish is linked to painting: plastic works that can be "framed" at the museum.
5. Carpentier developed his style of cannibalistic magical surrealism in France through the influence of Robert Desnos.
6. "Bucán" is a Taino word that designates a way to roast or cook meats, a barbecue. So, *Bucán de bucanes* would translate as "Barbecue of barbecues."
7. After comparing the banquet of the ex-first magistrate with the "bucán" of *El siglo de las luces*, Rita De Maessener explains: "Both arise spontaneously from the abundance of food. They are held in isolated spaces, an indefinite Caribbean

island and a Parisian attic. In both cases it is a transplanted meal, the "bucán" connoted with the French but originated in the Caribbean and a creole food in Paris, so the question arises of the difficulty and complexity of saying America and from where to say it. Both the bucán and the creole food present a festive character, but they also carry a violent or deadly bias: Is the Caribbean a festive song to be mourned? In both feasts, attention is paid to black, central in the Caribbean, and its problematic integration, since it questions and confirms at the same time certain hierarchical structures." (18)

8. Karlheinz Stierle evaluates this development when writing on Ariosto's *Orlando Furioso* and highlighting the mixed position of Torcuato Tasso's *Jerusalem Delivered*. In *Renaissance and Baroque*, Wölfflin tries to transfer the categories from baroque visual arts to literature in a way that recalls Costa Lima's analysis in *Mímesis: desafio ao pensamento* (*Mimesis: Imitation and Difference*) (1988).

9. Further information in Labriola (2007). See also Ortega's work on the Andean region in "The Discourse of Abundance" (1992).

10. A relevant study on this topic can be found in Earle (2012).

WORKS CITED

Ariosto, Lodovico. *Orlando Furioso*. Oxford UP, 1974.

Benjamin, Walter. *The Origin of the German Tragic Drama*. Translated by John Osborne, Verso, 1998.

Carpentier, Alejo. *Concierto barroco*. 1974. Andrés Bello, 1997.

———. *El recurso del método*. Siglo XXI, 1974.

———. *The Kingdom of this World*. Translated by Harriet de Onís, Farrar, 2006.

———. *El siglo de las luces*. Siglo XXI, 1984.

———. "Problemática de la actual novela latinoamericana." *Tientos y diferencias*, Arca, 1967, pp. 8–43.

Checa, Fernando, and José M. Morán. *El barroco*. Istmo, 1982.

Cheney, Peter. *Arte y naturaleza: El bodegón español en el Siglo de Oro*. Fundación Airtel, 1999.

Claudel, Paul. *The Tidings Brought to Mary: L'Annonce faite à Marie, a Drama*. H. Regnery, 1969.

Cornejo Polar, Antonio. *O condor voa: Literatura e cultura latino-americana*. Editora UFMG, 2000.

Costa Lima, Luiz. *Mímesis: Desafio ao pensamento*. Forense-Universitária, 1988.

Davenport, Guy. *Objects on a Table: Harmonious Disarray in Art and Literature*. Counterpoint, 1998.

Domingo, Xavier. *De la olla al mole*. Instituto de Cooperación Iberoamericana, 1984.

Earle, Rebecca. *The Body of the Conquistador: Food, Race and the Colonial Experience in Spanish America, 1492–1700*. Cambridge UP, 2012.

Forster, Edward M. *Aspects of the Novel*. Harcourt, Brace, 1929.

Foucault, Michel. *La arqueología del saber*. Siglo XXI, 1970.

González Echevarría, Roberto. "Modernidad, modernismo y nueva narrativa: El recurso del método." *Revista Interamericana de Bibliografía*, vol. 30, 1980, pp. 157–63.

Gumbrecht, Hans Ulrich. "The Future of Literary Studies?" *New Literary History*, vol. 26, no. 3, 1996, pp. 499–518.

Labriola, Rodrigo. *A fome dos outros: Literatura, comida e alteridade no século XVI*. EdUFF, 2007.

Lezama Lima, José. *Paradiso*. Letras cubanas, 1994.

Maeseneer, Rita De. "'El Bucán de los Bucanes' y *des mangeailles de sauvage*: Sobre dos festines en Alejo Carpentier." *CiberLetras: Revista de Crítica Literaria y de Cultura*, vol. 14, 2005. www.lehman.edu/faculty/guinazu/ciberletras/v14/demaeseneer.htm.

Ortega, Julio. "O *bodegón* e a mescla: Uma sintaxe transatlântica." *Alea: Estudios Neolatinos*, vol. 15, no. 1, 2013, pp. 100–14.

———. "The Discourse of Abundance." Translated by Nicolás Wey Gómez, *American Literary History*, vol. 4, no. 3, 1992, pp. 369–85.

Ortiz, Fernando. *Cuban Counterpoint: Tobacco and Sugar*. Duke UP, 1995.

Rama, Ángel. *Writing Across Cultures: Narrative Transculturation in Latin America*. Duke UP, 2012.

Reyes, Alfonso. *Memorias de cocina y bodega: Minutas*. Fondo de Cultura Económica, 2000.

Sarduy, Severo. *Ensayos generales sobre el Barroco*. Fondo de Cultura Económica, 1987.

Schneider, Norbert. *Naturaleza muerta*. Taschen Verlag, 1999.

Simmel, George. "Sociologia da refeição." *Estudos Históricos*, vol. 33, 2004, pp. 159–66.

Stierle, Karlheinz. *A ficção*. Translated by Luiz Costa Lima, Caetés, 2006.

Tasso, Torcuato. *Jerusalem Delivered (Gerusalemme Liberata)*. Edited and translated by Anthony M. Esolen, Johns Hopkins UP, 2000.

Todorov, Tzvetan. *La Conquista de América: La cuestión del otro*. Translated by Flora Botton Burlá, Siglo Veintiuno, 1987.

Wellbery, David. *Neo-retórica e desconstrução*. EdUERJ, 1998.

Wölfflin, Heinrich. *Renaissance and Baroque*. Cornell UP, 1966.

CHAPTER 4

Furniture and Equipment in the Royal Kitchens of Early Modern Spain

Carolyn A. Nadeau, *Illinois Wesleyan University*

IN THE OPENING words of the 1611 *Arte de cocina, pastelería, vizcochería y conservería* (*The Art of Cooking, Piemaking, Pastrymaking, and Preserving*), Francisco Martínez Montiño asserts that cleanliness and order should be the top priorities of any successful cook. As master cook and head of the kitchens for both Philip III and Philip IV of Spain, he begins his cookbook with an elegant visual image of the royal kitchen:[1] "Everything should be shining and hanging in its proper place, pieces should not be left around on the tables nor the wash area. The spits should be on their rack shining brightly, and the rolling pins and large spoons for blancmange, you should have on a board hanging with wooden pegs, like the ones found in pharmacies but much bigger and another one like this for sieves and cheesecloths" (1v).[2]

In this passage, readers begin to visualize the kitchen spaces and furniture, like tables and peg boards, and appliances, like spoons and strainers, that were necessary to prepare the 506 recipes and close to five thousand ingredients that are found within the pages of Martínez Montiño's masterpiece.[3] While much has already been written on *what* foodstuffs were produced and consumed in early modern Spain, this essay examines *how* dishes were prepared and what spaces and tools were used to prepare food at court.[4] The essay begins by signaling the priorities Martínez Montiño establishes in the cooking spaces of the royal kitchens, including access to water. It then turns to essential kitchen furnishings and heat sources and explains how cooking temperatures were identified without the use of thermometers. Moving from big kitchen items to medium and then small, the last two sections provide an account of prepware and serveware as well as hand-held utensils, which facilitates an understanding for readers of the evolution of kitchen apparatuses. By sharing data analysis of the hundreds of material objects described by the master cook in charge of the royal kitchen, my aim is to provide scholars and gastronomes today with an increased understanding of kitchen technology in early modern Spain and to contribute to the standardization of the material culture of early modern royal kitchens.

The most comprehensive work on early modern kitchen spaces and instruments to date is Peter Brears, *Cooking and Dining in Tutor and Early Stuart England*. Using archival, archaeological, and architectural sources, he brings his readers through the physical spaces and describes the material objects used in the preparation of all aspects of a meal. He makes brewing, baking, boiling, roasting, frying, stewing, pickling, and preserving vivid as he explains in detail the areas in which dishes were created and the appliances and utensils used to create them.[5] In Italy, Deborah Krohn has delved into Bartolomeo Scappi's *Opera* (1570) to examine the role of his twenty-seven exemplary illustrations of kitchen spaces and appliances. For the first time in the history of European cookbooks, Scappi provides his readers not only with recipes for preparing food, but also with visual images of the spaces and tools necessary for the accomplished cook.

In considering the spaces and contents of kitchens at the early modern Spanish court, María del Carmen Simón Palmer explains that sources are scarce (105). Other scholars, among them Carmen Abad Zardoya, have published essays on particular kitchen items found at court, but to date no one has examined Spanish royal kitchens in depth in the way that Brears does for England. Likewise, no one has examined a watershed text, like Krohn does for Scappi, to get a sense of how kitchen objects portray the shift in the secular expertise of the culinary arts. This essay is a first step in that direction as it codifies the furniture, appliances, and utensils that Martínez Montiño used in his cookbook that were present at court. To be sure, his illustrations are much more modest in scope than Scappi's—he includes just two types of spoons and folded paper for baked goods. However, when taken together with his written instructions, scholars today can visualize the layout of the royal kitchen and get a sense of the hundreds of objects used among the experts in early modern Spain.

Kitchen Spaces

Historians are familiar with the tradition of visual reproductions of kitchen design: from medieval manuscript reproductions of the eleventh-century *Tacuinum Sanitatis*, which indicate kitchens via a hearth and sparse kitchen detail, to German incunabula that represent crowded, busy kitchen spaces. Krohn explains that much like the later genre paintings of detailed kitchen scenes, these illuminated manuscripts and woodcuts seek to tell a story about kitchen life and provide visual imagery for the space within which those stories unfold. However, Krohn contends that in the late sixteenth century Bartolomeo Scappi's illustrations take on a completely different objective, one that is analytical and rational (91–97). Scappi's four illustrations of kitchen spaces are devoid of narrative; instead, he focuses on the functionality of the kitchen. Krohn notes that these images strive to "demonstrate the functions of furnishings, tools, or machines" (97). Martínez Montiño's description of his ideal kitchen space follows in this Scappi tradition. In the first chapter of the cookbook, his focus is on cleanliness and order, and, as we will see in these opening pages, he emphasizes both the openness of the space itself and its location with respect to the layout of the household.

Despite the fact that no images of the layout of Martínez Montiño's early seventeenth-century space survive today, we can get a sense for what it was like through his descriptions in the cookbook as he prioritizes the kitchen spaces and the necessary furnishings. First and foremost, Martínez Montiño insists on openness and prefers a single cooking area to separate rooms: "Some like to have a small room or scullery in the kitchen, but I am not one of them. Rather, there should be no corner of the kitchen that cannot be seen upon entering, except the wash area" (3r).[6] As noted here, the only area that should be separated from the rest of the kitchen space is the washroom. He explains further that the master cook should be able to see the entire kitchen from wherever he or she stands. Although Martínez Montiño's kitchen space differs from the multi-room kitchen seen in Bartolomeo Scappi's 1570 *Opera*, Figure 1 provides a sense of what Martínez Montiño is describing.

Regarding the kitchen's location with respect to the rest of the living spaces, he argues that kitchens should no longer be built in the basement: "If it were possible, no kitchen should be below house level, rather off to the side, under a wooden shelter, with no living quarters above it, unless it is vaulted, and if so, and has good light, it would be good" (2r).[7] This above-ground placement is also found in the 1740 kitchen plans that Manuel Losada laid out for a new palace design after the Alcázar burned down. He insists that the kitchen spaces be above ground on the east side of the palace and that they include drainage pipes that would lead to the basement.[8]

FIGURE 1. Plate of an early modern kitchen. Reproduction from Scappi's *Opera*. Appresso Michele Tramezzino, 1570, p. 921. Photo courtesy of the Getty Research Institute, via the Internet Archive. archive.org/details/operavenetiascapooscap.

Access to Water

The royal kitchen most certainly had direct access to a well. In a rudimentary drawing of a seventeenth-century kitchen, we see this type of access to fresh water on the far-right side of the illustration, behind the *tinaja* (big earthenware pot; see Figure 2). In his own work, Martínez Montiño mentions the use of a kitchen well in a recipe on tenderizing fowl (316v). For different kitchen areas, he notes two different ways of storing water: "Keep water in large earthenware vessels or in covered water tanks. You should have four to six jugs in a wooden pitcher stand so that the bottoms do not touch the kitchen floor. These should be glazed and have lids. The water from these jugs is used for all cooking, and the other water, for cleaning and scrubbing kitchen tools"(2r–2v).[9] Velazquez's well-known portrait, *El aguador de Sevilla* (*The Waterseller of Seville*), a detail of which is seen in Figure 3, provides scholars today with an excellent image

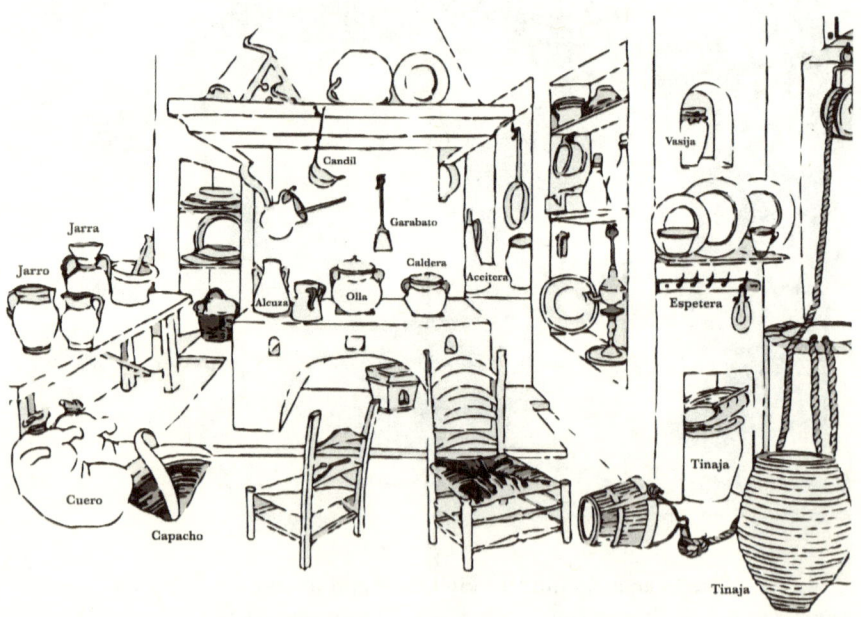

FIGURE 2. "La cocina. Vasijas y recipientes." Image courtesy of Centro Virtual Cervantes.

Furniture and Equipment in Royal Kitchens   121

FIGURE 3. Detail from *El aguador de Sevilla* (c. 1617–23) by Diego Velázquez. Apsley House Collection, www.english-heritage.org.uk/visit/places/apsley-house/history/collection.

FIGURE 4. A twentieth-century wooden *canterera*. Photograph by Tamorlan, "Cántaros en su cantarera," CC BY 3.0 license, commons.wikimedia.org/wiki/File:Cantarera_086.jpg.

of what Martínez Montiño is describing for cooking water. A more recent image of a wooden pitcher stand gives us a sense of what may have been in use in Martínez Montiño's kitchen so that the pitchers do not touch the floor (see Figure 4).

Kitchen Furnishing: Work Stations

In addition to explaining how to store water in different kitchen spaces, Martínez Montiño provides explicit detail for work stations, chopping blocks, and cutting boards, including their location within the kitchen, the ideal material and thickness, and how to care for them. Much attention is given to the *tajo* (chopping block) as he explains the characteristics of the best quality block:

> You should chop meat on chopping blocks made with black poplar. Although it seems like the wood should be black, it is actually white. They should be sawed from the trunk in pieces eight-fingers thick and should look like lemon wheels so that however you cut the meat, it will be against the grain and thus avoid splinters and other bits of wood. If you chop on cutting boards, even if they are from white ash, which is the best, if you do not chop very carefully, you will get splinters. (2v–3r)[10]

A reproduction of a *tajo* can be seen in a 1760 edition of Martínez Montiño's masterpiece (see Figure 5).[11]

Cutting boards are made from yet another wood, differing from both the white pine of the tables and the black poplar of the butcher's block. These boards are reinforced with a metal edge and have a ring attached to them so they can also hang on the peg board: "It is mandatory that dough boards be made of walnut and be at least an inch thick. They should be reinforced with metal edging on the corners so that they enclose almost the entire cutting-board edge. On one end, an iron ring on a hinge with an embedded button in the wood that can be moved around to hang the board. These boards

FIGURE 5. *El tajo*, in the lower left corner (marked "C"), reproduced from the front material of Francisco Martínez Montiño, *Arte de cocina, pastelería, vizcochería y conservería*. Juliana Carrasco, n.p. Photo by author, courtesy of Museo Massó (Bueu-Pontevedra), Spain.

should be hung in the part [of the kitchen] near the pastry table" (3r).[12] Martínez Montiño insists that instruments, including these cutting boards, should be hung in an organized fashion on a regularly bleached board in the most open part of the kitchen. He also insists that its location be close to the pastry station, which consists of a covered table or series of tables so that no dust falls on it, again emphasizing the importance of order and cleanliness.

In addition to tables, blocks, and boards, Martínez Montiño makes direct references to trunks for storing extras, small crates for towels and other kitchen linens, and boxes for storing spices. He carefully adds that it is beneficial to keep the spices separate and have them prepared in advance: "Spices should be in their bags or boxes, each one separate, and a teaspoon in each for seasoning with them.

Immediately fill them all up with spices that have been ground and sifted because you will get more from a pound this way than if you grind a pound and a half as needed" (6r).[13] Martínez Montiño's attention to properly storing spices and getting the most value from them speaks to his sense of economy in the kitchen.[14] Now that he has laid out basic kitchen spaces and furnishings in chapter 1 of his cookbook, he turns in chapter 2 to the recipes themselves, and in these instructions we find a wealth of information on kitchen appliances and utensils necessary to prepare meals at court.

Kitchen Furnishing: Heat Sources and Cooking Temperatures

Perhaps the most important kitchen furnishings are the ovens, or more broadly, the heat sources for cooking. In the 506 recipes, Martínez Montiño references these appliances 117 times (see Table 1 for a complete listing). He names a variety of ovens and methods of heating food. The *horno* (oven) is, of course, the most common, and sizes vary. For example, Martínez Montiño references the *hornillo* (small oven) in recipes for both stuffed lobster and roasted artichokes. He also distinguishes between bread, copper, and terracotta ovens.

The bread oven is referenced, not surprisingly, in recipes for bread, rolls, savory pies, and cookies, but there are no other defining features of this type of oven in terms of its material, its capacity, or its location in the kitchen. Often the bread oven and the copper oven can be used for the same purpose, as both retain even temperatures and both are used for baked goods. This similarity is seen in the recipe "Panecillos de colaciones" ("collation rolls"):[15] "While they are rising, heat the bread oven so that it is thoroughly warmed. . . . If you do not have a bread oven you can easily make them in a copper oven" (251r).[16] In this passage readers today note that Martínez Montiño is writing for a wider audience than only cooks at court, as he acknowledges that others may not have access to a bread oven and will have to use a smaller, portable one, like the copper oven he cites as an alternative.

One significant difference between these two ovens is their size. In his famous recipe "Olla podrida en pastel" ("A pie of hodgepodge stew"), readers get a sense of the relative sizes of different ovens: "place it in the baking oven because no copper oven would be able to hold it. Place it on a copper baking sheet, and do not remove it from the sheet until it is done baking" (101r).[17] Here he notes copper is used both for the oven and for the baking sheet. Specialty items, like *gubiletes* (molds) that are used to make "Huevos en puchero" ("Eggs in a stew pot"; 213v) or the *alcuzcucero* (couscoussier), are also made from copper. He also uses wide copper pans for "Sopa de huevos escalfados con leche" ("Milk sops with poached eggs"), and copper lids for providing top heat in custard recipes.

The third type of oven, *horno de barro* (terracotta oven), is used in ladyfinger recipes, which are the Queen's favorites, so that the cookies will come out dry: "Bake them in a clay oven, and they will come out a little firm and look like tablets. They will be flat and round like tortillas and not spongy. As I have said, they will look like tablets. Her Majesty the Queen our lady likes these little ladyfingers very much" (278v–279r).[18]

Turning for a moment to the raw material, "barro" ("terracotta") is commonly used for *cazuelas* (pots), *cazuelitas* (small pots), *cazolilla* (small sauce pan), *ollas* (pots), *platos* (plates), and other generic items listed as *pieza de barro* (terracotta dish) or *cosa de barro* (something terracotta). At times, he specifically references *glazed* terracotta that, like copper, is used in specialty items like the *dornajo* (glazed terracotta trough), used for salting venison (112r), or the *albornía* (big glazed terracotta pot in the shape of a cup), used for making merengue (268r).

Often modern readers feel at a loss for how to cook early modern recipes, as the temperatures are not explicitly stated in numbers as they are today. But, careful readers can begin to understand temperatures by comparing instructions for heat application among the different recipes. In fact, Martínez Montiño uses dozens of variations for applying heat. *A fuego manso*, *a poca lumbre*, and *lumbre mansa* describe *on low* or *on low heat*. He uses *horno templado* to explain a *thoroughly warmed oven* and *lumbre moderada abajo y arriba* for smaller, portable ovens that are moderately heated both above (with coals being placed on the lid) and below. And, of course, he also bakes *con mucha lumbre* (on high). Other times, oven temperatures are understood in terms of the outcome of a certain dish, for example, "ponla al fuego a cuajar" ("put it on the fire to set"; 69r) or "ponlo a perdigar en el horno" ("put it in the oven to parbake"; 237v).

For varying degrees of fire and flames he includes: *poquito, poco o manso, moderado, buena, caliéntese bien, no más de medio hervor* (very little, little or gentle, moderate, good, well heated, no more than moderate boil), and up the scale to *a mucha furia* (rapidly boiling), as is the case in a couple of recipes for boiling sugar. One of the most unique is, "al amor de la lumbre de manera que no se caliente, ni esté frío" ("near the heat so that it does not get too hot or too cold"; 270r). Most times the heat source is below the recipient, and at times trivets are used to provide extra care against burning the ingredients, as seen in recipes for blancmange and a sweet cream sauce (see Figure 5, marked "I" for a reproduction of a trivet). Many times, however, the heat comes from both below and above, for example in the case of the portable oven (known today as a Dutch oven). In fact, these portable ovens, like the *tortera* seen in Figure 5 (marked "O"), are designed with ridged lids so that they can easily hold embers, which are also described in varying degrees from cooler, grey embers to red-hot embers. Here, too, astute readers come to find that he makes subtle distinctions about the amount of heat with phrases like, "al fuego, poco lumbre abajo y poco encima" ("put it on low heat both above and below"; 71r) or "al fuego a poca lumbre abajo, y mucha encima" ("with low flame below and high flame above"; 136r). In one recipe, "Sustancias para enfermos" ("Consommé for the ill"), Martínez Montiño creates a circle of embers with the glass recipient in the middle.

Finally, in the peculiar recipe for roasting butter on a skewer, the flames are not underneath but in front of the skewer, much like a patient camper might roast the perfect marshmallow: "The rotisserie should be constantly rotating, and you should be continually adding breadcrumbs and sugar on top . . . the heat for roasting should

FIGURE 6. Plate of an outdoor kitchen in which the cook turns the rotisserie skewer resting low on the cob irons. Reproduction from Scappi's *Opera*, Appresso Michele Tramezzino, 1570, p. 932. Photo courtesy of the Getty Research Institute, via the Internet Archive. archive.org/stream/operavenetiascapooscap#page/n931/mode/2up.

not be directly below rather in front of it. It should be a good, clear charcoal flame" (264r).[19] Though Martínez Montiño lived centuries before the mechanization of oven temperatures, he takes care in describing both the intensity and the location of his heat sources. These seventeenth-century descriptions function much as our current terms "medium low" or "medium high" do when we describe cooking on the stovetop over an open flame.

Apart from ovens and open heat sources for pots and pans, the most cited kitchen furnishings for cooking food are the *asador* (roaster or rotisserie) and the *parrillas* (grill). The *asador* has multiple meanings. It refers to the bigger rotisserie oven, to a smaller roasting oven (again portable), and to the wide range of skewers or spikes themselves used in the rotisserie, the roaster, and on the grill. Among the specialty items associated with rotisseries are the *caballos*, also known as *caballitos* or *caballitos de hierro* (cob irons; see Figure 6). Essentially, they are a vertical structure whose primary purpose is to support a crossbar or rotisserie skewer. They usually have a variety of hooks that provide flexibility for how far the skewer is placed from the heat source.[20] Roasting and grilling occur in some two-dozen recipes for large and small game, domesticated meat, large and small poultry, and wild birds. By drawing out the language for heating food that Martínez Montiño uses throughout the cookbook, we can begin to demystify cooking temperatures and processes and get a clearer sense of how much heat was used when dealing with different dishes.

Kitchen Equipment

The hundreds of different pieces of kitchen equipment that Martínez Montiño references in his cookbook offer today's readers valuable information on the working of the early modern royal kitchens. Martínez Montiño himself recognizes the importance of these instruments in the opening chapter of his work: "One should try to have good tools, well-organized, both for regular use and for special occasions, such as tartlet pans, boat-shaped petit four molds, wide-mouthed pastry molds, pie pans, flat pieces, molds, and many other pieces for making different dishes" (1v).[21] These examples prepare the reader for the exciting array of specialty cookware. Furthermore, in this collection of data on more commonplace cookware, like pots and pans, we also discover a surprising amount of diversity in terms of their shapes and sizes and what ways and how often he used these pieces.

COOKWARE

Throughout his cookbook, Martínez Montiño mentions cookware 342 different times and employs thirty-five different varieties of pots, pans, sheets, and more. About half of those are specialty items used only once or twice in the cookbook. As seen in Table 2, the most popular piece of cookware is the *sartén* (frying pan), as versatile in the seventeenth century as it is today. Martínez Montiño uses it for just about everything: browning and braising meats, sautéing ingredients with minced onion and fatback, toasting nuts, reducing sauces, and of course frying anything from eggs to eggplant to deep-fried pastries.

Pots are also one of the most commonly used pieces of cookware in his kitchen, and among those, the *cazuela* and the *olla* are most often cited (respectively marked "D" and "E" in Figure 5). Although not evidenced in this image, these pots are generally considered two-handled vessels, as opposed to the single-handled frying pan, and are usually terracotta. The *cazuela* is wider and shallower than the deeper *olla*. Both are used for making stews and dishes served on sops; in addition, the *cazuela* is used for making casserole dishes, as is the case for the "Cazuela de truchas" ("Trout casserole"; 172v) or the "Cazuela de pies de puerco" ("Pig's feet casserole"; 197v–198r).

One creative way in which Martínez Montiño uses the *olla* is to place one pot on top of the other and seal them together with dough to create additional pressure for cooking. This technique is described in the recipe "Ánades estofadas" ("Stewed duck"): "Cover the lip of the pot with an edge made of dough, and place on top of this duck pot another pot filled with water so that the dough seals the pot very well. Set over grey embers so that it simmers" (28r).[22] This technique of sealing the pot with dough while placing another on top is a prototype for the pressure cooker that was designed later in the seventeenth century by French physicist Denis Papin.[23] Martínez Montiño uses this technique in several recipes.

Another pot is the *puchero*, which is similar to the *olla* in size. In the seventeenth century, the *puchero* usually had one handle and was made from terracotta, either glazed or not. And, like the *cazuela*, it was available in a variety of sizes. For today's audience, a *puchero* looks more like an oversized pitcher than a pot (see Figure 7). It is only used twice throughout the cookbook. In "Sustancias para enfermos" ("Consommé for the ill") it forms part of a *bain marie*, as it contains the consommé boiling in another, larger pot:

> The consommé explained with or without water can also be made in a tall glazed stew pot in water. Put the hen in as explained, cork the pot with a cork and a little dough, put it in a cauldron or big cooking pot. Place some stones around it so it does not move around, and fill it with water up to the neck of the stew pot. Put it on to cook, and let it cook for three hours, and the consommé will be done. (240r)[24]

This recipe also cites the *perol* (big cooking pot) or *caldero* (cauldron). The *perol* is rounded on the bottom, generally made of copper, and often used interchangeably with a *caldero*, *olla*, or *cazuela* (see Figure 8 for the first two). In the cookbook, the *perol* serves as a vessel for both prepping and cooking food; the majority of its uses are found in the preserving section in recipes such as "Peras secas cubiertas" ("Candied dried pear"; 294v–295r), "Cuartos de membrillos" ("Quartered quince"; 297v–298r), and "Nueces en conserva" ("Preserved walnuts"; 298v–299v).

Sometimes Martínez Montiño emphasizes the pot's material and, in this way, distinguishes it from another kitchen piece. Terracotta (appears in twenty recipes), copper (fifteen), glass (twelve, primarily in the section on preserves), and silver (eleven) are the most common

Furniture and Equipment in Royal Kitchens 131

FIGURE 7. Image of a *puchero*, early twentieth century, made from solid iron. Private collection. Photo by author.

cookware materials for the bigger pots and pans and their smaller companion sizes, the *ollita*, *cazuelita*, and *cazuelilla*, for example.

The *tortera* (portable oven) is a fascinating piece of cookware. It is used in forty-six different recipes that not only include stews or casseroles, like "Cazuela de arroz" ("Rice casserole"; 143v–144r) and "Calabaza rellena en el día de pescado" ("Stuffed squash for fish day"; 154v–155v), which today's reader would expect, but also for baking cookies like "Otra suerte de bizcochos secos" ("Another type of dry ladyfingers"; 276v). The lid plays a fundamental role in this piece of cookware, as Martínez Montiño often specifies that heat

FIGURE 8. The *perol* (above) and the *caldero* (below) were among the cookware inventory at court. Both are from the twentieth century but provide an idea of those from the seventeenth. From a private collection. Photos by author.

should be applied both above, that is on the lid, and below. Other times, such as when it is placed within an oven, the *tortera* functions as part of a double oven, as is the case with "Hojaldre con enjundía de puerco" ("Pork fat pastry"; 92r–94r) and "Un solomo de vaca relleno" ("Stuffed beef tenderloin"; 138v–139v).

Other pieces of cookware that play important roles in the royal kitchens are the *cazo* (large sauce pan) and its smaller companion, the *cacillo* or *cacito* (sauce pan). All these pieces usually have one handle, as opposed to the two of the *olla* and *cazuela*. The *cazo* and the *cacillo/cacito* are regularly cited as being used interchangeably with the two-handled versions. The *cazolilla* primarily refers to a small saucepan, for example, when making "Gilea de vino" ("wine jelly"; 268v–270v) or "Una cazolilla de ave para enfermo" ("Crustless poultry pie for the sick"; 303v–305r). But in the recipe "Cazolillas de manjar blanco" ("Blancmange tartlets"), the piece is actually a tartlet pan that is filled with custard and then placed in the oven to bake (142r–142v).

Specialty cookware items are those that appear only once or twice in the entire cookbook and fall into two categories. Some have a very specific use like the *alcuzcuero* (couscous maker) or the *gubiletes de cobre* (copper molds) used for shaping a sweet, scrambled egg dish. Others are similar to more common cookware items but differ in size and have a different name. The complete list of specialty items can be found in Table 3.

PREPWARE AND SERVEWARE

Prepware is defined as those non-handheld objects that are used in the preparation of dishes, and serveware are those objects used to hold food once it has been prepared and is ready to be sent to the table. The most commonly cited objects are found in Table 4, and of them the *tablero* (cutting board), discussed above, and the *almirez* (metallic mortar) are the two most often cited. We can find a reproduction of the *almirez* among the inventory of kitchen equipment found in the 1760 edition of Martínez Montiño's masterpiece, labeled "K," as seen in Figure 5. Used most often in baking, Martínez Montiño grinds nuts—including walnuts, pine nuts, chestnuts, and especially almonds—candied and preserved fruit, cheese and eggs, and hard-boiled yolks. He also uses the *almirez* for grinding herbs and spices, mashing fatty animal tissue, and thinning sauces. Generic prepware—*piezas* (pieces), *escudillas* (bowls), *vidrios* (glassware), and *vasijas* (vessels)—are commonly cited throughout the cookbook.

In the section on preserves, we see the only appearances of the *barreñón* (tub) or the *barreñoncillo* (small tub) and the *tabla* (board) or *tablilla* (small board). The first is used for boiling fruit in simple syrup for over a week, and the second is for layering sugar on fruit to candy it. The third is a special board used for cooling puree and checking its consistency or simply for drying candied squash: "put it on a board, and put it in the sun to dry until it is very dry" (294r).[25] Its smaller *tablilla* is also used for preserving fruit, specifically to test the sugar stage when making pomegranate jelly (296v–297r).

At times these items are not only used to prepare and/or serve dishes but also to cook them. This is certainly the case with the *plato* (plate or platter) and *platillo* (small plate), terms translated differently according to size and dependent on the context. At times *plato* is used in prepping, as in "Otra ave en alfitete frio" ("Another stuffed hen with puff pastry, room temperature"), in which Martínez Montiño builds the dish right on the plate. Other times it is actually used in the cooking process and most likely made from terracotta or metal. For example, in "Sopa dorada" ("Golden sops") he explains: "Put the plate over a low flame, dry, and add a little ground sugar on top. When the plate is very warm, add in enough stock to cover it half way and sprinkle more sugar on top. Cover it with another plate and let the bread stew" (68r).[26]

Throughout the cookbook the *plato* also serves as an instrument of measurement. For example, Martínez Montiño explains that on a certain *plato* one can fit two breasts of poultry (45r); three pounds of beef, unless the plate is small, then two pounds (65v–67r); eight portions of cream (74v); or four to five puff pastries (92r). *Platillo* functions in similar terms. Depending on the context, it can refer to serving a dish on a small plate or serving a small late-night dinner-size portion. It is most often used in reference to vegetable dishes, and sometimes Martínez Montiño offers an alternative of serving the dish as a main course. Another generic kitchen item, the *escudilla* (bowl), also often serves as a measuring device.

The most common item for packaging food for travel is the *cesta* (basket), as seen in recipes like "Besugos en escabeche al uso de Portugal" ("Pickled sea bream, as prepared in Portugal"; 191v–192r) or "Sardinas rellenas de escabeche" ("Pickled stuffed sardines"; 192r–193r). Baskets are also used for pressing elderberry flowers in preparation for making vinegar (257r).

In terms of the specialty times that are mentioned only once or twice in the cookbook, we can categorize them by their purposes: baskets and sacks for storage and transportation; the already mentioned items for preserving fruits, nuts, and other food items; different jars, pots, baskets, and bowls for baked goods; several items for couscous; and a handful of other specialty items like course linen for wrapping a boar's head before boiling, braided esparto for holding head cheese while it sets, or gravy boats for fish sauces. These specialty items are listed in Table 5. This extensive inventory of prepware and serveware gives us a strong sense of kitchen equipment and allows readers today to understand what was involved in food production at the early modern court. Although specialty items may be unique to those who could afford them, other more common pieces provide insight into what material objects were used not only at court but also in humbler households.

UTENSILS

To best understand the 416 handheld tools that Martínez Montiño references in his cookbook, I have broken them down into six essential categories according to their function:

1. to spread/stir, primarily spoons and spatulas;
2. to cut or puncture, such as knives, skewers, forks, and needles;

3. to separate, among which are a variety of sieves and cheesecloths;
4. to flatten, like rolling pins, mortars, and presses;
5. to seal/secure, including different threads and cloths; and
6. other specialty utensils, including paper products, instruments designed for specific baked goods and fried dough, and fennel sticks used as toothpicks. (See Table 6 for a complete listing.)

If one had to limit kitchen utensils to three essential items, they would be spoons (76), knives (31), and sieves (60). Martínez Montiño takes particular interest in the spoons and explains in both a special notice in the front material and later in the recipe "Bizcochos de harina de trigo" ("Ladyfingers with wheat flour") the importance of their different sizes and functions. He even writes in detail about illustrations he provides for two of the nine different types of spoons used throughout the work:

> Notice, on the size that cake spoons should be, which are illustrated at the end of the book.
>
> The large spoon with which you mix cake batter, should be a half yard, less three fingers long.[27] It should be one of the flat wooden types with an extra-long paddle, and the paddle should be thin and fairly shallow, and it should not be a wide paddle so that it will beat the eggs well. And if you want to beat the cake batter with two hands, like nuns do, then the spoon should have a wide, round paddle, because you cannot beat this way with a spoon with a narrow paddle.[28] The small spoon that is drawn at the back of the book is for ladling the batter into the paper cups and should not be used for anything else. (pro.)[29]

These illustrations are the first to appear in a Spanish cookbook and, combined with the prescriptive text, provide technical support for producing excellent baked goods (see Figure 9). Other spoons are described as having a single hole, multiple holes, made from silver, or dramatically wide. Beyond spoons and spatulas (see Figure 5, marked "N"), feathers are important for glazing pastries, laminating dough, sprinkling crusts with water or another liquid, or coating poultry with egg yolk.

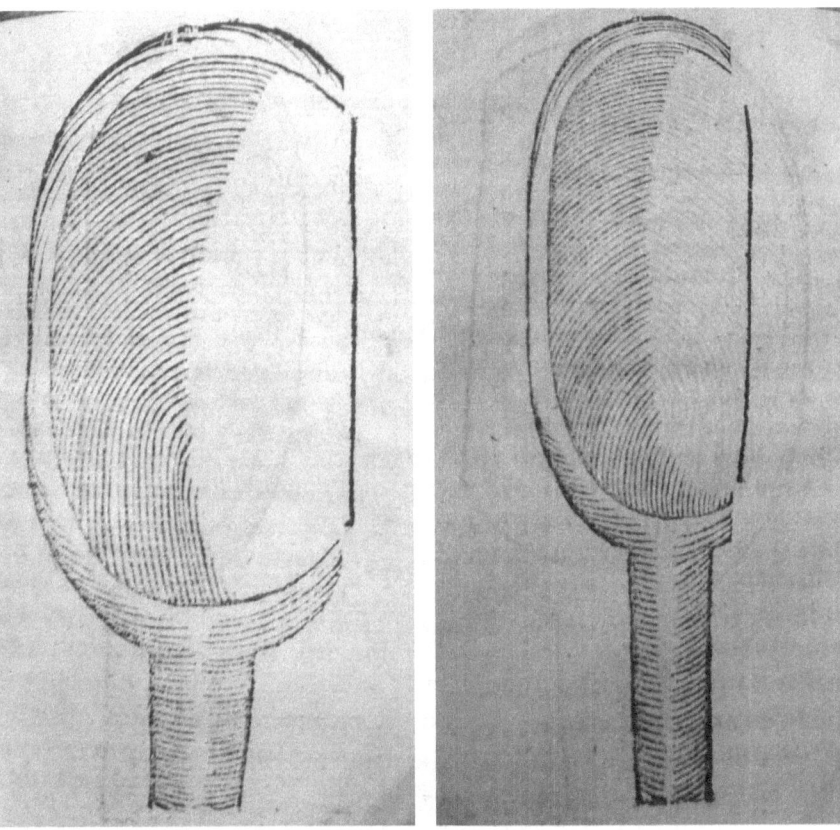

FIGURE 9. Large spoon (left) and small spoon (right), *Arte de cocina, pastelería, vizcochería y conservería*, Luis Sánchez, 1611, n. p. Images courtesy Lilly Library, Indiana University, Bloomington, Indiana.

Regarding knives and other related objects, specific instructions are provided for caring for the knives and sharpening them on Fridays or Saturdays because there is less to cut on those days. One of the more artistic ways Martínez Montiño uses a knife is for carving poultry. In the recipe "Cómo se han de aparar las aves en la cocina" ("How to present poultry in the kitchen"), he describes a series of fourteen cuts and turns while holding the bird with a fork in the air: "estos cortes todos se han de dar en el aire, sin que el capón llegue al plato" ("All of these slices should be done in the air without the capon touching the plate"; 286v). This description gives us a sense of the training and technical skill required to fulfill the duties of carver. The knife is not only used for carving but also at times for pounding, as is specified in the following instructions for preparing chicken breast: "golpearlas has con la vuelta del cuchillo" ("pound them out with the back of your knife"; 45r).

Martínez Montiño uses at least six different-sized sieves in addition to colanders, skimmers, and a wide variety of cloths for straining liquids. While the *cedazo* and *cedacillo* are by far the most popular, in his recipe for couscous he includes an *harnero* and an *harnerillo* so that the dough goes through a double-sifting process. Another specialty sieve, a *criba* (wide-hole sieve), is used for straining boiled squash before simple syrup is added and the pieces set out to dry (294r).

Paper is another common utensil and is used primarily as a liner for cookies and other treats. However, it is not uncommon to also find *en papillote* instructions, that is, for wrapping poultry in paper, greased with fat, to keep the bird moist as it cooks. The other utensils—mallets, presses, mortar, thread, cork, pins and needles, and more—are much less frequent in the cookbook. Finally, specialty instruments reveal that certain items were popular enough to require their own unique tool. This is the case for things like the *buñolera* (puff maker), *hierro a manera de hongo* (mushroom-shaped iron), which is designed for frying dough, or the *dedal* (thimble), used for cutting mini macarons.

In conclusion, studying material objects used and described in Martínez Montiño's 1611 cookbook provides scholars today with much valuable information. First, as a significant culinary artifact in its own right, this cookbook merits an in-depth study of the material objects found within its pages because such objects provide us with a deeper appreciation of not only *what* food was prepared but also *how* food was prepared in the early modern Spanish court. Second, by studying kitchen appliances and utensils we are able to uncover lost techniques that Martínez Montiño practiced and passed on to others. As a side note, it is important to remember that this cookbook was published at least two more times in Martínez Montiño's own lifetime, suggesting that it did have an immediate impact on its target audience. The combination of *vidrio* and *puchero* to create a bain-marie for making consommé, the different-sized *ollas* sealed with dough to build pressure for stewing duck, the series of *plumas* for spreading fat to laminate dough and create airy pastries, and the different sizes and types of paper used for cooking *en papillote* (wrapping a foodstuff in greased paper to maintain tenderness) are a few of these examples. Finally, delving into Martínez Montiño's work also brings to light the specialty items required in the preparation of certain dishes. I will mention the *alcuzcucero* (couscousier), *garabato* (spoon hook for puffs), and the *hierro a manera de hongo* (mushroom-shaped iron), as well as others listed in tables 5 and 6, as culinary curiosities that broaden our knowledge of cooking practices. In short, exploring the spaces and instruments of the early modern kitchen that Martínez Montiño includes in *Arte de cocina, pastelería, vizcochería y conservería* provides insight into Spain's social history and enables scholars today to delve deeper into understanding the material culture of food preparation at seventeenth-century court.

APPENDIX

TABLE 1. Kitchen furnishings in Martínez Montiño's cookbook

Kitchen furnishings	Translation	Count
caballos	cobb irons	1
hornillo	small oven	2
horno	oven	61
horno de barro	terracotta oven	2
horno de cobre	copper oven	6
horno de pan	bread oven	4
horno de pan o de cobre	bread or copper oven	1
ladrillo	brick	2
mesa	table	1
parrilla o asador	grill	1
parrillas	grill	33
pozo	well	1
tabla	board	2
trébedes	trivets	5
GRAND TOTAL		117

TABLE 2. Common cookware in Martínez Montiño's cookbook

Common cookware	Translation	Count
sartén	frying pan	67
cazuela	pot	55
olla	pot	49
tortera	portable oven	46
cazo	large sauce pan	41
cacillo	sauce pan	24
cacito	sauce pan	16
cobertera	lid	14
ollita	small pot	10
perol	big, round-bottomed cooking pot	9
cazolilla	small sauce pan or tartlet pan	6
hoja del horno	baking sheet	6
pieza de plata	silver piece	6
vidrio	glass	5
cajitas de papel	paper boxes	4
caldero	cauldron	4
GRAND TOTAL		362

TABLE 3. Specialty cookware pieces in Martínez Montiño's cookbook

Specialty cookware	Translation	Count
alcuzcucero	couscousier	1
almofia	basin	1
barquilla	barquette mold	1
barquillo	funnel-shaped vessel	1
barquino	leather flask	1
barreñón	tub	1
caldera	cauldron	1
cazolita	little sauce pan	1
cazuelilla	little pot	1
cazuelita	little pot	1
escudilleta	small bowl	1
graserilla	drip pan	1
gubiletes de cobre	copper molds	1
redoma	flask	1
redomilla	small flask	1
sartenilla	small frying pan	1
GRAND TOTAL		16

TABLE 4. Common prepware and serveware in Martínez Montiño's cookbook

Common prepware	Translation	Count
tablero	cutting board	75
almirez	metallic mortar	43
pieza	piece	20
escudilla	bowl	12
vidrio	glass	8
vasija	vessel	8
perol	round-bottomed bowl	7
barreñón	tub	5
caja	box	5
olla	pot	5
mortero	mortar	3
tabla	board	3
redomilla	small flask	1
sartenilla	small frying pan	1
Common serveware	Translation	Count
plato	plate	86
platillo	small plate	11
cesta	basket	4
GRAND TOTAL		295

TABLE 5. Specialty prepware and serveware in Martínez Montiño's cookbook

Specialty prepware and serveware	Translation	Count
For storage/transporting		
banasta	woven basket (for transporting venison)	2
paja de centeno	rye straw (for packaging food)	2
taleguilla	small sack (for transporting dried flowers)	1
For preserving		
barril	barrel (for pickling tuna)	2
tablilla	small board (to test sugar stage)	2
barreñón	tub (for making mustard)	1
barreñoncillo vidriado	small, glazed tub	1
berguera	fruit sieve (for candied fruit)	1
dornajo de barro	terracotta trough (for preserving venison)	1
pleita de esparto	braided esparto	1

(continued on next page)

Specialty prepware and serveware	Translation	Count
For baked goods		
Alorza	glazed terracotta jar (for preserved walnuts)	1
albornía	big glazed terracotta pot (for making merengue)	1
cestilla	small basket (for dough to rise)	1
librillo	earthenware bowl (for kneading dough)	1
For couscous		
almofía	basin (placed on top of simmering pot)	1
artesilla de palo	wooden trough	1
porcelana	porcelain dish (placed on top of simmering pot)	1
serilla redonda de las de Valencia	round, woven basket from Valencia	1
For other uses		
bacía	basin (for rinsing intestines)	2
angeo	course linen (to wrap boar head before boiling)	1
azucarero	sugar shaker	1
barquino de cuero	leather flask (for consommé for the ill)	1
Flamenquilla	medium size serving plate	1
Salserilla	gravy boat (for three different fish sauces)	1
trinchero	carving platter (for partridge)	1
GRAND TOTAL		30

TABLE 6. Utensils in Martínez Montiño's cookbook

Utensil	Translation	Total
	TO SPREAD/STIR	
Spoons		
cucharón	ladle; big spoon	43
cucharón de manjar blanco	blancmange spoon	6
cucharita	small spoon	9
cuchara	spoon	5
cuchara cerrada	regular spoon	3
cuchara de plata	silver spoon	2
cuchara espumadera	skimmer	2
cucharilla	small spoon	1
cucharoncito chiquito	very small spoon	1
remo de manjar blanco	blancmange paddle	1

Utensil	Translation	Total
Spatulas		
paleta	spatula	20
paletilla	small spatula	1
palillo spatula	spatula	1
For sprinkling		
plumas	feathers	17
hisopillo	hyssop brush	
TOTAL		115
	TO FLATTEN	
mortero	mortar	5
prensa	press	3
palo de masa	rolling pin	2
piedra	stone	2
plato	plate	2
mazo	mallet	1
palo	stick	1
prensilla	small press	1
TOTAL		17
	TO CUT/PUNCTURE	
For cutting		
cuchillo	knife	31
cortadera	trimmer	11
tijeras	scissors	1
rallo	grater	1
For skewering		
asador	spit, skewer	23
asadorcillo	small skewer	1
broqueta	broquette	6
broquetilla	small broquette	3
filete	small skewer	1
For puncturing		
tenedor	fork	7
tenedorcillo	small fork	1
alfiler	pin	4
mechadera	larding needle	4
dedal	thimble	1
punzón	awl	1
aguja	needle	3
TOTAL		99

(continued on next page)

Utensil	Translation	Total
	TO SEAL/SECURE	
Thread		
hilo	thread	10
hilo de bala	twine	1
cordel	cord	1
Cloth		
estopas	burlap	1
sedeña	linen cloth	1
Other		
corcho	cork	6
piedra	rock	1
TOTAL		21
	TO SEPARATE	
Sieves		
cedacillo	small sieve	22
cedazo	sieve	7
colador	colander	17
espumadera	skimmer	10
harnero	sieve	2
harnerillos	smaller sieve	1
criba	wide hole sieve	1
Cloths		
estameña	cheesecloth	25
paño	cloth	13
servilleta	napkin	11
mantel	tablecloth	5
manga	jelly bag	2
pañito	small cloth	2
lienzo	linen	1
lino	linen	1
toalla	towel	1
TOTAL		121
	SPECIALTY UTENSILS	
For containing		
papel	paper	25
papelillo	paper	3
pergamino	parchment	3
cama (de lino)	couche	1
ropa	cloth (for rising dough)	1

Utensil	Translation	Total
For shaping		
buñolera	puff maker	3
caña	reed (for bollo de rodilla)	1
cañutos de cañas	reed tubes	1
garabato	spoon hook (for puffs)	1
hierro a manera de hongo	mushroom-shaped iron	1
Other		
cosa que pese dos arrobas	two-pound weight	1
palillos para mondar los dientes	toothpicks	1
sello de la cortadera	seal on trimmer	1
TOTAL		43
GRAND TOTAL		416

NOTES

1. All translations from Martínez Montiño are my own.
2. "Puesto todo muy bien lucido y colgado por buena orden, que no anden las piezas rodando por las mesas, ni por el albañar. Los asadores en su lancera muy lucios, y los palos de masa, y cucharones de manjar blanco, has de tener en una tabla que estará colgada con unos clavos de palo torneados, como los tienen los Boticarios, que sean mucho mayores; y otro como éste, para cedacillos, y estameña."
3. In total, this work was published throughout Spain ten times in the seventeenth century, fourteen times in the eighteenth century, and five times in the nineteenth century until 1823. For more on the ingredients and recipes themselves in *Arte de cocina*, see Nadeau "Food Fit for a King."
4. Over the past thirty years, literally hundreds of articles and monographs have been written on early modern food consumption. See Campbell, Cruz Cruz, Nadeau (*Food Matters*), Pérez Samper, Sánchez Meco, and Valles Rojo, to name just a few.
5. Other scholars also examine the material objects of the kitchen to understand more fully the house as a work space (Whittle), how identities were crafted (Wall), or, as Sara Pennell explains, "as a major site for both consumption and its counterpart, accumulation, and thereby presented as an arena in which stability and continuity as ends of the consuming process were paramount" (202).
6. "Algunos son amigos de tener algún aposentillo, o recocina dentro de la cocina; mas yo no soy deste parecer, sino que no haya ningún rincón en la cocina, que no se vea en entrando por la puerta, salvo el albañar."

7. "Si fuese posible, no había de estar ninguna cocina debajo de ninguna casa, sino a un lado debajo de un cobertizo, de madera, que no hubiese encima vivienda de gente; salvo si es de bóveda, que con eso, y buena luz estará bien."
8. Losada's design provides detailed layouts of the different kitchen spaces, including a big oven and twelve small ones, a fountain with four spouts, a storage room for cured meats, different rooms for pastries and for candies (both with separate pantries for sugar and other baking goods, butter and flour, for example), a wine cellar, a storage unit, an ice locker, and all the necessary furnishings. For each area, he includes the dimensions and other necessary details. Although this design was conceived over one hundred years after Martínez Montiño's tenure at the palace, it provides a sense of what the layout of the palace kitchen space may have been (León Tello and Sanz Sanz 994–95).
9. "El agua la tendrás en tinajas, o en tinacos con sus cobertores: y tendrás cuatro o seis cántaros en una cantarera de palo, que no lleguen con los suelos al de la cocina. Estos sean vedriados con sus tapaderos; del agua de estos cántaros echarás a cocer todo lo que se hubiere de guisar, y la otra será para lavar, y fregar las herramientas."
10. "La carne picarás en tajos de trozos del álamo negro, que aunque parece que tendrá la madera negra, no la tiene sino blanca. Han de ser aserrados desde el tronco en unos trozos de ocho dedos de cantero, que parezcan ruedas de limón; porque adonde picares la carne esté la hebra derecha arriba, que de esa manera no sueltan género de madera: y si las picas en tableros, aunque sean blancos de fresno, que son los mejores, si no picas con mucho tiento, sacarás madera."
11. It should be noted that these illustrations first appear in Martínez Montiño's cookbook well over one hundred years after its first publication. Curiously, Don Pedro Joseph Alonso y Padilla, the enthusiastic *librero de la cámara del rey* (book vendor of the king's chamber), was the book vendor in charge of selling both this edition and the most recent edition of the popular *Nuevo arte de la cocina española* by Juan de Altamiras, first published in 1745, which includes the same illustration plate.
12. "Los tableros de masa, es forzoso que sean de nogal, y sean de poco más de una pulgada de cantero, y échales unas cantoneras de hierro por los bordes; de manera que vengan a cercar casi todo el tablero: y en la una punta una sortija de hierro en la bisagra, con un botoncillo embebido en la madera, que se anda al derredor para colgar el tablero. Estos tableros se han de colgar a la parte a donde está la mesa de la masa."
13. "Las especias anden en sus bolsas o cajas, cada cosa aparte, y una cucharita en ellas para sazonar con ella. Hínchanse de una vez de especias molidas y cernidas; porque aprovechará más una libra desta manera, que libra y media si se moliese a remiendos."
14. In the cookbook the most popular spices used are black pepper, ginger, nutmeg, clove, cinnamon, and saffron and appear in almost a full third of all recipes.
15. It is worth noting that in general *panaderos de corte* (court bakers) baked *paneci-*

llos (small loaf bread) that weighed half of a pound per loaf, while *panaderos de villa* (village bakers) regularly produced *pan* (bread) that weighed two pounds per loaf (Andrés Ucendo and Lanza García 69). *Colación* is a light meal allowed on days of fasting. It is usually eaten once a day and in the evening. In the early seventeenth century it was also a term used for a light afternoon or early evening meal.

16. "Entre tanto que se acaban de leudar, se caliente el horno de pan, de manera que esté muy bien templado . . . y si no tuvieres horno de pan, bien se podrán cocer en un horno de cobre."

17. "métalo en el horno de pan, porque no habrá horno de cobre tan grande que se pueda cocer dentro, y pondráslo sobre una hoja de horno de cobre."

18. "cuécelos en horno de barro, y saldrán tiesecillos, que parezcan tabletas, y saldrán llanos, y redondos como tortillas, y no esponjarán, y será, como digo a modo de tabletas. Su Majestad de la Reyna nuestra señora suele gustar destos bizcochillos."

19. "y ha de andar el asador muy redondo y ha de estar echando uno siempre pan rallado, y azucar por encima . . . la lumbre que ha de asar la manteca no ha de estar debajo, sino adelante, y ha de haber buena lumbre clara de tizos de carbon."

20. Martínez Montiño includes cob irons in his original recipe: "Cómo se puede asar una pella de manteca de vacas en el asador" ("How to roast a butterball on a spit"; 263v–265r).

21. "ha de tener buenas herramientas curiosas, para cosas particulares y trasordinarias, como son cazolillas, y barquillas, y gubiletes, torteras, piezas llanas, y moldes, y otras muchas piezas, para hacer diferencias de platos."

22. "luego pondrás un borde de masa a la olla, y asentarás otra ollita llena de agua sobre la olla de los anadones; de manera que ajuste muy bien con la masa, y ponla sobre un poco de rescoldo, de manera que cueza poco a poco."

23. For more information, see Abad Zardoya (89).

24. "La sustancia que está dicho del vidrio en seco, y de la del vidrio en agua, la podrás sacar en un puchero en agua vidriado un poco altillo: pondrás tu gallina como está dicho, y taparás el puchero con un corcho, y con un poco de masa, y ponlo en un perol, o caldero, con unas piedras a la redonda, porque no se trastorne: y luego hínchelo de agua hasta el cuello del puchero: luego dale lumbre, y cueza tres horas, y hallarás la sustancia hecha."

25. "y ponerlos en una tabla, y ponerlos a secar al sol hasta que estén secos."

26. "y pon el plato sobre un poco de lumbre así en seco, y échale un poco de azúcar molido por encima. Y cuando el plato esté bien caliente, échale caldo cuanto se bañe la sopa, y échale más azúcar por encima, y atápalo con otro plato, y déjalos estofar muy bien."

27. A *vara*, or a *yard*, was a standard unit of measurement used in early modern Spain, although, according to the Real Academia Española, the length varied between 768 and 912 millimeters or between two and a half and three feet. A

half *vara* would measure anywhere from fifteen to eighteen inches and Martínez Montiño's spoon, approximately thirteen to sixteen inches.

28. This reference to nuns stirring batter with two hands refers specifically to holding the spoon between the palms of two hands and quickly rubbing them together to create an airy batter. I am indebted to Vicky Hayward who shared with me the image of Marcela Osoro de Mendaro and Mari José "batiendo huevos, por el antiguo sistema llamado 'a dos manos de las monjas'" ("beating eggs the old-fashioned way called 'with two hands, nun style'") from José María Gorrotxategi Pikasarri's book *Historia de la confitería y repostería vasca* (271). In the *Diccionario general de bibliografía española*, the author also notes the peculiar comment on nuns using two hands to beat the batter: "la hondad del bizcocho de monja debe consistir en hallarse batido a dos manos" ("the thickness of the nun's sponge cake is the result of having been beaten with two hands"; Hidalgo 144).

29. "Advertencia, acerca de la medida que han de tener los cucharones para hacer bizcochos que están figurados al fin de la obra. El cucharón con que han de batir los bizcochos, ha de tener de largo media vara menos tres dedos. Ha de ser de unos cucharones llanos de pala, y un poco prolongados de la pala, y ha de ser delgada la pala, y un poquito honda, muy poco, y no ha de ser ancho de pala, porque corte bien los huevos. Y si quisieres batir los bizcochos con dos manos, como las monjas: en tal caso ha de ser la pala del cucharón ancha, y redonda; porque desta manera no se puede batir con cucharón angosto de pala. El cucharoncillo pequeño que va aquí dibujado al fin del libro, es, para poner el batido en los papelillos, que no ha de servir de otra cosa."

WORKS CITED

Abad Zardoya, Carmen. "Herramientas curiosas para cosas particulares y extraordinarias: tecnología, espacios y utillaje en la cocina histórica española." *La cocina en su tinta*, edited by Isabel Moyano and María del Carmen Simón Palmer, Servicio de Publicaciones de la Biblioteca Nacional de España, 2010, pp. 85–117.

Andrés Ucendo, José Ignacio, and Ramón Lanza García. "El abasto de pan en el Madrid del siglo XVII." *Studia Historica: Historia Moderna*, vol. 34, 2012, pp. 61–97.

Brears, Peter. *Cooking and Dining in Tudor and Early Stuart England*. Prospect Books, 2015.

Campbell, Jodi. *At the First Table: Food and Social Identity in Early Modern Spain*. U of Nebraska P, 2017.

"La cocina: Vasijas y recipients." Apéndices e ilustraciones. *Centro Virtual Cer-*

vantes. Accessed 28 Jan. 2018. cvc.cervantes.es/literatura/clasicos/quijote/introduccion/apendice/default.htm.

Cruz Cruz, Juan. *La cocina mediterránea en el inicio del Renacimiento*. La Val de Onsera, 1997.

En torno a la mesa: Tres siglos de formas y objetos en los Palacios y Monasterios Reales. Patrimonio Nacional, 2000.

Gorrotxategi Pikasarri, José María. *Historia de la confitería y repostería vasca*. Sendoa, 1987.

Hidalgo, Dionosio. *Diccionario general de bibliografía española*, vol. 1, Madrid, Escuelas Pías, 1862–1881.

Krohn, Deborah. *Food and Knowledge in Renaissance Italy*. Ashgate, 2015.

León Tello, Francisco José, and María Virginia Sanz Sanz. *Estética y teoría de la arquitectura en los tratados españoles del s. XVIII*. Editorial CSIC, 1994.

Martínez Montiño, Francisco. *Arte de cocina, pastelería, vizcochería y conservería*. Luis Sánchez, 1611. books.google.com. Accessed 29 Jan. 2018.

Nadeau, Carolyn. "Food Fit for a King: Exploring Royal Recipes in Francisco Martínez Montiño's 1611 Cookbook." Special Issue of *Bulletin of Spanish Studies: Food Cultural Studies and the Transhispanic World*, edited by Lara Anderson and Rebecca Ingram. Vol. 97, forthcoming.

———. *Food Matters: Alonso Quijano's Diet and the Discourse of Food in Early Modern Spain*. U of Toronto P, 2016.

Pennell, Sara. "'Pots and Pans History': The Material Culture of the Kitchen in Early Modern England." *Journal of Design History*, vol. 11, no. 3, 1998, pp. 201–16.

Pérez Samper, María de los Ángeles. *La alimentación en la España del Siglo de Oro. Domingo Hernández de Maceras: Libro del arte de Cocina*. La Val de Onsera, 1998.

Sánchez Meco, Gregorio. *El arte de la cocina en tiempos de Felipe II*. Concejalía de Cultura, 1998.

Scappi, Bartolomeo. *Opera*. Appresso Michele Tramezzino, 1570. Internet Archive 920/928. archive.org/stream/operavenetiascapooscap#page/n919/mode/2up.

Simón Palmer, María del Carmen. *La cocina de palacio 1561–1931*. Editorial Castalia, 1997.

Valles Rojo, Julio. *Cocina y alimentación en los siglos XVI y XVII*. Junta de Castilla y León, 2007.

Wall, Wendy. *Staging Domesticity: Household Work and English Identity in Early Modern Drama*. Cambridge UP, 2002.

Whittle, Jane. "The House as a Place of Work in Early Modern Rural England." *Home Cultures*, vol. 8, no. 2, 2011, pp. 133–50.

CHAPTER 5

Enlightened Meals
Literary Perspectives on Food in Eighteenth-Century Spain

María Ángeles Pérez Samper, *University of Barcelona*

The Paradoxes of Food: Benito Jerónimo Feijoo

FOLLOWING ENLIGHTENMENT IDEAS for economic development and reform, the great social and cultural developments that took place in Spain, as in other parts of Europe throughout the eighteenth century, concerned food production and consumption examined from cultural, economic, and social points of view.[1] Food was at the core of projects on agrarian reform, public and individual health, economy, and the social order. Many authors problematize the spread of luxury consumption, particular food practices considered markers for social distinction, and issues of food access, while highlighting the bridling power of reason over appetite.² Following Mennell, this chapter interrogates the ways in which food is used to construct identity and how food serves as an axis to examine issues of taste, social differentials, and intellectual ideas. It also engages the ideas proposed by Spary in considering the social significance of food practices and the link between food and the history of consumption. It highlights a variety of texts that help to better understand the complexities of food practices during the period. The chapter examines issues of social justice, hunger, and national identity in the works of Feijoo, Ramón de la Cruz, Clavijo y Fajardo, Meléndez Valdés, and Gregorio de Salas. It argues that eighteenth-century Spanish authors presented food as social paradox by which hunger and luxury consumption comingled and identified food as the crucible for discussions on modernity and cyclicity.

One of the best known eighteenth-century Spanish statesmen and philosophers, Gaspar Melchor de Jovellanos, framed some of the most pressing issues regarding agrarian reform within the subject of the social differentials that affected food accessibility. His "Informe sobre la Ley Agraria" ("Report on Agrarian Law") denounced the inverse economics that forced poor and lower-class families to spend the majority of their income on food, while the rich spent but a small fraction of their capital on foods that in fact included many luxury imported goods such as tea, coffee, and sherry wines, along with others from the Spanish colonies like sugar and cacao. That Jovellanos considered these practices as part of a pattern of overall conspicuous consumption on the part of the rich was underscored by his comments on the rich's partiality for other luxury household and personal items, which were almost always foreign (783). Benito Jerónimo Feijoo, one of the foremost figures of the Spanish Enlightenment and a keen and critical observer of his time, wrote with an emphasis on "the disabuse of common mistakes." Feijoo's magnum opus, especially his discourses in *Teatro crítico universal* (*Universal Critical Theatre*), published in nine volumes between 1726 and 1740, and the *Cartas eruditas y curiosas* (*Erudite and Curious Letters*), published in five volumes between 1742 and 1760, contain numerous insights into Spanish food in the Age of Enlightenment. A particular focus in Feijoo's work is that of the daily struggle for nourishment of large swaths of the population, which contrasted with the overspending of the well-off.[3] Undernourishment and periods of subsistence crises threatened large sections of the population throughout the century, for which Feijoo provided sharp commentary combined with eyewitness accounts:

> But lacking bread, oh God, how sad, how unfortunate, what a horrible theater is a whole kingdom! Everything is laments, everything is woe, all groans. The small places are depopulated, and the larger ones are filled with skeletons. Hunger is followed by disease, disease is followed by death; and how many deaths? [. . .] The things I saw happening in this city of Oviedo because of hunger, which this Principality suffered in 1710. In the roads, in the streets, on the thresholds of the houses, in those of the churches, lifeless swarms of the poor fell. (Feijoo 8: 416)[4]

Feijoo underscored that peasants bore the brunt of the work with little nourishment from the lowly food available to them: "In Galicia, Asturias, and Mountains of León. In these lands there are no hungrier or less sheltered people than the peasants. [. . .] Their food is a bit of black bread accompanied with some dairy or some vile legume, but all in such a small amount; barely once in a lifetime do they get up sated from the table" (8: 410). In contrast, Feijoo pointed to the paradox of the rich, who experienced an endless hunger for consumption that could never be satisfied and thus presented a perverse contrast with the hunger of physical need experienced by the poor: "If I say that the powerful are as hungry as the poor it will seem that I propose a new paradox, or at least a new enigma, and yet I tell the truth: The hungry poor man hungers for food: the satiated powerful man hungers for hunger itself" (1: 60).

Feijoo approached food choice and access as issues that separated two socioeconomic spheres, but he emphatically commented on the individual impact that food intake had on the creation of social capital and on the physiological effect of food, and particularly on taste, which engaged both the body and the intellect.⁵ Feijoo stressed that the social valuation of a food always played an important role in the development of personal taste. Expensive and difficult to access food products consumed by the powerful became fashionable and an object of desire. Through a phenomenon of emulation, everyone wanted to eat foods that were socially valued, considering them to be in good taste. On the other hand, the foods consumed by the poor and low classes or those associated with "primitive" or "uncivilized" people, independently from their nutritional value, were despised and rejected, thus making obvious the link between luxury consumption, high economic status, and civility:

> Many may not like a food at first but like it later because they hear that it is in fashion, or that it is put on the tables of the great lords; others, because they are told that it comes from remote lands and is sold at a high price. The opposite is also true: even when they like a food at first, they will begin to feel indifferent to it if they later hear that it is a rustic food, or ordinary food of uncultured and barbarous people. Such news aroused an apprehension, be it appreciative or contemplative, that changed their taste. (6: 360)

In an attempt to reconfigure the logic of the argument, Feijoo argued that, with the help of reason, it was possible to accept those foods rejected out of social and cultural prejudice, and he instead attempted to make obvious the situated and learned nature of food preferences: "The vices of apprehension are curable through reason. The man that looks at a food with annoyed disdain because it is not consumed in the area where he lives or because it is cheap or associated with ignorant and barbaric people can be easily persuaded with arguments showing that his dread is ill-founded" (6: 362). By presenting food choice as culturally patterned, Feijoo was able to make his point that tastes are overlapping, noting that taste needs to be contextualized, varying according to cultural uses associated with geography:

Many Northern peoples eat the meat of the bear, of the wolf, and of the fox; the Tartars that of the horse, the Arabians that of the camel; in parts of Africa they eat crocodiles and snakes. Do these all have bad taste? No, in fact they have good taste. They like the taste of those meats, and it is impossible for them to enjoy them if they taste bad, or rather, for the sense of taste to be bad, as it is clearly implied because it would be the same as it having and lacking delectable goodness. (6: 354–55)

Feijoo presented individual variance in taste along similar lines by relying on humoral theory, which claimed that each person had a different temperament that necessitated an individualized diet that also took into account personal food habits and preferences: "From a variety of temperaments comes the diversity of inclinations, and tastes. One likes a particular food, a second likes a different one; one likes a particular drink, a second prefers another; one likes cheerful music, another likes sad music, and so of everything else" (6: 356).[6] In line with the principles of humoral medicine, Feijoo emphasized the link between food and personalized health as one of the essential objectives when establishing the criteria for a correct diet: "Food that is beneficial for one, is harmful for another; its quantity, which for one is large, for another is small. The adequate proportion in the quantity and quality of the food for the temperament of each individual can only be known through individual experience, which the physician can only record by the account that is related to him" (1: 159). Such emphasis on the individual body made it possible to account for the changes in taste and the fluctuations between enjoyment and disgust, which end through repeated consumption and through habituation: "He looked at it at first as strange to the palate, and therefore as unpleasant, but habit removed that odious apprehension, and consequently made it palatable" (6: 359). At the same time, habit could generate tedium and thus the rejection of previously enjoyed foods: "On the contrary, many other times, and even very frequently, food that, consumed for a few days, is very gratifying becomes unpleasant when eaten continuously. The sensation on the palate is the same, as anyone who reflects upon this will experience himself, but the consideration of its repeated consumption prompts an annoying rejection, which makes it abhorrent" (6: 359). Thus, Feijoo argued for a harnessing of taste and food preferences through the application of reason and of an enlightened logic that emphasized both individual needs but also people's ability to take control of their food preferences while being aware of the socio-economic impact of their food practices.

The Comical *Sainetes* of Ramón de la Cruz: Between Jokes and Truths

On the public stage, eighteenth-century Spanish playwrights addressed what they presented as the unfair contrast between those who ate a lot and well and those who ate little and badly. In one of his short comic plays (*sainete*), entitled *El Hambriento de Nochebuena* (*The Hungry on Christmas Eve*) (*Colección de Sainetes* 1: 176–84), Ramón de la Cruz presented such a contrast by placing the most abundant and excellent banquet of the year, Christmas Eve dinner, at the home of a nobleman, a viscount, before the astonished and greedy eyes of a poor and famished character called Don Pajarilla, through whose gaze the overabundant table is presented:

> Gentlemen, I'm rabid with hunger / in such excessive degree, / that I would like to eat / with my eyes however much I find: / The soul and the heart / I'm after the gifts / that all castes of people / are bringing and taking./ What great number of bottles of liquor! / And of boxes! And of turkeys! / What great number of capons and chickens! Oh, bad fortune! For some, so much / and for me nothing?

In contrast, the gaze of the observer is presented through hunger, as the unfortunate Pajarilla declares himself so hungry that he dreams of mountains of food: "I am so hungry / that I could eat, fried, / seven thousand pairs of eggs, / six tons of fish, / three baskets of sea breams, / two loads of bread, with the mule, / basket and porter!" The great menu prepared at the viscount's house is depicted as the horn of national plenty available to the rich, the table being a rich map of regional foods that have been compiled for the enjoyment of a few:

> It has salads of all / the types God has raised, which is to say, I will eat a garden, / composed and seasoned. / There is half of Laredo / in sea breams, and all / the fish and delicious seafood / that may be found / Royal soups, pies; / all of Alicante's famed / nougat; all wines / subtlety has invented: / aromatic moonshine, sweets and fruits; / cakes and two thousand turkeys, / to finish dinner.

Shifting the religious nature of the celebration to that of consumption, the holiday is instead honored by singing a Christmas carol praising the long list of foods served at the plentiful table: "Jelly / perry / chorizos / pomegranates, oranges, / hake, salmon / sea bream, olives, cakes and candied citron, / purple cabbage. / Escarole. / Turkeys. / Marzipan. / Chickens, capons, / partridges, thrush, / nuts, pippin apples, / and a thousand other things. And long live Christmas." When Pajarilla sits at the table and the servants begin to serve, the spectacular culinary display turns his hunger into gluttony: "The first course is great! / Cakes soaked / in delicious wine ... / dried peaches and apricots / fresh salmon / four slices / are big! / These are good capons. / Rich bottles / nougat and sweets. / I am a glutton / for all desserts."

Beyond the social disparity between hunger and abundance, Ramón de la Cruz commented on yet another great contrast between the continuity of traditional cuisine, maintained by the popular classes, and the novelty of the grand French cuisine adopted by the upper classes, who dictated fashionable taste. Many authors problematized a divide that aligned French influences with the rich and their excesses and traditional foods with the lower classes, whom many presented as a repository of national traditions and identity. Ramón de la Cruz proposed an intermediate model characterized by the moderation dictated by enlightened philosophy in one of his most famous *sainetes*, *El Petimetre* (*The Dandy*) (*Colección de Sainetes* 1: 500–11). This intermediate model would allow the influences of Frenchified fashions but harnessed by moderation: "Yesterday I ate in a house / and the meal was even-handed: / there were no extravagances / of garnished soup, / nor of a squab per person. / There was a nice trencher / of vegetable stew, another of pasta, / a fricassee, a compote / and one or two roast chickens, / which for fifteen people at the table / is more than enough food."

In the significantly entitled *El cocinero* (*The Cook*) (*Ocho sainetes* 31–54), Ramón de la Cruz highlighted the cultural clash between foreign and national, the French cuisine in vogue and traditional Spanish cuisine that had arrived with the Bourbon dynasty in the Spanish throne at the very beginning of the eighteenth century. In the play, the author presents his argument as embodied by two chefs, one French and one Spanish. *El cocinero* humorously portrays the atmosphere of a kitchen in which Spanish and French chefs, all male, comingle. The play begins with a lively satire on the picaresque atmosphere of a kitchen:

This is a good job / that pays a good wage; / much eating and drinking, / with little work. / The best bites / stay here, / and the owner is happiest / the more he pays. / My good star / made me a cook, / for in the kitchens always / something sticks to one's hands. / Beware of roasts / with less rattle / one minces better, my friends. / Has that beef brisket already been dressed? / It already is / What wine is this? / Manchego / Pouf! / Tighten that dough! I have not seen limper arms.

The alternation between traditional and new dishes is presented throughout the work, marking that alternation between Spanish and French cuisines. It is significant that the splendid peasant turkey, a colonial food, is presented as a traditional product of the Spanish countryside and one that conveys the abundance of the rich man's table: "But what a tender and fat turkey! That neither Your Lordship, nor his father, nor his grandfather will have eaten better" and "I have brought a turkey that could feed a whole convent." On the other end of the spectrum lie the ingredients provided by the French cook: thirty chickens fattened on milk and tender bread crumbs, parsley, mushrooms, onions, capers, liver, and brains. The *sainete* culminates with the confrontation between the two cooks and the two cuisines, with a resounding victory of the Spanish over the French. The first chef states: "My master has great taste, that I may steal from him what I want, in putting two foreign stews on the table," to which the second replies: "You lie, for I don't like that. He neither likes it nor can he do so in good conscience."

The debate between gastronomic tradition and innovation aligned with a discourse on national identity was at the core of key eighteenth-century debates in Spain, as the triumph of French high cuisine gained ground and helped relegate Spanish cuisine to the popular sphere (Pérez Samper, "Recetarios manuscritos"). In this and other pieces, Ramón de la Cruz stressed the need to follow the trend of French foods until it reached an end, which was inevitably the disillusionment with French cuisine that would mark the return to traditional Spanish cuisine. In another *sainete*, *El abate diente-agudo* (*The Sharp-Toothed Abbot*) (*Ocho sainetes* 145–64), Ramón de la Cruz shows that the display of distinction actually had other bases and that home cooking could serve to display national gastronomic excellence through the usage of key regional products to which a high cultural, economic, and gastronomic value was attached and could thus give a distinction achieved through the display of consumption:

> Yesterday your brother invited me to eat a piece of beef from Aragon, which is the most beautiful morsel in the world. Here you will eat one like it.... Very well. Are you a fan of sweetbread pie? I die for it, and even more when it is made with the dough that your cook makes. My friend, today's dish is good Galician sweet bacon with tomatoes. Bravo! You are a brave gentleman, and it is not flattery, for everyone is saying it. If one does not treat oneself right, what

do you want your money for? Everyone should think that way. And what large trout I expect from Barco de Ávila! And how beautiful they are! I am only sorry that they have not arrived yet. Oh, sir, it's not good to eat so much in one day. (150)

In this work, Ramón de la Cruz combines a commentary on social distinction as something achieved not only by the kind of table one keeps but also by those who sit around it, as one of the characters explains: the character, talent, and honor of the guests distinguish a table. Significantly, gender considerations appear aligned with notions of distinction and domesticity by placing capital differentials on the superior foreign male cook and the inferior female home cook. When a table displayed the food prepared by a foreign male cook, social distinction was fully achieved, as it marked both gustatory and intellectual taste. In contrast, food prepared by female hands could never satisfy a "learned" ("erudito") hunger, for, being "unrefined" ("grosero") and insipid, it lacked "taste":

GRANADINA. Is it not worth more eating your stew at home than going to the homes of others to taste their soup without being invited?
GARRIDO. Men of my character, of my grace and my talent honor any table where we appear at noon. A hundred ladies and forty friends I have whining because I continuously refuse to eat their soup with them.
GRANADINA. And if you go, you will be branded as a sponger. Stay at home, because your little stew is good, and in taking out the three quarters of mutton, we can have roast.
GARRIDO. And then what will we have for dinner?
GRANADINA. Soup.
GARRIDO. My mistress, as long as he cannot keep a cook, a man remains rebuffed, and usually hungry; because women's cooking is for those of us who have a learned taste, insipid and unrefined. And today I have a hunger capable of honoring the most opulent banquet. (147–48)

In contrast with the private sphere of the home, inns and taverns were hubs for a sociability that was coded as one of the keystones of "enlightenment" in Spain, as they were in other parts of Europe (Albrecht). Cafés were viewed as equalizing spaces where the different social classes mixed, helping them become a great public success and the setting for many well-known plays. Ramón de la Cruz set his one-act comedy, *El Café de Barcelona*, in a Barcelona café. The play had been commissioned by the Captain General and was performed in Barcelona in the newly built theater on the Ramblas, in order to celebrate King Carlos III's saint's day in 1788. The cast of characters reflect the variety of people meeting at cafés during the period, women and men of all social classes and any geographical origin, Spanish or foreign. The plays are also valuable sources for the practices of commensality in public spaces and for information on the food and drink consumed at the cafés. In Ramón de la Cruz's play, some drink coffee or milk, others chocolate, wine, or punch, some also eat biscuits or bread from Mallorca:

> At the first table will be sitting the Lady with the abbé, leaning back with her hand on her cheek, as if she were angry, and he will be drinking chocolate from one of the two cups they have been served. At the second table will sit the officer, gazettes in hand. The coffee maid, standing nearby, will be singing loudly, and the officer will be following in a low voice, as if learning the Catalan song he is following. At the third table will sit the mayor (that is *batlle* in Catalan) only with a bottle and a glass, bread from Mallorca, etc. At the fourth table will sit the attractive Andalusian woman, with the hairdresser serving some drink, biscuits, etc. The café's waiter comes and goes, serving what's necessary. (*El Café de Barcelona* 3)

In contrast, more traditional public spaces like taverns (*tabernas*) and inns (*fondas*) were presented as the repository of tradition and associated with the lower classes, and many texts during the period characterize the food served in them accordingly. In his *sainete Los bandos del Avapiés*, Ramón de la Cruz presents the food and drink of a

Madrid tavern—bread, wine, sardines, and peppers: "It was the case that one day I saw that he entered the house of Pedro the innkeeper, and with her went Perdulario the cobbler, behind them I entered; they asked to drink, they drank; they asked for bread, they asked for sardines, and peppers for dessert; and when paying, Perdulario said: 'I have no money' (*Colección de Sainetes*, 1: 292).

Thus, tradition and innovation were viewed as coexisting in the private and public spheres, mixing and at the same time confronting two cuisines: the Spanish, seen as the repository of tradition and popular tastes, and the modern, embodied by the French influences introduced by the new Bourbon dynasty that had ascended to the Spanish throne with King Felipe V at the beginning of the century. The two different cultures, the foreign French backed by the prestige from the monarchy and thus the upper classes, and the traditional Spanish, embodied by the popular classes, became differential ways to mark or erase social distinction (Pérez Samper, *Mesas y cocinas*). However, such values assigned to foreign and Spanish cuisines would not go uncontested.

Against Refreshments and Other Gastronomic Fashions: José Clavijo y Fajardo

Few things achieved greater success than *refrescos* (refreshments) in the Spanish food scene of the eighteenth century. A refresco was a small meal that served to indicate social standing through a display of abundance and refinement and played a transcendental cultural role in the sociability of the upper classes. At the same time, few events centered around food were more polemical than the refresco, which became the touchstone for debates on Spanish tradition and the economics of the upper class's conspicuous consumption, particularly as it was seen in connection to the quest for social distinction. The *Diccionario de Autoridades de la Real Academia Española* offers the first definition of the word "refresco" as "Moderate amount of food, or restorative food that is taken to strengthen oneself and continue to work, or overcome fatigue." But the initial meaning had evolved, as seen in the second definition: "It is also used to refer to a refreshment of drinks, sweets, and chocolate served to fete guests or other visitors." (entry *refresco*, vol. 3).[7] The refresco consisted mainly of sweets, with chocolate always taking the center stage of the celebration, but there was also entertainment in the form of music, dancing, and card games. Refrescos played a symbolic role, projecting a lifestyle characterized by luxury, pleasure, and refinement.

Despite its enormous popularity, or precisely because of it, there were many critics of the excesses that the practice of refrescos caused. José Clavijo y Fajardo, a famous journalist, ranted against refrescos in his newspaper *El Pensador*, which was dedicated to social critique and to the denunciation of customs that he considered antiquated or irrational. Clavijo acknowledged that the roots of the refresco practice were ingrained in Spanish identity, but he believed that it had become such a quintessential marker of socioeconomic standing that many who would want to abandon the practice did not dare to do so: "Refrescos, this peculiar puerility of our nation, [...] the terrible ill-will that I have for them, they are one of the simplicities that we have more generally established, and one that many sane people wish to abandon. But how does one dare to banish this socially sanctioned treat?" (238). Clavijo further denounced refresco as the unreasonable but fashionable outgrowth of a practice more fit to serve the needs of growing children than those of respectable adults:

> Refrescos are already considered as a snack, as a treat, or as one and another together, but it seems they should be seen rather as an object worthy of the request of some school children than of the attention of women of reason and of serious and bearded men; but as it is, all, without distinction of sex or age, look at this puerility as a very important matter, and they have reduced it to formality and etiquette, with rules and unalterable ceremonies. (238–39)

Thus, refresco had been coded as the epitome of both social distinction and luxury consumption that marked the upper classes and followed a precise ceremonial that some authors parodied. Clavijo's description of a refresco, although full of irony, provides a good sense of the ritual:

> It is barely seven o'clock in the winter, eight o'clock in the summer, when in houses that hold regular gatherings, and even in those where only a few people get together, the bell is rung calling all to *refresco*. Behold three or four pages carrying salvers, plates, and trays. One page begins to lighten the weight, distributing dishes to all, according to the ceremonial order established, which instructs that preference be given, as it is right to do, to bonnets and shawls, over hats and toupees. Another page parades in front of all the people in the room, who take a plate from him, with the exception of a few, who excuse themselves with a nod either because they have refreshed themselves in another house, where the ceremony has been held earlier, or because they do not like this kind of hospitality, or to distinguish themselves from others, for there are all sorts of people. After the plates follows the tray with sugar or sweets called "of small plate." If the former, the damage is less, for its cost is lower, and less also is the time lost in this ridiculous ceremonial, but when they bring the latter, men may well have patience, go to sleep, or go for a walk, sure that there will be time for everything. (239–41)

Finally came chocolate, the climax of the refresco and the great passion of eighteenth-century Spanish society, the chocolate that delighted everyone and that was the object of everyone's desire (Pérez Samper, "The Early Modern Food Revolution"), making the wait unbearable: "The sweets have just been distributed to all: then comes the water, and later follows the chocolate with buns, biscuits, etc., again water is passed around, and so ends this long, annoying ceremony" (Clavijo 241). Clavijo accused those who participated in refrescos of transforming what should have been a warm reception into an interested obligation and of helping incur the hosts into disproportionate expenses that unbalanced domestic resources:

Is not it really a mockery to see the gravity of the *refresco*? Would it be possible to believe, if we did not see it, that to quench one's thirst so much formality and apparatus were needed? And if this is the case in the daily refreshments, what is there in those of etiquette? [. . .] Can you be so foolish as to spend your fortune on these childish gifts? So houses are consumed, and annihilated, for they are turned into confectionery shops. This daily lavishness usually adds up to the same sum as that needed to support the family. (242–43)

A further object of Clavijo's critique was the waste of the time that the refresco, which provided a means to allow the pleasurable passage of time without occupation or concern, inherently occasioned: "The time they occupy is not one of the minor inconveniences of refreshments. In those houses where there is a function of music, dance, or theater is where the waste of time is more obvious. The more solemn the function is, the more so is the refreshment, and the greater the time that is uselessly spent. The refreshment gets the biggest and best part of the night" (245–46). Clavijo sought to refocus on the social value attached to the participation in a refresco by emphasizing the importance of social interaction and intellectual exchange and seeking a diminution of the role played by sociability based on a consumption that, significantly, he gendered feminine:

> There is a more powerful reason in favor of refreshments. Ladies particularly found a part of their vanity in the number of people who go to their homes. The better the refresco they customarily offer, the better and more splendidly attended it is; therefore, it is natural for them to take pains in offering a treat whose consequences flatter their self-esteem. But forgive me if I tell you that this is a mistake that they pay with their own money. We have a natural inclination to seek the interaction and companionship of our fellow human beings. Where we find a pleasant society, we will go without being asked and without it being necessary for us to be given anything as it is commonly done. (239–41)

Instead, Clavijo championed the traditional practice of hospitality (*agasajo*), which he counterposed to the fashionable refresco in an argument based on semantics. Clavijo considered *agasajo* as preferable because it referred to the reason for the celebration and not to its gastronomic content. One of the meanings (number three) of the word *agasajo* in the *Diccionario de Autoridades* lists a definition very close to that of *refresco*: "It is also the term for the refreshment of sweets and drinks that in the evenings is served to house visitors and in other functions" (entry *agasajo*, vol. 1). Significantly, Clavijo presents *refresco* as a traditional *agasajo* whose values have been inverted by a fashion that the upper classes follow as a means to attain social distinction but that is privately loathed for its negative impact on home economics:

> Formerly it was called an *agasajo*, and even today it is called so in various parts, and among certain people, what at court and among the fashionable people is called "*refresco*" [...] I will conclude, then, with a reflection, which now occurs to me. If Your Grace gives this letter to the public, as you did with the prior, it will be read in more than four houses, whose owners are eager to shake off the yoke of the *refresco* but do not dare to bring about such change. The reading will end, the refreshment will be brought in, and there will be some more discussion about this letter (*Discurso*). The owners of the house, despite their desire and knowledge of the matter, will maintain that my letter is ridiculous, to avoid being marked as miserly, and those present, whose greater number would feel it very much if they were to be deprived of this small meal, will approve of my letter, blaspheming the fashion of the *refresco*, but gobbling everything up just the same. (248–50)

For related reasons, Clavijo also criticized another great gastronomic social celebration: the wedding banquet, which he saw as similarly plagued with conspicuous consumption and extravagant spending due in part to the perceived need to enlist foreign hands:[8]

They call a cook of the new cuisine and a confectioner, both among the most famous (if the houses do not have their own, or do not have first-rate ones and they need to seek advice), and they agree on the price of the dinner and *refresco*, in which the businessmen do not fall short. It is a time of rejoicing and an occasion for showing off, and it is time for sparing no expense. This happens once in a lifetime, says the one who is paying: help me shine, and let us spare no expense. So they shake hands; one does not need to be a duke in order to spend four or six thousand pesos in one day. Cooks and confectioners know that a wedding and *refresco* may take ten or twelve years to pay, for which reason they are encouraged to make the bill a little longer than they customarily do out of habit and inclination so that the total comes out right in the end. (54–55)

The need to make a prominent display of economic standing and make a show of conspicuous consumption led the hosts to overspend, but the guests had competing interests as they looked to fulfill similar self-fashioning goals and establish themselves as superior. For this reason, the food and entertainment offering could never fulfill the expectations of the guests, who were infinitely dissatisfied with the food served, which they could never find luxurious or abundant enough. Endless criticism during the event commented on the macaroni cake, the fashionable dish indispensable in a good wedding banquet, which was invariably cold, the strawberries not in season, and the sweets scarce:

Regardless of how much care is placed or how much money might be spent, there is always something to criticize. They say that everything has been good (exclaims a prim lady): That may well be, but what I know is that I wanted to taste macaroni cake and found it to be stone cold. It cannot be denied (says another who takes pride in being a critic) that everything has been superb, but the strawberry drink is not in season: the milk sorbet would have been better if it had been served two minutes earlier, and the sweets have not been in the abundance as I had hoped. Abundance? (replies another lady); abundance indeed! They have been very stingy, and very miserly.

The first tray could not get to where I was, and the second just brought about three pounds of sweets, for which reason I was not able to fulfill my obligations with those in my circle, and it was necessary to send to the sweet shop for more and baptize those as wedding sweets. (55–56)

Thus, Clavijo presented a different form of a paradox of plenty, in which the extreme abundance and luxury offered by the host could never match the ever-superior needs of their guests, overabundance and luxury being a pursuit that could never be fulfilled and failed to deliver its promise of social distinction. As an alternative, Clavijo attempted to promote moderate abundance, "an abundance that is well understood, discreet, and not disproportionate." As an alternative to the pressures of luxury consumption, he proposed fraternity and citizenship that took the upper classes away from their vicious circles and instead entered another social factor: the needs of the poor who could not afford to eat:

I have decided to make better use of the money that I should have spent in *refresco*, banquet, and music in keeping with the custom among men of my class. I know that there are a lot of poor people [. . .] I cannot ignore that all are my brothers and that, if I have not ended up in their situation, it has been one more benefit that I owe to providence. For this reason, to not take compassion of their misery and contribute to their relief as a man, as a Christian, and as a good citizen would make me seem to be made out of stone. (61–62)

The ever-present contrast between hunger and abundance would remain a recurrent theme among eighteenth-century authors, sometimes counterposing the urban rich and poor.[9] They also served to draw differentials along the lines of other dichotomies inherited from previous centuries, such as the distinction between city life, exposed to foreign and luxurious tastes, and a life in the countryside that was portrayed as both a pastoral ideal and a repository of the traditions closer to the land that gave the nation its character.

Eating in the Country: Juan Meléndez Valdés and Francisco Gregorio de Salas

In his poem "The Philosopher in the Country" ("El filósofo en el campo"; *Poesías*), written in 1794 as the French Revolution was revealing the contradictions of the Enlightenment, the Extremaduran Juan Meléndez Valdés (1754–1817) focused his social criticism on the contrast between the countryside and the city. Meléndez Valdés built upon the long classical tradition carried on by the Renaissance and baroque periods of praising a simple country life and censuring that of the court, a topic that he had earlier presented in an idealized form. He sent his work to Jovellanos, who received it on June 19, which seems to indicate that Jovellanos's plan for agrarian reform ("Informe en el Expediente de la Ley Agraria") may have been indirectly at the root of its composition. In Meléndez Valdés's poem, the contrast between court and peasant life is aligned with socioeconomic differentials that mark the distance between the privileged guests of opulent tables and the poor people who have no bread to give their children:

> Oh Fabio, Fabio! / in the golden halls / between the brocade and rich draperies, / the foot treading carved pavements, / how badly the courtier judges the poor man! / What evil around the opulent table, / covered with deadly delicacies, / bait of gluttony and fiery lasciviousness, / from the unhappy the cries are heard! / He lacks bread, he is surrounded by the hungry / swarm of his sad children, / squalid, plunged into misery; / and perhaps his grieving wife has just, / woe is she! given the fatherland another poor wretch, / a victim from that moment destined / to the serf's indigence and opprobrium; / and there in the court, in scandalous luxury / swimming in abundance, the sybarite laughs / between perfumes and festive toasts, / and with his laughter insults the poor's misfortune. (238)

The poem's entire structure is built around the contrast between the useless and exploitative upper classes living luxuriously without doing anything and the people of the countryside, who work hard to produce food that is inequitably distributed. The peasants, who should be proud of the piles of golden grain, have to settle for humble, even miserable, tables, lacking even the bread made with the wheat they grow:

> Far away, from the reaper the song sounds / besides the soft bleating of the flock / that the shepherd leads to the gentle shade, / and the sublime sun at the zenith points out / the time of rest; to home returns, / bathed in useful sweat, the husband / from the dusty threshing plot; the family / sits around the humble table. / Oh, if it was not made so poor by the yoke / of a barbarous, insensible steward! / But robbed by his avaricious hand, / the real torture of Tantalus / here, Fabio, you would see: the heaps / of golden grain they can see in front of them, / reward that Heaven to his labor dispenses, / and the miserable lack even bread. / But, oh good God!, to the opprobrium of the rich, / their heart with reverent hymns / give you thanks for so few gifts, / and is constant in trusting your fond love. (242–43)

The focus on the golden grain and bread is especially strong because of the enormous importance that bread was assigned as the fundamental staple and of particular importance as the basic food of the popular classes. Bread was the food par excellence, consumed every day by everyone. However, even such a basic staple served to mark socioeconomic differentials, as white wheat bread was reserved for the rich, while the common people were left with brown wheat bread, which was considered inferior. In his poetry, Meléndez broadens the contrast, adding other sectors to agriculture by involving commerce and the trade in foreign luxury goods. The privileged classes did not settle for bread and local foods but rather sought exotic products, which involved long sea voyages that were extremely difficult and full of dangers in order to get spices like cinnamon, highly valued since antiquity and brought from distant Asian islands. Other fashionable imported commodities included coffee, which originated in Ethiopia, but in the eighteenth century, it was a colonial product brought to Spain from American soil, where its cultivation had been successfully introduced:

Admire their patient suffering, / or rather cry seeing them naked, / emaciated, hungry, stooped, / exhaling their dying sigh / under the immense burden that on their shoulders / luck placed. The unhappy sails off, / leaving his home, and facing the storms / of the immense ocean, so that luxury / may feed your gluttony, and so that his proud disgust, / may bring you the perfumed coffee that Moca gives / or the cinnamon of Ceylon. (246)

Whether it was sailing out on the seas or opening furrows in the earth, it was always the lower classes that sustained society with their work and effort. It was those hardworking people who produced "the golden ear of wheat that feeds," despite being despised by the idle sybarites who took advantage of them: "That bitter sweat that floods / the long furrows that their plow forms / is the golden ear of wheat that feeds, / Fabio, the courtier's comfortable idleness. / Without it, the pale hunger . . . And we dare scorn them?" (246–47).

Meléndez Valdés concludes his poem with a philosophical and moral reflection once more counterposing the uselessness of so many fashionable inventions with the fundamental importance of the true necessities again exemplified by "the heap of ripe grains" that staved off hunger: "What is the worth of so many strange inventions / of our insane pride, compared / with the heap of ripe grains / that the farmer grew? We weak children, / would fast meet our end in hunger and tears / without the help of his strong arms" (247). Thus, Meléndez Valdés makes wheat the axis around which social differentials are built because it is the primordial food and the source of broad contrasts between hunger and abundance and between white and brown bread, marking the abyss that separates the rich conspicuous consumers and the productive poor that labor close to the land.

While the rural world was the scene of much hard work and suffering, it was also a place of joy and celebration for Francisco Gregorio de Salas (1729–1808), a poet from the region of Extremadura and a long-time resident of Madrid, where he remembered his native land with regret. In his *Observatorio rústico*, a very popular work that went through ten editions between 1772 and 1830, he followed the same classic line of contempt of court and praise of countryside, lauding the simple pleasures of the peasants: the "tender and fresh bread, though dark, healthy and very tasty" (49), the fresh eggs, the fruits picked from the trees, the vegetables from one's own orchard, and the lamb from one's own flock, the honey from one's own hives (50–51). His work included the praises of the daily stew pot, rendered in the version of the Extremaduran countryside: "I see my gardener, / who waters with his own hand / the cabbage, the cardoon, the celery, and the lettuce / [. . .] / He will pull up an onion / to put in the pot, / which cooks with the garlic, the turnips, the cabbage, and the jerky; / whose dry cured meat / he prefers to the partridge and the chicken" (71–72). Although the peasant diet was simple, there were plenty of opportunities to enjoy abundance and pleasure: "To celebrate the religious guest, / in the pleasant delicious field / they arrange the afternoon snack, / carrying with a boast / the recent kid / cooked in a tasty cochifrito,[10] / some roasted lamb, / a rabbit pie, / and a piece of well-cooked beef / in a well-stocked provisions box, / a wineskin, / and a seasoned piece of bacon" (111).

In the rural world, gastronomic celebrations also reached their maximum expression in the wedding banquets. Although they did not have the French innovations so fashionable in the cities, the feasts in the countryside were not far behind in quantity and quality. The beginning was promising: "a cake soaked in red wine; / and a sweet ripe orange, [. . .] and with raisins and almonds garnished. / Among the tasty loaves of breads are scattered / some ornate, white ring-shaped bread / made from extra fine flour" (97–98). The main dishes were a display of abundance and variety:

> The food on the table is piled up, / a partridge and rabbit per person; / without counting the kid or the lamb, / the veal, the beef, and the mutton, / admirable trout, barbels, and eels, / and many other healthy foods; / or some seasoned pickled dishes / of bogas and other fish, prepared / with aged laurel leaves, /[. . .] / and some empanadas / of graceful edges adorned; / chickens, turkeys, and many other birds, / tender, fattened, big, and soft. (98–99)

If plenty and good were the savory dishes, the best were the sweets. In Gregorio de Salas's relation, the most traditional and popular specialties are favored. The list is long: "curly sweet fritters," "white and fresh buttery milk, / covered with a dense and thick cream," "white ricotta and fresh cheese," "a basket of choice fruits," "a large and transparent honeycomb," "a bucket / of exquisite junket, / that shames and humiliates / the cream, the milk and almond custard and the soft egg custard," "a box / of white jam," "the fresh butter on tender buns," "a salad, / surrounded by many hard / fat, fresh, pure eggs, / and covered with sweet candied citron, / pimpernel, cress, and tarragon," "a plate of olives seasoned / with thyme and oregano," "some tender tasty radishes," "and some sweet liquor wines" (100–103).[11] Gregorio de Salas clearly looked to propose the cornucopia of country foods, of which he extolls not only their abundance but also their taste, more pure and intense and more reflective of the land that gives its qualities. The lavish description of country food is intended to appeal not only to the intellect but also to the appetites of his readers, thus inciting a hunger that attempts to draw them from the court to the country, from the foreign exotic to the national and traditional foods of the land. His celebration of the peasant calendar and the cyclicity that marks country life similarly allows the author to celebrate the annual gastronomic cycle. The author evokes the autumn grape harvest and the new wine: "and as they arrive, / and unload the ripe grape, / in my clean wine presses, / with skillful singular devices, / they crush it, and cheerfully I see / running with great cleanliness / the sweet must of the healthy grapes, / to the wide bosom of my vats; / and of the purest and most delicious wine / in my deep cellars enclosed, / I reserve the most aged and exquisite / for my own use and appetite" (33). It was also of the utmost importance to preserve the fruit for the autumn and winter months, thus lengthening a production concentrated in the spring and summer:

> Then I set out to separate in heaps / the fruits of the winter, and prepare, / in white and folded paper, / sweet mirabelle plums, / healthy damson plums; / and hang the good / thick bergamots, / from my

old half-broken beams, / along with the most seasoned grapes from Jaén, / the melons, the quinces, the pomegranates; / tending on very thick straw / cider apples, oranges, and pippin apples; / and leaving the largest figs / scattered on the drying trays under the sun, / together with everything else that in comfortable interval / serves to bring me pleasure in December. (34)

Following a well-established calendar that placed Christmas Eve at the center of the celebration of the season, Gregorio de Salas emphasizes the celebratory aspect of food in spite of the fasting and abstinence that the Church prescribed for the day, a prescription not always strictly respected, because the joy of the Feast of the Nativity of Jesus usually prevailed and allowed a festive dinner, accompanied by all kinds of fruits and sweets:

When the cold winter is already midway, / in icy December, / the pleasurable Christmas celebration arrives, / and in its happy night the neighbors / meet in the house of the old / closest landed relative, / and without any fear or scruple / to break the faithful and holy fast, / through abuse and inveterate custom, / authorized by time, / they take the amplest collations, / which are in fact their dinners and lunches. / At the table are served in several dishes, / with simple apparatus, / mead, grape syrup, and grape preserves, / jelly, nut bread, and pine-nut candy, / a golden soup / of white honey and crushed almond, / honey nougat, and donuts, / and sweet yellow pippin apples, / grapes, pear apples, chestnuts, and pomegranates, and plenty of fresh salads; / being the last dessert and treat / a large platter of nuts, / of pine nuts, walnuts, and hazelnuts, / and other tasty and very healthy fruits; / without missing some delicious wine / seasoned with fragrant cinnamon; / and eating and drinking freely, / they entertain the night cheerfully. (57–58)[12]

Later, the poet offers a list of typical dishes that were consumed in the spring in Extremadura's villages during Easter: "Easter arrives, and on this happy day / the majordomo of a confraternity

/ usually gives me a whole quarter / of the fattest mutton, / some ornate ring-shaped bread, / and a great empanada, / a sweet leg of good pork, / with a large pitcher of delicious wine" (60). In contrast with the city, the country is presented as particularly reflective of the passage of time, the arrival of seasonal products, and the traditional dishes of each festivity that marked a calendar full of gastronomic celebrations. The seasonal cyclicity of nature was superimposed to the liturgical cycle, both of them sanctioned by tradition. The enduring popularity of Gregorio de Salas's *Observatorio rústico*, encouraging a turn toward the local, is witness to the draw that such accounts had on the reading public, an interest that was fed not only through literary texts but also through texts on agrarian and economic reform.

As this chapter has shown, eighteenth-century Spanish authors present a perspective on food that is often organized around the axis of place, drawing continuous lines between the city and the country, which lie at both ends of a spectrum that links food to soil. More problematic is the divergence between the national and the foreign, which had at its core the paradox of having a new monarchy lead the country in the adoption of foreign influences and customs that many saw as eroding traditional food practices related to the land. In addition, the Enlightened period was viewed as marked by socioeconomic differentials, opposing attitudes toward tradition and toward the luxury consumption that marked the distinction of the upper classes but was detrimental to others. Thus, the overabundance of the rich was portrayed as being built on the backs of the poor and of the peasants who grew foods that were inequitably distributed. Social distinction and physical need for nourishment were thus debated as contrasting and keystone issues in Spanish Enlightenment texts.

NOTES

Translated by Ana M. Gómez-Bravo and Matthew Kullberg.

1. See for example the work of Mennell; Spary; Von Hoffmann; and the studies collected in Morton.
2. For the concept of distinction and economic and cultural capital, see Bourdieu. On the relationship between food and science during the Enlightenment, see Spary. On various aspects of consumption, history, and luxury, see Berry; Brewer and Porter; Miller.
3. On the issues concerning food scarcity and eating habits, see Flandrin and Montanari.
4. For an overview of some of the main issues regarding eighteenth-century food in Spain, see Pérez Samper, as well as Sánchez Meco.
5. For a study of the understanding of taste, see Gigante; Gronow; Von Hoffmann.
6. On humoral theory and Galenic medicine, see Chapters 1 and 2 in this book.
7. In his famous cookbook *Arte de Repostería*, Juan de la Mata provided instructions for the preparation of refrescos that help us understand the standard offering for different numbers of guests, the "[m]anner that should be observed when serving a general refresco, and explanation of dressing tables in ten different ways" (ch. 41).
8. On a personal level, Clavijo showed himself to be very much against weddings. The fact that in 1764 he had broken his engagement with Lisette Caron, sister of the French playwright Pierre-Agustin de Beaumarchais, along with the enormous scandal that was unleashed and that caused his fall from grace and the loss of his jobs, could have influenced his negative view of the celebration of marriage.
9. For a study of the contrasts between hunger and abundance present elsewhere in Europe, see Montanari.
10. Shepherd's stew often made with the meat of kid or lamb that is first boiled and then fried with spices, vinegar, and *pimentón*.
11. "enroscados buñuelos," "blanca y fresca leche mantecosa, / cubierta de una espesa y gruesa nata," "el blanco requesón y el queso fresco," "algún cesto de frutas escogidas," "un panal crecido y transparente," "una herrada / de esquisita cuajada, / que avergüenza y humilla / a la crema, al manjar y a la natilla," "una caja / de blanca confitura," "la reciente manteca en tiernos bollos," "una ensalada, / rodeada de muchos huevos duros / gordos, frescos y puros, / y cubierta de dulces acitrones, / pimpinelas, mastuerzos y estragones," "un plato de aceitunas sazonadas, / con tomillo y orégano adobadas," "algunos tiernos rábanos sabrosos," "y algunos dulces vinos generosos."

12. "Quando ya el frío invierno va mediado, / en el Diciembre helado, / llegan las regaladas navidades, / y en su noche feliz las vecindades / se juntan en la casa del anciano / hacendado pariente más cercano, / y sin miedo ni escrúpulo ninguno / de quebrantar el fiel y santo ayuno, / por abuso y costumbre inveterada, / del tiempo autorizada, / hacen las colaciones más cumplidas, / que suelen ser sus cenas y comidas. / Á la mesa se sirve en varios platos, / con simples aparatos, / el aguamiel, arrope, y el uvate, / la jalea, alajú, y el piñonate, / una sopa dorada / de blanca miel y almendra machacada, / el turrón de melcocha, y las rosquillas, / y las dulces camuesas amarillas, / uvas, peros, castañas y granadas, / y abundantes y frescas ensaladas; / siendo el último postre y agasajo / una crecida fuente del cascajo, / de los piñones, nueces y avellanas, / y otras frutas sabrosas y muy sanas; / sin que falte algún vino regalado / con fragante canela aderezado; / y comiendo y bebiendo francamente, / entretienen la noche alegremente."

WORKS CITED

Albrecht, Peter. "Coffee-Drinking as a Symbol of Social Change in Continental Europe in the Seventeenth and Eighteenth Centuries." *Studies in Eighteenth-Century Culture*, vol. 18, 1988, pp. 91–103.

Berry, Christopher J. *The Idea of Luxury: A Conceptual and Historical Investigation*. Cambridge UP, 1994.

Bourdieu, Pierre. *Distinction: A Social Critique of the Judgement of Taste*. Translated by Richard Nice, Harvard UP, 1996.

Brewer, John, and Roy Porter, editors. *Consumption and the World of Goods*. Routledge, 1992.

Clavijo y Fajardo, José. *El Pensador*, vol. 5, Madrid, Joaquín Ibarra, 1767.

Cruz, Ramón de la. *Colección de Sainetes, tanto impresos como inéditos, con un discurso preliminar de Agustín Durán*. Madrid, Yenes, 1843. 2 vols.

———. *Ocho sainetes inéditos de Don Ramón de la Cruz*, edited by Charles Emil Kany, U of California P, 1925.

———. *El Café de Barcelona*. Barcelona, Francisco Genéras, 1788.

Diccionario de autoridades. Real Academia Española. 1726–1739. Vols. I–VI. Facsimile Edition, Gredos, 1963. 3 vols.

Feijoo, Benito Jerónimo. *Teatro crítico universal*. Madrid, 1726–1740. 9 vols.

Flandrin, Jean-Louis, and Montanari, Massimo. *Food: A Culinary History*. Translated by Albert Sonnenfeld, Columbia UP, 1999.

Gigante, Denise. *Taste: A Literary History*. Yale UP, 2005.

Gregorio de Salas, Francisco. *Observatorio rústico*. Madrid, Repullés, 1816.
Gronow, Jukka. "Need, Taste and Pleasure: Understanding Food and Consumption." *Palatable Worlds: Sociocultural Food Studies*, edited by Elisabeth L. Fürst, Ritva Prättälä, Marianne Ekström, Lotte Holm, and Unni Kjærnes, Solum Verlag, 1991, pp. 33–52.

———. *The Sociology of Taste*. Routledge, 1997.

Jovellanos, Gaspar Melchor de. "Informe de Ley Agraria." *Obras Completas*, vol. 10, "Escritos económicos," edited by Vicente Llombart Rosa and Joaquín Ocampo Suárez-Valdés, Ayuntamiento de Gijón, Instituto Feijoo de Estudios del Siglo XVIII, KRK Ediciones, 2008, pp. 693–826.

Mata, Juan de la. *Arte de la Repostería*. Madrid, Antonio Marín, 1747.

Meléndez Valdés, Juan. *Poesías*, vol. 3, Madrid, Imprenta Real, 1821. 4 vols.

———. *Batilo: Égloga en alabanza de la vida del campo premiada por la Real Academia Española*. Madrid, D. Joachin Ibarra, 1780.

Mennell, Stephen. *All Manners of Food: Eating and Taste in England and France from the Middle Ages to the Present*. U of Illinois P, 2006.

Miller, Daniel. "Consumption as the Vanguard of History: A Polemic by Way of an Introduction." *Acknowledging Consumption: A Review of New Studies*, edited by Daniel Miller, Routledge, 1995, pp. 1–57.

Montanari, Massimo. *La Fame e l'abbondanza: Storia dell'alimentazione in Europa*. Laterza, 2012.

Morton, Timothy, editor. *Cultures of Taste/Theories of Appetite: Eating Romanticism*. Palgrave Macmillan, 2004.

Pérez Samper, María Ángeles. *Mesas y cocinas en la España del Ssiglo XVIII*. Trea, 2011.

———. "Recetarios manuscritos de la España moderna." *Cincinnati Romance Review*, Special Issue: *Writing About Food: Culinary literature in the Hispanic World*, edited by María Paz Moreno, vol. 33, 2012, pp. 27–58.

———. "The Early Modern Food Revolution: A Perspective from the Iberian Atlantic." *Global Goods and the Spanish Empire, 1492–1824: Circulation, Resistance, and Diversity*, edited by Bethany Aram and Bartolomé Yun-Casalilla, Palgrave Macmillan, 2014, pp. 17–37.

Sánchez Meco, Gregorio. *Sabores del pasado: La cocina en tiempos de Carlos III*. Sar Aljandría, 2017.

Spary, E. C. *Eating the Enlightenment: Food and the Sciences in Paris*. U of Chicago P, 2012.

Von Hoffmann, Viktoria. *From Gluttony to Enlightenment: The World of Taste in Early Modern Europe*. U of Illinois, 2016.

CHAPTER 6

Madrid

Cuisine as Cultural Melting Pot

María del Carmen Simón Palmer, *Spanish National Research Council (CSIC)*

T HE STUDY OF a national cuisine involves a cultural perspective that should take into account the synergies created by different elements. These elements include environmental considerations such as the native production of certain foods, the centuries-old techniques used in specific geographic areas, as well as the people who turned cooking into a profession. This chapter attempts to show how different national cuisines blended in Madrid and the cultural and political circumstances that facilitated the adoption of other cuisines, particularly that of Italy, making Spain's capital an international melting pot.

The Cuisine of the Powerful

From the moment Madrid was proclaimed as Spain's capital in 1561, the monarchs were almost always served by foreigners. It was not until the Enlightenment, at the end of the eighteenth century, that the great chefs would become independent and create their own businesses to cater to an increasingly larger bourgeoisie.

The table of the monarchs of the House of Austria represented the empire's greatness and therefore had to imitate that of King Solomon. The table etiquette followed in the royal palace or Alcázar was Burgundian, and the names of the different food-related posts and departments (called "de boca") were German. Documents tell us that some cooks of King Felipe II were "Germans of Flanders," and the queens, who until the nineteenth century came from other countries, would always have an extraordinary influence on eating habits. Isabel de Valois's cook was a Frenchman, Valentín Hori, and in 1615 Charles de Villaneuve arrived as part of the retinue of Isabel de Borbón, wife of Felipe IV. From then on, France and Germany's influence alternated in the royal kitchen according to the queen consort's nationality. These cooks' economic conditions present a relationship that is directly inverse to that of their masters. During the years when the Spanish Court was the center of Europe and the royal table monopolized attention, the cooks lived in an unfortunate situation. Their written complaints about wage payment delays serve as proof of their troubles. In addition, they showed their surprise at the use of strange ingredients such as the "greens" in the salads of the German queens, or the queens' whim for having their own "pleasure cooks" that they brought with them from their own countries. Table dressing included damask or German tablecloths imported from Flanders until King Felipe V's reign at a very high cost because of the taxes required in the various countries they passed through en route to the Alcázar. Along with the consumption of local refreshments and wines, the wines preferred by the monarchs in the Golden Age were those of the Bordeaux, Rhine, and Champagne regions.[1]

The arrival of the Bourbons to the Spanish throne brought a profound change in kitchen management with the consequent anger of the Spanish palace staff, who felt marginalized before the so-called

"French family," as the servants Felipe V brought with him became known. This displeasure was shared by the queen's ladies, who showed it in the dinner celebrated in Figueras in September 1701, after the wedding of King Felipe V and Luisa Gabriela de Saboya. The Duke of Saint Simón relates how the dishes that were to be served in that banquet were in equal parts Spanish and French, something that displeased the Spanish ladies, who used different pretexts, including the heat of the dishes and the awkwardness in their delivery, to make sure that no French dish reached the table (222). Nevertheless, the command of the French cooks could not be stopped, greatly improving the functioning of the royal kitchen with quarterly contracts, work shifts, and secure retirement. They also established fixed prices for special dishes and became suppliers, which helped them to stop hurting financially. The menus were enriched with sauces and new products. The Abbe Alberoni confessed that in order to flatter Queen Isabel de Farnesio he brought her "succulent Italian sausages," as well as Parma wine and macaroni. Bologna sausage appeared among the desserts as often as did Parma ham, served on its own or with chicken or stuffed in bread. Caserta cheese and coffee were also brought from Italy at that time.

Contrary to what happened in France during the French Revolution, the cooks' guild in Spain never intervened in politics. However, in the nineteenth century, once King Fernando VII returned to Spain, those who had served under King José Bonaparte underwent a purge, since some of the cooks were found to have shown their loyalty to the dethroned monarch José Bonaparte "during the usurpation," as documents held in the Royal Palace archives attest. Pérez Galdós mentions in *La Corte de Carlos IV* that "the body of cooks followed the whole country in the path traced by the directors of the Fernandist party." Pérez Galdós stresses the patriotic attitude of "that handful of braves, whose pots were, so to speak, the palate of the kings of Spain, to some extent arbiters of their welfare, if not of their existence." Although many of them were old and peaceful servants, "they still followed the water seller Pedro Collado, spy of the monarch [. . .] in all the lower regions of the Palace" (*La Corte de Carlos IV* 274–75).

In the nineteenth century cooks were still employed exclusively in rich mansions because of their high fees. The cook was a luxury employee who had worked in the best European houses and pushed his resumé in order to be hired by the palace superintendent. Although he considered it an honor to be accepted, the cook set a number of conditions, including the amount of compensation in case of dismissal and the option of leaving his job if he did not agree with the internal functioning of the kitchen, as studied by Simón Palmer (*La cocina de Palacio*). Although his was still a very difficult job, it became simplified once the service *a la rusa / à la russe* (in Russian style), was introduced in Spain in the middle of the nineteenth century under Queen Isabel II's reign. Prince Kourakin, ambassador of Tsar Alexander I, brought this new dining model to France in 1809. After diners were seated at the table, the menu was read out loud, though later it became distributed in print form. The dishes were brought to the table sequentially, which significantly reduced their number, instead of being set at the table all at once as they had been before. Moneyed aristocracy, like blood aristocracy, competed in giving the best banquets, and some houses became famous for the generosity of their hosts, who threw the doors open to all their friends, as was the case of the Marquis of Salamanca.

The Cuisine of the Bourgeois

There exists an important terminological confusion when naming the different places dedicated to serving food, perpetuated in the *Diccionario de la Academia Española*, which does not adequately differentiate them. Whereas in the Golden Age there were *tabernas*, *hosterías*, *figones*, and *mesones*, in the Enlightenment the term *fonda* encompassed both a type of lodging that usually included food and eating establishments that only served food. In *Montes de Oca*, Pérez Galdós explains that in the 1840s, "The exotic word *restaurant* was not yet a common term in Spanish: we said '*fonda*' and 'eating in a *fonda*,' and *fondas* were lodgings with food and assistance, as well as dining rooms without board" (1).² Madrid's Archivo de la Villa holds the 1753 City Hall order (*Sobre limitación*) attempting to limit the number of *hosterías*, *bodegones*, and *figones*, which involved visits to these establishments and a survey that revealed there were twenty *bodegones*, four *hosterías*, and one *figón* in the whole capital. During the reign of King Fernando VI, the guild of *hosteleros*, heirs to the old *figoneros*, became organized, creating its own statutes, which were approved and published in 1758, in anticipation of what the *hosteleros* felt was going to be an invasion of professionals from other countries. The new regulations stipulated a check on the personal and professional background of those who aspired to open a business. They also required the candidate to pass an examination before the guild's delegates, during which he would make three different dishes: a dish made with dough, a roast, and a stew (Simón Palmer, "Evolución" 337).³

Out of concern over the news that arrived in 1792 of the French revolutionaries, Spanish authorities stipulated that it was necessary to obtain a license from the mayor's hall before opening a restaurant, a café, or any such business, following the legal compilation known as *Novísima Recopilación* (in Pacheco 383; book 3, title 19, law 27). A visit to the establishment was required in order to verify that it was clean, that its offices or premises were well constructed to avoid fires, and that they were stocked with cookware and pots that were not harmful to health. In those that were authorized, gambling, reading gazettes or other newsprint, and smoking were prohibited. Patrons were also required to avoid "dishonorable" conversations, including those relating to "government" matters and those against any citizen, for which the offenders would receive the corresponding punishment. The rooms of the establishment were to be used for serving food and drink to the public and should always be open to all, without allowing the use of hidden or interior rooms. In his *Manual de Madrid*, Mesonero Romanos notes that, in addition to inns, a multitude of grocery stores and *figones* serving meals and lunches to the less-affluent class "with all convenience" were scattered throughout Madrid. There were likewise many shops selling fortified wines or overseas goods, as well as famous patisseries and beautiful confectioner's shops located on every street, which allowed one to restore any lost strength: "In these stores you will find comfort, cleanliness, and good will from their owners" (64).

With the proliferation of eating establishments fell the reputation of chefs, and negative testimonies on the subject abound, including Larra's well-known article "La fonda nueva," in which he comments ironically about some of their "novelties": "They will then give us a soup they call 'herb soup,' which could not have a more allusive name; Italian-style cow stew, which is a new thing; roasted veal, which is an everyday thing; wine from the fountain; bruised olives; a fry of brains and mutton trotters, a chicken left over from yesterday, and some desserts that we will leave to be served tomorrow." Larra had eaten in fondas for three years and could not understand why it was not possible to eat for less than six or seven *duros*, a price that neither the badly decorated places nor the service or drinks could justify. There were continuous criticisms about the poor quality of low-priced meals in Madrid and about the apparent necessity to order à la carte expensive items like oysters from Ostende, wine from Grave, lobster, and boar's head, delicacies that could not be dispensed with when trying to treat a friend. The newspaper *La Iberia* blamed the government on August 7, 1860, "because it is the first to take its official guests to Lhardy." Dining rooms were choice places for political activity. In the nineteenth century many government representatives lived in fondas, and their dining rooms were their preferred meeting places. This led municipal authorities to tighten the conditions under which they would allow meetings during the revolutionary periods.

The Italian Initiative

Until the eighteenth century, heading the kitchens of the palace or those of a grandee of Spain was considered the height of a cook's professional career, but there came a time when professional cooks chose to become independent and autonomous. The political situation played a key role in this shift. The arrival to the throne of Spain of King Carlos III brought with it the cooks of nobles who returned to the court with the monarch, leading to the ascendance of Italian cuisine in Madrid, a change that until now has been little studied. As it had occurred in other cultural and social developments, there arose the paradox of an overwhelming French influence after the Spanish War of Independence and a diminished Italian influence, which resurfaced in a more discreet way toward the end of the century. The triumph of the new current coincided with King Fernando VII's death and Queen Regent María Cristina de Borbón's rise to power. At that time there were also many outsiders, a fraction of them foreigners, who would play an essential role. The liberals returning from England and France occupied positions of maximum importance in politics and culture, and they naturally took into account the new developments taking place outside Spain, with which they had become very familiar. A survey of the Spanish press of the period allows for a study of Parisian restaurants through the detailed descriptions given by Spanish authors, dazzled by their quality and attesting to their having dined there. At the same time, authors like Mesonero Romanos in "Las costumbres de Madrid," included in his *Escenas y tipos matritenses*, ridiculed those foreigners, especially the French, who came to court and only visited the establishments of their fellow countrymen: "Getting up, for example, the next day, and after having had forty-eight columns of newspaper print arrived by mail for breakfast, he goes through the shortest route to *Mr. Monie's* house to take a bath; then to lunch *chez Genieys*; then to the *Petibon* hall, or to *Rouget's* shop; from there to the embassy" (2). Foreign-run businesses that facilitated sociability were of great importance for culinary developments as well as social life. In *Montes de Oca*, Pérez Galdós acknowledged the innovations introduced by Italians, including good service manners and cleanliness, as well as the written list of dishes on offer that substituted for the list that had previously been merely recited by the waiter, "headed by *ordubres*, strange version of the term *hors d'œuvre*" (4). The merit of fixing the price of twelve *reales* for a series of dishes stands out: "with that they adapted to the national poverty and secured a public made up almost entirely of employees and soldiers with petty salaries, of penniless rake, or of families that began to like the vanity of eating out on important or celebratory days" (4).

The first consequence of the 1758 implementation of professional regulations for cooks was union members' reaction to the attempt by two Italians to settle in the city capital without complying with union rules. The requests presented in 1760 by José Barberán to open an establishment in the Carrera de San Jerónimo and by Antonio and José Gippini to be authorized in a location close to the Church of San Sebastián were welcomed by the Board of Mayors of House and Court, but the leaders of the Guild of Figoneros protested angrily, arguing that there was no need to create new establishments whose owners, in addition, had not even passed the examinations and tests that were required for nationals. Their claims were heard, and the Italians had to present proof of their professional experience as cooks and as heads of establishments that both provided lodging for distinguished gentlemen and had a café and restaurant open to the public. They tried to improve the existing offerings, and in a short time they managed to place themselves on par with the best, and in both cases they passed into Spain's literary and political history. Furthermore, as managers, they created the first family-owned hospitality companies that drove the modernization of Spanish cuisine.

LA FONTANA DE ORO

In 1760, José Cilio and José Barberán signed the deed that transferred to José Barberán the Gentlemen Inn House (Casa Posada de Caballeros), known as La Fontana de Oro when owned by Cilio (*Licencia* fol. 360). The house was in Carrera de San Jerónimo, on the corner of Calle del Baño. On April 15 of that same year the newspaper *Diario Noticioso* announced that the owner was opening a boarding house with a set menu (*mesa redonda*) at the Real Sitio de Aranjuez. Madrid's main hoteliers would follow suit in Aranjuez and in other royal sites to attend to the courtiers who followed the monarchs when on holiday. The Hoteliers' Guild required Barberán to take the necessary steps to obtain a legal permit and to explain the reason for leaving his homeland, the city of Verona in the Republic of Venice. After certifying, with the help of three witnesses, his legal status, his not having any contagious disease, and his arriving at the court with the only purpose of earning a living, Barberán passed the corresponding examination by cooking the three required dishes. The Guild's tribunal considered him "skillful and competent for the practice and exercise of Master Hotelier, having executed them with the requisite cleanliness and ease" (*Licencia* fol. 360). He obtained the license for his establishment on August 1, 1760. There, he offered two set-menu tables, one set at ten *reales* and the other at five *reales*, not including the wine. Those dining at the latter table had to arrive at half past twelve every day wearing a wig. They ate soup, an abundant *cocido*,[4] an entrée, and seasonal desserts. Very soon his reputation as an excellent cook spread and attracted a lot of visitors to his restaurant. In 1762, the Gippini family, who owned the Fonda de San Sebastián, bought La Fontana de Oro from José Barberán. When discussing the restaurants of his time, Larra pointed out that La Fontana de Oro was a model establishment in the first years of its operation. However, in his similarly named work *La Fontana de Oro* (1870), Pérez Galdós describes the place in unflattering terms: small, asymmetrical, low, with exposed beams and decorated with terrible taste (20–26).

Upon the arrival of the Constitutional Triennium in 1820, the café became the main meeting place for the most exalted young liberal politicians. Numerous writers have left descriptions and accounts of the public sessions held there. In *La Fontana de Oro*, Galdós explains that the café had two sections: one that functioned as a café and another that was used for political purposes and which formed an angle. In the latter section, during the early years the speaker would climb up on a table and make his speech, but the audience was so large that a platform for the speaker was built and benches were placed. Among those who attended the sessions were young people who had participated in the making of the Constitution of 1812, while other attendees had grown up during the first absolutist years of Fernando VII and were opposed to a conservative regime.

La Fontana de Oro and La Cruz de Malta were the two cafés that were preferred by Masonic lodge members to celebrate their meetings. The Patriotic Society of La Fontana de Oro moved to the first floor in order to avoid confrontations, but they were so raucous that they would drive away the clientele, even though the owner "was looking for a balance between patriotism and business," according to Galdós. The uproar reached its maximum during the banquet held in honor of General Riego's triumph. One of those who went up to the stand was Antonio Alcalá Galiano, who in his memoirs acknowledged his youthful exaltation: "the toasts were frequent; we sang, we shouted, and with the heat of the strong drink, that of the room and of our enthusiasm, the heads were several notches above their natural seat" (338). Such atmosphere was increasingly worrying to the authorities, and on December 27, 1819, the Marquis of Cerralbo commanded that on the columns of the cafés La Fontana de Oro and Café de Malta an order be posted demanding the release of the names of those who were scheduled to speak on any given day. The order was copied by the Marquis of Miraflores in his *Apuntes*: "Those individuals who want to meet periodically in a public place to discuss political matters and to cooperate in their reciprocal education may do so with prior knowledge of the local superior authority, which shall be responsible for any abuses and shall take the measures it deems appropriate, not excluding the suppression of meetings" (81). In 1821, Juan Antonio Gippini, owner of the café La Fontana de Oro, was arrested and held in solitary confinement in Madrid's prison by order of the political chief. Charges were brought against him that would later be published because he failed to follow orders. His social influence was clear when the next day he was released on bail and, even further, when the prosecutor saw no reason to hold a trial, and the judge, Ángel Fernández de los Ríos, gave a warning to those who had arrested him. Thus, Gippini complained of an "attack against his individual freedom and arbitrary detention." After the Trienio Liberal (Liberal Triennium), with the persecution brought on by the second absolutist period, these activities ended, and La Fontana de Oro had to devote itself to music and dances to attract customers. The establishment fell into decline, and it only managed to come back to life when the French Monier bought it and remodeled it.

LA FONDA DE SAN SEBASTIÁN

On June 8, 1765, brothers Juan Antonio and José María Gippini, natives of Milan, went to the governor of the Consejo de Castilla (Council of Castile) because they intended to establish "a *hostería* in this city, similar to those of Italy, with the same characteristics and with the same title as those already in existence in Barcelona, Cádiz, Puerto de Santa María, and Seville; where many people might be served, in tables d'hôte with a set menu for boarders (*mesas redondas*) and in tables for other clients" (*Solicitud* fols. 607–17). They argued that La Fontana de Oro was the only one in existence, and it was not enough, especially when holding special functions. They had rented a house on Calle Atocha, in front of the Church of San Sebastián, belonging to the Prince of Las Torres. On July 5, 1765, the Gippini brothers declared themselves ready to be included in the guild of hoteliers and to pay as members the three hundred *reales* that would allow them to work. They also attempted to justify the fact that their establishment did not keep the required distance from another nearby. They believed that it was not plausible that the "distinguished people" who were bound to go to their place might instead go to the other *hosterías*, and they highlighted the importance of having a plentiful supply of food: "for it would be advisable to have enough food in view of the next royal functions" (*Solicitud* fols. 607–17). The representatives of the Guild insisted on their passing the exam regardless of how much experience they had, "which did not mean they wanted to expel them," although they recognized that in the case of the Gippini brothers, "their thirst seems insatiable, being unable to care for or be present in all their fondas and having the intention of taking the money out of the country and they already having a house next to the Church of San Sebastián" (*Causa*). As recorded in the Archivo Histórico, Juan Gippini bore the title of "master of hospitality" in 1767 and assured that his house was the most accredited in the city. In addition to being a center of meeting and lodging, fondas like Gippini's could house commercial transactions: On December 3, 1798, the *Diario de Avisos* announced the sale of two violins, an Amatus and a Stradivarius, by Juan José Gippini.

La Fonda de San Sebastián is remembered in Spanish literary history for having been the location of a famous gathering attended by prominent Italian and Spanish writers. The playwright Leandro Fernández de Moratín gave an account of these meetings, their participants, and the topics they discussed in the life of his father Don Nicolás (*Vida de don Nicolás Fernández de Moratín*, 1846). There were Italian participants like Gippini, owner of the fonda, as well as some friends of his, including a doctor, Mariano Pizzi, and the Neapolitan Pedro Napoli Signorelli, author of a valuable *Historia crítica de los teatros*. Among the Spanish attending were the authors Moratín, Ayala, Cadalso, Iriarte, and others. What he might not have fully gathered at the time was the transcendental importance that such interaction had for the mutual knowledge of both literatures, Spanish and Italian. Without making it explicit, Leandro Fernández de Moratín set one of his most famous comedies, *La Comedia Nueva*, or *El Café*, in this fonda. After this period La Fonda de San Sebastián would not rise to notoriety again, surviving only as a café until the mid-twentieth century, with some mentions in Galdós' *Un faccioso más y algunos frailes menos* and *La Primera República*, as a meeting place for some politicians. On January 8, 1892, Dr. Thebussem stated in an article in *La Ilustración Española y Americana* that a member of the Gippini family left with Count d'Artois when the latter returned to France and came to be his *Maître d'Hotel Confiseur* when the count became Charles X.

LA CRUZ DE MALTA

In 1763, the Posada de los Caballeros de Malta was situated on Calle Silva, with the sign of the Grand Cross of Malta on its portal. On December 9, 1771, the *Diario Noticioso* announced its transfer to Calle Alcalá 6. Its owner, Pedro Visoni, served "with all tidiness, promptness, and cleanliness" meals made "for anyone" and had coffee rooms with all sorts of beverages and liqueurs. In 1801, King Carlos IV bought this and other neighboring houses, situated in the area where part of the Ministry of Education stands today, and the fonda was moved to Calle Caballero de Gracia, where its name became La Cruz de Malta. Like La Fontana de Oro, it became the center of patriotic societies during the liberal period and, like Gippini, its owner is cited in 1822, in the Royal Court (Audiencia) accusing it, along with others, of "infringement of law and edict on public meetings and gatherings on the nights of December 17 to 30, 1820," as published in the *Diario de Madrid* on July 24, 1822. Mesonero Romanos provides a description of such meetings during the Liberal Triennium in his *Memorias de un setentón*:

> Another meeting took place in the fonda-café of the Great Cross of Malta, on Calle Caballero de Gracia, next to the Oratory, but this retained rather its former character as a musical café (*café cantante*), with the exception that in between the programmed duos and cavatinas, readings of patriotic verses were now improvised. From the tribune, they delivered harangues that were quite scabrous, and among raptures and toasts, vows and oaths from all members of the lively crowd, concluded the whole by intoning Riego's Anthem (*Himno de Riego*). (233)

La Cruz de Malta regularly hosted wealthy liberal guests and exalted youth and adolescents, as cafés in truth were vehicles for the transmission of the political ideas of patriotic societies such as *Landaburiana*, which was banned in 1823. On September 9, 1824, the *Diario de Madrid* announced that La Cruz de Malta had hired one of the best French cooks and that it offered a menu as well as meals by special order. While La Fontana de Oro had been bought by the French Monier, La Cruz de Malta ended up in the hands of Genyeis, another famous French businessman. Paradoxically, after King Fernando VII's death and Queen Regent María Cristina de Borbón's acendency, French influence prevailed while Italian influence slowly decreased.

A PARENTHESIS: PEROTE AND LOPRESTI'S FONDA ESPAÑOLA

The so-called "Fonda Española" of the Italians Perote and Lopresti became famous through Benito Pérez Galdós' depiction in *Montes de Oca*, where one of the characters, Don José del Milagro, is presented as a regular customer. The Fonda Española was located in front of the Basilios Convent on Calle Desengaño and is first documented in 1850, later than the events described in Galdós' work. At that time, the Fonda Española was catering the buffet of the Liceo Matritense during its masquerade balls. Galdós situates the Fonda Española in Calle Abada in a gloomy space with the odor and signs of a Masonic lodge: "a low floor with two gratings on the street side and entrance through the building's main door. The building's entrance was wide, with a baseboard of black and white tiles like a chessboard, well-lit at night by a two-light lantern, but dark late at night, raising the risk of stumbles, which were sometimes serious" (3).

The Fonda Española followed the French schedule, "serving the main meal at night, but omitting the *cocido* from the menu. Mid-day, they served six- and eight-*real* lunches, with fried eggs and one or two dishes, and the invariable dessert of raisins and almonds with the addition of a bun from the bakery" (6). As for its specialties, Galdós highlights the Valencian and Milanese rice dishes, the cod in red sauce, the lamb with peas, the red sea bream cooked Madrid style, the Italian macaroni, the *pepitoria* (chicken in an egg-yolk sauce), and especially the coarse stews (*guisotes*) of fish and seafood cooked Provençal or Genovese style. The wines were suited "to the clientele's modest means and were limited to the reds of Arganda or Valdepeñas, and to a familiar and inexpensive sherry for the Sunday libertines and for those revelers who went out late at night with or without women" (5). The water was advertised as being from the Fuente del Berro,[5] but it was actually brought from the lesser-quality fountains of Academia or Escalinata. Galdós praises Lopresti for popularizing such delicacies, "putting them within the reach of those with scarce means, proving their knowledge of their profession, as well as the paternal equity of their prices" (5).

Eusebio Blasco tells that, in 1853, on the day of the premiere of the zarzuela *La Estrella de Madrid*, its authors, the musician Arrieta and his friend Ayala, wanting to assuage their fear of failure, went out to eat at "Perona's famous fonda, whence they came out very ready to face any setbacks" (182). The last news about Fonda Española dates from March 29, 1875. On that day, Pedro González de Velasco, a doctor and anthropologist and founder of the Museum of Anthropology, offered a dinner for more than fifty journalists in the Fonda Española at seven in the evening to celebrate King Alfonso XII's inauguration of the museum. The next day the press remarked on the elegant table, "set with the taste that this justly accredited establishment always displays," as published on March 31, 1875, in *El Genio Médico-Quirúrgico*.

However, a new kind of eating establishment was rapidly making its appearance. Within the space of a few years, the new *hoteles*, bearing such names as *France, París, Campos Elíseos, Rusia, Inglés*, etc., became preeminent thanks to their gastronomic offerings. The geographic allusions of their names might invite the assumption that there was a strong influx of foreign nationals. However, there is no evidence that any of the above *hoteles* had a foreign owner, and the phenomenon can be considered a passing fad. Italians did continue to have a strong presence in Madrid's gastronomic landscape. They were now grouped in companies that were not exclusively family owned. They founded and managed some of the main *hoteles* in the center of the capital, placing them on par with those of other European countries. In their restaurants they welcomed national and foreign aristocrats, politicians, artists, and intellectuals.

HOTEL DE LAS CUATRO NACIONES

The site of the Hotel de Las Cuatro Naciones, located on Calle del Arenal numbers nineteen to twenty-three, belonged to *La Peninsular* Insurance Society (Sociedad de Seguros Mutuos *La Peninsular*). Its general director, the lawyer José Indalecio Caso, signed the lease agreement with Juan Bautista Borella (*Escritura de mobiliario* fol. 2537), a professional fonda manager, or *fondista*, on December 31, 1872. The hotel had been operating on that site since February of that year. Borella acted on behalf of several people, including his brothers José, Pedro, and Luis, who had fondas and pastry shops of their own, the fondistas Durio y Durio, born in Civiasco, located in the Italian Province of Novara, and the only Spaniard, José Mejorada González, a real-estate owner. The lease was for four years with the option to extend it by mutual agreement, as was done until 1892. On January 14, 1873, the newspaper *La Iberia* gave an account of the copious lunch offered by the owner of the "sumptuous" Hotel de Las Cuatro Naciones to several journalists of various political ideals, in spite of which "cordiality and friendship prevailed." Much like the Gippini family, the Borellas were an Italian saga of fondistas who had begun as cooks and had with time become hotel owners. A long time before, they had first settled in Barcelona and later in Zaragoza.

The Hotel de las Cuatro Naciones went down in literary history thanks to Ecuadorian author Juan Montalvo, who opposed General Veintemilla's dictatorship. In *Catilinaria: Sexta*, Montalvo provided a satire of Veintemilla when the politician fled to Europe and arrived in Madrid. Veintemilla was lodged in the Hotel de las Cuatro Naciones, where he also dined, boasting of his wealth, only to end up asking Borella for money and leaving without returning the two thousand *duros* he owed. Montalvo puts the following words in Borella's mouth: "You would not believe how that rogue stole from me: food; wines charged to his account; cognac charged to his account; cigars charged to his account. Even what I asked him to pay in silver he would add to that list of more than two thousand *pesos*. That is what he is, a thief: you were wrong to listen to him" (18). And he concludes: "He acted as though he owned the pastry shop, the cellars, and even the drawers and chests belonging to the owner of the Hotel de las Cuatro Naciones" (19). Years later, in his *Autobiografía*, Rubén Darío, an admirer of Montalvo, acknowledged the double celebrity of the Hotel de las Cuatro Naciones, first because of its excellent cooks, whom he compares to the mythical Vatel, "although they are incapable of culinary suicide," and second and most particularly because of its renown among literary enthusiasts. As Darío points out, one of Montalvo's most terrible attacks on the "stricken" former president of Ecuador Ignacio de Veintemilla occurred in this hotel. During the summer of 1892, Rubén Darío stayed at the Hotel de las Cuatro Naciones, where also lived "for fifteen years, more or less, in a modest apartment, the prestigious encyclopedic man, the ever-young wise man, the Catholic, the academic, the most remarkable Marcelino Menéndez y Pelayo" (115). In *Un viaje a Madrid*, Leopoldo Alas (Clarín) muses on Menéndez y Pelayo's choice of this hotel. According to Clarín, Menéndez Pelayo must have arrived at the Estación del Norte train station absorbed in his thoughts and allowed the first porter he found to take him to the Hotel de las Cuatro Naciones, where he stayed. Clarín describes the dining room, which was on the ground floor, almost on the street: "carts roll by just a few steps away with a horrendous din, making the windows tremble; the street vendors shout without restraint, the children cause a racket, hawking newspapers, the din is as if you were in the middle of Calle del Arenal" (23). In such an environment and with the door of the street a meter away from his back, without feeling the cold that came in:

> Marcelino Menéndez Pelayo eats lunch in a hurry, and at the same time reads a new book with untrimmed edges, which he trims with a knife. Entering and leaving are French, Italian, and German commission agents, a main element in this fonda; some candidates (as it could not be otherwise) for representatives to the Cortes; and in the middle of the confusion and noise, he studies and meditates like an ascetic in the *Thebaid*. Occasionally he raises his eyes, takes a pause

from his reading and eating in order to swallow a bite and digest an idea; he smiles, but not at the English commissioner facing him, but rather at the thoughts that are boiling in his brain. (23–24)

Clarín assures that he studied not only while eating but also while sleeping. Finally, on May 22, 1892, Juan Bautista Borella transferred or subleased the buildings and sold all the stock and furniture to his former partners, Pedro and Luis Durio y Durio, reserving some rooms for himself and his family.

HOTEL DE ROMA

On November 1, 1881, the newspaper *El Imparcial* announced the opening of the new Hotel de Roma located on Calle Caballero de Gracia, as well as the banquet offered by its owners in honor of the press. It was not until 1884 that the document establishing it as a business was signed to the name of Yotti and Company (*Escritura para la explotación* fol. 635), which included the Italian Félix Yotti, a fondista, and some Spaniards. Members of various diplomatic corps, particularly those from Latin American countries, liked to frequent the restaurant. In its dining room important banquets were celebrated, like the one given by the faculty of medicine in honor of Ramón y Cajal when he was invited by the Royal Society of Sciences of London to give the opening speech at the beginning of a new academic year, as described in the newspaper *El Liberal* on April 1, 1894. According to another newspaper, *El Día*, on March 31, 1894, Madrid councilmen treated the minister of the interior, the governor, and the mayor of Madrid to a banquet in the restaurant in order "to show that their infighting had been put to an end."

HOTEL DE PARÍS

After the demolition of the Church of Buen Suceso in the Puerta del Sol, speculation soon began about the site's fate. On December 5, 1863, the newspaper *La Época* clarified that the new house that was being built had not been leased to any company. Rather, it had been leased to the Fallola brothers to set up a fonda called Gran Hotel de París, which would occupy the mezzanine and all four floors of the house; it remained in the hands of the brothers until its sale in 1895 to the Baena company. The hotel had its entrance on Calle Alcalá 2, and on its second floor there was a large dining room that became famous for its French cuisine. Much like the Gippini and the Borella clans had done before, the Fallola brothers created branches of their hotel in Seville, Cádiz, and Córdoba, where it was called Hotel Suisse. The Fallolas were also in charge of managing the large buildings destined to be fondas and lodgings in Alhama de Aragón. In the newspaper advertisements they published in both Spanish and French, they stated that they could compete with the best establishments from abroad because of the good organization of the building, their cuisine, a fixed-menu service at five in the afternoon, special services, good treatment, and even their fair prices. According to an article in the newspaper *La Iberia* published on May 27, 1866, the eldest son of the owner of the Gran Fonda de París, José Fallola, Italian by birth, "full of holy enthusiasm for the unity of his country," had left for Italy with the aim of enlisting in Garibaldi's battalions. Years later, this young man, César Fallola, married the daughter of a Spanish senator.

The Fallola brothers were considered important members of Madrid society at the time, as well as well-known businessmen and collectors of art and trinkets. In 1878, José Fallola, owner and director of the Hotel de París, donated a sixteenth-century earthen jar in Mudéjar style to the Archeological Museum, which selected this piece for exhibition in the Spanish pavilion at the Exposition Universelle in Paris, according to an article published in *La Revista de Archivos, Bibliotecas y Museos* on July 5, 1878. In 1876, a royal order authorized Federico Fallola to build a tram line on the public road that went from Madrid to the royal site of El Pardo. In that same year he built a second line to the area of La Florida, where he had a restaurant and a dairy. According to an article published in the *Gaceta de los caminos de hierro* on May 7, 1876, in previous years Federico Fallola had acquired shares in the company dedicated to the extraction and sale of snow from Guadarrama (Compañía de los neveros del Guadarrama). In 1880, together with the count of Locatelli, he requested a license to set up a public grain market in Las Vistillas. Thus, Federico became a full-time businessman and left the management of the hotel to José. For this reason, by 1883 the hotel is listed as belonging to Fallola and Company.

On January 21, 1887, José Fallola y Ricci passed away, after having been awarded the honors Encomienda de Carlos III and the Encomienda de Isabel la Católica. The notice published by the newspaper *El Liberal* on January 25 lists the names of Fallola y Ricci's family members and those of his Hotel de París business partners, as well as his address in the hotel and the details of his funeral in the Sacramental of San Isidro. On February 26, 1887, two months after his death, the newspaper *El Pabellón Nacional* announced the Hotel de París as property of Fallola, Baena, and Company. On February 28, 1897, a decade after Fallola's death, the hotel was owned solely by Baena and Company. The hotel's gastronomic excellence continued under the new ownership after Fallola's death, including the owners' annual tradition of treating their numerous guests to a splendid banquet. The newspaper *La Iberia* published the French menu of the banquet served on January 2, 1888: "Buitres de Santogne. -Consommé Princesse. -Rissoles á la Montobant. -Saumon a la Chambord. -Filets de boeuf á la Rossini. -Foiegras á la Belle-vue. -Punch au Champagne. -Cépes sautés a la bordelaise. -Dindonneaux flanquées de bécasses. -Roull-Pudding. -Glace Walewsky." Many notable people met in the restaurant over the years, from the extraordinary envoy of the emperor of Japan, who arrived in 1876 to meet with King Alfonso XII, to authors, artists, and politicians such as Pío Baroja, Zuloaga, Anglada Camarasa, Anatole France, and the Maharaja of Kapurthala.

Toward the beginning of the twentieth century things changed dramatically in Madrid. The big hotels like the Ritz or the Palace that started to appear were no longer family initiatives but branches of large international companies with powerful Spanish shareholders, including the royal family. The first chef of the Ritz was the Spanish Félix Ruiz del Castillo, trained in France and England. The famous cook and author Teodoro Bardají also worked there, and his cookbook *La cocina de Ellas* was financed by the hotel. In 1912, two years after the opening of the Ritz, the Palace Hotel opened its doors on the other side of the Plaza de Neptuno, and the style of its grill room and its restaurant, with capacity for two thousand people, was now English. Spaniards like Ignacio Domenech, Bardají, Serra, and many others broadened their cultural training, created professional magazines and schools, and trained with great kitchen masters. A new wave of change had once again been set in motion.

NOTES

Translated by Ana M. Gómez-Bravo and Matthew Kullberg.

1. See Simón Palmer, *La cocina de Palacio*.
2. In the inns, in addition to admitting guests, meals were served from ten *reales* per place setting. The hostels were smaller and cheaper restaurants, where meals were on offer from six *reales*.
3. On the changing status of professional cooks, see also Simón Palmer, "El estatuto del cocinero."
4. Cocido is a brothy stew made with a variety of fresh and cured meats, chickpeas, and vegetables served in three stages, or *vuelcos*: a soup made with broth and fine noodles, or *fideos*; a vegetable and chickpea platter; and a meat platter.
5. Fuente del Berro was the water that the monarchs drank daily in the palace since the date it was purchased by King Felipe IV.

WORKS CITED

Alas, Leopoldo (Clarín). *Folletos literarios: Un viaje a Madrid*. Madrid, Librería de Fernando Fé, 1886.
Alcalá Galiano, Antonio. *Memorias: Recuerdos de un anciano*. Madrid, Librería Viuda de Hernando y Compañía, 1890.
Bardají, Teodoro. *La cocina de Ellas*. La Val de Onsera, 2002.

Blasco, Eusebio. *Mis contemporáneos*. Librería Editorial Leopoldo Martínez, 1905.
Causa formada contra Don Juan Antonio Gippini, dueño del café de la Fontana de Oro. Madrid, Imprenta de R. Aguado, 1821.
Darío, Rubén. *Autobiografía*. Casa Editorial Maucci, 1915.
Escritura para la explotación de un hotel por la Sociedad Yotti y Compañía. 1884. Archivo Histórico de Protocolos. Tomo 35309.
Escritura de mobiliario y subarriendo a D. Juan Bautista Borella. 1872. Archivo Histórico de Protocolos. Tomo 31422.
Fernández de Moratín, Leandro. *La Comedia Nueva; El sí De Las niñas*. Crítica, 1994.
———. *Vida de don Nicolás Fernández de Moratín*. Madrid, Rivadeneyra, 1846.
Larra, Mariano José de. "La fonda nueva." Madrid, *La Revista Española*, 23 Aug. 1833.
Licencia concedida a don José Barberán como maestro hostelero para abrir el local de la Fontana de Oro-1760. Archivo Histórico Nacional. Consejos, Libro 1347-E.
Mesonero Romanos, Ramón de. "Las costumbres de Madrid." *Escenas y tipos matritenses*. Madrid, Imprenta y Litografía de Gaspar Roig, 1851.
———. *Manual de Madrid*. Madrid, Imprenta de D. M. de Burgos, 1831.
———. *Memorias de un setentón, natural y vecino de Madrid*. Renacimiento, 1926.
Miraflores, Marqués de. *Apuntes histórico-críticos para escribir la historia de la revolución en España*. London, Ricardo Taylor, 1834.
Montalvo, Juan. *Catilinarias: Sexta*. Panamá, Imprenta La Estrella de Panamá, 1881.
Pacheco, Joaquín Francisco, et al. *Los Códigos españoles Concordados y Anotados*, vol. 7: *Novísima Recopilación de las Leyes de España*, Madrid, Rivadeneyra, 1850.
Pérez Galdós, Benito. *La Corte de Carlos IV*. Crítica, 1995.
———. *Un faccioso más y algunos frailes menos. Episodios Nacionales*, vol. 5, Fundación José Antonio De Castro, 2006.
———. *La Fontana de Oro*. Madrid, La Guirnalda, 1870.
———. *Montes de Oca: Episodio Nacional. Obras*. Madrid, Est. Tip. de la Viuda e Hijos de Tello, 1900.
———. *La Primera república*. Alianza Editorial, 1980.
Saint Simon, Duc de. *Memoires completes et authentiques du Duc de Saint Simon*, vol 3, Paris, Hachette, 1856.
Simón Palmer, María del Carmen. *La cocina de Palacio 1561–932*. Castalia, 1997.
———. "El estatuto del cocinero: Su evolución en el tiempo." *Food & History*, vol. 4, 2006, pp. 255–76.

———. "Evolución de la profesión de cocinero: Del primer estatuto a la primera exposición culinaria en Madrid (1758–1921)." *Anales del Instituto de Estudios Madrileños*, vol. 51, 2011, pp. 337–58.

Sobre limitación de hosterías, bodegones, figones, juegos de trucos y de bochas. 1753. Archivo de Villa. Secretaria. 2-244-6.

Solicitud de Juan Antonio Gippini para ser incluido en el Gremio de Hosteleros. Archivo Histórico Nacional. Sala de Alcaldes, libro de Gobierno de 1768.

CHAPTER 7

Beyond the Recipes
Authorship, Text, and Context in Canonical Spanish Cookbooks

María Paz Moreno, *University of Cincinnati*

WHAT, REALLY, IS a cookbook? Is it a text composed with merely a practical purpose, or does it allow, as any other text, for a variety of interpretations and can therefore serve more than one purpose? What is the author's motivation for producing it? Do cookbook authors have a style that is unique to each of them, a personal voice? Several critics have explored these questions, looking into issues of discourse, gender, race, or power and addressing the kinds of inquiries that are commonplace when analyzing traditional literary works. A pioneer at proposing new ways of looking at recipe books, Susan Leonardi argued in her 1989 article "Recipes for Reading: Summer Pasta, Lobster à la Riseholme, and Key Lime Pie" that a recipe is a form of text and should therefore be studied as such within its context. For this critic, a recipe is "an embedded discourse, and like other embedded discourses, it can have a variety of relationships with its frame, or its bed," relationships that are key to understanding "the significance of this discourse as a narrative strategy" (340). It is this dialogue between the recipe, the cookbook, their context, and the role of the author as narrator that constitutes the focus of this article, which looks at several canonical Spanish culinary texts to better understand the relationship between the authorial voice and the genre of the cookbook within the Spanish context in particular.

A number of valuable studies have followed Leonardi and delved into the complexity and rich potential of analyzing cookbooks, providing readings that illuminate them from a number of perspectives. Studies such as *Eat My Words: Reading Women's Lives Through the Cookbooks They Wrote* by Janet Theophano have been seminal to helping us understand issues of authorship and autobiography in many of these texts. *The Recipe Reader*, edited by Janet Floyd and Laurel Forster is another work of reference, collecting a number of essays on recipe interpretation using contemporary critical tools, seeking to "demonstrate the multiple ways in which the recipe illuminates the cultural worlds in which it appears, and constitutes a textual form worthy of study in its own right" (1). In the area of Spanish culinary literature, Lara Anderson's valuable analytical approach, problematizing the idea of nation building through the ideology embedded in Spanish cookbooks, is worthy of mention. The work of Carolyn Nadeau has also pointed Spanish Golden Age literary studies in interesting new directions.

In *De la página al plato: El libro de cocina en España* (2012), I proposed reading "between the lines" of both canonical and non-canonical, published and unpublished Spanish cookbooks in order to unlock alternative readings and meanings by considering issues of author identity and purpose, gender, and class, as well as contextual and socio-historical aspects. The idea that *a cookbook is more than a cookbook* is a powerful premise. It allows us to look at these books as a specific genre with its own formulas and purposes, ranging from the autobiographical to the ideological, which can be important sources of historical information. The following pages are a development of those ideas, where I present several texts to offer a critical reading focusing on issues of authorship and context. For this essay I have chosen four specific cookery books, dating from the seventeenth century to the mid-twentieth century, for their relevance as representative of the issues mentioned earlier: Francisco Martínez Montiño's *Arte de cocina, pastelería, vizcochería y conservería* (1611), Juan de Altamiras's *Nuevo arte de cocina* (1745), María Mestayer de Echagüe's *La cocina completa* (1940), and Ignasi Doménech's *Cocina de recursos: Deseo mi comida* (1941). All of these cookbooks and the cuisine they portray are profoundly tied to their historical and social contexts. Their authors show a strong sense of authorship and pride for their work, and they are great examples of the cookbook author's role and the concept of authorship in culinary works. A detailed look at these texts, spanning from the seventeenth to the twentieth centuries, can provide us with valuable insights into the role played by food and cooking in Spanish society throughout several centuries: Martínez Montiño's book portrays the food of the royalty and the nobility during a time of power and influence for the Spanish crown, while Altamiras's presents the more modest food of commoners and religious orders. In contrast, the 1940 book by Mestayer de Echagüe is a great example of early twentieth century Spanish cuisine, written by not only one of the few female authors in the history of Spanish cuisine but also one of the most prominent. Finally, Doménech's cookbook is an exceptional document of the Spanish Civil War's impact on the everyday lives and diets of regular citizens. Other cookbooks will also be mentioned here for comparison of reference, although not analyzed in depth, given the scope of this study. As Carolyn Nadeau points out, "when studied as a genre, cultural values emerge through the patterns of foodstuffs, cooking methods, and presentations that recur. [. . .] there is no one fixed meaning in cookbooks" (3). The idea that cookbooks are texts, and as such are open to interpretation, is the basis of my analysis. The readings provided here illustrate the richness of interpretation that this genre allows.

Cookbooks and Authorial Voice

As Janet Theophano has argued, an individual cookbook "is not only the creation of one person but a social context from which a singular voice emerges" (116). Theophano considers these texts "celebrations of identity," since they are depositories of cultural identity, they preserve the author's identity and their relationships with others in their social circle, and they tell us what was eaten at the time in which they were written (8). This is certainly true in the case of the books chosen for this study, where the author's voice comes through loud and clear, making these texts not only instruction manuals about how to cook but also texts that tell us a great deal about the authors' motivation, purpose, and circumstances. Authorial pride is one of the elements that all cookbooks presented here have in common.

The *Arte de cocina, pastelería, vizcochería y conservería*, published by Francisco Martínez Montiño in 1611, is a major canonical text of Spanish culinary literature, since it constitutes a prime example of the type of cuisine the European royalty enjoyed during the seventeenth century. Martínez Montiño worked as a cook at the court of King Felipe III, and over the years he became very prominent at the Spanish court. His book was influential at the time and became a primary reference work for several centuries of cooks. It was reedited many times during the seventeenth, eighteenth, and nineteenth centuries. The prologue shows the author's awareness of both the symbolic and the concrete benefits that could potentially result from choosing cooking as a profession. Access to power circles and the opportunity to gain the confidence of the monarchs and the nobility were very important intangible benefits, and Montiño wrote his book to help and educate those who wished to become cooks for the elite. To that effect, his prologue emphasizes the possibilities for a successful career for those who followed his example and teachings. The motivation behind putting his knowledge in writing is explained in detail in the opening pages of the *Arte de cocina*:

There are no books by which those who serve the kitchen can turn to for guidance, and everything is entrusted to memory [...]. And what has encouraged me to write is to have served so many years to His Majesty the King and to have been charged with the greatest things my art can produce, which have been offered in the royal palace, to the satisfaction of my chiefs; and because I am very inclined to teach, and great officials have developed under my tutelage. (qtd. in Moreno, *Madrid* 108)[1]

This prologue provides us with valuable information about the author's reasons for producing his book. First, he states the need for such a work, since there were no other reference manuals for those seeking guidance in the craft of cooking. Martínez Montiño also mentions—without specifics—"another book" recently published, which he despises, criticizing it for being a copy of others and full of erroneous information. He is referring to Diego Granado's *Libro del arte de cocina*, a work published in 1599 that contained a large number of recipes, many of which seemed blatantly copied from several sources. Montiño attacks Granado and his book in very harsh terms, accusing it of being "so flawed that whoever uses it will be ruined. It is composed by an official that hardly anyone at this Court knows" and stating of the recipes, "not only are they not good, not should they be made, but furthermore it was impertinent to write them at all" (qtd. in Moreno, *Madrid* 107). In Pierre Bordieu's terms, this could be viewed as a fight for *symbolic capital*, an idea that Peter Naccarato and Kathleen LeBesco have adapted to culinary studies to develop the concept of *culinary capital*, focusing on food practices as a means to access benefits in the social sphere. For Bordieu, who himself builds on Karl Marx's ideas on economic capital, certain social practices are conducive to the earning of economic, social, cultural, and symbolic capital, which can result in status and power within their social systems (Naccarato and LeBesco 2). It is in this context that Montiño's high status as the king's cook matters. His word carried considerable weight, given that he had vastly more culinary capital than his rival, and this criticism clearly had an effect on

Granado's reputation and the reception of his book. After the publication of Martínez Montiño's book, Granado's, which had enjoyed moderate success during the previous decade, fell into obscurity. His prestige vanished, and his *Libro del arte de cocina* was quickly forgotten.

Martínez Montiño makes great efforts to legitimate his authority, mentioning his vocation of educating others and his goal of helping the royalty and nobility eat well while not wasting food or incurring unnecessary expenses. Among the many reasons he cites for his writing the book, he includes "because I have been asked by many people." He also points to an altruistic motivation: "what I intend is that anyone who wants to take advantage of this, learns all things easily."[2] In addition, he states that all the recipes are his, and many of them are of his own invention, having been tested and perfected by him over the years. This emphasis on experience is important, as it is one of the pillars that sustain his authority as an expert in the field. For Martínez Montiño, cooking was an art, as the title of his book implies, but also an important skill that could be learned. To that effect, his manual contains not only recipes, but also discussions on the qualities required from a good cook, such as having a pleasant and neat appearance, as well as detailed instructions on how to maintain a clean kitchen, the proper way to serve food at the table, and even the appropriate composition of royal menus. Martínez Montiño's cooking was clearly intended for the court and was aimed at pleasing the palate of kings and nobility. This is obvious in the ingredients he uses: abundant and varied types of meats (boar, duck, turkey, lamb, pork, Cornish hens, even pigeon), as well as many expensive spices, which were out of reach for the majority of the population. Gaining the esteem of these influential members of society could guarantee tremendous symbolic and material benefits in seventeenth-century Spain. By asserting that his teachings had already given proven results, and that "great officials" had been educated under his direction, the author further strengthens his authority and status. Anyone who follows his book's advice, Montiño tells us, can also achieve the status (i.e., the culinary capital) that he enjoys.

A different type of cuisine, aimed for a wider audience, is presented in *Nuevo arte de cocina, sacado de la escuela de la experiencia económica* by Juan de Altamiras. First published in 1745, Altamiras's book constitutes a prime example of Spanish conventual cooking, and it quickly became a standard reference for both cooks and cookbook authors for the next several centuries. A text of lasting influence, it was reedited five times during the author's lifetime and reached twenty editions by the year 1901 (the first translation of this book into English was published only recently, in 2017, edited by Vicky Hayward). The name Juan de Altamiras (sometimes spelled "Altimiras") was actually the pseudonym of Franciscan friar Raimundo Gómez, who worked as a cook for his religious congregation at the convent of San Diego in the city of Zaragoza. Given that the Franciscan order was devoted to helping the poor, and feeding them was one of their main charitable endeavors, *Nuevo arte de cocina* offers a valuable portrait of eighteenth-century popular cooking. In contrast to the exotic royal cuisine that Martínez Montiño's work portrayed, Altamiras's cookbook presents us with humble, affordable fare made from simple dishes, declaring that it was not his intention "to write about exquisite ways to cook, since there are already many books given to light by the cooks of the monarchs, but the execution of their teaching is costly, as if dictated by a silver tongue; rather, in this one the golden tongue of charity can be heard" (qtd. in Moreno, *De la página al plato* 93).[3]

The distinction made by the author between courtly cooking and the simple fare presented in his own work, inspired by charity and with the goal of being nutritious yet affordable, is highly significant. The cuisine of the upper classes, to which he refers here by mentioning "a silver tongue," was very different from the one Altamiras cultivated. Monastic cooking was characterized by using humble ingredients, little meat, and abundant vegetables grown in the monasteries' gardens. As we know, meat was often restricted, especially during Lent and other occasions dictated by the religious calendar. Soups and stews made with vegetables and grains, as well as eggs, cheese, bread, and wine, were at the core of monastic cuisine.

Altamiras's unpretentious cooking style reflects the popular cuisine that the majority of the population was eating at the time, based on affordable ingredients and simple preparations (Pérez Samper 59). His religious inspiration and his awareness for whom his cooking was meant are also evidenced by the author's admonition to his readers, emphasizing the importance of not wasting any food: "always think of how to employ what is left over, because it is often useful for something else, and the poor (following Christ's example, who after having fed five thousand men, asked to gather what was left) must make use of everything" (142).[4]

The author's humility extends to his purpose for writing the book, humbly downplaying its importance and mission while asking for the experts' kindness: "I ask the intelligent to look with kind eyes at this little work, for it is good only for apprentices" (prologue).[5] Despite the author's humility, his voice comes across very clearly in this book, revealing a highly intelligent and kind-hearted individual with a deep knowledge of both culinary matters and human nature, as well as an acute sense of humor. Aside from the abundant advice about the importance of cleanliness in the kitchen and the good sense and honesty required to be a good cook, Altamiras often makes humorous comments when providing recipes, such as this one with regards to a drink made from barley: "It is good for those who study a lot, because it is fresh, according to the opinion of many. Good reward for studying, to eat barley, and food of a rare quality, to be common to both wise men and asses" (49).[6]

Juan de Altamiras's cookbook is a product of its time, as it illustrates its gastronomic legacy and the influences that have shaped Spain's cuisine over the centuries. The Arabic legacy, common to all Spanish cookbooks since the Middle Ages and a reflection of the previous centuries of Muslim occupation in the Iberian Peninsula, can be appreciated here in the frequent use of spices, such as cinnamon or saffron, the numerous sweets included, and the recipe titles, such as "gallina a la morisca" ("hen Morisco-style"). The appearance of some foods from the New World is also significant, as foodstuffs like potatoes, tomatoes, peppers, and chocolate were slowly starting to make their way into European diets. Most of these foods (with the exception of chocolate), became common first among the lower classes, since the upper classes and royalty took longer to incorporate New World foods into their diet, guided by a certain mistrust of these novelties. Interestingly, Altamiras includes here several recipes containing tomatoes, along with instructions to preserve such an exotic and novel ingredient all year by submerging them in olive oil. This is the first mention of tomatoes in a Spanish cookbook. (Antonio Latini had previously mentioned them in a cookbook published in Italy, *Lo scalco alla moderna,* in 1694.) In 1747, another Spanish author, Juan de Mata, included in his *Arte de repostería* the first recipes for tomato sauce in a Spanish cookbook. Slowly, the incorporation of foods from the Americas set in motion an authentic revolution that affected the food of the entire world, well beyond Spain and the rest of Europe, reaching as far as Africa and Asia; the case of Asian cuisine is representative of this influence, impossible today without the presence of chili peppers.

During the nineteenth century, Spain saw France as the model for all cultural aspects, whether it was literature, philosophy, or science. This trend also extended to cuisine, causing Spaniards to look down on their own culinary traditions and favoring French dishes and cooking techniques instead. A few Spanish intellectuals started to denounce this trend at the end of the nineteenth century and beginning of the twentieth, writing about the idea of a national cuisine that would be specifically Spanish. They called for a new appreciation of autochthonous cuisines and an effort to preserve Spain's traditional dishes, while vindicating Spain's gastronomic identity as distinctive, and even superior, to the French. Cookbooks such as *La cocina española antigua* (1913) by prominent novelist Emilia Pardo Bazán, *El practicón* (1894) by Ángel Muro, and the writings of Mariano Pardo de Figueroa, better known by his pen name, Dr. Thebussem, exemplify this trend among Spanish intellectuals. Emilia Pardo Bazán, for example, compiled in her famous 1913 cookbook an exhaustive catalogue of Spanish regional dishes, declaring the urgency of preserving Spain's national cuisine as an endangered cultural treasure. For his part, Doctor Thebussem published a number of very influential essays in which he called, in his peculiarly erudite and ironic style, for the appreciation of Spain's original cuisine, highlighting the importance of recovering its own culinary history and identity while steering away from French influences. He famously decried the use of French terms to refer to dishes that already had a Spanish name, and he is credited with convincing King Alfonso XIII to change the language of the banquet menus at the Royal Palace from French to Spanish. Nevertheless, despite these efforts to change the perceptions around Spanish cuisine, most of the cookbooks of this time were still heavily indebted to French cooking manuals, sometimes being direct translations or borrowing heavily from them. This is where a figure like María Mestayer de Echagüe, better known by her pen name of Marquesa de Parabere, comes in. She is an essential figure who embodies the shift in Spanish cuisine that would take place during the first half of the twentieth century. Even though her cooking still showed some of the French influences that were so prevalent in the previous century, Mestayer incorporated numerous dishes from her native Basque region as well as many other traditional recipes from other parts of Spain. Her indefatigable work over decades as a major figure in Spanish cuisine contributed greatly to the recuperation and revalorization of Spain's own culinary tradition.

We know a great deal about Marquesa de Parabere's life. Born in Bilbao in 1878, her full name was María Manuela Eugenia Carolina Mestayer Jacquet. Born to a wealthy family, she was the daughter of the French consul in Spain. She was not a Marquise, as her pen name would suggest, although it is believed the real Marquis of Parabere, Joaquín Aguirre Echagüe, was her husband's cousin and allowed her to use the nobility title as a pseudonym. María Mestayer de Echagüe was self-educated as a cook, learning and reading avidly about food and cooking for years. She was also a brave entrepreneur, opening and running two successful restaurants, although they were both eventually forced to close by the difficult circumstances of Spain in the 1930s and 1940s. She became an extraordinary force in Spain's culinary panorama, publishing numerous cookbooks and several volumes of culinary history while accumulating a considerable personal library on the subject in the process. Originally from the Basque Country, she moved to Madrid—defying her husband's opposition—to open a restaurant, Parabere, which became highly successful and gave her a reputation among the city's food lovers and intellectuals. Unfortunately, the venture came to an end in 1936 with the beginning of the Spanish Civil War. Even though she reopened the restaurant briefly after the war, the business was not able to survive the tough postwar years of food shortages and economic disaster. Once the Parabere closed permanently, Mestayer devoted her time and energy to writing an ambitious work of culinary history, left unfinished at her death in 1949.

María Mestayer de Echagüe is best known as a cookbook author for her most ambitious work, *La cocina completa*, first published in 1933 and reedited as an expanded, two-volume version in 1940 with the subtitle "Enciclopedia culinaria" ("Culinary Encyclopedia"). The book was reedited numerous times during the 1940s and the decades that followed. The dishes contained in this book range from the sophisticated to the simple, and from the costly to the affordable, which was no doubt one of the reasons for its success at the time, appealing to readers from every social class. It was also a great resource for the millions of women struggling to feed their families during the 1940s, given the constraints of the postwar rationing policies imposed by Francisco Franco's government. *La cocina completa* contains numerous classic Basque dishes such as *bacalao a la vizcaína* (salt cod Vizcaya style) or the traditional *marmitako* (Basque tuna stew), French desserts like *marrons glacés* (candied chestnuts), and also quintessential Spanish dishes like *cocido* (chickpea and meat stew). Her recipe for this dish is rich—she describes it as "a very complete *cocido*"—and includes a wide variety of meats, acknowledging, however, that "it goes without saying that many ingredients can be omitted—for economic reasons or for any other cause, making it in a simpler manner" (138).[7] She also devotes an entire chapter to using the leftover meat from the *cocido*, providing recipes for several dishes of nutritious new creations.

In the prologue to *La cocina completa*, Mestayer emphasizes that she has tested all the recipes included in the book. Her desire to acquire culinary capital is evident when she engages in what we today would call "name dropping," providing a long list of respected and well-known cooks who had, according to her, approved her book. She states that these recipes "have earned the approval of such excellent and renowned cooks as Teodoro Bardají, Francisco Mullor, Salvador Bandrés, Francisco Roig Riera, Rondossini, Juan Kavigné, Dumont-Lespine, M. Bernard, H. Pellaprat, Gastón Derys, and others" (9). It is highly significant that the long list contains exclusively male colleagues, both Spanish and French, thus highlighting her international reputation. The fact that there are no women on that list underscores the rarity of females in the group of elite cooks at the time, as well as the importance of Mestayer's achievement of being accepted into this exclusive, male-dominated professional space. While virtually every woman was taught how to cook, and many became very accomplished at it, the professional arena was mostly closed to them, and their cooking was almost always relegated to the confines of the home, seen as merely part of their domestic duties.

On *La cocina completa*'s opening page, the reader finds a poem written by Basque lawyer and gastronome Pedro Eguillor, dedicated with much praise to Mestayer, whom he calls "Great master of the culinary art and culinary literature in Spain."[8] The dedication and poem are followed by the author's prologue, where Mestayer makes it very clear that she is the sole author and that the book is the result of over twenty years of compiling and testing recipes (9). As the title of the book implies, and as is evidenced by the use of the adjective "complete," this is an ambitious work. Indeed, Mestayer's comprehensive volume, over nine hundred pages long, is extremely detailed and contains instructions and information about cooking utensils, techniques, types of dishes, table protocol, and even cuts of meat. The point of her writing style and confident authorial voice was to make her stature as an authority in the field unquestionable. It is not surprising that a woman had to vehemently establish her credentials in order to gain the culinary capital needed to be respected, and it should also not surprise us that, in addition to her numerous cookbooks, Mestayer de Echagüe undertook the monumental task of writing a *Historia de la gastronomía* (*History of Gastronomy*). In this 1943 work, she emphasizes again her many years of experience in the field and mentions her extensive personal library, showing great authorial pride and erudition and, in sum, going to great lengths to construct an authorial persona.

As a result of all her publications and years of work, the Marquise of Parabere became very well known in her time. As mentioned earlier, *La cocina completa* was for decades a must-have in every Spanish house, and it is still a very popular book that continues to be reedited today. Considered a main reference for those interested in traditional Spanish dishes, it is viewed as a classic, perhaps because as Theophano reminds us, cookbooks often serve "as a place for readers to remember a way of life no longer in existence or to enter a nostalgic re-creation of a past culture that persists mostly in memory" (8). To the modern audience, these recipes from the 1940s have the appeal of the past, fueled by a nostalgia for our mothers' or grandmothers' cooking at a time when preparing food was perhaps a simpler affair, and meals played an important role in family bonding.

Another truly extraordinary cookbook is *Cocina de recursos: Deseo mi comida* by Catalan chef Ignacio Doménech. Written during the 1936–1939 Spanish Civil War and published in 1941, it is unlike any other cookbooks published in Spain's history. Not only does it contain remarkable recipes that show the author's genius and resourcefulness, but it is also a sort of *memoir* of the war and postwar years, since a narrative voice throughout the text provides us with a firsthand account of the wartime hardships. Doménech achieved considerable fame in his lifetime as a professional chef, cookbook author, cooking-school director and teacher, and editor of the first cooking magazine in Spain, *El gorro blanco*. As a chef, he worked for members of the nobility, diplomats, and other wealthy clients in London, Paris, and Madrid. He was a major figure in the Spanish culinary world during the 1920s, with numerous books under his belt that contributed to consolidating his reputation. Doménech was always opinionated and clearly proud of his work, and his deep sense of authorship is evident in all of his writings, as the prologue to his *La nueva cocina elegante española* shows. First published in 1915, the prologue makes it clear to readers that the book was not "just one more cookbook—and please forgive the lack of modesty in this assertion—it is the minimum product of thirty years of consecutive work" (6). He mentions the importance of cooking manuals as major contributions to progress and the advancement of humankind, asserting that "the publication of a cookbook should be seen, examined, and praised with the same fruition, with the same interest, with the same curiosity with which we look at all artifacts that are invented and perfected for the comfort, respite or enjoyment of Humankind" (6).[9]

Doménech's sense of purpose is evident in all his published works, in which he often mentions his commitment to bettering the lives of his readers and his goal of popularizing the culinary arts. During the years 1936–1938, however, this prominent cook faced the same grim reality as all other Spaniards, a ravaging civil war resulting in thousands of deaths, destruction, food scarcity, and widespread hunger. These terrible circumstances compelled him to write a cookbook that would help his fellow citizens. The resulting work is one of the most amazing testimonies of the Spanish Civil War from the perspective of an individual citizen, a text that shows the hunger dynamics that were the reality for the majority of the country, both during the war and in the years that followed. Combining essays and recipes, *Cocina de recursos* is a complex book with more than one purpose, and its author declares different intentions throughout the work: On one hand, he emphasizes the purpose of documenting the historic moment as one of his main goals; on the other, he expresses his desire to "help his countrymen" in such difficult circumstances, providing them with ideas to feed themselves in adverse circumstances. But there is also a clear intention of denunciation in this work, manifested in the numerous occasions in which Doménech describes with stark realism the brutal food shortages he finds on his journey through numerous Barcelona restaurants. He tells us about restaurants without food, bread rationing, starving children, hungry dogs unsuccessfully looking for scraps under the tables, skilled cooks who disguise the food or ingeniously "stretch" ingredients to achieve the miracle of the loaves and fishes. Throughout his book, the author shows a vein of social writing: deeply committed to portraying reality, indirectly denouncing the uprising led by General Francisco Franco and the resulting war. On numerous occasions, for example, the author expresses his indignation at the high prices of staple foods such as milk, eggs, and bread, repeatedly comparing prices before and after the uprising. The impossibility of directly criticizing the Franco regime leads Doménech to articulate a double discourse throughout the book, on the one hand praising the regime and Franco, declared a great "savior" of the country; on the other hand presenting the devastating effects of the war and the immense suffering it caused to the population. The construction of "an identifiable authorial persona with whom the reader not only *can* agree or argue but is encouraged to agree or argue" (Leonardi 342) is evident in this work, as the reader empathizes with the author, bonding over the tragedy of collective hunger. This bond must have been obvious for his contemporary readers, who endured the same difficult circumstances and were able to find solutions in this cookbook to the food shortages and rationing present in 1940s Spain. It is clear, then, that authorship and purpose are deeply intertwined in this work, as are the author's memories embedded throughout. As Floyd and Forster argue:

> The recipe, in its intertextuality, is also itself a narrative which can engage the reader or cook in a "conversation" about culture and history in which the recipe and its context provide part of the text and the reader imagines (or even eats) the rest. It is open to subjective intervention and interpretation, putting the reader in contact with the writer, making personal connections with a cultural moment or a community, and allowing the reader to interpolate herself into the text, making the narrative her own. [. . .] Thus, the recipe, besides

being a narrative in itself, offers us stories too: of family sagas and community records, of historical and cultural moments of change, and also personal stories and narratives of self. (2)

Conclusions

The authorial voice comes through with confidence in all of these works (often in the prologues, but also throughout the works themselves), telling us a great deal about the authors of these books and their motivation to write them. The relationships between these cookbooks and their context and the discourse that each articulates highlight the dynamics between cooking and society, cooking and history, and cooking and authorial identity, among others. There are, as we have shown, multiple possibilities of interpretation behind each cookbook. The comparison between these two sets of books, two dating to premodern times and the other two to the modern era, shows significant differences in the concept and meaning of a cookbook and its goals. For instance, there is a notable evolution in the profile of the authorial voice, its target audience, and the culinary capital that it can expect to obtain through the writing of a cookbook. Also, with the popularization of books and printing in the modern era, and the distribution of texts becoming more widespread and accessible to more readers, the profile of the reader changed too, from professional male court cooks or members of religious congregations to domestic cooks of every gender and social status. While Martínez Montiño's and Altamiras's books were conceived as educational manuals for professional cooks (be they at the court or in the monastery), María Mestayer's and Ignacio Doménech's were written mostly for the home cook, in a time when cooking had become a democratized activity and women's voices were starting to be heard in the professional culinary arena. Of these authors, Altamiras and Doménech seem to show the greatest awareness and empathy for their audience, using their skills and knowledge to help others in times of hardship. Especially in the case of Doménech, the book breaks free from the format limitations of the genre, creating a text with a hybrid form, which presents itself as a cookbook but is in reality a collection of memories embedded among the recipes.

As the preceding pages have shown, all of these cookbooks establish a dialogue between text and context, articulated through the recipes, ingredients, and techniques they contain, as well as the advice they give and the manner in which they reflect (and conform to or defy) the social norms of their time. Their prologues, where the authorial voice comes through uninhibited, greatly illuminate the social, political, and historical frame around them. In addition, the voices of their authors establish a direct dialogue with the reader, using the bonding power of food to seek their audience's approval, confidence, and support, in pursuit of the much-desired culinary capital.

NOTES

1. "no haber libros por donde se puedan guiar los que sirven el oficio de la cocina, y que todo se encarga á la memoria. [. . .] Y lo que me ha animado á escribirlo es haber servido tantos años al Rey N. S., y habérseme encargado las mayores cosas de mi arte que se han ofrecido en el real palacio, con satisfacción de mis jefes; y por ser yo muy inclinado á enseñar, porque han salido con mi exemplo grandes oficiales." (Martínez Montiño, Prologue).
2. "lo que pretendo es que cualquier persona que se quiera aprovechar de este, acierte las cosas con mucha facilidad" (prologue). All translations are mine unless indicated otherwise.
3. "No es mi intento escribir modos exquisitos de guisar, que para este fin ya hay muchos Libros, que dieron á luz Cocineros de Monarchas, pero la execución de su doctrina es tan costosa, como dictada por lengua de plata; en esta suena más la lengua de oro de la Caridad" (Prologue).
4. "Siempre has de discurrir el empleo de lo que te sobre; porque muchas veces lo que sobra, viene bien para otra cosa, y los pobres (á exemplo de Christo, que después de haver socorrido a cinco mil hombres, mandó que se recogiese lo que havía sobrado) deben aprovecharlo todo."
5. "Pido a los inteligentes que miren con buenos ojos esta Obrilla, pues es buena solamente para los Aprendices."

6. "es buena para los que estudian mucho, porque es fresca, según la opinión de muchos. Buen premio del estudio, comer cebada; y rara calidad de alimento, ser común á sabios y borricos."
7. "Desde luego queda sobrentendido que se podrán suprimir muchos de sus componentes (por razones económicas o por cualquier otro motivo), dejándole muy reducido."
8. The complete dedication reads: "A la gran maestra del arte y literatura culinaria de España, la distinguida señora Doña María Mestayer de Echagüe, en prueba de admiración profunda y respetuoso afecto."
9. "Por esta causa, la aparición de un libro de cocina debiera ser mirado, examinado y ensalzado con la misma fruición, con el mismo interés, con análoga curiosidad con que se miran, examinan y ensalzan cuantos artefactos se inventan y perfeccionan para comodidad, descanso y recreo de la Humanidad" (6).

WORKS CITED

Altamiras, Juan de. *Nuevo arte de cocina, sacado de la escuela de la experiencia económica*. Barcelona, Imprenta Don Juan de Bézares, 1758.

Anderson, Lara. *Cooking Up the Nation: Spanish Culinary Texts and Culinary Nationalization in the Late Nineteenth and Early Twentieth Century*. Tamesis, 2013.

Doménech, Ignacio. *Cocina de recursos: Deseo mi comida*. Quintilla, Cardona y Cía. Editores, 1941.

———. *La nueva cocina elegante española; El tratado más práctico y completo de cocina, pastelería, repostería y refrescos*. Imprenta Helénica, 1920.

Floyd, Janet, and Laurel Forster, editors. *The Recipe Reader: Narratives, Contexts, Traditions*. Ashgate, 2003.

Granado, Diego. *Libro del arte de cozina*. Salamanca, Casa de Antonia Ramírez, 1607.

Hayward, Vicky. *New Art of Cookery: A Spanish Friar's Kitchen Notebook by Juan Altamiras*. Rowman and Littlefield, 2017.

Latini, Antonio. *Lo scalco alla moderna*. Biblioteca Culinaria; Appunti di Gastronomia, 1993.

Leonardi, Susan J. "Recipes for Reading: Summer Pasta, Lobster à la Riseholme, and Key Lime Pie." *PMLA*, vol. 104, no. 3, 1989, pp. 340–47.

Martínez Montiño, Francisco. *Arte de cocina, pastelería, vizcochería, y conservería*. Madrid, Luis Sánchez, 1611.

Mata, Juan de. *Arte de repostería*. Madrid, Imp. de Joseph García Lanza, 1791.
Mestayer de Echagüe, María. *La cocina completa*. Espasa-Calpe, 1940.
———. *Historia de la gastronomía (Esbozos)*. Espasa-Calpe, 1943.
Moreno, María Paz. *De la página al plato: El libro de cocina en España*. Trea, 2012.
———. *Madrid: A Culinary History*. Rowman and Littlefield, 2017.
Muro, Ángel. *El Practicón*. Tusquets, 1997.
Naccarato, Peter, and Kathleen LeBesco. *Culinary Capital*. Berg, 2012.
Nadeau, Carolyn A. *Food Matters: Alonso Quijano's Diet and the Discourse of Food in Early Modern Spain*. U of Toronto P, 2016.
Pardo Bazán, Emilia. *La cocina española antigua*. Sociedad Anónima Renacimiento, 1913.
Pardo de Figueroa, Mariano (Doctor Thebussem). *La mesa moderna: Cartas sobre el comedor y la cocina cambiadas entre el doctor Thebussem y Un cocinero de S. M.* Madrid, Librerías de Fernando Fe, 1888.
Pérez Samper, María de los Ángeles. *La alimentación en la España del Siglo de Oro*. La Val de Onsera, 1998.
Theophano, Janet. *Eat My Words: Reading Women's Lives through the Cookbooks They Wrote*. Palgrave, 2002.

CHAPTER 8

Cooks and Ladies

The Writing of Culinary Knowledge in Argentina in the Late Nineteenth and Early Twentieth Centuries

Paula Caldo, *National Scientific and Technical Research Council, National University of Rosario, Argentina*

Two key editorial events had an important impact on the Argentinean reading public at the turn of the twentieth century. The first was the publication of the cookbook *La perfecta cocinera argentina* in 1888 under the author's name of Teófila Benavento by Jacobo Peuser printing press. Later, in 1914, a new cookbook, *La cocinera criolla y recetario curativo doméstico* was published in Barcelona by Luis Gili. Its author appeared under the name of a lady called Marta who hailed from the city of Santa Fe in Argentina.

There are several common denominators in the editorial phenomenon of cookbook publishing during the period. First, these publications are exclusively designed for the transmission of culinary knowledge; second, despite their apparent eclecticism, the texts attempt to gather recipes for dishes that were already favored in Argentina; and third, their authors tend to use a pseudonym, opening the question of their identity. This chapter will look at different aspects of the cookbook editorial phenomenon in Argentina at the turn of the twentieth century as well as the methodological implications for its analysis.

Food historians have pointed out the risks involved in using cookbooks to document culinary practices (Flandrin and Montanari; Arcondo; Remedi; Caldo). There are important questions regarding the use of cookbooks: Are the written recipes they contain the ones that people actually used when cooking? In historical perspective, were books always accessible, or was their impact limited to a literate audience who could afford to buy them? Did those who cooked know how to read, and, conversely, were those who could read and write interested in improving their culinary knowledge? Asking these questions helps further refine the issues at stake when studying cookbooks, highlighting the need to examine the practices involved in food writing, including those of authorship and gender and the social politics of cookbook publishing.

The turn of the twentieth century is characterized by a wealth of self-narratives written by the Argentinian literate bourgeoisie (Arfuch). This period is rich in *costumbrista* essays, memoires, and memory books that open a vantage point from which to examine the daily practices and sociability of affluent Argentinians. The recurrent references to *culinaria* (cooking) and food mark them as socially acceptable topics in conversation and writing at the time. A display of knowledge of the culinary preferences of cultures abroad was a way to present oneself as a sybaritic world traveler. For these reasons, gastronomy appears as a recurring topic in the writings of the self during this period, helping unveil a wealth of information about cookbook writing and its authors.

The culinary experiences carried out by Argentine women have slowly generated research of crucial value that serves as a frame of reference to the reflections expressed in this chapter. Female culinary writing was part of the knowledge and skills of female domesticity, and it was disseminated in handwritten documents that were at times transformed into editorial products focused on guiding the practices of everyday and home cooking. Marcela Fugardo's work on the manuscript recipe notebook of María Varela in 1880 presents the patrimonial, formative, and domestic value of a pioneering experience that articulates writing, recipes, and female agency. María, a renowned figure in Buenos Aires social circles, compiled typical late nineteenth century recipes in her spare time and in the privacy of her domestic sphere. Rebekah Pite has carried out research on the life and work of the economist Petrona C. de Gandulfo, writing from the provincial periphery and popular sectors, who became known as a cooking expert in the 1930s, continuing to work until her death in the 1990s. If María Varela is the oldest indicator of Argentine female cookbook writing, Petrona comes forth as the *ecónoma* (corporate home economist) who made culinary knowledge and its attendant practices a women's trade. Between the handwritten strokes of one and the media and political versatility of the other lie a series of cookbooks published by women who, perhaps fearing being called pedantic, hid their names under pseudonyms. The following pages are dedicated to them.

La Cocinera Criolla: Marta/Mercedes

We find "Marta," the author of *La cocinera criolla y recetario curativo doméstico*, in *Recuerdos de antaño*, a memoir filled with anecdotes written by one of her paternal cousins, Elvira Aldao de Díaz (1858–1950). Elvira describes everyday moments of her childhood and youth in which she recounts her family vacations in the country with praise and eloquence. When recalling the delicacies prepared by "La negra Manuela" ("Black Manuela"), she comments:

But what Dona Manuela prepared most exquisitely was the most genuine dish from Santa Fe: homemade duck in a dark, almost black, sauce of peanuts roasted and crushed into pieces. How sorry I am not to remember the strange name of that provincial dish, perhaps now disappeared even from the city of Santa Fe itself. Perhaps not; maybe the recipe is in the renowned cooking guide—whose title I want to recall but escapes me—published by my interesting cousin Mercedes Cullen de Aldao, with the purpose widely achieved (for the editions follow each other in rapid succession), to contribute resources . . . , to finish a temple instead of resorting to the devotion of the faithful, she aroused their appetite, presenting recipes of exquisite delicacies. (238–39)

If she had had on hand the book written by "Marta," whom we can now identify as Mercedes Cullen de Aldao, Elvira could have specified that the recipe for "duck with black or dark sauce" was the "Tulpo de pato" found in the 1923 edition of *La cocina criolla* and in later reprints. The recipe reads: "Put a little oil and fat in the pot, add chopped onion, tomatoes, peppers, salt, pepper, and broth; after the sauce has cooked for a while, add the duck cut up in different pieces; cook over low heat and add finely chopped peanuts and a little sugar before serving. It can also be made with beef" (Marta, 1923; 19). In 1926, 1928, and 1931 reprints, the recipe still appears on page nineteen. However, the 1942 edition appeared under a new editorial imprint, with a change in print quality and an increase in content.[1]

Mercedes was born on September 22, 1865, in the city of Santa Fe, capital of the Argentinian province of the same name. Her parents were Tomás Cullen y Rodríguez del Fresno and Josefa Comas. The couple had nine children who would grow up to occupy important leading positions in the politics of the province of Santa Fe, as well as in public life, in various associations and in sociability practices. The Cullen-Comas women repeatedly assumed the presidency and secretariat of the local Sociedad de Beneficencia (Welfare Society). Due to their proximity to political power, they managed initiatives to shelter those in need. Mercedes was the daughter, goddaughter, and sister of governors, mayors, and government representatives, as well as of prestigious doctors and lawyers. It is important to highlight Mercedes's ties to Catholicism and charity, as they could have provided the impetus for the publication of *La cocinera criolla*. As a practicing Catholic, Mercedes took part in various activities and contributed to the aid of the underprivileged sectors of society. Mercedes was committed to the work of the Hospital de la Caridad, at that time led by one of her brothers, and planned the construction of a chapel on the hospital premises. In 1913, in order to raise funds for the chapel, Mercedes set out to compile and publish a cookbook. In that year, she left for Barcelona carrying the manuscript of *La cocinera criolla* in her chests. How had she managed to gather those recipes? By tapping into two different resources: on the one hand, the knowledge of the family cook in Villa Aldao (province of Santa Fe), and on the other, her sybarite friends and relatives and their travels, with all their culinary secrets. This mode of compilation caused the book to have, word for word, some of the same recipes as those found in other cookbooks in circulation at the time. In some recipes, *La cocinera criolla* reproduces the exact texts from other cookbooks, such as *La cocina familiar*, published under the pseudonym "U. P. de S." by the printing company La Facultad (Buenos Aires) in 1914; *El arte de cocinar*, edited by the Congregación de Las Hijas de María y Santa Filomena de Tucumán (Congregation of the Daughters of Mary and Santa Filomena de Tucumán) in 1914 (city of San Miguel de Tucumán); and Teófila Benavento's cookbook. The idea of plagiarism was not operative among women, and recipes circulated, going by word of mouth, from handwritten kitchen notebooks to other such notebooks, and, finally, from book to book. It is important to note how differently women and men understood "plagiarism" in light of the complaints by the cook Francisco Figueredo against women as "thieves" of the intellectual property of the recipes (Caldo, *Libros, cocina e inmigración*).

Carrying her manuscript materials with her, Mercedes arrived in Barcelona and immediately managed to find a printer for a book that aimed to capture the interest of the Argentine public. The book was so successful that five thousand copies of the first volume were printed in 1914, while another five thousand copies of the second volume were printed the following year. A second printing followed a year later after the first printing had quickly sold out. The author's identity was hidden under the pseudonym "Marta" (see Batticuore). This pseudonym had been suggested by Monsignor Romero as an explicit allusion to the biblical Martha (*Marta* in the Spanish version of the Bible), the sister of Mary and Lazarus who had cooked for Jesus during his visit (Damianovich). This *cocinera criolla* that the book evoked was therefore a mix of Catholic lady and matron from Santa Fe. Over time, the culinary guide she published would be modified in both content and form. If the 1914 edition was dedicated to traditional Argentinian cuisine, the 1915 edition included even more of those traditional recipes. "Marta" herself clarified that the recipes in this new volume had not been included in the previous edition because she had not managed to send them from Santa Fe to her editor in Barcelona on time. After the delay due to the distance between the two cities, the new recipes were compiled in a book called *La cocinera criolla (Tomo segundo) y recetario curativo doméstico*. The publication of the book had fulfilled its two goals of raising sufficient funds to start the construction of the Hospital de la Caridad chapel and, secondarily, of becoming a useful text for households and housewives. Santa Fe and Argentine tables had accepted the proposal of *La cocinera criolla* with pleasure.

The Perfect Argentine Cook: Teófila/Susana

Much like in Marta's case, Teófila's identity is similarly revealed through family memoirs. In 1978, Mariano Apellániz, one of Teófila's grandchildren, wrote a *costumbrista* book in which he described, among other things, the practices of sociability that took place in the house of his great grandmother, Joaquina Arana de Torres. The book is entitled after her house address: *Callao 1730 y su época*. Joaquina Arana was the mother of Susana Torres de Castex, and the latter is the woman who hides under the pseudonym Teófila. As Apellániz explains to his children:

> Your great-grandmother's bent for the culinary arts is well known. She signed her famous book *La perfecta cocina argentina* with the pseudonym Teófila Benavento, the name of one of her first cooks. In relation to the practice of the culinary arts, I related an anecdote to you (very amusingly, as expected). Pototo was spending some time in Paris. She had rented an apartment. A few days after her arrival in the City of Light, she ran into her great friend Carlos Pellegrini, and the following conversation took place: "Here you have me, Susana, fed up with French food and yearning for *pucherete* and *humitas*." "Very well, gringo, tomorrow I'll expect you and Carolina for lunch. I'll do the cooking." Early the next day Pototo went to the kitchen and set to work, masterfully cutting some steaks before the eyes of the delivery woman who had arrived with an order that would complete the lunch. (90)

Her maiden name was Susana Torres, while "de Castex" was added after her marriage, but her relatives had called her "Pototo" since childhood. However, when she had the chance of publishing a cookbook she chose a pseudonym that was the name of a real professional cook, Teófila Benavento. Her choice of a pseudonym was most likely due to the limitations placed by the publishing world on female authors. A pseudonym may function as a riddle that hides and protects the subject of authorship (Caldo, "La mujer"). This function may have been more pronounced in prescriptive texts such as cookbooks, whose exclusive purpose was to transmit culinary recipes. Despite this, the titles of the recipes are a repository of clues as to their author's identity. A plausible reason for such authorial traces in the narrative of recipes may be found in the empirical and oral nature of the transmission of cooking instructions, as any notes written by the recipient would convey allusions to the woman narrating them (Giard). For example, we find several recipes with the qualifier "Joaquinita," as in "Empanadas Joaquinita, Tortas santafecinas Joaquinita" or "Tortas porteñas Joaquinita." Joaquina was the name of Susana's mother and one of her daughters. Similarly, the recipe for "Ecrivisses Teófila Benavento" clearly references the professional cook whose name served as Susana's pseudonym, while the recipe for "Susi fondants" perhaps refers to Susana herself. These names may be understood as signs of ownership/authorship as well as playful winks at the reader.

Toward end of the twentieth century, Mariano, Susana's grandson, reviewed his ancestors' sociability practices in the city of Buenos Aires. In his story, his grandmother stood out as an exception. Among other things, she was passionate about good food and became a gastronomy enthusiast. Of robust frame (she was obese), this Buenos Aires lady entered the kitchen to satiate her own appetite as much as to regale her loved ones. In their home, Susana and her husband planned the construction of a kitchen with huge windows overlooking the garden, thought to be one of the first of its kind in the city.

But, who was Susana Torres? We know that she was born in 1866 and died in 1937, seventy-one years later. Both by birth and by choice, she always resided in Buenos Aires, a city that at that time was beginning to move slowly but steadily toward urban, political, and cultural modernization. The ruling classes were shaping an architecture that promoted spaces for a thriving urban sociability that was ultimately fueled by the economic resources brought by land ownership. At the turn of the twentieth century, sociability in Buenos Aires followed rules of urbanity and civility that were greatly influenced by protocols, tastes, and manners imported from France. Paris, its food, its parties, its aromas, its musical tastes, its shows, and its fashion were the model of inspiration for the ladies and young women of Buenos Aires society. Nevertheless, French influences were combined with practices taken from other European countries, and customs like the English five o'clock tea were faithfully adopted (Barrán; Losada). Along with the tea, all sorts of English pastries were served (e.g., scones, fruit pudding, apple tarts, auntie's cakes, etc.).

In the midst of this restless and active social scene, Susana learned to understand and interpret the world. Her father, Gregorio Torres, was a prominent landowner but also a politician and personal friend of the twice-elected president, Julio Argentino Roca. Her father's commitment to politics was helped by the intense social life of her mother, Joaquina Arana de Torres (1840–1940), who stood out as a prominent host of Buenos Aires evenings. Susana was greatly influenced by European customs and modes of living, which she followed throughout her single and married life. In 1884 Susana married a young doctor named Mariano Castex. The union was blessed in Iglesia de la Merced and celebrated with a sumptuous party in her parents' house. Susana Torres de Castex and her husband had five children, three daughters and two sons.

The Torres-Arana residence became the epicenter of the most lavish Buenos Aires evenings. Through these celebrations passed prestigious personages from the world of politics and Argentine culture. On these occasions, Susana and her mother, Joaquina, officiated as hostesses. Susana distinguished herself among the women of her time, as she spoke several languages fluently and frequently traveled to Europe, where she stood out as a soiree hostess for her European friends and other Argentine travelers abroad. Susana was exceptional as much for her simple and little ornamented wardrobe as for her fondness for smoking, taking snuff, playing billiards, and practicing sports such as hunting, fishing, and boxing. In addition, she refused to be part of charitable associations, preferring to spend her time in soirees centered around discussions on music, art, and other topics.

Despite her uniqueness, she never ventured into the academic or business worlds, remaining in her roles as mother of five children and wife of a doctor whose profession included attending to mothers and giving professional advice on motherhood, which Susana often contradicted. Thus, while her husband cited a number of risks in breastfeeding, Susana breastfed all her children. Despite her extravagant tastes, her controversial practices, and her questions, Susana was a dedicated wife and mother. As stated above, their residence was distinguished by a detail that is key to the focus of this chapter: *the kitchen*, a space that served as a test laboratory for the recipes.

Like Marta (Mercedes Cullen), Susana's only publishing experience was with *La perfecta cocina argentina*. The publishing house Jacobo Peuser, founded in 1881, did the printing, the lithography, and the binding of the cookbook and would continue doing so until the second decade of the twentieth century. They were pocket editions (11 cm high by 1.5 cm deep), bound in brown cloth, sewn, with the cover bearing the book title and author's name in golden letters. The book was published in this format through almost twenty reprints, and the same 413 recipes from the first printing were included until the 1901 edition. In the 1920s, 216 new recipes were added to those of the first editions. Even in its last edition, published posthumously, a number of recipes were added. Regardless of the actual quality of cookbook editions, the practical uses to which they were destined were detrimental to their durability, making it difficult to find extant copies of all the various reprints. Nevertheless, the limited number of those reprints available enables us to assess the number of published recipes, the increase in their number, and the frequency of reprints.

Though Teófila's cookbook became an instant bestseller, early editions provide little contextual information on the topic of women's relation to cuisine, the author's identity, or her sources of culinary knowledge. In fact, *La perfecta cocinera* does not even include a prologue explaining its content and intent and leaves out any customary form of advice, description of urbanity rules, or help in solving the problems of the modern home. The book is quite literally an alphabetical guide to cooking recipes, starting with "A" ("alfajores") and ending with "Y" ("yema quemada"). Each recipe provides a summary description of cooking steps and a list of ingredients. However, the titles of the recipes do contain some allusive references to the author's compilatory work. References to recipe "donors" are inserted through a particular turn of phrase that becomes more evident in successive reprints. Thus, in many titles of the original 413 recipes we find allusions to female contributors, including these examples: "Bizcochuelo á lo *Laurita*," "Bizcochuelo de *Avelina*," "Bacalao vizcaíno á lo *Josefa*," "Escabeche *Antonina*," "Marmelada *Juana* de damasco," "Pan francés *María*," "Palitos *Betty*," "Pasteles á lo *María Juana*," "Ris de veau *Isabel* (mollejas de vaca)," "Torta *Elena* con almendras," "Torta inglesa *Matilde* o Torta *Betty* (con levadura)" (emphasis added). It is not explained whether the allusive names are meant to recognize the intellectual property of the recipe's author or are rather intended as a tribute to the person mentioned. It should also be noted that some men are similarly mentioned, as may be seen for example in "Pasta de membrillo a lo *tío José*," "Pan *Alberto*, de carne, á la alemana," and "Perdices a la *Teofilón*" (emphasis added).

Nevertheless, starting in the 1920s, 216 new recipes were incorporated, with many displaying new ways of naming those creative collaborators by, for example, adding references after the title in between parentheses, as in "Baño blanco para coscorrones (María)," "Pan francés (María)," "Bocadillos de papa (Andrea)," "Carbonada (Andrea)," "Carbonada (Josefa)," "Dulce de tomates (Damasia Barreto)," "Dulce de leche (Barreto)," "Pastel de choclo (Barreto)," "Mazacote de tomate (Barreto)," "Dulce de durazno (Enriqueta)," "Dulce de leche (Genoveva, el mejor)," "Empanadas tucumanas (Josefa)," "Huevos (Carmen)," "Yema dura para yemas (Carmen)," "Merengues (Juana)," "Perdices en escabeche (Adriana)," and "Crêpe de Viena (Emilia)." These parenthetical mentions may be understood as direct indications of the cookbook's contributors.

Susana Torres (Teófila) traveled widely, making new acquaintances and enjoying good food. In the conversations held in her social circles, there was talk of the day's menu and other discussion of food, providing Susana with information that was translated into the wealth of recipes she offered for the Argentines' gastronomic enjoyment. While her pseudonym allowed her to recreate and copy from that patrimony of knowledge and pleasure called cuisine, she could not avoid the duty of mentioning the creative cooks she knew. Cookbook writing is textured much like a puff pastry, made up of many layers in which different voices become inserted. Some of these voices were inaudible, allowing cookbook authors to replicate them freely, but others, more solid, demanded to be cited. Registering the name of the creative cook implied removing cuisine from an intangible and collective patrimony and inscribing it in the register of personal ownership. In this way, the many women who wrote about cuisine and inscribed themselves in it using modern technologies leveraged orally reproduced traditions. The performative force of discourse thus played a significant role in the writing and agency of female bodies and subjectivities.

Final Reflection: On Recipes, Cookbooks, and Writing Practices

Claude Fischler explained, "There is currently no known culture that is completely devoid of an apparatus of food categories and rules, that knows no prescription or interdiction concerning what to eat, what not to eat, and how one needs to eat" (58–59). These prescriptions, once adopted, are preserved by means of memory or writing. The recipes designed to regulate food preparation make up a body of knowledge that is useful not only for daily diet but also for special public events and celebrations. While daily cooking in the home was women's work (that of housewives and female servants), the production and writing of culinary knowledge was for a long time in male hands (Revel). Similarly, home cooking was within the purview of women, be they housewives or female servants, while the cooking outside of the home was the domain of men, who headed professional kitchens (Caldo, *Libros*). This professionalization of cooking is directly related to the publication of cookbooks, which only belatedly acknowledged female authorship. The participation of well-heeled ladies in food writing at first brought an emphasis on food as an object of consumption and less so on cooking (Goody). Early twentieth century cookbooks in Argentina resulted from the necessary collaboration between ladies and female cooks by trade. This collaboration enabled the creation of a written record of everyday cuisine and helped make recipes the imprint of material culture. Thus, the first cookbook authors in Argentina were bourgeois ladies who had the necessary resources to compile and publish books, but their content was the product of a collaborative effort. Female writers and cooks combined their knowledge and skills to write and publish books about cooking (Caldo, *Un cachito de cocinera*), as seen in the two cases that have been outlined here. In this vein, there are six particular features of the period between 1888 and 1914 that must be underscored:

First, this period shows the gradual importance that culinary knowledge began to gain in the publishing market and in Argentine culture in general. Recipe books were hardbound, sewn, printed in heavyweight paper, with print runs of five thousand copies, although devoid of images (with the exception of some covers, as in Marta's cookbook). They were books worthy of libraries, but not yet "kitchen-table drawer cookbooks."

Second, the internal organization of cookbooks saw changes that reflected their evolution as artifacts. In 1888, Teófila organized her recipes alphabetically, while in 1914 Marta perfected a system for organizing recipes according to gastronomic principles. One of the first divisions distinguished typical criollo dishes from those belonging to a cosmopolitan cuisine. For example, *chanfaina, chatasca, carbonada, mazamorra, locro, empanadas regionales,* the various types of *humita*, as well as *tamales, tortas fritas, chipá,* and the different kinds of *tulpo* (the longed-for dark peanut sauce) coexisted with rice (casserole, risottos, etc.), *cazuelas* (fish, red meats, vegetables, etc.), different kinds of pasta (macaroni, tagliatelle, gnocchi, ravioli), *tortas, dulces, salsas,* etc. This first classification was followed by a second differentiation between sweet and savory recipes. Finally, a third line of recipes was divided according to ages (for children), the state of health or illness, and festivities in general or religious holidays (i.e., fasts, Easter, Christmas, etc.).

Third, recipes of French origin, mainly in Teófila's cookbook, make apparent the prestige of French cuisine. This may be explained by the author's social circles, her travels, and her frequent tasting of the so-called haute cuisine, mainly French. Recipes in this category include: "Canapés de patê de fois," "Soufflé," "Soubise," "Salsa à la Maître d'Hôtel," "Sauce Printannière," "Supreme de Partiz," "Soupe a la Reine," "Vol-au-vent," "Velouté de venera," "Riz de veau," "Chaud-froid de Volaille," "Potage Velor," "Perdices aux choux," "Bordelaise," "Pâte brisée," "Gateau de Boyer," "Croquets," and "Pollo a la bonne femme." Although to a lesser extent, recipes from the English-speaking world also make an appearance: "Beefsteak à la Arly," "American Cocktail," "Sandwiches," and "Caraway Seed."

Fourth, in some cases recipes are grouped according to a general category with shifting components. For example, in the revised editions we find more than sixty recipes for "tortas." These vary in the quantity of their ingredients and in the way they are combined or cooked, though they all contain sugar, eggs, some type of fat, and flour (*tortas, bizcochuelos, masitas,* and *gateau*). The same is true of other categories, such as the fifteen recipes for "guisos," a variety of soups (dry, liquid, etc.), *pucheros, cremas,* etc. Thus, a menu was conceptualized as a sum of general categories that are to be further refined according to their ingredients or cooking methods. The dishes favored for lunch or dinner are red meats, fowl (partridge, duck, small birds, pigeons, chicken), fish (pejerrey or odontesthes bonariensis, eel, cod), soups, sauces, purées, vegetable salads, and the classics of criolla cuisine: *locro, chanfaina, puchero, guiso, empanadas,* and puddings. Pasta appears very rarely and mostly as part of the soups: tagliatelle, macaroni, ravioli, gnocchi, and cannelloni. However, the different categories of sweet recipes are presented under the general categories of *tortas,* cakes, pastries, and *alfajores.* Individual recipes within each category are differentiated through the use of a particular name or a variation in the ingredients or cooking methods (baking, boiling, frying, etc.). The mix of traditional Argentine recipes with others taken from international cuisine needs to be underscored here. Similarly, the emphasis on animal protein and the rare appearance of pasta and other dishes seen as less prestigious make it apparent that the cookbooks catered to the tastes of upper middle class households.

Fifth, the written style of the recipes provides essential clues regarding authorship and compilatory methods. As noted before, cookbooks appear under the pseudonym of a cook (i.e., Teófila and Marta) that hides the name of the actual author, Mercedes and Susana.

These cookbooks appear as collaborative efforts that translate into recipe compilations rather than single-authored texts. They are the result of female work that involves not only the lady and her cook, but also friends, relatives, and other cooks as well as cookbooks. The many hands that helped write are evident in the heterogeneous mode of composition, as the cookbook includes recipes with directions on procedures, ingredients, and weights and measures that don't follow one single norm. Specifically, the same page may contain measures stated in kilos, ounces, pounds, or grams or include "kneading" as one of steps while the same action may also appear expressed through the verb *sobar*. Recipes are written as a narrative describing the procedures for the preparation and cooking of food. Ingredients are merely mentioned in the narrative, using their generic terms and in some cases listing a brand name in lower case and as a synonym of the generic term. A recurrent example is that of baking powder, expressed as follows: "two spoonfuls of royal." Such practice is meaningful as it points to a cuisine that had not yet been dominated by a consumer society (Caldo, "Recetas"). Nevertheless, the advancing action of such a consumer society becomes more obvious in subsequent editions. For example, both Marta and Teófila detail the process of preparing turtle soup. *La perfecta cocinera argentina* (1888) indicates that one should cook in salted water "a turtle," meaning the whole animal, whereas years later, in 1914, that same recipe in *La cocinera criolla* called for "a can of turtle soup." Canned goods are representative of the consumer society and packaged-food industry that were budding in 1914 (Goody). Such details as they appear scattered in the pages of cookbooks provide valuable information on the changing habits of an increasingly consumeristic society as well as the impact of the food industry on the eating habits of the Argentine upper middle classes.

Sixth, it is essential to consider the role of the cook. As stated before, cookbooks place greater importance on the person executing the recipes than on ingredients or procedures. For this reason, this cuisine may be seen as based on "human traction," as the secret of its success relies on the actions of those who cook. Many of the recipes begin with a mention of the way the ingredients may be gathered (picking the vegetables or fruits from the garden or killing the animal from which the meat or blood will be obtained). The cook's keen eye is key to selecting the best ingredients, relying on his or her knowledge of the seasons and the best criteria for their selection. The cook for whom these cookbooks are written lacks technology and sophisticated tools such as blenders or choppers and is relying on hand work. The available equipment is minimal and includes such basics as cans used as molds, a rolling pin, or a wire whisk. Cooking relies on the hard work of the cook and the kitchen help, as may be seen, for example, in the "Bombones de chocolate" recipe, in which Teófila Benavento instructs: "Chocolate should be softened on the stove; white icing like the one used for 'Masitas con baño' should be made and some of it mixed with chocolate. One person makes a little ball of white icing, and another puts the chocolate on top of it; [the little balls are] then bathed in thick hot caramel syrup and left to cool" (1901; 17). In another example, the recipe for "Pan con grasa" suggests: "If there are two or three people to knead the dough, let each of them take one piece . . . . It is better if two or three people help because it is hot, and the dough starts to rise quickly" (1901; 105–6).

In sum, when studying these recipes we find that the writing is characterized by a disparity in references to units of weight and measure, a lack of uniformity in the vocabulary used that makes it appear anarchical, ambiguity in presenting cooking utensils and devices, as well as a lack of precision in the cooking times, favoring directions such as "eyeing it," "to taste," and "just a pinch."

These six points mark the profile of the written culinary knowledge of an era. Marta-Mercedes and Teófila-Susana saw fit to publish their cooking recipes in Argentina at the turn of the twentieth century. These cookbooks were not the only ones of their kind, but they helped shape a growing editorial niche. Handwritten notes and notebooks and those compiled by ladies were often transformed into editorial products for purposes that were not exclusively culinary. These cookbooks became focal points that provided topics of conversation during the period. Their authors had to first present themselves as literate women and then move to build a place for themselves in the publishing market in order to claim ownership of the subject and load it with meaningful content. Along the way, a varied set of actors gave a miscellaneous character to the sources of culinary knowledge. While such knowledge defies complete appropriation, it rewards collective efforts by writers and cooks, which, through the compilatory and writing process, become inextricably linked.

NOTES

Translated by Ana M. Gómez-Bravo and Matthew Kullberg.

1. The 528 recipes in the 1915 edition increased to 1076 recipes in 1926 and to 1104 recipes in 1942.

WORKS CITED

Aldao, Elvira. *Recuerdos de antaño*. Jacobo Peuser, 1931.
Apellániz, Mariano. *Callao 1730 y su época*. Edición de autor, 1978.
Arcondo, Aníbal. *Historia de la alimentación en Argentina: Desde los orígenes hasta 1920*. Ferreyra editor, 2002.
Arfuch, Leonor. *El espacio biográfico: Dilemas de la subjetividad contemporánea*. Fondo de Cultura Económica, 2002.
Barrán, José Pedro. *Historia de la sensibilidad en el Uruguay*. Ediciones de la Banda Oriental, 2008. 2 vols.
Batticuore, Graciela. *La mujer romántica: Lectoras, autoras y escritoras en la Argentina: 1830–1870*. Edhasa, 2005.
Benavento, Teófila. *La perfecta cocinera argentina*. Casa Editora de Jacobo Peuser, 1901, 1923.
———. *La perfecta cocinera argentina*. Obras del Divino Rostro, 1940.
Caldo, Paula. *Un cachito de cocinera: Mujeres, libros y recetas de cocina en la Argentina de fines del siglo XIX y principios del XX*. Casagrande, 2017.
———. "La mujer detrás de pseudónimo, reflexiones en torno a una pesquisa de historia con mujeres." *Género y documentación: Relectura sobre fuentes y archivos*, edited by Jaqueline Vassallo, Yolanda de Paz Trueba, and Paula

Caldo, Brujas, 2016, pp. 139–54.

———. *Libros, cocina e inmigración: Una propuesta culinaria con aires rosarinos.* El Ombú Bonsái, 2014.

———. "Recetas, ecónomas, marcas y publicidades: La educación de las mujeres cocineras de la sociedad del consumo. Argentina, 1920–1945." *Arenal: Revista de historia de las mujeres*, vol. 20, no. 1, 2013, pp. 159–90.

Damianovich, Alejandro. *José María Cullen: Altruismo y gestión sanitaria antes del Estado de Bienestar.* Talleres Gráficos de Imprenta Lux S.A., 2003.

Fischler, Claude. *El (h)omnívoro: El gusto, la cocina y el cuerpo.* Anagrama, 1995.

Flandrin, Jean Louis, and Massimo Montanari. *Historia de la alimentación.* Trea, 1996.

Fugardo, Marcela. *Un recetario familiar rioplatense: Cuaderno de recetas de María Varela. Patrimonio inmaterial de San Isidro.* Maizal, 2018.

Giard, Luce. "Hacer de comer." *La invención de lo cotidiano II: Habitar, cocinar*, edited by Michel de Certeau, Luce Giard, and Pierre Mayol, U Iberoamericana de Estudios Superiores de Occidente, 2006, pp. 151–256.

Goody, Jack. *Cocina, cuisine y clase: Estudios de sociología comparada.* Gedisa, 1995.

Losada, Leandro. *La alta sociedad en la Buenos Aires de la Belle-Époque: Sociabilidad, estilos de vida e identidades.* Siglo veintiuno, 2008.

———. *Historia de las élites en la Argentina: Desde la conquista hasta el surgimiento del peronismo.* Sudamericana, 2009.

Marta. *La cocinera criolla y recetario curativo doméstico.* Luis Gili Librero, 1916, 1923, 1926, 1931.

———. *La cocinera criolla: Otras cocinas y recetario curativo doméstico.* 1914.

Pite, Rebekah. *La mesa está servida: Doña Petrona C de Gandulfo y la domesticidad en la Argentina del siglo XX.* Edhasa, 2016.

Remedi, Fernando. *Dime qué comes y cómo lo comes y te diré quién eres: Una historia social del consumo alimentario en la modernización argentina. Córdoba, 1870–1930.* Centro de Estudios Históricos "Prof. Carlos S. A. Segreti," 2006.

Revel, Jean-Francois. *Un festín en palabras: Historia literaria de la sensibilidad gastronómica desde la antigüedad hasta nuestros días.* Tusquets, 1995.

CHAPTER 9

The Evolution of Mexican Cuisine

Five Gastronomical Seasons, Mole, Pozole, Tamal, Tortilla, *and* Chile Relleno

Adolfo Castañón, *Mexican Academy of Language*

A FEW YEARS AGO, on August 6, 2007, the political-culinary manifesto "Campaign in defense of native corn starts in the Historical Center" was published in *La Jornada* and signed by numerous authors, artists, intellectuals, actors, teachers, and plain citizens. The manifesto alerted the government and the general population to the grave dangers and serious material and political risks that the use of transgenic or GMO corn posed for our national economy and identity. The purpose of this movement was to take corn and beans out of the agriculture chapter of the North American Free Trade Agreement (NAFTA/ALENA).

The manifesto, promoted by authors and gastronomes Marco Buenrostro and Cristina Barros and supported by renowned intellectuals such as Miguel León-Portilla, is one additional though decisive episode in a long and persistent battle that dates back at least to the Conquest of Mexico. It was not only arms and shields that collided, but also pots and pans; wooden and iron spoons; grinding stones and mortars; corn and wheat; pork, beef, dog, and iguana meats and—alas!—human flesh; chile and spices; pulque made from the maguey and wine; milk and chocolate. While grains and legumes such as rice and European beans (*alubias*) were coming to Mexico, tomatoes, tobacco, American beans (*frijoles*), potatoes, and nopal cacti were traveling to Europe.

Along with the bedroom, the kitchen was the space for exchange, transfer, and commerce par excellence. "Donde hay maíz, hay país; Donde hay tortilla, hay patria" ("Where there is corn, there is country; Where there is tortilla, there is homeland") are meaningful expressions of the powerful and deeply rooted customs that have risen the banner of a Mexican national identity over political upheaval. Such identity is in the process of acquiring self-consciousness, as is suggested in José Luis Juárez López's title *La lenta emergencia de la comida mexicana: Ambigüedades criollas 1750–1800* (*The Slow Emergence of Mexican Food: Creole Ambiguities 1750–1800*). It could be said that Mexican cuisine emerges dish by dish as it feels threatened, exiled, discriminated against, rejected, or distorted when, like its corn, it is also turned transgenic, transmexican.

On the upper level of the old Jardín de Plantas (Plant Garden) situated near the Austerlitz station in Paris lies a melancholic museum. Extinct species, animals that have disappeared from Earth such as the saber-toothed cat, the dodo bird, and certain varieties of the royal eagle, are on display there. Shouldn't there also be an exhibit of our conjectural cuisine and of extinct gastronomies?

It is a well-known fact that languages disappear at a vertiginous pace. This is addressed in the interdisciplinary project "Enduring Voices" that attempts to compile a sort of linguistic testament of the planet, as reported in the *New York Times* (Grau 38). A less-noticed fact is that each language carries a sort of shadow, a particular culinary expression, a gastronomy. How many cuisines must have disappeared, and how many more are on the brink of vanishing? How many dishes, cheeses, and drinks have become extinct in the course of history? How many modes of food preparation have been erased? Each day a cuisine is lost, each day a gastronomic sensibility disappears, each night the name and use of an herb, essential for a particular dish, is forgotten. I ask myself these questions and many more when I face the title of this essay, "The Evolution of Mexican Cuisine." Can we talk about a Mexican cuisine? Isn't this designation a conceptual abuse that allows us to place easy nametags on a multiform and protean reality?

A bibliographical proof of the diversity of Mexican cuisine may be found in the series published by the National Council for Culture and the Arts (Consejo Nacional para la Cultura y las Artes) and the Advisory Office for Popular, Indigenous, and Urban Cultures (Dirección General de Culturas Populares, Indígenas y Urbanas), which gathers previously scattered gastronomic information from all geographic points in Mexico into forty volumes. There are also many collections of recipes, notebooks, dictionaries, and cookbooks that include old documents, both previously published and unpublished. In addition, there are editorial projects intended to make information widely available. These include the *Encyclopedic Dictionary of Mexican Gastronomy* (*Diccionario Enciclopédico de la gastronomía mexicana*) by Ricardo Muñoz Zurita, and the ten-volume *Mexican Cuisine Through the Centuries* (*Cocina mexicana a través de los siglos*) written by several renowned authors (Krauze and González de la Vara). Also deserving of mention is the *Gastronomic Song-Book of Mexico* (*El que come y canta: Cancionero gastronómico de México*) by Aline Desentis Otárola, which documents the profound literary and musical relationship that Mexican popular culture has with the world of food.

Does Mexican cuisine, if we can refer to it as an entity, initiate its history the first time that American ingredients were combined with native elements, when *mestizaje* (miscegenation) first occurred? Or should it be dated at an earlier time? Sophie D. Coe, historian, anthropologist and author of *America's First Cuisines* (translated into Spanish as *Las primeras cocinas de América*), dates early Mexican cuisine to thousands of years before the Conquest. Further, Coe disproves the notion of the proverbial isolation among Native American cultures through her analysis of documentary and archeological evidence.

Perhaps it is not redundant to say that Mexican cuisine is born with the entity, later identity, called Mexico, which is in its turn the product of a long process of combinations, fusions, chemical transformations, and grafting. Much like its geography and its material and symbolic institution, cuisine is a space traversed by history, tense with conflict, wounded with the arrow of social, religious, and political contradictions. For example, in the culture of the "New Spain" there exists an obvious correspondence between baroque architecture—those seventeenth-century golden altars and literary forms, close to Góngora, of Juana Inés de la Cruz—and gastronomy (giving the sumptuous *mole* a liturgical habit).

The "Prehistoric" Age

The history of Mexican cuisine, or of Mexican cuisines, could be subject to a periodization that combines the evolution of language and that of literary and artistic styles with the action of communication and domination.

We should begin with a remote prehistoric age dating farther back than the discovery of the hybrid or genetic hybrid that is corn and its siblings, the domesticated frijol and chile. That age is characterized by hunting, fishing, gathering, and the use of weeds, wild herbs, and plants. Bernardino de Sahagún, in his *Universal History of the Things of New Spain*, or *Florentine Codex* (*Historia Universal de las cosas de Nueva España*), and Francisco Hernández, in *History of the Plants of New Spain* (*Historia de las plantas de Nueva España*), listed more than two hundred new plants, but Francisco Espinosa García and José Sarukhán list several thousand in their *Handbook of Wild Plants from the Valley of*

Mexico (*Manual de malezas del Valle de México*), including wild mushrooms and fruits, in particular those of the cucurbits like pumpkin and chayote, much valued by José Antonio Alzate and eighteenth-century Jesuits. From this remote age, the future will preserve the use of edible herbs like *quelite* (which may include amaranth, pigweed, or other herbs), *quintonil*, purslane, nopal, wild tomato, and all sorts of edible mushrooms such as *clavitos* and *pajaritos*, and even hallucinogenic mushrooms, which experts such as Gordon Wasson prefer to call "entheogens." From the thick subsoil come the different types of chile or capsicum (the proverbial "I am like the green chile, hot but tasty") as well as the multitude of medicinal plants that also function as condiments, which include epazote, sage, aloe vera, cilantro, rue, and many others.

In his discussion about *Relación de Michoacán*, written in the Purépecha language in the sixteenth century, novelist and essayist J. M. Le Clézio pointed out that mestizaje, at least in gastronomy, took place before the Conquest:

> The main event in purépecha history [...is the] moment [in which] Michoacán civilization crystalizes and begins to "take root"; in the *Relación de Michoacán* they are mentioned by the *petáutli* between the tenth and eleventh centuries as an encounter around the intimate event of a meal: ". . . and the fisherman was sweating from roasting fish and he kept giving them fish as he was roasting, and they ate that fish and said: 'it is true, it has good flavor.' And as the chichimecas ate all sorts of game, [. . .] they took a rabbit out of their nets and put it on the fire, and after it had been roasted they skinned it and set out the roasted rabbit and told the fisherman: 'islander, eat some of this, and see what flavor it has, for we hunted it.' And as the fisherman put a bite-sized piece of the rabbit in his mouth, the chichimecas asked him: 'so islander, how does what you are eating taste?' He answered: 'Lord, this is real food; it is not a matter of bread, because although fish is good food, it reeks and becomes boring; but this food of yours does not reek, but it is real food.'" (Le Clézio 113–14)

Corn, Taco, Pinole

For our purposes, history begins with the discovery of corn, the cultivation of which brought a true agricultural revolution that revolved around its grain. From corn prepared with nixtamal comes masa, the goddess mother of the paradise of *tortillas, tacos, sopes, tlacoyos, quesadillas, chivichangas, gorditas, tamales, tostadas, corundas,* and drinks like *atole* or *chileatole*. Even the plague of the corn plant, *huitlacoche* (a sort of vegetable tumor that thrives like a violet-colored parasite), is food when properly cooked and seasoned. Boiled corn goes into *pozole*; corncobs toasted or roasted are those delicacies called *elotes*. Corn is also eaten as popcorn and boiled and seasoned with herbs; the boiled corn kernels are consumed as *esquites*.

Furthermore, there is the enormous variety of tacos that can be stuffed with practically anything: *tlacoyos* and *quesadillas*, but also tortillas filled with fish or meat like *empanadas* (turnovers) fried in fat (*baril huah* or *cayil huah* in Mayan) or simply browned in a pan or *comal*: "chanchanes." The most reliable reference on this topic is José N. Iturriaga's *De tacos, tamales y tortas,* which stands out for its juicy chapter on "Indigenous Tacos." These tend to be regional specialties that sound eccentric and unique because they stem from a "cuisine of hunger" poised to invent foods where there are seemingly none: tacos filled with *charales* (small lake fish, Chirostoma), maguey worms, *acociles* (freshwater crayfish), *escamoles* (ant larvae and pupae), crickets or grasshoppers, live *jumiles* (a kind of beetle), *ahuaucles* (aquatic fly eggs), *quelite, manjúa* (just born fish and crustacean larvae), ants, *gusano elotero* (corn earworm), *toritos* or *periquitos* (avocado leaf pests), nopal worms, *xonhues xaue* (fragrant bugs), *aneneztli* (dragonfly larvae), *chicharras de guamúchil* (cicada of the *guamúchil* tree), *gusanos barrenadores* (fly larvae that feed on the flesh of live animals), *ticocos* (larvae from dead wood) or *cuauhocuilín* (wood worm eggs), *huenches* (strawberry tree butterfly catterpillars), and *cuetlas* or *tepolchichic* (spotted and horned caterpillars or larvae of the so-called deadman's butterfly).

There are subtle varieties of corn cuisine. Alfonso Reyes associates the corn masa drink, *pinole*, with the "sensual tickling of the diminutive ... which, in a display of tact, dresses up fleas and makes up a wedding party with them" and with the very "miracle of the Holy Host" that "joins in a slight pretext of matter the power of God." And he adds:

> The technique of the minute, when applied to the palate, would make us talk about "pinole," the last residue of the grinding of grain: corn, *cacahuacintle*, or fluffy white maize that has been previously toasted, ground in the *metate* with cinnamon and *piloncillo*, which is black sugar before it is refined. This treat exists in the limits of matter, on the brink of being mistaken for one's breath. Breath alone is needed to absorb or reject it, and for that reason our proverb says, "One can't whistle and eat pinole," which is the same as: "One can't be in the procession and tolling the bells." The person who eats pinole, like the one who eats *polvorones* (a crumbly shortbread cookie), has to keep the mouth shut; and he who doesn't know when to close it, will choke because—as people say—"it hits you in the uvula." (Reyes, *Memorias* 110)

In that relatively remote history a distinction could be drawn between a rural and peasant cuisine and an urban and cosmopolitan or transregional cuisine that equally appeared among the Mayas, the Aztecs, and the Nahuas of the high plateaus. From its beginnings, so-called Mexican cuisine was basically "[a] peasant cuisine elevated to the level of a sophisticated art," as Diana Kennedy states in *The Cuisines of Mexico* (qtd. in Pilcher, *Vivan* 19). But to talk about a rural cuisine is to talk about a cuisine of hunger. The Mexican culinary bastion is indeed anchored in precariousness and poverty, but it turns such conditions into parameters for a secondary level of food preparation: it is acceptable to eat everything, such as insects, flowers, stems, herbs, plants, seedlings, legumes, fruit; animals like deer or rat, iguana or snake, those that fly, like ducks, or those that swim, like shrimp or carp. Drinks are made from agave, maguey, fruit peels (*tepache* is made from fermented pineapple rind), corn, and obviously chocolate. That cuisine of hunger involves an inventive grammar and a syntax that creates the basic elements—corn, frijol, chile, tomato, agave, chocolate—that would be like the vowels of a discourse in permanent transformation and adaptation. Even though the Conquest or encounter between two worlds fertilized the culinary arts on both sides of the Atlantic, it also kept alive and safe, as though in a sort of greenhouse or vivarium, numerous culinary and gathering practices. To a large extent, this was possible because of the racism and classism that for a long time, until well into the nineteenth century, viewed with contempt basic national foods like corn, chile, pulque, frijol, or tomato, which were fundamental in the configuration not only of a transregional diet but also for the very identity of Mexico. In pre-Hispanic times, plebeians and lords were eating what was fundamentally the same diet, although the rich also consumed exotic foods brought from other geographic regions.

Pre-Hispanic Cuisine

The country of Mexico shares its name with a city originally situated on an extensive lake system, with one salt-water and several fresh-water lakes, that spreads from Texcoco to the city of Mexico Tenochtitlán, so called because of the small but fierce tribe of the Aztec Mexica that had settled on an islet there. The Mexicas were the last group of the nahuas, hailing from the distant land of Aztlán.

When the Spaniards arrived, the island of Tenochtitlán had five thousand inhabitants who fed on agricultural products, game, fresh fish, ducks (*chichicuilotes*), and insects (*chapulines*) that were transported along with other products in canoes arriving from various places. Conquistador Hernán Cortés describes one of the markets in Tenochtitlán:

There is a street for game, where they sell every species of birds found in the country, such as hens, partridges, quails, wild ducks, fly-catchers, widgeons, turtle-doves, pigeons, reedbirds, parrots, sparrows, eagles, hawks, sparrowhawks, and kestrels. They sell the skins of some of these birds of prey with their feathers, head, beak, and claws. They also sell rabbits, hares, deer, and small dogs, which are castrated and raised for eating. There are also streets of herb-sellers where you will find all the kinds of roots and medicinal herbs that grow in the country.... There are all kinds of green vegetables, especially onions, leeks, garlic, cress, watercress, borage, sorrel, cardoons, and golden thistle. There are all sorts of fruits, including cherries and plums that are similar to those from Spain. They sell bees' honey and wax, and honey made from the stalks of corn, which are as honey-like and sweet as sugar-cane; and honey from a plant that in other islands is called maguey, which is much better than fruit syrup (*arrope*).... They sell pies made with fowl and fish *empanadas*. They sell hen and goose eggs, and eggs of all the other birds I have mentioned in great quantity. They sell ready-cooked egg omelettes. Finally, [it must be said that] everything that can be found throughout the whole country is sold in these markets, which in addition to those already mentioned are so numerous and so diverse that I cannot name them all in order to avoid prolixity and also because I cannot recall them all or don't know how to write their names. (Spanish text in Cortés 235–36)

In his prodigious *Visión de Anáhuac*, Alfoso Reyes gives his own gloss of *La historia verdadera de la conquista de la Nueva España* (*The True History of the Conquest of New Spain*):

The buzzing and noise of the square—says Bernal Díaz—astonishes those who have been to Constantinople and Rome. It is like a dizziness of the senses, like a Breughel dream, where the allegories of matter gain a spiritual warmth. In picturesque bewilderment, the conquistador comes and goes through the streets of the fair and preserves among his memories the emotion of a rare and pulsating chaos: forms that fuse together; colors burst like flares; the appetite wakens to the spicy scent of the herbs and spices. From the tray spills out a whole paradise of fruit: color spheres, transparent ampoules, bunches of spears, scaly pineapples, and leafy hearts. In the round trays of sardines spin silver and saffron reflections, fin trimmings and brush tails; out of a barrel comes the beastly head of the fish, all astonishment with its big moustache. (29–30)

Aztecs were an extremely religious (that is, scrupulous) people, and the first of their fruits were offered to the gods and goddesses of their pantheon. The excavations of the Templo Mayor (Main Temple) undertaken in the last few years by a sophisticated and multidisciplinary team of archeologists headed by Eduardo Matos Moctezuma confirmed, not without surprise, the boldest hypotheses on the extent of the military and commercial empire ruled by the Aztecs. Conch shells, skeletons of fish only found in deep ocean waters, and bones from birds and reptiles that are only found in coastal areas confirm notions of the extension of the territory dominated by an empire that, due to its vast scale, could be termed cosmopolitan, as it received and assimilated products and practices that were widely spread throughout all Mesoamerica. A history of contemporary Mexican gastronomy must record the formal candlelit dinner that in 1990 Eduardo Matos offered to a select number of guests at the Templo Mayor. In an unpublished recorded statement, Eduardo Matos recounted:

> Years ago we offered a banquet for ninety-nine guests with nine pre-Hispanic dishes cooked by Patricia Quintana (a great chef), where the number nine corresponded to the nine steps to Mictlán [Aztec underworld]. The guest number one hundred was death, and for this reason there was one empty chair. There were chants in Nahua performed by a children's choir, and the cups from which we drank were broken much like it had been done with household goods every fifty-two years. Among the guests were Bertha and José Luis Cuevas and many more. The table was shaped like a cross to symbolize the

four directions of the universe. It took place on a side of the Templo Mayor, in Santa Teresa la Antigua (because the guests could not all fit in the Templo Mayor).

It can be said that the long trajectory of Mexican cuisine starts in those vast *tianguis* or markets (like today's Tlatelolco market, La Lagunilla and Tepito), where products from a vast extension of the Mesoamerican continent were mixed and combined. It would be fitting to say that before entering the realm of history, the cuisines of Mexico spread out geographically like the foothills of a great mountain and came to converge in a symbolic center thanks to the military and commercial exercise of the wondrous empire that was able to raise the extinct torches of such other cultures as the Teotihuacan or the Olmec.

The use of Nahuatl spread to what Alexander von Humboldt would later call "Mexican America" and went on to become a sort of lingua franca that was dominant throughout that vast territory. Nahuatl prevailed over many regional languages, defeating other less powerful cultures. It may be supposed that, much like the use of Nahuatl overtook other languages (though with exceptions like the Tarasco and the Zapotec), the other side of the tongue, cuisine, also imposed its customs and utensils, along with culinary techniques that were Nahua's own in content and form. Similarly, it may be assumed that, in turn, the Nahuatl absorbed the habits and customs of other peoples.

Corn and Tamal

As has been stated before, a prehistory, or rather an epoch previous to that of the great urban settlements, spread out as a backdrop of a wild and nomadic era before domestication. "Domestication," a word that is more commonly used in reference to animals, can explain, when referring to corn, why this plant was deified and symbolically inscribed in the pre-Hispanic religious pantheon.

Each time period, each month, was presided over by a god or goddess to whom gifts and offerings were presented. Each god was due a specific gastronomic gift; each god was adored—by way of the mouth—with a dish and a drink. Man was made of corn, as the Quiché say in *Popol Vuh*: "the making, the modeling of our first mother-father, with yellow corn, white corn alone for the flesh, food alone for the human legs and arms, for our first fathers" (164). Maize, *imix*, is the name of the first day in the Mayan calendar, and the image of the calendar glyph shows a breast, symbol of the original food.

Corn can be white, yellow, red, blue, violet. Its transformation into a food first requires a process called *nixtamal* or *mixtamal*, as well as a *metate*, a flat stone that works as a mortar with the help of a cylinder. For many centuries until well into the nineteenth, when the process became mechanized, grinding corn in the *metate* was a woman's daily work: "Each morning she returned to the stone on hands and knees, with back sloped as if she herself were a *metate* wielded by some tyrannical maize goddess" (Pilcher, *Que vivan* 101), or as though the metate were the name of "another Aztec deity, another sacrificial stone" (Reyes, *Memorias* 92).

Once ground, corn is used to make tortillas and tamales. What is a tamal? "To the one who is born to be a tamal, heaven gives the leaves" ("Al que nace para tamal, del cielo le caen las hojas"). Tamal is made with a corn masa that is ground on a *metate* and later spread out and stuffed; it is wrapped in corn husks or banana leaves and steamed. Tamales come in various sizes. Their shape can be elongated or square. Tamales range from those made in the North, stuffed with shredded meat, to the titanic *zacahuiles*, which can encase a turkey, a pig, and a hen. Tamales can be wrapped in corn husks (as they do in the high plateaus and the North) and in banana leaves (as done in the Southeast and the Gulf Coast). They can be stuffed with adobo, iguana, deer, turkey, pheasant, *tepezcuintle* (lowland paca), beans, white beans, *chaya* (tree spinach), and starting in the sixteenth century, pork and beef. They can be cooked buried underground, steamed, or using the "pib" method (cooked in buried dirt ovens).

There are several different kinds of tamal in Yucatán: *Chachacuahes*, made with achiote, thus the doubling of the syllable *chac*; *polcanes*, small corn cakes that are made to resemble a snake head; and *dzotobichayes*, cakes made with corn masa mixed with *chaya*. In Chiapas we find *jacuané*, a tamal made with masa and stuffed with pureed beans and pulverized shrimp heads, the whole wrapped in *acuyo* and *hoja santa* (Mexican pepperleaf) leaves. In the Northeastern part of Mexico, in the mountains of La Huasteca region, along the borders of the states of Veracruz, Hidalgo, San Luis, and Tamaulipas, they make *zacahuil*, a gigantic tamal that envelops a small pig or a whole turkey. The *zacahuil* is steamed in an underground oven and eaten in situ. The formidable tamal, wrapped in banana leaves and seasoned, is lowered onto a plank where it is left to cook as though in a *barbacoa*. When it emerges from the earth's belly, it is consumed by pinching out portions with the bare fingers. This dish is eaten in the festivity honoring the dead, functioning as an institution in which the community is founded. In the area spanning from Aguascalientes to Monterrey in the North, there are thin and small tamales thickly stuffed in a corn layer. The tamales of Oaxaca, Tabasco, and Yucatán in the Southeast resemble the Venezuelan *hayacas* and may be filled with mole and chicken but also, much as is done in Venezuela, with complex minced fillings. It is said that the creole *hayaca*, cooked in Venezuela and Colombia, gathered in a single dish the generous leftovers of the rich Creoles' brimming tables.

Preparing corn masa for tamales is long and tedious work. In the early 1950s, the Mexican company Herdez invented processed flour ready for canning: the *tamalina*, which met with great success and is now a registered trademark that has given way to a prosperous industry. In addition to *tamalina*, there are other processed products such as *maicena* that may be used to prepare tamales. Tamalina, much like the Doña María brand of industrially prepared mole, is mostly consumed outside Mexico by the Mexican emigrants moving to neighboring states such as California, Texas, and New Mexico or even farther north, to Chicago and Canada. It can also be found in some cosmopolitan supermarkets in Europe, specifically those in Paris, Madrid, and Frankfurt.

The mechanization of corn grinding took many years to master. Starting at the turn of the twentieth century, growing industrialization first helped improve the grinding processes and then made possible the mass production of tortillas for initiatives financed by entrepreneurs like Rodolfo Celorio. Mechanization and industrialization processes were more or less simultaneous with the political and social movement known as the Mexican Revolution, whose ideologues advocated for the industrialization of rural areas and for rural values. Further, these advocates supported ad-hoc education programs that would train agricultural engineers in the latest technologies. One such program was established in the famous University of Chapingo, which today houses some little-known murals by Diego Rivera, among which are *Tierra fecunda, con las fuerzas naturales controladas por el hombre* (Fertile Earth, with Natural Forces Controlled by Man; 1926) and *La sangre de los mártires revolucionarios fertilizando la tierra* (Blood of Revolutionary Martyrs Fertilizing the Earth; 1926). It is in this context that waves of nationalist affirmation ensued, bringing out rural cuisine from the shadows of the oral tradition and situating it as crown and center of national pride. Professional cooks like Josefina Velásquez de León, Mayita, Salvador Novo, and Sodi-Pallares, as well as plastic artists Diego Rivera and Frida Kahlo, participated in the mission of "saving the tongue (*lengua*/language) with the tongue" and redeeming the country through the transformation of its cuisine and its language. This movement carried a revolutionary impetus, since Mexican cuisine had not been considered its own entity and had been viewed as only marginal, regional, susceptible to discrimination and rejection.

The Colony and Mole

During colonial times, the cooking done in convents and the palaces of the viceroyalty was mainly a Spanish or Iberian cuisine that had been transported to America. The Mexican cuisine that was emerging, sprouting, so to speak, from among the rocks, prospered along the city walls, in the periphery of the rural world that was slowly being colonized, and in the interstices of recipes.

The *guajolote* or *pavo* (turkey) was considered an unworthy food, if not dirty, during colonial times, although later in nineteenth-century Jalisco it came to be called "governor," perhaps because this watchful and flamboyant bird rules the farmyard. The tomato was regarded with suspicion in Europe until well into the nineteenth century. Beans (frijoles), tamales, and tortillas, which the Marchioness of Calderón de la Barca could only tolerate when freshly made, were synonymous with indigenous, peasant, and poor food. Nopales and *tunas* (prickly pears) have only recently been added to the official tables in Mexico.

It is said that mole was invented by Sister Andrea in the convent of Santa Rosa in Puebla de los Ángeles. Artemio de Valle-Arizpe relates the origin of this dish in a narrative that is as polychromatic as a Talavera tile. According to Alfonso Reyes, the labyrinthine recipe for mole produces "a changing brightness of aromas and flavors, like a new iridescent tail that stands for the one that [the turkey] has lost in its last hour" (*Memorias* 113). The walls of the labyrinth that is the *mole poblano* are made of toasted *pasilla* chile, pieces of bread and tortillas fried in lard, chocolate, toasted chile seeds, sesame seeds, vinegar, sugar, spices, ancho chile, garlic, laurel leaf, dephlegmated onion, *tornillo chile*, plums, *perón* apples, and about half a liter of sherry.

Mole is both creole and mestizo, while evoking the Turk, proverbial enemy of Christendom, due to its use of pine nuts and pecans that are mixed in the grind. Mole is eaten with an escort of cured pulque made with hazelnut and banana. There are those who maintain that mole is a sort of Mexican curry, a product of the three centuries that the viceroyalty of New Spain was in contact with the Philippines. In addition to mole poblano or red mole, Oaxaca has black, green, yellow, and red mole, as well as *pipián* (made with ground pumpkin seeds), *manchamanteles*, and the red, yellow, and orange *achiotes* that speak to the Mexican need to envelop meats in sauces and cover them with eye-catching colors. A further mention should be made of the mole made with goat rump that is eaten in the area around Tehuacán, Puebla. In addition to the heavy mole or *pipián* sauces, there are everyday light sauces made with tomato, tomatillo, chile, and water.

The Manila Galleon is said to have traveled every year between Acapulco and the Philippines, so named in honor of King Felipe II. This commercial route brought to Mexico rice and *manchamanteles*, that succulent combination of tropical fruits and aromatic chiles that helps round out the blend of China's sweet and sour sauces as well as that of mole. In its turn, when paired with beans, rice would form that perfect marriage of "Moors and Christians" (*moros y cristianos*, or rice and beans) that is one of the bases of Caribbean and Southeastern Mexican cuisines. The poet Manuel José Othón has left a delicious description of mole as the protagonist of a popular Mexican banquet in his short story "Una fiesta casera" ("A Home Feast") (111–20). Much like other elements of Mexican cuisine, mole has gone from being ground on a stone *metate* and *molcajete* to the mechanical and electric mill and packaged in cans or glass jars for commercial purposes: Herdez and Doña María are two of the brands of industrially made mole.

Pozole

The following lines may serve as a transition to the section on pozole: "También llegó un guajolote, / pero convertido en mole / y llegó también al trote / un cochino hecho pozole" ("So came a turkey / though turned into mole / and trotting by also came / a pig made into pozole"; Mendoza 725). We can add a quote from *Los de abajo* (*The Underdogs*), where a figurative use of the term is used to imply that there has been no fight: "Vente ya, loco, que al fin no hubo pozole" ("Come already, you madman, for in the end there was no pozole"; Azuela 198).

When describing the celebration in honor of the god Xipe, Franciscan friar and chronicler Bernardino de Sahagún states that the captives were sacrificed by being skinned alive and adds that the elders called *quaquacuilli* later took the bodies to the community area or *calpulco*, where the captive's owner had made his vow or promise. There they divided the captive's body and sent Moctezuma a thigh to eat, and the rest was distributed among the other principal people and the relatives. The flesh was eaten at the house of the person who had captured the dead man. They boiled the flesh with corn and served everyone a piece of the flesh in a deep bowl or *cajete* along with some broth and boiled corn. That meal was called *tlacatlaolli*. After the meal came drunkenness. Thus, pozole was the dish that was prepared for the celebration of Xipe Totec among the Aztecs. It was a sacred food that joined the flesh of the skinned, sacrificed in honor of the god, with corn, divine flesh. Sowing, harvesting, and preparing corn were in and of themselves natural processes, as well as allusive to rituals symbolizing the creation, death, and resurrection of God. We may recall, along with Fernando del Paso in his preface to *Douceur et passion de la cuisine mexicaine*, that if the Aztecs practiced ritual cannibalism on the night of San Bartolomé, "Men who were not cannibals ate the liver and heart of Huguenots and made 'ear fricassé'" (21).

But with the arrival of the Spanish, pork would substitute for human flesh in the dish. Today pozole is cooked everywhere, and it is considered a good hangover cure for habitual drunkenness. Pozole is a stew made with tender corn, pork, and chile. A popular saying in relation to a silly person goes, "What a good head for pozole" ("Qué buena cabeza para un potzoli"). Pozole or *potzoli*, as it is called in Michoacán, is made only with a certain type of corn (the one called *cacahuazintle*) that is soaked for one day and one night. Afterward, it is set to boil with or without pork, according to preference. In some places in Michoacán it is made with pig trotters.

Pozole must be prepared by first soaking white corn kernels that have had their tip cap removed. It is then boiled lightly and cooked with the meat in one piece and a pig's head; thus, the expression "each head is a different pozole" ("cada cabeza, un pozole"). Thursday is the best day to make pozole because it is tastiest eaten on Friday and Saturday after it has been reheated. There is a certain familial resemblance between pozole and Spanish *cocido*, which became very well acclimated and adapted not only in Mexico but throughout the Americas, thus proving the profound unity of the "other" Spanish tongue. In Yucatán, pozole is only mentioned as a drink. According to the *Diccionario de mejicanismos* (*Dictionary of Mexican Terms*) by Francisco J. Santamaría and Joaquín García Icazbalceta, "pozole with a snout" ("pozole con trompa") is a "familiar expression in Guanajuato meaning gossip, mess, story, or rumor. 'To be like the pozole of Sayula, of pure snout, of pure mouth' is a figurative and injurious expression that is used to scorn braggarts or the loudmouthed (the comparison is ingenious because it is said that the pozole of Sayula, in Jalisco, is made only with pig's head)" (886).

Pozole is an atlas or museum, a *tianguis*, a market where meat, corn, radishes, lettuce or cabbage, oregano, chile, onions, and lime coexist. It is a living and warm metaphor of concord and national consciousness: an image of the national pact that exists before the country is created. Pozole is—always—coming to be.

Each region in Mexico prepares pozole differently: in Guerrero it has sardines, in Sinaloa it has shrimp, in the Plateau it is cooked with pork or chicken, but never, curiously enough, with beef, which leads us to a new digression. Mexican female cooks tend to be conservative. It should not be assumed that they would deviate from the traditional recipes and cook, for example, beef pozole. Any such request would be regarded with suspicion. One day I asked Irma, the house cook, to make pozole with beef, but it was impossible. She boiled corn as she always did; she then boiled beef and left up to us the grave responsibility of mixing those two boiled dishes into one. For her the request had been a profanation.

Insects

The use of insects in Mexican cuisine is tenacious and enduring: *chapulines*, grasshoppers roasted with lime and *piquín* chile, are to this day served as garnish and appetizer in Oaxaca and in Mexico City; *acociles*, small freshwater crayfish, are eaten in tacos; *jumiles*, a kind of beetle (from the Nahuatl *xomitl*), are devoured alive in Morelos, in a tortilla or with a sauce, or dried and toasted; *escamoles* (ant lavae) are eaten in various parts of Jalisco and Oaxaca; the agave plant is the source of mezcal as well as the maguey worm, which is sometimes added to bottles of mezcal. There are various books on the delicate matters of entomophagy and entomophobia, among which we may highlight the amusing *Insectos comestibles, entre el gusto y la aversión* (*Edible Insects: Between Pleasure and Aversion*) by Federico Arana. The author notes a singular development of our time: the diverse and prosperous markets of edible insects spread throughout Canada and the United States, as exemplified by the Food Insects Festival of North America and the journal *The Food Insects Newsletter*, an initiative by Professor Florence V. Dunkel.

Cookbooks

Gastronomic discourse, writing about food and cuisine, crosses over to literature. In the first place, there are recipe books mostly produced by women. In convents, anonymous nuns put together recipe collections or diet books during the three centuries that comprise the colonial period. However, it is also the case that authors like Fernando del Paso and Socorro (Gordillo) del Paso have written their own cookbooks individually or as part of a team. Strictly speaking, there are no cookbooks among the pre- and post-Hispanic codices. However, the copious allusions and gastronomic attributions found for each deity make—why not?—those sacred books of ancient Mexico cookbooks also. The recipe book must involve a vast and detailed research in— there is no other way to put it—oral culture. The plate, pan, pot, and frying pan may be seen as the stage, the battlefield between the outside and the inside, as well as the area for the combat among the diverse interiors and the diverse social classes and regions. Italo Calvino portrayed Mexican cuisine in that light in the pages of his book *Bajo el sol jaguar* (*Under a Jaguar Sun*). According to Calvino, Mexican cuisine results "from a battlefield between the aggressive ferocity of the old gods of the high plateau and the sinuous overabundance of baroque religion" (in Paso, *La cocina mexicana* 20). But as Paso reminds us, ferocity was present on both sides, and blood ran in the *autos-da-fé* and "over the skin of the sinister Spanish Christs" (24).

Beyond the isolated mentions of dishes, fruits, or vegetables in poems, novels, and short stories, from Sor Juana and Gutiérrez Nájera to Tablado, Novo, Reyes, or even the emotional and sentimental Laura Esquivel, other authors have focused on the subject of cuisine. Five recent ones may be highlighted: *Las memorias de cocina y bodega* (*Memoirs of Kitchen and Cellar*), as well as the poem "Minuta" ("Menu"), both by Alfonso Reyes; *La cocina mexicana* (*Mexican Cuisine*) by Salvador Novo; *Nueva guía de descarriados* (*New Guide for the Stray*) by José Fuentes Mares, as well as the work by historian Luis González y González, author of several essays on the cuisine of Michoacán collected in *La querencia*. Finally, *Libro de cocina: Convento de San Jerónimo* (*The Cookbook of the Convent of San Jerónimo*) deserves mention; it is thought to contain recipes selected and copied by Sor Juana Inés de la Cruz. The edition of this cookbook edited by Josefina Muriel and Guadalupe Pérez San Vicente is headed by this sonnet, which I cannot but copy here:

> Lisonjeando, oh hermana, a mi amor propio
> me conceptúo formar esta escritura
> del Libro de cocina y ¡qué locura!
> concluirla y luego vi lo mal que copio.
> De nada sirve el cuidado propio
> para que salga llena de hermosura,
> pues por falta de ingenio y de cultura,
> un rasgo no he hecho que no salga impropio.
> Así ha sido, hermana, ¿pero qué senda
> podrá tomar el que con tal servicio
> su grande voluntad quiso se entienda?
> ¿Qué ha de hacer? Suplicaros que, propicia,
> apartando los ojos de la ofrenda
> su deseo recibáis en sacrificio (Sor Juana Inés de la Cruz 11)

Flattering, my pride, sister,
I think of giving shape to this writing
of the Cookbook and, what madness!,
conclude it, and soon I saw how poorly I copy.
Proper care is no use
when trying to make it come out full of beauty,
because lacking wit and education,
I have not made a stroke that is not unbecoming.
It has been so, sister, but what path
may be taken by the one who wants
his great will to be understood with such service?
What can he do? Just to beg that, propitious,
averting the eyes from the offering,
you may accept his wish as sacrifice.

Though it is a well-known and proven fact that the conquistadors and colonizers tried Mexican cuisine with wonder (sometimes with fascination and other times with resigned repugnance), it is also clear that they brought with them a taste for all Spanish and European things and that they tried to adapt Mexican culinary matter to their molds and norms. Salvador Novo states that the origin of Mexican cuisine may be dated to the moment in which the first Spaniard ate the first pork taco, or rather, as Guadalupe Rivera proposes, it may be seen as a mere game of the imagination: "It was the 'cochinita pibil' from the Yucatan Peninsula when the achiote, *Kukub* or marinade used to prepare the armadillo *huetch* of the indigenous tradition, was substituted by the sour oranges that the Spaniards brought along with other citrus" (xv).

What we now call Mexican cuisine is the result of a set of processes of hybridization, miscegenation, grafting, adaptation, and fusion not only between two races or two civilizations, Spanish and indigenous, but also among diverse regions and geographies. These mixtures and combinations took place in the fertile space of the kitchens and stoves first dominated by women. Recipe books have been published in Mexico since the early dates of the colonial period.

Most of them came from convent kitchens (Castelló Yturbide et al.). Examples may be found in *Un acercamiento a la comida novohispana: Segundo miércoles de cuaresma en el Convento Jerónimo de San Lorenzo* (*An Introduction to Food in New Spain: Second Wednesday during Lent in the Hieronymite Convent of San Lorenzo*; Mexico, 1628) or in *Viandas y fatigas para el recibimiento del arzobispo Alonso Núñez de Haro y Peralta* (*Viands and Travails for the Welcoming of Archbishop Alonso Núñez de Haro y Peralta*; Puebla, 1722) (see Bazarte). Even though in principle all nuns were daughters of God, those who were Spanish and Creole were given wheat bread, chocolate, and the occasional viand of pork, hen, or turkey meat, while mestiza nuns, maids, and indigenous female youth were instead given *atole*, corn, beans, and chile.

Mexican history may be deciphered against the backdrop of the conventual cuisine produced by a viceroyalty of filigree, to allude once more to an expression coined by Alfonso Reyes. But it will not be the history of the nation made in deeds of arms and military prowess but rather the murmured and whispered history of the motherland or the homeland, the slow pulse of culinary preparation, of mastication and digestion. In the space of the conventual kitchen of the sixteenth, seventeenth, and eighteenth centuries, it may be seen how, even if there were idols behind the altars as suggested by Anita Brenner, likewise the pots, *metates*, and mills lent themselves to the disguise of taste. Proof of such actions is found in some Inquisitorial processes, where cuisine and witchcraft (Camarena), gastronomy and traditional medicine could go hand in hand. Chiles could be used to make a good sauce or to feed a cleansing smoke, an egg could be used for nourishment or to be rubbed over the body of a child afflicted by evil eye, menstrual blood could be added to chocolate in order to "rope in a man," and finally *toloache* (poisonous flowering plants), mushrooms, peyote, and *oliliuqui* (snakeplant), which are highly toxic, were prepared in the same cooking spaces.

However, the recipes of strictly indigenous foods or those of indigenous origin would take centuries to cross the limits of decency and move from an oral transmission mainly performed by women to the domain of written culture. These indigenous foods include *tamales*, *atole, tacos, sopes, garnachas, tlacoyos, quesadillas, chivichangas, gorditas, chilaquiles*, chiles, sauces, and the *chiles rellenos* derived from them, wild herbs (*quintonil* and purslane), wild mushrooms, iguanas, birds and lake fowl, flowers (squash and *colorín* or coral tree), as well as drinks such as *pulque, mezcal*, and *tepache*. It would not be until well into the nineteenth century that a cuisine of corn, chiles, and mole started to timidly appear, as this cuisine had been considered from an almost racist and slightly discriminatory perspective since colonial times. It had been seen as the cuisine of the Indians, a cuisine without memory, dependent on the fragile web of oral transmission. Mexican cuisine would have to wait until the twentieth century and the Mexican Revolution to affirm itself with dignity and pride, as cultural sovereignty.

Mexican cuisine has three roots: the indigenous, the Castilian cuisine of the sixteenth century, and other European cuisines such as French. There are four periodicals that took on the dissemination of a *Mexican* culinary education or *paideia* in nineteenth-century Mexico: *Semanario Económico de México* (1810), *La semana de las señoritas mexicanas* (1850–1852), *El Diario del Hogar* (1882–1909), and the monumental *Nuevo Cocinero Mexicano en forma de Diccionario* (1888) (Díaz y de Ovando and Schneider).

Among nineteenth-century Mexican authors, the work of Guillermo Prieto (1818–1897) stands out when undertaking an archeology of taste and diet. In *Memoria de mis tiempos* (*Memoirs of my Times*; 1828–1853), Prieto unravels a *costumbrista* thread through neighborhoods, slums, city squares, markets, *tianguis*, tenements, fandango parties, wedding celebrations, and feasts of the fortunate and less fortunate inhabitants of Mexico City. The work of another author, Manuel Payno, helps reconstruct the ephemeral temples of Mexican taste. In *Los bandidos de Río Frío* (*The Bandits of Río Frío*), which takes place around 1810–1830, Payno relates a rancher's diet during that time:

> Landowner don Pedro Martín de Olañeta, upon opening his eyes at five in the morning, had it brought to him while still in bed a thick and hot chocolate along with an accompaniment of estribo or *rosca* [ring-shaped bread]. At ten o'clock he ate a lunch of white rice, roast

mutton tenderloin, well-fried beans, and a glass of pulque. At half past three he was ready to eat: broth with lime and green chiles, noodle or bread soup, which he mixed in a plate; the *puchero* [stew] with a Castile squash, meatballs, carrot torte, or some other dish, along with fruit bought in Volador Square: oranges, lemons, bananas, and apples, which were never missing from his table. At six in the evening he was served chocolate, and at eleven he was served dinner. (in Díaz y de Ovando and Schneider xv)

Similar information may be gleaned from parts of Luis G. Inclán's novel *Astucia* (*Astuteness*), as well as from costumbrist narratives like the gastrophile and convivial depiction that poet Manuel José Othón produced in his previously cited short story "Una fiesta casera."

In its encyclopedic recipe collection, the 1888 *Nuevo Cocinero Mexicano: En forma de Diccionario* (*New Mexican Cook in the Form of a Dictionary*) features various ways to cook autochthonous Mexican dishes like *guazontle* (or *huazontle*, a green leafy vegetable), *chichicuilotes*, and *apipitzca*, also waterfowl, as well as *auauhtle* (mosquito eggs) (Rivera 370–71; 250–51; 35; 47). It also provides recipes for "ensaladas de nopalitos" ("nopal salads"; 298), "ensalada de xitomate que llaman aguacamole" ("tomato salad called aguacamole"; 297), "ensalada de alcauciles" ("alcaucil salad"; 297–98), as well as various methods for preparing and stuffing tamales (813–15).

In 1845, fourteen years later, Mariano Galván Rivera's printing press published the *Diccionario de cocina, o Nuevo cocinero mexicano en forma de Dicionario* (*Dictionary of Cuisine, or New Mexican Cook in the Form of a Dictionary*). In 1855, it went through a second, expanded printing with added plates; and in 1858 it was further enriched with additional recipes, plates, and appendices. Finally, the 1888 edition includes French, Spanish, and other European recipes adapted to suit Mexican taste and tradition. Indigenous cuisine and the cuisine of corn is accepted, with reservations. For example, when referring to tamales made with *capulín* (Mexican black cherry) or beans, it warns "that they are not in the best taste, nor are they usually served at decent tables; rather, they are served to satisfy a whim only rarely, and they are those made by the indigenous people. Our young ladies do not make them themselves though they customarily make those of other classes" (Díaz y de Ovando and Schneider xxv).

The 1888 *Nuevo cocinero mexicano, en forma de Diccionario* justifies its title by listing in its encyclopedic recipe collection the various ways to cook *axolotl, apipitzca, chichicuilote, acuaci (acocil), anahutle,* and *cacaloxochitl* (frangipani or plumeria) salad. It also includes some recipes for tamales, but none for pozole. However, it does list recipes for turkey cooked in different moles (common, black, yellow, green, and red moles and *clemole,* or guajillo chile soup). Publishing the recipes in the form of a dictionary likely made it easier for the authors and editors, who were one and the same in this case, to disguise and present as acceptable such dishes as an omelet made with mosquito eggs harvested in lakes, inserting the recipe among other more conventional ones.

Perhaps one of the defining characteristics of Mexican mentality is an ambiguity about its own tradition. On the one hand, Mexicans can be proud about the wealth and variety of Mexican indigenous foods and quote with self-complacency and long detail Hernán Cortés's letters (*Cartas de Relación*) in which, as we have seen, Cortés shows himself seduced by the markets in Tenochtitlán. On the other hand, those memories would not prevent the indigenous roots of Mexican cuisine to be either omitted from conventional recipe collections or duly segregated under the denomination of indigenous or indigenist cuisine. Pulque, tortilla, mole, and chile were regarded with suspicion and reserve. On August 29, 1897, an editorial published in the newspaper *El Imparcial*, humorously signed with the pseudonym "Guajolote" ("Turkey"), commented on the subject of chiles: "Learned hygienists advise a parsimonious use, even in *nogada*, of that other enemy of the soul [the chile], which united with the national liqueur [pulque] and the tortilla works as fuel for the untiring machine of the proletarians and even of those who are not" (in Pilcher, *Vivan* 116).

Corn was called a cursed grain by Porfirista historian and sociologist Francisco Bulnes in *El porvenir de las naciones hispanoamericanas ante las conquistas recientes de Europa y los Estados Unidos (The Future of Spanish-American Nations before Recent Conquests by Europe and the United States*; 1899). In Bulnes's opinion, corn was responsible, alongside pulque, on which he also wrote a treatise, for the apathy and passivity of the Mexican national character: "history teaches us that the race of wheat is the only one that is truly progressive" and "corn has been the eternal pacifier of American indigenous races and the founder of its repulsion against becoming civilized" (*El pulque* 119). Bulnes was not the only one to hold such views. In *El génesis del crimen en México: Estudio de psiquiatría social* (*The Genesis of Crime in Mexico: Study on Social Psychiatry*; 1901), Mexican sociologist Julio Guerrero detailed with morbid minutiae the indecorous living conditions of the urban poor, as well as their "abominable" diet consisting of mosquito larvae—the same that the Count of la Cortina had recommended as an exceptional delicacy to the Marchioness of Calderón de la Barca—and tamales stuffed with a whole fish. But the true enemy was not the tamales or the mosquito tortes, but pulque, the drink made from the maguey. Pulque was also great business. In the nineteenth century there were hundreds of pulque establishments, or *pulquerías*, in Mexico City fed by dozens of haciendas and ranches, as stated in Manuel Payno's "Memoria sobre el maguey en México y sus diversos productos" ("Report on Maguey and Its Different Products in Mexico"; Payno, "México" 133–52, 159–61).

Female sociability played a key role in the constitution of a Mexican national cuisine. As an example, the case of María Luisa Soto Murguiondo de Cossío, wife of a rancher from Hidalgo, is worth mentioning. In her cookbook *Recetario de cocina mexicana* (*Cookbook of Mexican Cuisine*), written at the end of the nineteenth century, she included the recipes of three other women, her grandmother, her aunt Gabriela, and Virginia, a neighbor friend, and copied recipes from a book borrowed from a friend. The commerce in culinary secrets went beyond family boundaries, even those of the extended family, and with the help of the Church was turned into a motor for sociability and politics, as witnessed by various community cookbooks compiled as fundraisers for different charities, like an orphanage in Guadalajara or the construction of churches like San Rafael or San Vicente de Paul. Such was the impetus behind Vicenta Torres de Rubio's famous *Manual de Cocina Michoacana* (*Manual of Michoacana Cuisine*; 1896). This book, a pioneer work for many reasons, was originally written by Doña Vicenta Torres along with Manuel Pacheco. They decided to request from their acquaintances and friends: "your contributions, very particularly, begging that you may be so kind as to transmit some that you may deem appropriate among the thousand curiosities that you have in relation to the culinary arts. Please send each recipe written and signed, since we would like to include them alongside your name for the greater renown of the State to which we proudly belong and for the increased prestige of our book" (39).

They did not have to wait long for an answer, as around fifty contributions arrived not only from Michoacán, Guanajuato, and Jalisco, but also from Mexico City, San Luis Potosí, Aguascalientes, and even Nuevo Laredo. Vicenta Torres's is a pioneering cookbook for yet another reason: it includes regional and indigenous recipes like tamales or *corundas* from Zacapú, *atapakuas* (Purepecha salsa), the cordial *gorditas* from the mountains, *nacatamales*, and *toqueres* treats (fresh corn tortillas). The book benefited from the generous participation of women from all over the country, including the woman from Celaya who sent the recipe for "nopalitos de la hervica" ("prickly pear cactus of hervica"), the reader from Nuevo Laredo who submitted her "gallinas del gastrónomo fronterizo" ("hens of the frontier gastronome"), and one from Guadalajara who sent her recipe for a stew of "cordero en salsa verde" ("lamb in green sauce").

The modes of operation of female sociability are an indication or tip of the iceberg suggesting the extent to which labyrinthine family networks have been preserved and refined thanks to the work of what anthropologists Larissa Lomnitz and Marisol Pérez have termed "centralizing women," heirs to the female encomienda owners (*encomenderas*) studied by historian Josefina Muriel. These networks functioned like directories or contact books that were linked to each other and enabled the channeling of social capital within both the well-to-do classes and the less-fortunate ones. These networks carry the survival of a maternal rule, of a hidden politics of gynecocracy that avails itself of kitchen tools in order to regulate the social pulse, as may be seen more recently in Laura Esquivel's *Como agua para chocolate* (*Like Water for Chocolate*; 1989).

Chile Relleno and Other Chiles

Chile relleno makes its triumphal entrance in Mexican history at the crowning of Agustín de Iturbide as emperor, when he is presented with a delicacy that bears the three colors of the Mexican national flag: the green of the chile, the white of the *nogada* sauce, and the red of the pomegranate seeds. We know that chile relleno was one of the most common dishes at the beginning of the nineteenth century because there was a municipal order that forbade its consumption, though, needless to say, the order was not heeded. Chile relleno could be considered an emblem of the mestizaje and coexistence in place during the three long centuries of the viceroyalty. In principle, chile poblano, optionally deveined and dephlegmated, is used to make the dish. In order to be dephlegmated, the chile must be slowly roasted at a low temperature. Once the skin of the chile blisters, it is wrapped in a plastic bag and left to "sweat" so that it can be easily peeled. A *picadillo* or hash of minced red meat (half pork and half beef) that has been previously prepared is used to stuff the pepper. Chiles in *nogada* sauce are not usually battered. They are just bathed in the *nogada* sauce, made with shelled and minced walnuts and cream. After they are covered in the sauce, the chiles are sprinkled with pomegranate seeds. When they are to be battered, chiles rellenos are floured and dipped in egg whites that have been beaten until stiff. Once coated, they are fried until golden. After they finish frying and any excess oil is removed, they are served covered in tomato broth. Chile relleno is a complexly textured dish with several layers of flavor: the stuffing, the chile, the flour and egg coating, the tomato sauce. There are also those who add a bit of cream. Due to the diversity of its ingredients, some have seen in the chile relleno in *nogada* sauce a metaphor for national unity. Among pre-Hispanic peoples, chile was used as a food and as a medicine against parasites, as a flavor enhancer, and as a tincture. It was used to make sauces, pestos, adobos, dressings, and poultices, and it was served raw, roasted, boiled, marinated, and fried. Chile is one of the foundations on which Mexican culture and gastronomy rest.

In Mexico, to speak with truth is to speak "al chile," and it is true that chile relleno is one of the peaks of Mexican gastronomy. As Chef Ricardo Muñoz Zurita states in his beautiful book on the subject, *Los chiles rellenos en México* (*Chiles rellenos in Mexico*): "How long did it take for someone to have the brilliant idea of stuffing a chile, a capsicum? How long did it take to come up with the idea of peeling it before using it? How long must [it] have been . . . [before] someone thought of wrapping them in a damp napkin? . . . Who thought about covering them with a batter and then immersing them in broth? . . . When did chiles begin to be eaten cold? When were they gratineed?" (10)

Chipotle chiles (from Tlaxcala), poblanos, jalapeños, *mecos, chipotles tamarindo, ixcatic,* and the very hot habaneros in Yucatán, the *perones* or *manzanos* in Guanajuato, almost all varieties may be stuffed, including *chile de California, chile Ana heiva,* and *chile verde del norte,* with the curious exception of the bell pepper, which Mexicans disdain as unfit for stuffing. In fact, chiles rellenos can be classified according to their stuffing:

> Today a great many varieties of chiles rellenos are prepared from coast to coast and from one national border to another. However, they are cooked most in the center of the country. The poblano is the chile par excellence to be stuffed with various ingredients such as *picadillos* (minced stuffing), cheeses, vegetables, shellfish, and fowl. The many varieties of rellenos invite to be categorized into different groups, with *picadillos* being the most extensive due to the sheer number of ingredients that are mixed with pork, beef, or a combination of both meats, or with chicken, which also occupies an important place in that group. Then there are the cheeses, the

most common of which are those from Puebla, fresh cheese, cheese from Oaxaca, Chihuahua, as well as basket cheese (*queso de canasto*). Lastly, there are the vegetables, the most used of which are *calabacitas* (zucchini), squash blossoms, and fresh corn kernels combined in different proportions. There are also many recipes for stuffing using shellfish, which are generally considered luxurious, in which shrimp are considered the protagonists and crab meat, oysters, or octopi play the supporting role. (Muñoz Zurita, *Los chiles rellenos en México* 12)

Still, as stated before, the pinnacle, the Everest of this category is the mysterious and albino chile *en nogada* adorned with pomegranate seeds sprinkled over the white hill of a *nogada* sauce made with walnuts and cream. Indisputably, stuffed with anything, cold, warm, or hot, chile relleno bears in its stuffing aphrodisiac properties, as is well known by readers of Laura Esquivel, who describes the cooking technique in her peculiar style in *Como agua para chocolate*.

In a well-known anecdote, when general Charles de Gaulle visited Mexico, he boasted in front of President Adolfo López Mateos that even though France was a small country compared to Mexico, it was not easy to govern as it had over two hundred kinds of cheese. López Mateos remained unperturbed and replied that Mexico had over two hundred varieties of chile. Both men laughed, understanding that they were each leaders of a vast gastronomic wealth that was not always easily governable.

Does Mexican Cuisine Have a Future?

Mexican cuisine has a history, is itself history. The various steps toward modernization that have affected it, and sometimes made it stronger, have been reviewed here. A clear proof of the processes of inscription into history may be found in the cookbook that the laborers and workers of the Federal Electric Commission (Comisión Federal de Electricidad) put together when they were forced to cook in places with difficult access, camps, substations, and electric and thermoelectric plants, using the heat from turbines, forges, and melting pots. The recipe for "rabbit with chiltepin chile" ("conejo al chiltepín") is an example of an intrepid cuisine that, without losing its local accent, reaches far beyond its region of origin:

RABBIT WITH CHILTEPIN

Rabbit is very "xoquioso" (gamy, strong tasting): it has a particular smell that is not very pleasant, so it has to be dephlegmated. In order to remove the "xoquío" (strong smell), the rabbit needs to be soaked for one day and one night; [the soaking must be done] in equal parts of water and pulque in which [the rabbit] must be completely submerged.

INGREDIENTS NEEDED:
A skinned and gutted rabbit
A head of garlic
A medium onion
1 kg. chile chiltepin (chile piquín)
Oil for frying
½ liter pulque

IT IS PREPARED THUS:

The rabbit is dephlegmated in the water and pulque on a low flame until the liquid has evaporated; once dephlegmated, it is quartered. The garlic and onion are finely minced and fried; once they become translucent, the rabbit is added. Lastly the tomato and chile chiltepin are added; the whole is seasoned with a little bit of salt and left over a medium flame until the rabbit meat becomes tender. The resulting broth should be very thick. (*Un toque* 47)

NOTE

Translated by Ana M. Gómez-Bravo and Matthew Kullberg.

WORKS CITED

Arana, Federico. *Insectos comestibles: Entre el gusto y la aversión*. UNAM, 2006.
Azuela, Mariano. *Los de abajo: Novela de la revolución mexicana*. FCE, 1993.
Bazarte Martínez, Alicia. *Un acercamiento a la comida novohispana: Segundo miércoles de Cuaresma en el Convento Jerónimo de San Lorenzo, México, 1628. Viandas y fatigas para el recibimiento del arzobispo Alonso Núñez de Haro y Peralta, Puebla, 1772*. Instituto Politécnico Nacional, 2006.
Brenner, Anita. *Idols behind Altars*. Payson and Clarke, 1929.
Bulnes, Francisco. *El porvenir de las naciones latinoamericanas ante las recientes conquistas de Europa y Norteamérica (estructura y evolución de un continente)*. México, Imprenta de Mariano Nava, 1899.
———. *El pulque: Estudio científico*. Antigua Imprenta de Murguía, 1909.
Calvino, Italo. *Bajo el sol jaguar*. Tusquets, 1989.
Camarena Castellanos, Ricardo. *Catálogo de textos marginados novohispanos: Inquisición; Archivo General de la Nación (México: siglos XVIII y XIX)*. El Colegio de México, 1992.
Castelló Yturbide, Teresa, et al. *Delicias de antaño: Historia y recetas de los conventos mexicanos*. Océano Landucci, 2000.
Coe, Sophie D. *America's First Cuisines*. U of Texas P, 1994.
Cortés, Hernán. *Cartas de relación*. Castalia, 1993.
Desentis Otárola, Aline. *El que come y canta: Cancionero gastronómico de México*. Lecturas Mexicanas, 1999.
Díaz y de Ovando, Clementina, and Luis M. Schneider. *Arte culinario mexicano, siglo XIX: Recetario*. Fundación de Investigaciones Sociales, 1986.
Dunkel, Florence V, editor. *The Food Insects Newsletter*. Aardvark Global P, 2009.
Espinosa García, Francisco Javier, and José Sarukhán Kérmez. *Manual de malezas del valle de México: Claves, descripciones e ilustraciones*. UNAM, 1997.
Esquivel, Laura. *Como agua para chocolate: Novela en entregas mensuales con recetas, amores y remedios caseros*. Planeta, 1989.
Fuentes Mares, José. *Nueva guía de descarriados*. J. Mortiz, 1978.
Galván Rivera, Mariano. *Diccionario de cocina, o El nuevo cocinero mexicano en forma de diccionario*. México, Imprenta de I. Cumplido, 1845.

González y González, Luis. *La querencia*. Clío, 1997.
Grau, Anna. "La torre de Babel se viene abajo." *ABC*, Science and Future Section, 30 Sept. 2007, www.abc.es/hemeroteca/historico-20-09-2007/abc/Sociedad/la-torre-de-babel-se-viene-abajo_164891980002.html.
Guerrero, Julio. *La génesis del crimen en México: Estudio de psiquiatría social*. Bouret, 1901.
Hernández, Francisco, Isaac Ochoterena, and José Rojo. *Historia de las plantas de Nueva España*. Imprenta Universitaria, 1942.
Inclán, Luis G. *Astucia, el jefe de los hermanos de la hoja o los charros contrabandistas de la rama: Novela histórica de costumbres mexicanas con episodios originales*. Porrúa, 1987.
Iturriaga, José N. *De tacos, tamales y tortas*. Diana, 1987.
Juárez López, José Luis. *La lenta emergencia de la comida mexicana: Ambigüedades criollas 1750–1800*. Porrúa, 2000.
Kennedy, Diana. *The Essential Cuisines of México*. Clarkson Potter, 2000.
Krauze, Enrique, and Fernán González de la Vara, editors. *La cocina mexicana a través de los siglos*. Clío / Fundación Herdez, 1996–1997.
Le Clézio, Jean M. "Universalidad de la relación de Michoacán en Jerónimo de Alcalá." *Relación de las ceremonias y ritos y población y gobernación de los indios de la provincia de Michoacán*, edited by Jerónimo Alcalá and Moisés Franco Mendoza, El Colegio de Michoacán, 2000, pp. 107–19.
Lomnitz, Larissa Adler de, and Marisol Pérez Lizaur. *Una familia de la elite mexicana: Parentesco, clase y cultura, 1820–1980*. Alianza Editorial Mexicana, 1993.
Mendoza, Vicente T. *El romance español y el corrido mexicano*. Universidad Nacional Autónoma de México, 1997.
Muñoz Zurita, Ricardo. *Los chiles rellenos en México: Antología de recetas*. UNAM, 2001.
———. *Diccionario enciclopédico de la gastronomía mexicana*. Larousse, 2000.
Novo, Salvador. *Cocina mexicana; o, Historia gastronómica de la ciudad de México*. Porrúa, 1967.
Nuevo cocinero mexicano en forma de diccionario (1888). Porrúa, 2007.
Othón, Manuel José. *Cuentos completos de Manuel José Othón*. Compiled and edited by Joaquín Antonio Peñalosa. Universidad Autónoma de San Luis de Potosí, 2001.
Paso, Fernando del. *Douceur et passion de la cuisine mexicaine: 151 recettes et 46 menus*. Les Editions de l'aube, 1993.
Paso, Fernando del, and Socorro del Paso. *La cocina mexicana de Socorro y Fernando del Paso*. Diana, 2003.
Paul, Carlos, and Bertha T. Ramírez. "Arranca en el centro histórico la campaña en defensa del maíz nativo." *La Jornada*, 6 Aug. 2007, www.jornada.com.mx/2007/08/06/index.php?section=cultura&article=a09n1cul.

Payno, Manuel. *Los bandidos de Río Frío*. Porrúa, 1945.
———. "México y sus diversos productos." *Obras completas*, vol. 17, notes by Boris Rosen, CONACULTA, 2006.
Pilcher, Jeffrey M. *Vivan los tamales!: La comida y la construcción de la identidad mexicana*. Reina Roja/ CIESA/ CONACULTA, 2001.
———. *Que vivan los tamales!: Food and the Making of the Mexican Identity*. U of New Mexico P, 1998.
Popol Vuh: The Mayan Book of the Dawn and Life. Translated by Dennis Teddlock, Simon and Schuster, 1986.
Prieto, Guillermo. *Memoria de mis tiempos*. Patria, 1969.
Reyes, Alfonso. *Memorias de cocina y bodega; Minuta*. Tezontle Cocina/ FCE, 1989.
———. *Visión de Anáhuac. 1519*. Impr. Nuevo Mundo, 1953.
Rivera, Guadalupe. *Nuevo cocinero mexicano: En forma de diccionario*. Porrúa, 1992.
Sahagún, Bernardino de. *Historia universal de las cosas de la Nueva España*. Giunti, 1996.
Santamaría, Francisco Javier, and Joaquín García Icazbalceta. *Diccionario de mejicanismos*. Porrúa, 1974.
Sor Juana Inés de la Cruz. *Libro de cocina: Convento de San Jerónimo*, edited by Josefina Muriel and Guadalupe Pérez San Vicente, Instituto Mexiquense de Cultura, 2000.
Soto Murguiondo de Cossío, María Luisa. *Recetario de cocina mexicana*. Vargas Rea, 1968.
Torres de Rubio, Vicenta. *Manual de la cocina michoacana*. 1896. Gobierno del Estado de Michoacán/ Fundación Herdez/ U Michoacana de San Nicolás Hidalgo, 2004.
Un toque de sabor: Tradición de los trabajadores de Luz y Fuerza del Centro. Luz y Fuerza del Centro, 1999.
Valle-Arizpe, Artemio de. "El mole." *El Universal*, 14 Aug. 1927.
Wasson, R. Gordon. *Persephones's Quest: Entheogens and the Origins of Religion*. Yale UP, 1986.

CHAPTER 10

What the Palate Knows
Nicaragua's Culinary Cultures

Sergio Ramírez

NICARAGUA'S CULINARY TRADITION was created on the rural stoves, in the kitchens of the haciendas, and in the neighborhoods and villages where indigenous people, people of African descent, *mulatos*, and poor mestizos were the majority. Also of key importance from early colonial times, the kitchens of the most prominent families were in the hands of Spanish greenhorn (*chapetones*) and criollos, as well as male and female African cooks, slaves, and freedmen who arrived from the Iberian Peninsula with their masters.

These kitchens also counted on female indigenous cooks, who were the repositories of ancestral secrets that were exclusive to women, because in aboriginal cultures men kept away from the stoves and the markets, or *tianguis*, from which men were excluded by law. Even today, the word *cuque*, an Anglicism meaning "the cook," evokes dubious masculinity. And thus, this system became culturally ingrained. Pablo Lévy, in his *Geographical and Economic Notes of the Republic of Nicaragua*, states: "Cooking is always done by women. We will say in the article on industry what we think of their talent, as well as of several indigenous specialties in confectionery, charcuterie, and pastry" (270).

Indigenous women introduced unknown staples to the Spanish palate, including the use of mature maize in its infinite varieties, as well as tender corn on the cob (*elotes*), and unripened corn cob (*chilotes*); potatoes and sweet potatoes; beans, chilies, and bell pepper (*chiltomas*); winter squashes such as *ayotes*, *pipianes*, and *chayotes* (*sechium edule*); avocados, vanilla, and tomatoes, which from that point on would be inseparable from onions; and cacao, also henceforth inseparable from sugar and milk. At the same time, an immense variety of fruits were put on the table to be eaten fresh or as sweet preserves: pineapples, papayas, *jocotes* (*spondias purpurea*), *nancites* (*byrsonima crassifolia*), sapotes, loquats, *mameyes* (*pouteria sapota*), guavas, inga fruits, sweet-sops, and soursops, a few of which are also used to make sweet liqueurs.

While the palates of wealthy Spaniards recalled happy culinary experiences, others who were needy and came looking for a better life remembered eating only wheat porridge, for which they found an equivalent in a traditional hot-corn beverage of Mesoamerican origin called corn *atole*, and the emaciated stews made primarily with bones and hard bits of bread. Both in the Iberian Peninsula and the rest of Europe, the food of the poor was substandard compared to that of the higher classes. Social classes were strictly separated by the foods available to them: Asian spices were used to marinate meats and were worth as much as gold—so much as to have inspired the venture of America; nib sugar, so expensive and rare that it was only sold in pharmacies; oxen meat, rams, pork, and capons were scarce among the less fortunate, who had to settle for eggs, milk, butter, or tripe, lungs, and some *botifarra* sausage, as is depicted in picaresque literature. Cacao underwent a similar socioeconomic transformation, being first consumed only by the indigenous upper castes in Mesoamerica and by the privileged in Europe after their arrival.

African slaves and freedmen brought with them the tastes and traditions of the food they had left behind, including plantains, bananas, and sugar cane, crops imported into Nicaragua by colonizers from Africa and the Caribbean. Africans also brought eating habits and cooking techniques for various tubers, the wrapping of meats in banana leaves, and *revoltijo*, or hodgepodge. Previously unknown products that became everyday food, for example sour milk, very popular in Nicaragua, would not exist without the arrival of dairy cows from Europe. Sour milk would become a slave meal in the US South, as can be read in Mark Twain's novel *Pudd'nhead Wilson* (1894), which tells the story of a female slave named Roxy who switches her son Tom with the master's son, Chambers, so that Tom does not grow up as a slave. Roxy feeds her own child the best and most delicious foods and gives the other child sour milk without sugar, among other despicable foods.

Successive and incessant stages of adjustment, blending, weights, and counterweights are needed to form a traditional cuisine. New immigration waves, taste preferences, availability of raw materials, particular climates and crops further influence its development, and it is shaped through times of scarcity or abundance. The processes that shape a cuisine are always directed toward improving taste, even in the everyday food of ordinary people. "Personal touches" only survive if they are able to enter the mainstream of collective taste, even if they come from wealthier cuisines. This is what happened in Nicaragua.

What we call Nicaraguan cuisine is a hybrid of constant fusions that have been operating since before the conquistadors set foot on Nicaraguan soil. We know that this territory was always a meeting place, from the North to the South of the continent and to the Caribbean islands. Chorotega and Nahuatl cuisines are among the first to have been established. Then came Aztec influences, brought by commercial traffic from the empire, as well as influences from Mayan cuisine and the eating habits of Caribs, Arawakas, Tainos, and the various tribes that emigrated from the South, like the Chibchas, just to name a few. The mixing process continued after conquest and colonization, as aboriginal cuisine mixed with that which came from Spain and Africa to form new combinations. All the new African and Spanish elements entered the Pacific coast through the Caribbean, bringing with them the Taino culinary culture, along with the Taino language.

It is a myth that Nicaragua's only cuisine with African influences is that of the Caribbean coast, or Atlantic coast as it is usually called, which has a history of its own and includes contributions from indigenous peoples such as Miskitos, Sumos, Ramas, Africans, insular Afro-Caribbeans such as the Garifuna and Jamaicans, Creoles, and Europeans, especially Britons. Given the lack of communication, both territorial and cultural, between both parts of Nicaragua, the influences of Nicaraguan Caribbean cuisine were transferred to the Pacific coast not only late, but also poorly. Coconut oil based dishes, such as the *rondón* (derived from the English "run-down"), were viewed for many years with reluctance, and others, such as *guabul*, a milkshake of fermented bananas, were received with disgust. On the other hand, certain Pacific dishes, such as the *mondongo* soup, the *nacatamal*, a *tamal* stuffed with pork or chicken and other ingredients, and all the food that included pork and beef, were more easily accepted by mestizo immigration and became more popular at the end of the nineteenth century. Nevertheless, there was always some common denominator between Atlantic and Pacific cuisines, such as turtle meat and eggs, turtles being abundant on both coasts as well as in lakes and lagoons. Fish and seafood of all kinds were also popular, as were various ways of preparing plantains and unripe bananas, or *guineos*.

The key elements of African cuisine did not enter the Pacific through the Escondido River, the Grande de Matagalpa River, or on the back of a mule via the rare horse paths. Rather, from colonial times until the late-nineteenth century, slaves were transported through the San Juan River and Lake Nicaragua to the slave market in the port of Granada. Slaves were brought from the Strait of Magellan and from Lima to El Realejo, where there was another slave market in addition to the one in El Viejo. In the *vigorón*, another important Nicaraguan dish, the Caribbean cassava meets the peninsular *chicharrón*, served over banana leaves adorned with a simple and tasty salad of tomato, cabbage, scallops, and vinegar. The salad is made even better if black bananas and whole pequin peppers are added. The academic Carlos Mántica Abaunza agrees that the *vigorón* began as the food of slaves. *Mondongo* is an African word from the Kikongo-Kongo language, although the *Diccionario de la Real Academia Española* (*Dictionary of the Royal Spanish Academy*) says it comes from *mondejo*, which in turn would come from the word *bondujo*, meaning gut or belly. Miriam Gomes, in her article "African Blacks in Argentine Culture," identifies the *mondongo* as one of the most essential culinary contributions of African slaves. Nicaraguan *mondongo* soup, along with its variants, is also found in Peru, Colombia, Venezuela, Honduras, and Costa Rica, where it is prepared in the same way as in Nicaragua. In the *mondongo* soup we find beef tripe, which is never sufficiently washed, along with the *ayote*, *chayotes*, cocoyam, and indigenous *pipianes*, plus Caribbean cassava, African plantains, and European cabbage.

José Coronel Urtecho describes turtle stew in his *Elogio de la cocina nicaragüense* (*Praise of Nicaraguan Cuisine*), writing "more mestizo than indigenous, what the dish suggests, above all, is the direct influence of *mulato* cooks on the haciendas near the lakes and their tributary rivers" (32). The complex preparation of turtle stew, with its abundance of ingredients that never lose their harmony, suggests a *horror vacui*, the fear of emptiness or bareness that characterizes baroque art. The kitchen often became a sort of baroque art space, as can be seen in our *ajiaco*, where corn, *quelite* leaf (*quelite* comes from the Nahuatl language *quilitl*, and it refers to several edible wild herbs when tender), ripe banana, pineapple, *jocotes*, and pork meat coexist. But such an abundance is also found in other dishes of indigenous origin, in which the main components are reptiles, iguanas, and black iguanas, which are never eaten without garnish and ornaments, seasonings and sauces. After skinning them, they are boiled or roasted, and go to the table with rich side dishes.

One of the decisive elements of African food culture that became a Nicaraguan food, just as in the whole of the Caribbean, was the banana or *Musa*, a family that includes the plantain (*Musa paradisiaca*) and the *banano* (*Musa cavendishii*). The word *musa* comes from a family of languages to which the Wolof and the Mandingo belong, as well as the *guineo* (*Musa sapientum*), a word that comes from the Arab name "Guinea" that designates several African countries. The *guinea* for Nicaraguans refers to the top of the banana tree cluster. The banana was brought from Spain by conquerors in 1516. When the first slaves arrived, they found a familiar food in the varieties commonly called banana, plantain, and *guineo* (of which many varieties exist: *guineo dominico*, *guineo chancho*, also called square *guineo*, the lady *guineo*, pink *guineo*, apple *guineo*, and the black guineo, excellent for pickling). The banana itself did not take root in Central America until late in the nineteenth century, when the United Fruit Company's extensive crops emerged. Nicaraguans learned to eat the banana in different ways: green or ripe, roasted on embers, or fried in slices like *tostones*, sliced bananas that are sautéed, ground, and later fried, named in memory of an old colonial coin minted in the sixteenth century, and known in other parts of America as *patacón*. The banana reaches its peak in the *maduro en gloria* (glorious ripeness), another of our baroque dishes with elements of sweetness, in which the ripened bananas, already sliced and fried, are oven-baked with cheese, cream, and cinnamon bark. *Maduro en gloria* has its most humble but no less delicious expression in *peoresnada*, literally meaning "better than nothing" in Spanish, where banana mash fried in lard rendered from pork rinds comes together in the pot with the same mash that remains from the rinds. In the Dominican Republic and Puerto Rico, a typical African dish is the *mofongo*, derived from Cocola cuisine and prepared on a base of ground green bananas and scrambled with ground pork rinds.

The yucca or cassava, originally from the Caribbean and bearing a Taino name, was cultivated in some of its varieties by the Miskito indigenous peoples. Gonzalo Fernández de Oviedo y Valdés mentions it as a food of the Pacific populations: "and there in Nicaragua there is more care in this regard to agriculture than in any other part of the Indies where I have been, like corn or cotton, or cassava, or any other sustenance" (*Historia general* 285). Cassava was quickly adopted by African immigrants who were already accustomed to eating similar tubers, such as taro (*malanga*) and yam; the taste for cassava became as emblematic in Nicaragua as the taste for the banana. Boiled and fried, cassava is an essential ingredient of the *carne en vaho* (meaning "meat in mist," it is a Nicaraguan dish consisting of a mix of meat, green plantains, and yucca cooked in banana leaves) and *vigorón*, a mix of cabbage salad, boiled cassava, and fried pork rinds, or *chicharrones*, as well as beef soups and *mondongo* soup. It is also used to cook fritters, made with cassava dough, stirred with shredded cheese, and fried with lard, then bathed in delicate sweet panela honey and garnished with cinnamon bark. While making fritters is a technique inherited from the Iberian-Arab culinary tradition, the use of cassava makes them a hybrid, mixed with the African culinary traditions.

The expansion of sugarcane crops, brought to Nicaragua by the Spanish settlers in the sixteenth century, precipitated the arrival of a large number of slaves to the Caribbean. Sugarcane was ground in animal-powered *trapiches*, mills made of wooden rollers used to extract juice from fruits, which produced the juice called *guarapo* or African *Kikongo*, which means "fermented drink," though the term *guarapo* may well come from the Quechua *waru* with the same meaning. *Guarapo* is a drink in itself and is also the base of the sweet panela loaf as well as the liquor *aguardiente*, commonly called *guaro*, a word also derived from *guar(ap)o*. A common drink among black slaves in the Dominican Republic, *guarapo* was also the favorite drink of people of African descent, and especially of the *bozales*, in colonized Peru. Meaning "muzzle," the *bozales* were black slaves recently brought from Africa who did not understand any local language, customs, or orders. Two types of *guarapo* were distinguished: the sweet *guarapito*, drunk by black women, and the *achichadito*, a more vigorous drink preferred by black men. As the mayor of Cartagena states in the process of the beatification of St. Peter Claver: "It was the year 1652, there was a widow's shop where a certain drink called *guarapo* was sold. I went with Manuel López; we found a great contest of blacks in that store" (Splendiani and Aristazábal 198). *Panela* loaf, also called *rapadura* or *raspadura*, was sold in Nicaragua as two loaves tied together and wrapped in dried banana leaves or *chagüite*. It was commonly used in the colony to sweeten food and drink. This contrasts with pre-Hispanic sweetening practices, when only bee honey was employed, and with our present-day use of sulfated sugar as a sweetening agent. Honey used to cover the fritters, and *bienmesabe*, literally meaning "it tastes good to me," was obtained by melting panela loaf. *Bienmesabes* are traditional candies served during the Celebrations of the Virgin Mary and are made of small slices of fried green banana, soaked in the same honey. *Bienmesabes* are a delight derived from the various species of banana trees, the *trapiches*, and lard.

Cooking food wrapped in leaves was a typical practice of both aboriginal and slave cuisine. The many varieties of tamales, typical of Mesoamerica, soon adopted the leaves of the banana tree as the wrapping, although maize leaf, or *tusa*, was still used for some foods like tamales made with tender maize, called *yoltamales*, and Nicaraguan little tamales stuffed with chicken meat or rooster, called *montucas*. In sub-Saharan Africa the *kwanga* is a cassava bread cooked in banana leaves, steamed or roasted. Meats and fish such as *ajomba*, from Central Africa, are cooked in the same way. A recipe for *ajomba* indicates the steps to make the wrapping after placing the meat on the leaves: "Fold the banana leaves into a wrapping two or three layers thick and tie it with a thin string. Steam husks, or grill them in the broiler or oven. After approximately one hour, carefully open the package and check that the meat is done. If it is not done yet, close the package and continue cooking" ("Dos recetas de África Central"). This practice is the origin of the preparation of the unsurpassable *carne en vaho*, one of the flagship dishes of Nicaraguan cuisine. To prepare this dish, steamed (*al vapor* or *al vaho*) jerky is placed in a pot with a bed of wood chips or small branches that will protect the food from direct heat. Once the base is set, the pot is lined with banana leaves, which are used to wrap peeled yuccas, green and ripe plantains with their peels, and, finally, strips of salted and sun-dried *cecina* (jerky) garnished with tomato, garlic, and onion. The whole is then left to cook or steam. The essential component of *carne en vaho* is *cecina*, a product of the colonial cattle ranch, but the banana-leaf wrappings and the green and ripe plantains that complement the meat are of African descent, while the yucca or cassava recalls indigenous flavors. In Venezuela it is customary to use banana leaves to wrap *hallacas*, a Christmas dish made of corn dough, meat, sweet peppers, onions, pickles, capers, olives, and almonds, similar to a *nacatamal*. The same leaf is used to wrap fish to be cooked directly on the fire, and also milk curd. All these uses are also common in Nicaragua. On the other hand, the intimate kinship between the *carne en vaho* and the rundown, typical of Nicaraguan Caribbean cuisine, is not gratuitous. When making Nicaraguan run-down, beef can be substituted for fish or turtle meat. Coconut oil is an essential element of its composition.

Corn is consumed in many different forms, including *totoposte*, made with corn, butter, and salt. It was the peasant soldier's staple food throughout Nicaragua's chronic civil wars because it can last for months in a backpack without rotting. The use of maize extends far beyond its role as a survival food and is an essential component in more than three hundred dishes described in my dictionary (Ramírez): cooked and roasted *elotes*; fresh and brined chilotes; *nacatamales*, *yoltamales*, simple tamales, also good as travel provisions, and tamales stuffed with panela or bean candy. Maize is employed in many of the sauces we have already mentioned, such as moles, seasonings, and *pinoles*, like the sublime *pinole* of tortoise. It is also used in soups made of sardines, in donuts, and in refreshments, like a drink called *tiste* made with toasted corn flour, cocoa, annatto, and sugar; *chingue*, made from half-toasted corn, with cinnamon, sugar, and water; and *pozol*, usually prepared with white or purple corn.

Hot drinks such as *tibio*, made with cooked pinole, or the *pinole*, which can also be drunk cold, and sweet *atoles* like *chilate* (a type of *atole* prepared with purple corn, milk, sugar, and cloves that are simmered) are made with maize, as are fermented beverages (*chichas*) and aguardientes such as *cususa*. Many baked goods also use maize, including breads like donuts and the *cosa de horno* (made with corn flour and cooked in an oven); cakes, such as *marquesote* (made of flour, rice, or corn, with egg and sugar, baked) and *perrerreque* (a variety of *cosa de horno* made of tender corn and cheese); and sweets, such as *nuéganos* (made from purple corn flour and sugar honey and cooked with lard over low heat) and *alfajores* (whose dough is made with cassava or corn flour, sugarloaf, pineapple, and ginger).

Nicaraguan meat soup incorporates almost the same vegetables as *mondongo* soup. There are several varieties of this soup, which is descended from Spanish *puchero* and *cocido* or the Catalan *carn d'olla*. Since colonial times, Nicaragua (like Spain) has boasted an abundance of cattle farms, which made possible the culinary dominance of red meat dishes such as *carne en vaho*, *mondongo*, cooked in a metal grate where fat drips onto the embers; loins, ribeye, steak tenderloin, and stewed meat; and ground-meat stuffing, such as the *mano de piedra*, a prepared cut of meat that is usually cooked, and *salpicones*, which are shredded or ground meat, as side dishes of meat soups. These different meat preparations give Nicaraguan cuisine its carnivorous character. Beef soup gets its color from the boiling of different kinds of meat, or meat soups, including soup with bones, like the flat bone of *chombón* and the meaty middle rib bone. *Cecina*, ribs, filet, and brisket, all of which add fat to the soup, may be boiled beforehand with garlic, sweet pepper, and onion. The soup is accompanied by a wide variety of products from the Nicaraguan countryside. Such sides consist of a wide assortment of vegetables that when served do not follow any specific culinary practice but rather depend on the particular season, region, and individual taste of the cook. In addition to meat, tubers, and other vegetables, meat soup can be made with some thirty ingredients that may include: green and ripe plantains, cassava, cabbage, cocoyam, *elotes* and *chilotes*, *ayote*, *chayotes*, potatoes, *pipianes*, *jocotes*, mimbro fruits, guava seeds, onions, *chiltoma*, tomatoes, cilantro, peppermint, and celery, among others. At the end of the cooking process, when the prolonged boil has removed all aromas, salt and the juice of a sour orange are typically added. A small side dish next to the soup dish with pequin peppers marinated in onion and vinegar or, even better, a small dish of magical *chilero*, which is food seasoning prepared with vinegar, chilies, onions, and some vegetables usually kept in a glass jar, served alongside the soup makes the flavors pop in the mouth.

Similar to the *feijoada*, a Brazilian dish with beans and pork as essential ingredients, the *revoltijo* (hodgepodge) is another result of the slave kitchen, where all sorts of ingredients would be combined in a pot. Slaves developed the habit of stirring aboriginal beans (*frijoles*) with rice brought from Asia, resulting in a dish called *gallopinto*. Shredded meat and virtually any leftovers may be added to *gallopinto*, which is then refried to make a dish commonly eaten throughout Central America and the Caribbean, where it receives other names such as *moros y cristianos* (Moors and Christians) or *congrí* in Cuba, although Nicaraguans usually vehemently insist that it is exclusive to Nicaraguan cuisine. The typical Nicaraguan hodgepodge is prepared with red beans, a variety inherited from pre-Columbian agriculture. Beans are also eaten fried, ground, cooked, or boiled with salt, as filling in tamales, and in the famous bean soup with hen eggs sprinkled with cheese, or even as dessert, as in the *anté de frijol*. The *anté* or *antes* is a colonial dish of Spanish origin made of sponge cake bathed in a mixture of sugar syrup and fruit pulp. It is decorated with nuts or pieces of the same fruit with which it was made.

Many ingredients come together in the hodgepodge, because in camps slaves had to use their hands or basic spoons to take food from the pot. Many had to eat at the same time from the same pot. In *Nicaragua: Its People, Scenery, Monuments, and the Proposed Interoceanic Canal*, Ephraim G. Squier offers a description of the hodgepodge that the sailors of Lake Nicaragua, among whom there were undoubtedly mestizos, *zambos*, and *mulatos*, used to eat around 1850:

> Every bongo, on leaving the interior takes on board a large number of plantains, not yet fully ripe, and which are therefore called *verdes*. These are detached from the stalk, "corded up" in the bow of the boat, and constitute the principal food for the men. A few that are nearly

or quite ripe, called *maduros*, are also taken on board for immediate use. Beside these, there is a box of jerked beef, or what the Americans ironically called yard beef—i.e., beef cut in long strips and dried in the sun. Some bottles of *manteca* (lard), or a quantity of leaf fat and a bag of rice are added, and then the substantial supplies for the voyage are complete. The cookery is very simple. Stakes are driven in the ground to support the kettle, in which they first put a portion of fat, next a layer of *plátanos verdes* from which the skin has been stripped, then a layer of beef cut in small pieces, a calabash of rice, and so on until the kettle is filled [. . .]. When the mess in the kettle is cooked, each one fills his calabash, and with his fingers or a cocoa-nut spoon disposes of it at his leisure. As the "yard beef" has always a most suspicious odor, I could bring myself to taste the content of the kettle but once. I must do the sailors the justice to say that it was not an unsavory dish. It is always arranged to have half a kettle full of the mix, to which the men help themselves at their pleasure. (94)

It was in the stoves and especially in the poor kitchens of Nicaragua where the meat, bacon, and lard of the Iberian Peninsula found the maize dough, annatto, and tomato of the aboriginal people alongside the plantain leaves of the Africans to create the *nacatamal*, a dish of pre-Columbian origins. Foreign ingredients from overseas such as rice, raisins, prunes, olives, and capers in brine would later be added to make the dish a truly baroque creation of different coincidences, but of indigenous origin. Pork has largely displaced aboriginal meats (deer, turkey, lowland paca, iguana) in the original nacatamal dish, although it is possible, albeit rare, to find *nacatamal* made with the meat of such animals, many of which are endangered. *Cecina* may also be used instead of pork, as in *tamugas* from Masatepe. The *tamuga* is made with pork, chicken, beef, or fish, which is prepared a day before and seasoned with garlic, onion, vinegar, and annatto. Rice is cooked with lard before carrot pieces are added.

Where the three traditions of cooking and eating—Indigenous, Spanish, and African—met and intermixed, the Spanish component was the most elaborate and was thus the one that offered greater complexities, even when prepared in the poorer kitchens. Spanish cuisine is the only one that uses frying. As was the case in the Iberian Peninsula itself, and indeed throughout Europe, Spanish cuisine rapidly adopted corn, cacao, tomatoes, cushaw squash, vanilla, pineapple, and potatoes as common ingredients. Potatoes would later become a staple that helped in times of famine, as its cultivation proved resistant to harsh winters.

It should also be noted that Nicaragua was throughout colonial times a depopulated province, quite isolated and forgotten. The main contingent of Spanish colonizers, Andalusian, Extremaduran, and Castilian, settled in the first decades of the colonization (1520–1530), with no significant subsequent migratory waves. There was no migration of Catalans, Basques, or Galicians, owners of sublime regional cuisines, to Nicaragua. Other countries received a constant influx of immigrants from the different regions of the Iberian Peninsula, as was the case of Costa Rica and, above all, Cuba, where African slaves continued to arrive until the nineteenth century. However, such varied migrations did not translate in either case to a cuisine superior to Nicaragua's.

Iberian contributions to Nicaraguan cuisine were foundational and fixed but left out two of its key elements, olive oil and wine, and therefore olive groves and vineyards. Nevertheless, other basic Spanish elements were adopted from the outset: cattle, pigs, poultry and eggs, flour (although wheat crops would not prosper), onion and garlic, and soon after, Asian and African crops such as rice, sugar cane, and plantain brought by the colonizers themselves. It is surely due to a lack of subsequent immigration waves that Nicaragua did not receive the Spanish omelet, which appeared in the Iberian Peninsula after the arrival of the potato from America, ready to complement beaten hen eggs. Though Nicaragua never managed to become a producer of wheat, the consumption of bread fully entered into the culinary customs of the country in one of its best forms, French bread. A roll rounded off at the ends is eaten with breakfast as well as a series of small bread rolls stuck to one another in both sweet and salty varieties. French breads multiplied in Nicaragua's artisanal ovens, where various cornbreads were also baked, including the bread we call *cosa de horno*. The fundamental provisions of the Nicaraguan table are: corn tortilla (of Native American origin), ember-roasted or cooked plantain (of African origin), and wheat-flour bread (of Spanish origin). All are used equally in any meal. The tortilla is traditionally as large as the size of the *comal* (a clay or metal disk that is used to make corn tortillas or roast coffee or cocoa beans) in which it is cooked; the *comalera* tortilla serves as an edible dish on which beans or meat are usually placed. Tortillas may also be layered on top of each other and serve as the conveyance for mopping up juices, just like bread or plantains.

As mentioned above, Spain introduced the novelty of frying, an art unknown to aborigines and African slaves and still used excessively in Nicaraguan cuisine. Given that olive groves are not native to Nicaragua's landscape, olive oil was always an expensive imported product in colonial times. Therefore, it was neither customarily used in salad dressing nor commonly consumed. For this reason, frying was done from the beginning with thick pork lard, a daily extravagance that communicated a touch of unique flavor to everything that fell into the pan. Cursed now as unhealthy, pork lard was not expelled from kitchens until the middle of the twentieth century, with the arrival of the cotton crop, which brought cottonseed oil as an industrially manufactured derivative product.

Eventually, butter claimed sovereignty in Nicaraguan cuisine, and everything began to be fried in it. Green and ripe plantains; all kinds of tubers and vegetables, from cassava and potatoes to chayote; *chancletas* (a Central American dish mainly prepared with chayote); and food prepared with different vegetables such as *pipián*, chayote, and potatoes, called *pescozones*; pork itself and bacon, beef steaks, and chicken pieces—all were fried. Other meats already incorporated into the aboriginal diet also passed into the realm of butter: poultry, wild game, and fish, which were eaten in great variety upon the arrival of the Spaniards, at least in the coastal settlements. This is what Gonzalo Fernández de Oviedo recalls in *Historia general y natural de las Indias* (*Misfortunes and Shipwrecks in the Seas of the Indies*) as he writes about the table set for the cacique of Tesoatega in Chinandega: "A single indigenous woman came and brought a three-foot earthenware pot full of fish, and a fig tree with buns made of corn and another with water . . . and just as he was seated, the same Indian came back and gave him water, and washed his hands and face and ate slowly. And when the cacique began to eat, other Indian women brought food to the main men, fish as well, and they sat down together to eat" (qtd. in Incer 377).

Both butter and corn could frequently be found in the pinole batter in which both saltwater and freshwater fish were fried: guabina or trahira (*Hoplias malabaricus*), mojarras, guapotes (*Parachromis managuensis*), a singular fish without bones, or fish native to the *Tipitapa* from which the spine is extracted with surgical precision. Fish is fried in pinole and covered with a sauce of pre-Hispanic onions and tomatoes crushed in the *metate*, a Nicaraguan grinding stone. Native Americans were wise in their use of sauces, to which butter was later added: moles, sauces originally used in Mexican cuisine that usually contain fruit, chili pepper, nuts, and spices like black pepper, cinnamon, and cumin; pinoles; *pebres*, or seasonings intended for meats, poultry, fish, and reptiles; and sauces made from tomatoes, sweet pepper, cacao, and chili pepper. There has always been a wide variety of such sauces in Nicaragua. Others were made from a base of crushed maize ground in the *metate*. These sauces include iguana pinole and deer pinole, which are closely related to *pebres* such as the iguana *pebre* and the turtle *pebre*, not to mention the frequent *guacamol*, made with avocados. Finally, fried street food or *fritanga* (sold outside in parks and squares, on sidewalks, at entrances of police stations, courts, and public offices, in schools and universities, cinemas, galleries, and at circuses and other shows) employs butter in many inventive ways. The name *fritanga* now designates even what is not fried, as described by Alberto Vogl in *Nicaragua con Amor y Humor* (*Nicaragua with Love and Humor*):

> On charcoal burners, classic *tenamastes*[1] make their *fritangas*: Rich slices of ripe and green bananas, fried pork chops, cooked hen, stuffed meat, delicious beans, burst rice, *pipián* and chayote stews, soup, cho-

rizo with egg, roasted meat, *carne en vaho*, fish, fritters, warm tortillas, *pinolillo*,[2] coffee, *chibola*.[3] For those so inclined, there is armadillo, deer, Paslama or turtle eggs, oysters, iguana, and of course *nacatamales*, *mondongo*, and *moronga*, all of exquisite taste and well-cooked. [. . .] There is also fried cheese, eaten with banana slices and a salad of cabbage and pickled tomatoes, and the small but effective pequin pepper; *chicharrones* and fried pork, red pork with cassava, tinted with annatto, chorizos with annatto, *vigorón*, empanadas of ripe banana, enchiladas, *repochetas*,[4] *tostones*,[5] *chancletas* and *pescozones*. (127)

The habit of eating in the street at all times has to do with the *tianguis*, aboriginal markets established outdoors in the squares. The traditions associated with street food, from which the *fritanga* is derived, were deeply rooted in the second half of the nineteenth century, as Pablo Lévy testifies:

> The diet of the poor class presents three dismal particulars regarding hygiene which so powerfully influences the regular increase of the population, and consequently of the prosperity of the country that they should seriously draw the attention of the administration. The first is IRREGULARITY in diet: Nicaraguan people eat at all times, anything that is provided between the accustomed times is accepted and quietly eaten; there is also much irregularity in the amount of food consumed at each time. The second peculiarity refers to the QUALITY of food: plantains, beans, and cheese, which are the basis of food for the people, are harmful foods when eaten exclusively, and are non-nutritious anyways. [. . .] The last peculiarity refers to QUANTITY, which is totally insufficient. (227)

From the perspective of a European visitor such as Lévy, food hygiene was lacking, particularly among the poorer classes, but Lévy states that:

> A particular character of the household administration of poor families is not having provisions; every day they buy what is needed to eat in small portions. Many women, too poor to have maids, and

yet too proud or lazy to cook, not only live this way, buying every day what they need for their sustenance, but also order ready-made food for themselves and their families. This is so common that it has resulted in the growth of a particular type of commerce, grocery stores sell food in small portions, not only raw edibles of all types, but also cooked. (226)

Going daily to the market or the grocery store has to do with scarcity of income, as Lévy recognizes, and is a custom imposed more by necessity than force, along with the habit of buying on credit until one's paycheck arrives. Even today buying ready-made foods such as cooked beans or pre-made food is a popular practice, especially among the elderly and those who live alone. Lévy also tells us how the families of moderate means sat to eat at the table:

> The general characteristics of Nicaraguan food are sobriety and uniformity. The cuisine has lard as its universal base, and except for the poorest people, they generally eat sitting at a table covered with a tablecloth, but the use of napkin is very little known. There are some irregularities in the use of spoon, fork, and knife; however, only very ordinary people eat with their hands. A large number of people have learned from North Americans the custom of bringing food to the mouth with the point of a knife. Many eat without drinking, and only after eating do they drink water; others drink chocolate or coffee. (224–25)

In a footnote, Lévy adds that, "sociological data are essential, although childish in appearance. At various points in Spanish America, in Mexico for example, a large number of families, although very well off, eat on the ground, on a bed mat, and with their fingers. There is interest in knowing that Nicaragua, on this count, leads many of its sister nations" (225). What was normally eaten, then? Beef, above all, as we know. "There is no other meat than that of beef or pork, and very few vegetables," Lévy says (226). In fact, beef continues to be the primary meat consumed in Nicaragua. Lévy adds that:

Fish is not as common as you might think when considering the hydrographic provisions of the territory. There is almost never small game; with the exception of deer, which is eaten frequently. The poor quality of the vinegar and oils prepared in the country prevents the manufacturing of preserves that use them, and condiments are reduced almost exclusively to pickles, olives, and sardines. The pepper called chili, of such an abusive use in other countries of Spanish America, is almost entirely neglected in Nicaragua; instead, an unexpected condiment is used in Indigenous cuisine: the annatto. (226)

Annatto is essential to so many dishes: rice, red pork, and sausages. Since the arrival of the pig to Nicaragua, a diverse population learned to prepare sausages (which are part of the *fritanga* realm) made of pork meat flavored richly with annatto and other spices. They are seasoned inside cow casings rinsed until transparent; once stuffed, they are tied in balls with strips of banana leaf to be eaten fried, roasted, or scrambled with hen eggs. The *morongas*, an African word that became the name of a traditional peninsular black pudding made with the blood of the same pig, were marinated and seasoned in the same way: "*morongas* or *morcillas* are not at all unworthy of their Spanish ancestors, but rather are somewhat superior; they are combined with the *telilla*[6] of the same pig and with grains of rice, which give it consistency and improve its taste" (Coronel Urtecho 31).

Wine was used mainly for consecration as part of the Catholic mass and was only within the reach of those few families who could pay the luxury of its importation from Spain. Therefore, wine was replaced by the harsh flavor of *guaro* extracted from the sugarcane, *guaro lija* or *guarón*, which is harsh for the uvula. *Guaro* replaced *chicha* as the alcoholic beverage of choice in the festivities and drunkenness of pre-Columbian times. As Fernández de Oviedo recalls, "*chicha* or wine that they make of corn was very strong and somewhat acidic, its color seems like chicken soup, when one or two egg yolks are diluted in it" (Incer 353). Today, *chicha* is usually found as a soda in a slightly fermented form, except when it rises to the category of *cususa*, the corn-derived spirit of clandestine distillation that is always prosecuted by the government. There is a *cususa* made in Camoapa that has the magnificent name of *morir soñando*, to die dreaming. During colonial times, Bishop Vílchez y Cabrera wanted to forbid the revelries of *mulatos* in the *fandangos* not only because of the blatant lasciviousness of the dances, but also due to the prodigality with which they drank the "aguardiente that they call 'of the land' and that they make in their houses or buy in the tobacco shop for eight *reales* per jar at its most expensive" (Cardenal 189). If it was made at home, the liquor was *cususa*. If it was purchased in a tobacco shop, it was *guaro lija*. But both led to the machete (an instrument of labor in agricultural tasks used mainly for cutting sugarcane) to be used as a weapon in drunken brawls: "he who drinks *guaro* kills with a machete," the journalist Gabry Rivas states (qtd. in Coronel 31).

In the realm of candy and desserts, Nicaragua has a sumptuous delight: a type of syrup and a dessert of cooked fruits with panela or sugar, called *curbasá*, a word of mysterious etymology that not even the most learned philologists have dared to explain. Typically eaten during Lent, when summer fruits are harvested in Nicaragua, *curbasá* reveals the most refined culinary imagination. Throughout Lent, preserves made from different fruits are prepared in advance, including mangos, *jocotes*, tomatoes, green papayas, mameyes, cashews, and redcurrants. Pickled *nancites*, tamarind and fig leaves, cinnamon sticks, and cloves are often added to these delicious concoctions to achieve a balanced mixture of flavors. Some are gently sweet while others are acidic, but each fruit preserve boasts its own taste and color, sometimes darkened by panela, or, when made with white sugar, pleasing to the eye with an amber and golden sheen.

Curbasá has evolved from two culinary traditions, one Iberian, the other African. A direct antecedent of the *curbasá* in the colonial kitchen appears in *Lybro de cocyna* of Guatemala (*The Cookbook*; 1844), with recipes written for "dry preserves and preserves in syrup" made with peaches, apples, tomatoes, figs, pineapple, apricot, watermelon, melon, pumpkins, granadillas, soursop, sweet potatoes, and other similar fruits that are previously boiled with sugar and cinnamon sticks. Dry preserves or marmalades are made with oranges, lemons, citron, limes, and other citric fruits that lose their bitter taste after being boiled. Once boiled, these fruits are cooked in clarified sugar in the same proportions used in syrup preserves, with the addition of cinnamon sticks once the preserves are set. *Calandraca* is a similar Easter preserve found in the African cuisine of Colombia's Caribbean coast. It is also called *mongo-mongo*, a name that refers to one of the four great African tribes along with the Bantu, the Kongos, and the Zande, who live mainly in Zaire. It is made with mangoes, ripe plantains, sweet potatoes, pineapples, guavas, tomatoes, mamey, and coconuts; cinnamon, clove, anise, and allspice are added to the honey of panela with which it is sweetened.

One cannot speak of Nicaraguan cuisine—or any other, for that matter—in the past tense. Nicaragua's culinary tradition is one that moves and changes, subject to the permanent mutation of invention, external influences, such as the Chinese or Italian immigration in Nicaragua, exoduses and exiles that have also inspired a Nicaraguan cuisine outside its borders: the cuisine of nostalgia. When abroad, tradition somehow freezes because from afar the eyes only perceive that which the country may have lost. Yet, at the same time, culinary tradition is subject to dynamic innovation as it adapts, like the language, to variations within the local environment, starting with the ingredients. Replacements, modifications, and new contributions are discovered and employed, such as the *Tres leches* (three milks) dessert or the *Siete mares* (seven seas) soup, which includes all kinds of fish and seafood. An abundant selection of cooking websites and cookbooks by Nicaraguans living abroad, mainly in the United States, can be found online.

But the cuisine that is made within Nicaragua also varies because it has modernized and also, unfortunately, has become impoverished. Many of the dishes of our culinary tradition have disappeared or are in the process of extinction. In many ways, my dictionary (2014) aims to rescue this essential part of our culture that is falling into oblivion, for a dish that is not cooked for a long time soon becomes an extinct dish. The causes of such culinary extinction vary, and we should not wholly blame the importation of foreign ways of eating, such as the fast-food culture from the United States. Because of the times and the changes within our society, traditional cooking is losing its essential artisanal quality. Many traditional dishes are difficult to execute, and, because they require skill, time, and patience, no longer belong to Nicaraguan daily life. The cooks who master the art of preparing them are few. The ingredients are expensive, as well as scarce.

The shortage of ingredients that are necessary to prepare traditional Nicaraguan dishes may be attributed to several factors, the most important of which is simply their disappearance, as is the case of *piñuela* (*Bromelia karatas*), which was once used in hedges on rural properties but today is almost non-existent. Its acidic fruit is used to prepare the *motasatol*, a dessert prepared with the *piñuela* fruit, corn flour, sugar, cinnamon, and ground plantains. Likewise, in the case of *pinol de venado* (deer pinole), the deer, along with many other wild animals like armadillo, lowland paca, and agouti have also irremediably vanished. There were still deer in the foothills of the volcano Santiago some years ago, as I recall from childhood memories, when the hunters came to my father's shop to buy batteries for their head lamps and 0.22 bullets for their Winchester rifles. Another example is turtle eggs, which are justly banned from harvesting and the subject of flourishing campaigns of spawning protection and turtle reproduction so that they may prosper.

Nicaragua has a rich heritage that is no less substantial than diverse. Cuisine is a matter of the palate but also of smell and sight, making it a feast of the senses. "Tell me what you eat and I'll tell you who you are," says Brillat-Savarin in *The Physiology of Taste*. If we want to know who we are, we have to know what we eat. We must know the origin of what we eat, and who ate before us. And we have to know how they ate, and how they brought together their tastes and their needs.

NOTES

Chapter translated by Rafael Climent-Espino, reviewed by Gabrielle Miller. This chapter is based on the comprehensive study on Nicaraguan cuisine published in Spanish in Ramírez (2014), particularly its introduction, which this chapter closely follows.

1. Each of the three stones that form the stove and on which the cooking pot is placed.
2. A cacao-based traditional Nicaraguan drink made with sweet cornmeal.
3. Chibola dough is made with flour, egg, butter, water, salt, yeast, and vanilla.
4. This fritanga is common throughout Nicaragua. It is made with tortillas, mashed beans, grated cheese, coleslaw, onions, and tomato sauce.
5. The tostón is a small piece of bread fried in oil or toasted, which serves to accompany soups, creams, and stews; it is also eaten at breakfast, for a snack, and as an accompaniment to hot drinks.
6. Retraction of a membrane that lines the viscera, called peritoneum.

WORKS CITED

Brillat-Savarin, Jean A. *The Physiology of Taste, or, Meditations on Transcendental Gastronomy*. Heritage P, 1949.

Cardenal Tellería, Marco A. *Nicaragua y su historia, 1502–1936: Cronología del acontecer histórico y construcción de la nación nicaragüense*. Banco Mercantil, 2001.

Coronel Urtecho, José. "Elogio de la cocina nicaragüense." *Revista Conservadora*, 31 May 1962.

Diccionario de la Real Academia Española. Real Academia Española, 1984.

"Dos recetas de Africa Central." Taringa, 6 Aug. 2011. www.taringa.net/+entusiastasdeafrica/dos-recetas-de-africa-central_rkkx7.

Fernández de Oviedo y Valdés, Gonzalo. *Misfortunes and Shipwrecks in the Seas of the Indies, Islands, and Mainland of the Ocean Sea (1513–1548)*. Translated and edited by Glen F. Dille, UP of Florida, 2011.

———. *Historia general y natural de las Indias, islas y tierra firme del mar océano*. Imprenta de la Real Academia de la Historia, 1851.

Gomes, Miriam V. "Los negros africanos en la cultura argentina." *Página Digital*, 14 Aug. 2005.

Incer Barquero, Jaime. *Descubrimiento, conquista y exploración de Nicaragua*. Colección Cultural de Centro América, 2002.

Lévy, Pablo. *Notas geográficas y económicas de la República de Nicaragua*. Introduction and notes by Jaime Incer Barquero, Fondo de Promoción Cultural del Banco de América, 1976.

Lybro de cocyna, que contiene el modo de hacer los pucheros, sopas, guizos, nogadas, salsas, tortas, pasteles, marquezotes, quezadias, dulces tamales, tamalitos, pastelitos, biscotelas, y otras cosas. En Guatemala copiado á 7 de diciembre de 1844. Prólogo de Luis Luján Munoz. Centro de Estudios Folklóricos, Universidad de San Carlos de Guatemala, 1972.

Mántica Abaunza, Carlos, and Alicia Casco Guido. *El habla nicaragüense y otros ensayos*. Hispamer, 2007.

Ramírez, Sergio. *Lo que sabe el paladar: Diccionario de los alimentos de Nicaragua donde se ponen y anotan las cosas de los reinos naturales que el gusto regala, artes con que cocinan y sazonan, y todo lo demás que buenamente se corresponde*. Hispamer, 2014.

Splendiani, Ana M., and Tulio Aristazábal. *Proceso de beatificación y canonización de San Pedro Claver*. Centro Editorial Javeriano, 2002.

Squier, Ephraim G. *Nicaragua: Its People, Scenery, Monuments, and the Proposed Interoceanic Canal: With Numerous Original Maps and Illustrations*, vol. 1, New York, D. Appleton, 1852.

Twain, Mark. *Pudd'nhead Wilson and Those Extraordinary Twins*. Harper, 1922.

Vogl Baldizón, Alberto. *Nicaragua con amor y humor*. Ministerio de Cultura, 1977.

CHAPTER 11

A Gastrocritical Reading of Miguel Ángel Asturias's Early Narrative

Legends of Guatemala, The President, *and* Men of Maize

Rafael Climent-Espino, *Baylor University*

THE EARLY WORK of the Guatemalan writer Miguel Ángel Asturias has been widely studied by prominent scholars in Spanish American literature. Well-informed essays have provided an in-depth analysis of *Legends of Guatemala* (1930), *The President* (1946), and *Men of Maize* (1949).[1] Nevertheless, those studies tangentially address an increasingly important theme that appears in Asturias's narrative since *Legends of Guatemala*, a topic that underlies most of his work: food. This essay aims to analyze how food interacts with ethnicity, gender, and social class in the early narrative of the Nobel Prize for Literature laureate Miguel Ángel Asturias, one of the most lauded Latin American writers of the twentieth century.

In the last decades, works relating to humanities and food studies are growing in importance. Food production and consumption provide relevant information about the social structure and specific roles that subjects play within society. Food places the individual in relation with other members of the community and sheds light on social hierarchies. The act of eating is related to us individually and socially, since the idea of sharing food is linked to that of group belonging. The need to eat points to the social nature of the culinary act, to commensalism and its centrality in any type of group activity (Goody 12–17). Additionally, there are works that refer to food as an important factor of human knowledge from philosophical and psychological perspectives. For instance, Deane W. Curtin, who investigates the relationship between food, culinary arts and women, argues that the experience that the individual has with food constitutes her/him as a person. Eating is an activity that we share with animals, but the production, elaboration, transaction, and consumption of food is a distinctive cultural human practice that reflects social stratification (14).

Gastrocriticism (Tobin) and gastro-politics (Appadurai) are the two main theoretical frameworks used in this study. They both place food and everything related to the culinary act at the center of cultural studies. With the attention that studies of daily life have received since the second quarter of the twentieth century, prominent anthropologists like Claude Lévi-Strauss and Jack Goody took a particular interest in the aspects of food as it relates to the humanities. The term "gastrocriticism" was coined by Ronald Tobin, who proposed that this discipline, "tries to study the relevance for a literary work of the multiple connotations of eating and drinking in the social, racial, geographical, identity, historical, sexual, anthropological, religious, philosophical, medical, cultural, psychological, ideological-political, generic, and linguistic aspects" (qtd. in De Maeseneer, *Devorando* 24). This theoretical approach:

presupposes a vast undertaking of research in human sciences that explores the connections between alimentation and art. It belongs and appeals to history—cultural history, economic history, history of mentality and daily life, and history of art—, sociology, civility and gallantry, alimentation and cookbooks, medicine, nutrition and dietary questions and health, literary criticism and semiotics, psychoanalysis and philosophy, gender studies, and, particularly *anthropology*. Gastrocriticism serves to understand the fact that the poet and the cook work both to create a metamorphosis and an illusion. (De Maeseneer, "The Aesthetic of Hunger" 30)

Indeed, anthropological research on food has provided relevant concepts for food studies to better analyze its role in both real and fictional contexts. Gastrocriticism comprises a wide range of fields from which to approach the culinary act and food representations within the arts. Among those concepts, Arjun Appadurai's anthropological notion of gastro-politics is valuable to analyzing how characters relate to food and how race, class, and gender are variables that matter when studying social dynamics in relation to it. Since food is a contributing factor in shaping social hierarchies in *The President* and *Men of Maize*, gastro-politics enables reflection on its role as a main subtext in those novels. Thus, gastro-politics is a useful tool to analyze the relationship of need between characters and food, since it offers unique information on social issues in the fictional universe. Approaching the text from this perspective shows how social relationships and practices are reflected in fiction through food. For the purpose of literary criticism, I propose to consider Appadurai's gastro-politics within the more comprehensive concept of gastrocriticism. To explain gatro-politics, Appadurai states that: "The general semiotic properties of food take particularly intense forms in the context of gastro-politics—where food is the medium, and sometimes the message, of conflict. In South Asia, where beliefs about food encode a complex set of social and moral propositions, food serves two diametrically opposed semiotic functions: it can either homogenize the actors who transact in it, or it can serve to heterogenize them" (494). He concludes that: "By gastro-politics I mean conflict or competition over specific cultural or economic resources as it emerges in social transactions around food. In this sense, gastro-politics is a common feature of many cultures" (495).

Food is the medium, and sometimes the message, of conflict. As I will show, this statement can be applied, to a great extent, to the action taking place in *Men of Maize* and *The President*. *Men of Maize* presents a subaltern group, the Mayas, and a hegemonic group, the Ladino. The negative reaction of the Mayas to the Ladino must be understood within the counter-hegemonic cultural practices framework in Central America.[2] Through this concept, the conflicts of interest between ethnic groups—Mayas versus Ladino—and the symbolic transactions related to food production and consumption can be unveiled.[3]

Central American society has constituted and bridged gender and social differences through foodways, which are eating habits and culinary practices including production, elaboration, distribution, consumption, and access to food.[4] Controlling food production means controlling satiation or scarcity, and depending on who controls it, it can be used to defy or consolidate a status quo. Furthermore, social customs such as the meaning that surrounds the act of eating, alimentary exchange, the consumption of alcohol, or the division of labor have depicted male and female roles, identity, and structures of power. I aim to show how in Miguel Ángel Asturias's early narrative, characters define their social relationship in food-centered productive roles. Social inequality is depicted through food production and consumption in Asturias's fiction. It is also shown that symbolic comparisons related to food are a common rhetorical tool used by the writer to draw a detailed panorama of Guatemalan society at that time.

Legends of Guatemala and the Mythical Connotations of Food

Just by understanding some main aspects of the Mayan idiosyncrasy, it will be possible to undertake a profound reading of Asturias's narrative. Due to the strong influence of the Mayan cosmogony's most important codices in his work, namely *Popol Vuh* and *Chilam Balam*, maize and natural elements have a clear presence in *Legends of Guatemala*, his first critically acclaimed book.[5] In *Popol Vuh*, maize has extraordinary symbolic connotations. The voice used in *Popol Vuh* is very similar to the narrative voice in *Legends of Guatemala*; it is a third person omniscient narrator with Mayan background or with deeply assimilated Mayan beliefs; a sort of wise ancestral voice who speaks from the knowledge and teachings of the Mayan tradition assuming the close link between nature and food in that mythical context.[6] Alejandro Lanoël-d'Aussenac asserts that: "Maize, as the sacred sustenance of life and the primordial element of Mayan mythology, is quoted repeatedly in a literal or metaphorical way throughout the text of *Legends of Guatemala*" (Asturias, *Leyendas* 67). Mayan cosmogony is tightly related to natural elements, which are idolized and revered.[7] Mayan civilization has imbued food with religious and cosmological significations. Rural traditions become important to understanding the ritual processes—sowing, harvesting, etc.—to acquiring food from the fields, from Mother Earth. The complexity of Mayan symbolic thought in relation to natural elements, and therefore to food, must be taken into consideration when analyzing Asturias's texts to comprehend how meaningful food is in social dynamics within his literary universe.[8]

During his stay in Paris, Asturias reviewed in depth the most important texts of the Mayan culture, *Popol Vuh* and *Chilam Balam*, becoming an expert on them. It is also important to note that when Asturias was five years old: "he moved to Salamá, and he frequents the mansion of his maternal grandfather [...] where he comes in contact for the first time with the natives of his country and with the natural world. There, he is in the care of the young Indian Lola Reyes, his nanny, whose stories immerse him in the world of indigenous myths and legends"[9] (Asturias, *El señor presidente*, 2000; 483). Later, as an adult, Asturias profoundly studied other scriptures of Mayan origin such as *Annals of the Cakchiquels* (1571) and *Rabinal Achí* (fifteenth century). In *Popol Vuh* (1550), Mayan traditional beliefs establish that the genesis of the human being is in the ear of corn. *Legends of Guatemala* incorporates those sources of magical and mythical knowledge. In *Legends*, gods and humans are related through food, which becomes a point of contact between the divine and the earthly: "The multitude licks the earth to bless it" (47). Since Asturias is rewriting myths of the Mayan cosmogony, *Legends of Guatemala* must be considered a mythopoetic text. These fictions offer a positive perspective of the fruits of the earth. Thus, in "Legend of the Volcano" it is asserted that "for the first, men were given the knowledge that there is not bad fruit; all are blood of the earth, rendered sweet or sour according to the tree that bears it" (59). In "Legend of La Tatuana," Father Almond, a significant name, "knew the name of all curing-plants" (68). The personification of natural elements is a constant in *Legends of Guatemala*, and it culminates in "Legend of the Treasure of the Flowering Place." In this legend, natural elements are personified, and humans are vegetalized: "Boats ferrying people in multicolored clothing that gave them the appearance of plants" (79).

Maize appears in *Legends of Guatemala* with different connotations. In relation to time, "Don Chepe and Niña Tina keep track of my years with kernels of corn" (52); since Maya people consider their own genesis to be in maize, it makes sense to count years with corn kernels. This idea also appears in *Men of Maize* (93). Maize is linked to genesis, so different spirits and deities are invoked: "Hail Beauties of the Day, giant Masters, Heart of Sky, of Earth, Providers of Yellow and Green. Providers of Daughters, of Sons! Return to us, scatter green, yellow, give life, existence to my children, my offspring! May they be engendered, may your supporters be born, your nurturers" (Asturias, *Legends* 53–54). Green and yellow, the color of corn cobs, are praised together with the ancestral attributes that maize has in the Mayan tradition: genesis, fertility, offspring, and nurturing.[10] Their own people are made with maize, that is why "trickles of blood run down the tree trunks. [. . .] Under the love of almond trees the clay smells of woman's flesh" (54). The earth seems to be bleeding, there is a personification of natural elements, and the forest becomes a living being: "In the darkness, wondrous, absurd images were looming up: eyes, hands, stomachs, jaws. Numerous generations of men pulled their skins off to cover the jungle with it. Unexpectedly I found myself in a forest of human trees: the stones were seeing, the leaves were speaking, the waters were laughing, and the sun, moon, stars, heaven and earth were moving under their own volition" (55). This metamorphosis from vegetation to human, or vice versa, makes nature acquire a different status in the Mayan people's understanding of life, one in which human beings are part of nature in relation to its flora and fauna and where food plays a main role. And so it is represented in *Legends of Guatemala* and *Men of Maize*.

Men of Maize: Confronted Ways of Understanding Food and Nature

The historical context in which Asturias wrote *Men of Maize* is relevant to understanding why food production is such an important theme within the novel.[11] Asturias started writing the novel in 1945, shortly after the US–backed dictator Jorge Ubico resigned as president in 1944. After Ubico, Juan José Arévalo, the first elected president of Guatemala (1945–1951) implemented a series of social reforms, among them an agrarian reform that included the return of the dispossessed land, expropriated by Ubico in favor of the United Fruit Company, to the Mayas.[12] Asturias supported these reforms and wrote *Men of Maize* under Arévalo's government.[13] Asturias fictionalizes the reforms that Arévalo was driving by extoling the power of the Maya community and by showing the progressive reality that Arévalo had in mind for Guatemala.

Food symbolism in *Men of Maize* must be understood in the same mythical context as in *Legends of Guatemala*. In *Men of Maize*, two different understandings of nature clash head-on with each other, forming the main conflict. The Mayans' mythical perspective is essentially respectful of their ancestral thoughts on nature and its cycles of productivity. They believe nature is a superior spiritual provider that should be respected at all cost. On the contrary, for the Ladino people nature is a space that must be subordinated, a resource for material and economic profit that can be exploited as much as possible. They represent a capitalist and exploitative vision of land and corn.[14] Thus, the struggle for control over potential corn fields between these two groups drives the action. In Central America, the term Ladino refers to mestizos who only speak Spanish.[15] For the purpose of this essay, it is significant that the Ladino people are racially, linguistically, and therefore culturally different from the Mayans: two ethnic groups in confrontation. Both fight fiercely to control corn production. Appadurai's aforementioned words, "Food is the medium, and sometimes the message, of conflict" (494), fit within the plot of *Men of Maize*. In the novel, there is an attempt to murder Gaspar Ilom, whose self-sacrifice of throwing himself into the river will cause the rite of corn cultivation to continue. Ilom, a Mayan main protagonist, asserts at the very beginning of the novel: "Sown to be eaten [maize] is the sacred sustenance of the men who were made of maize. Sown to make money it means famine for the men who were made of maize" (5–6). Thus, in order to avoid famine, Gaspar decides to kill Ladino maize growers who are damaging the earth by burning the forest to grow maize.[16] This is the main conflict developed within the novel. Because of Gaspar Ilom's Mayan background, he cannot consider maize as a mere good to sell; maize has a symbolic character—a "sacred sustenance"—that passes from generation to generation and whose roots can be found in the mythical genesis of the Mayans.[17] Maize is a permanent symbolic food in Mayan culture (Cruz Cruz 17–20). In *Men of Maize*, Ladino people and maizegrowers do not operate within Gaspar Ilom's symbolic pattern. Those Mayans who know the sacred attributes of the land and help the Ladinos to exploit the land are considered traitors. They create their own curse by renouncing old Mayan teachings. In the novel, this was the case with Señor Tomás Machojón, who married a Ladino woman, Vaca Manuela Machojón.

Food activities provide relevant information on social roles within the Mayan community, as can be seen in this important passage from *Men of Maize*:

Adolescents with faces like unpainted tortilla gourds played among old people, among the women, among the men, among the bonfires, among the cooks sinking calabash ladles into great pots of pulique, sancocho, chicken stew, and pipian, to fill the glazed earthenware bowls the guests kept passing and passing and passing and passing, without ever confusing the orders, whether pipian, stew, or pulique. The women in charge of the red chili sprinkled drops of huaque chili like spots of blood into bowls of tawny soup swimming with spiny chayote halves, skins intact, chunks of meat, pacayas, melting potatoes, and tender guicoy squashes shaped like shells, and handfuls of string beans, and strips of root chayote, all with coriander, salt, garlic, and tomato to taste. And they sprinkled red chili over bowls of rice and chicken stew, seven chickens, nine white chickens. The tamale-makers, blackened by the smoke, took banana-leaf bundles tied with reed strands out of bubbling earthenware tubs and opened with a trice. Those who served the open tamales, the ones ready to eat, were sweating as though exposed to the sun, after standing so long taking the blistering steam from the boiled maize dough full in their faces, those brilliant red packages with meat inside, snares set for folk who eat the tamale and end up sucking their fingers and exchanging confidences with their neighbors. (16)

Paraphrasing Appadurai's aforementioned words in relation to literary analysis, food encodes a complex set of social propositions. Literary critics must try to decode what at first may seem like a meaningless description of food. This quote offers a sort of *costumbrista* description marked by a realistic depiction of a regional way of preparing and consuming food. Although lost in translation, in the original text in Spanish we find that cooks (*cocineras*), tamale-makers (*tamaleras*), and tamale-servers are all women. This fact shows a social division of work in relation to food and gender. Meanwhile men are in charge of strength trades, agriculture, working on food production, and hunting; women take care of the house and children and prepare foods. One could argue that the Mayan public space is a masculine one, while the house is feminine. The complexity of the described scene must be analyzed, as it provides much information on social aspects of food elaboration and consumption in the Mayan community.

Asturias's depiction of the scene does not miss any detail. On one hand, the beginning of the quote explains that preparing and consuming food are group activities, opportunities for the members of the community to talk to each other regardless of gender and age; adolescents, old people, women and men, are all together. Eating and sharing food means a common celebration where all can participate. This "eating together" reinforces personal and family ties, group and ethnic identity. On the other hand, these types of activities ensure the intergenerational passage not only of culinary knowledge but also of the gender roles associated with the preparation and service of food. In addition, the emphasis on the redness of chili "like spots of blood" and the specific number of chickens—"seven chickens, nine white chickens"—confers the scene ritualistic connotations.[18]

Finally, the last part of the quote points out that they "end up sucking their fingers."[19] The Spanish introduced cutlery and table manners during the colonial period. By describing how Mayan people eat with their hands, Asturias emphasizes the differences between ethnic groups in showing how Mayan people keep their traditions in contrast with the Europeanized Ladinos who use cutlery to eat. Eating with the fingers is not a minor detail when analyzing food. For the Mayans, the importance of food is found in its link to nature. Therefore, physically touching the food establishes a closeness between Mayans and nature that has been lost for other ethnic groups. In relation to ethnicity, it is meaningful that most of the food is boiled or roasted. Although there is some fried food, which was introduced by the Spanish, the indigenous people of America had not produced vegetable oil and did not use animal fat to cook with until the Spanish arrival. These facts show that they continue using Mayan culinary techniques and skills. The description of the banquet goes on:

> Guests are put at their ease as they eat their tamales, so much so they soon have no qualms about trying their companion's or asking for another, like Gaspar's brash guerrillas as they asked the serving

women, slipping in a pinch or two, only to have their hands brushed aside or answering with slaps, "Let's have another one, missy...!" Large tamales, red ones and black ones, the red ones salted, the black ones filled with turkey, sugar, and almonds; and smaller ones like acolytes in white maize-leaf surplices, and other of purple amaranth, pink choreque flowers, loroco seeds, or pita and pumpkin flowers; and tamales with aniseed and tamales with green maize ears, like the soft unhardened flesh of little maize boys. "Let's have another one, missy...!" The women were eating things that looked like roseapples of maize dough brushed with milk, little tamales colored with cochimeal and subtly perfumed. "Let's have another one, missy...!" The cooks wiped the backs of their hands across their foreheads to put their hair away. Now and then they used their hands to wipe their noses, streaming with the smoke and the tamales. (17)

These two quotes from *Men of Maize* show tamales and tortillas made of corn as main dishes of the Mayan diet, and dishes made with hot pepper (*chile*), corn, and different varieties of beans are the main foods consumed in the Mayan community. There are clear gender roles in relation to food. While the men sit and eat, the women prepare the food and serve it to them, reinforcing the idea of a patriarchal society. The demanding and constant repetition of the sentence "Let's have another one, missy...!" emphasizes this role of female servitude in contrast to male gluttony. In this context, an abusive behavior of Gaspar's men with the female servers is described: "they reach out their hands to touch their *meats*," where "meats" (*carnes*) refers to servers' bodies.[20] This reference to meat is not naïve in a patriarchal context: women are also "meats" prepared to be consumed by men. Asturias establishes a parallelism between two basic necessities: eating and sex. While the food appetite is being satiated with the help of female servers, the men are also trying to find out if the female servers would be willing to help satiate their sexual appetite. During the exchange between the men and the female servers, the food is suggestively cooking: "dried beef seasoned with sour oranges, lots of salt and lots of sun, *meat* contorted in the fire as though the animal had come back to life and were being burned alive" (emphasis added; 17).²¹ This "contorted and burning meat," which is literally on fire, emphasizes the sexual connotations of the scene as well as the women's passive role as food and sexual servers.

The offer of foods increases in the last part of Asturias's description of this impressive Mayan banquet where traditional Guatemalan dishes and products are consumed:²²

> Other eyes were devouring other dishes. Roasted calabashes. Yucca with cheese. Oxtails with chili sauce, so sweet it seemed like calabash honey. Meat fritters sweating with red-hot chili. Those drinking chilate finished off their gourds as though they were putting them on as masks, so eager were they to taste the last salty dregs. The atole was served in round bowls, slightly mauve, slightly acid. The atole made of whey and maize tasted like eloatole, and the ground atole tasted like cane sugar. The boiling fat made rain bubbles in tortilla dishes steadily losing the glory of fried bananas, served whole and covered in mead to women who were already flocking and twittering to taste the cinnamon-flavored milk and rice, plums in syrup, and coyoles in honey. (17–18)

The common consumption of food mentioned in these quotes affirms the group's ethnicity. Fried food is not common, though it does signify an external influence in their culinary habits. It is important to note that this passage about the banquet is one of the most detailed culinary passages in Asturias's fiction. A brief overview of the food being eaten provides relevant information about the characters' background. Thus, for instance, we find pots of pulique, pipian, red chili, spiny chayote, pacayas, potatoes, guicoy squashes, root chayote, tomato, tamale, maize, turkey or *chumpipe*, purple amaranth, pink choreque flowers, loroco seeds, pita and pumpkin flowers, roseapples of maize dough, yucca, chilate, atole, coyoles in honey, etc. All these foods clearly connote a strong Mayan identity. The *pipian* used to be served in religious and political ceremonies, such as celebrating a change of tribal leadership.²³

The extensive enumerations and detailed descriptions of food provide the reader with an overflowing cornucopia of animals and vegetables, a compendium of Maya food, a literature of the senses with valuable information on original products of Central America. In addition, the traditional Mayan dishes mentioned establish the limits of Guatemalan national cuisine.[24] The exposed variety of dishes can even be considered exaggerated; in his introduction to the novel, José Mejía points out that: "The banquet that precedes the killing of the Indians of Ilom is a typical example of Asturias's delirious baroque style. The orgiastic abundance of food concurs with the proliferation of images, in the description of the delicacies and the agitation of the scene" (*Hombres de maíz* 36).[25] On one hand, the passage describing the banquet can be considered a sort of abbreviated cookbook of traditional Mayan cuisine. On the other, it ratifies the importance of food within Asturias's narrative. Ultimately, it shows Miguel Ángel Asturias as a well-informed writer in culinary matters.

Eating and drinking are not just described as delightful actions in *Men of Maize*. Shortly after this magnificent banquet, Vaca Manuela Machojón tries to poison Gaspar Ilom: "The two white roots dyed the amber liquid the man at the underground feast held in his hands. He did not see the reflections of the white roots, and when he drank from it he turned pale, gesticulated, and fell writhing to the ground, feeling as though his intestines were ripping him open, his mouth foaming, his tongue purple, his eyes staring, his nails almost black against his fingers yellow in the moonlight" (20). Poisoning can be considered the manipulation of food with bad intentions. The cheerful atmosphere of the sumptuous banquet sharply contrasts with this assassination attempt. The ingestion of some herbs can be deadly, a fact that is evidenced when Colonel Godoy's men later advise him against eating purslane soup: "When a man is in danger, like the colonel sentenced to die come the seventh fire, wanting to eat purslane is a bad sign" (97). There are also superstitious beliefs related to eating and drinking. Talking about the Mayan wisdom of nature, Asturias asserts that: "Their practical knowledge had progressed a great deal. There were botanists and zoologists who knew the secrets of medical plants possessing curative properties unknown in our times" (*Guatemalan Sociology* 69). The use of plants, foods, and natural elements can be a source of joy, but also, as poisoning attempts show, a source of sorrow. This is one of the main messages of the novel. Gaspar saves his life by jumping into the river, its water acting as a purifying element.[26]

There is a clear opposition between the use of natural elements. In the Maya banquet, plants and animals are used to eat and celebrate, which contrasts with the Ladino Manuela Vaca Machojón's use of "white roots" to poison and kill Gaspar Ilom. Those "white" roots can also be read from a racial perspective as someone of non-Mayan origin, as "white" or Ladino. I propose to understand this opposition as a *mise en abyme* of the whole novel as it relates to the aforementioned conflict between the Mayans' and Ladinos' understanding and use of nature.[27] *Mise en abyme* is a reduplication of a concept but applied to the text as a whole. Asturias uses the representation of food preparation as a rhetorical device to show the tensions between two ethnic groups within the novel.

The President: Hunger and Power, Food and Social Class

Though the appearance of food in *The President* is not as important as in *Men of Maize*, its presence is still used to emphasize relevant topics within the novel: power, cruelty, and status quo. Food representations in *The President* vary substantially from those in *Legends of Guatemala* and *Men of Maize,* in which the action is performed in rural areas. In *The President*, most of the story develops in a city with an overbearing totalitarian atmosphere.[28] Within fiction, those in power use food scarcity as a method for manipulating the population into accepting their ideas. Hunger is a weapon of control, and it increases the value of food. The beginning of the novel shows the craving for food as the driving force of fiction in a sordid setting:

The beggars were shuffling past the market eating-houses [. . .] [they] slept like thieves, with their heads on the bags containing their worldly goods: left-over scraps of meat, worn-out shoes, candle-ends, handfuls of cooked rice wrapped in old newspapers, oranges and rotten bananas [. . .] they were miserly with their scraps, and would rather give them to the dogs than to their companions of misfortune. Having satisfied their hunger [. . .] they threw themselves on the ground and sank into sad, agitated dreams—nightmares in which they saw famished pigs, thin women, maimed dogs [. . .] the sobs of a blind woman dreaming that she was covered in flies and suspended from a hook like a piece of meat in a butcher's shop. (7–8)

This excerpt highlights poverty. It also presents a fight for food while offering relevant information about characters: they belong to a low social class and suffer starvation. Beggars do not share food, and, even in their nightmares, hunger plays a main role—famished pigs, thin women. Hunger is not just in their reality, but also in their unconscious. They fear being treated like food, "like a piece of meat in a butcher's shop." This angst of "being eaten" is repeated throughout the novel. Beggars seem to be the literal "scraps" of society:

[The Zany] sank on a heap of rubbish, like someone who has reached his bed at last, and fell asleep. Above the dunghill was a spider's web of dead trees, covered with turkey-buzzards; when they saw the Zany lying there motionless, the black birds of prey fixed him with their bluish eyes and settled on the ground beside him, hopping all around him [. . .] in a macabre dance. A savage croaking gave the signal for the attack. The Zany got to his feet as he woke, prepared to defend himself. One of the boldest birds has fastened its beak in his upper lip piercing it right through the teeth like a dart, while the other carnivores disputed as to which should have his eyes and his heart. The bird which had hold of his lip struggled to tear off the morsel, caring nothing that its prey was alive. (19)

The scene described is extremely macabre. The fact that the Zany is in a landfill and he is about to be eaten by turkey buzzards can be compared with the aforementioned beggars fighting and eating scraps. This comparison animalizes beggars, who battle for food. Both the beggars and the turkey buzzards seem to fight for different scraps. Turkey buzzards appear with frequency in the story as symbols of death. Food representation emphasizes the sordid atmosphere depicted throughout the novel. Again, it is worthy to remember Appadurai's words: "Food is the medium, and sometimes the message, of conflict" (494). In this novel food represents a constant conflict due to its scarcity, and references to starvation are widespread in the text (Asturias, *The President* 9, 13, 110, 115).

Appadurai asserts that "to one or another degree, food transactions serve to regulate rank, reify roles, and signify privileges" (508). Food functions to remind characters of their social status. This is clear within the novel where military rank and hierarchy up to the all-powerful president is extremely relevant.[29] Thus, for instance, when General Canales escapes, his daughter Camila goes to live with Don Miguel Angel Face, a supporter of the president who sexually desires her. In a report to the president, Angel Face's cook informs the president that: "her master seemed very pleased and gave her orders to go out as soon as the shops opened and buy preserves, liqueurs, biscuits, and sweets, because a young lady of good family was coming to live with him" (65). Women cook for powerful men in their role as household servants. The food consumed by the upper class strongly contrasts with the food eaten by lower classes and beggars. Food is clearly marking social class within *The President*.

The cruelty and cynicism that the president and his supporters embrace to maintain the status quo is limitless. Doctor Barreño, called "that swine" by the president, denounces that a hundred and forty soldiers were poisoned by drinking soda-water because the chief of military hygiene wanted to get rich by buying the cheapest sodium sulfate from a soda-water factory. As in *Men of Maize* where Gaspar Ilom drank venom, Asturias presents another scene of poisoning through drink. The president animalizes Doctor Barreño by calling him "swine." When the denouncement comes to the president he personally talks to the doctor: "I am not going to stand the good name of my government being depreciated by gossiping medical quacks, even to the smallest degree" (31). Later on, while the president is quietly eating supper in the dining-room, a general informs him that "that swine" was unable to stand the two hundred lashes sentenced by the president: "The President was at that moment helping himself to fried potatoes, and the maid-servant holding the dish began to tremble. 'Why are you trembling?' her master scolded her" (35). The president seems unaware of his cruelty, as the man's death has no effect on him. By contrast, it has an important effect on his maid-servant, who, almost in tears, clarifies to the president: "the General says he couldn't stand it because he died!" (36), to which the president replies: "Well, what of it? Bring the next course!" (36), in the last sentence of the chapter. The peaceful, pleasant, and serene scene of the president eating is powerfully contrasted against the cruel and violent death of Doctor Barreño. That final sentence, "Bring the next course!," can be understood literally, but it can also be read as satire, a challenge to anyone who dares to disobey or even bother him as did "that swine," already devoured by a hungry president, eaten by a cannibal state.

Readers realize that the society portrayed in *The President* is degraded. Decades of brutality, coercion, and ideological persecution have damaged the state from top to bottom. The last scene I analyze is one of the cruelest. Fedina, a secondary character, is taken to prison. Her husband knows General Eusebio Canales, who has a warrant out for his arrest. The police torture Fedina to extricate the whereabouts of the general, of which she has no knowledge. Fedina recently had a newborn baby boy. Though incarcerated, Fedina "found some comfort in thinking on her child [. . .] as if she still carried him in her womb" (108). She fantasizes about her son's baptism: "She planned to celebrate the occasion with tamal and chocolate for breakfast, Valencian rice and stew for midday, cinnamon water, almond syrup, ices, and wafers in the evening" (108). These comforting thoughts vanish little by little because of the urgency of hunger:

"She sat up slowly. She was hungry. Who would suckle her child?" (110). Though she does not know anything about General Canales, Fedina is tortured and questioned by the judge advocate general: "A door opened some way off and a baby's crying was heard. Passionate, despairing crying. [. . .] 'He is crying of hunger and he'll die of hunger if you don't tell me where the general is'" (115). Fedina fights the soldiers to get her baby and, almost naked, implores the judge: "Let me feed my little boy. Listen, he hardly has the strength to cry anymore; listen, he's dying" (115). After hours of questions and torture: "they left her lying unconscious on the ground. A viscous stream was coming from her lips, and milk whiter than lime itself was flowing from her breasts" (117). Later on, they took her to the cell where "she watched her frozen, dying baby, lying as limp as a rag doll in his mother's lap. [. . .] He was growing cold. They couldn't possibly let an innocent creature die like this" (117). The mother is the first innate connection to food. If breastfeeding symbolizes motherly love, tenderness, and nurture, the mandatory weaning that leads to her son's death symbolizes the opposite: hatred, hunger, cruelty, and bestiality. The fact that the baby boy dies when his mom was capable of feeding him makes this scene the cruelest of the novel.

Beyond offering substantial information on food practices in Guatemala, Asturias's masterly usage of food representations in *Legends of Guatemala*, *Men of Maize*, and *The President* emphasizes key points to create a suitable atmosphere in which to portray his characters, highlight their personalities, and even point out their defects. In all these narratives Asturias underlines a clear fight of the Maya population to preserve their costumes and traditions against the constant challenge of Ladino people who want to appropriate their lands in order to exploit them economically. That is why the food, fruits of the land, plays a main symbolic role within these narratives. A close reading and analysis of food in Asturias's stories unveils important information about his plots and characters. Food practices also have a relevant role in Asturias's three following novels that comprise *The Banana Trilogy*: *Strong Wind*, *The Green Pope*, and *The Eyes of the Interred*.

NOTES

1. I am referring to scholarly works on Asturias by Gerald Martin, Seymour Menton, Eladia Leon Hill, and Giuseppe Bellini.
2. I use Gayatri Spivak's widely known idea of "subaltern"(90–104) as well as Boaventura de Sousa Santos's concept of "counter-hegemonic practices" developed in his *Toward a New Legal Common Sense* (278–80).
3. In my as yet unpublished work, "On Banana Exploitation Narrative: Food Depictions in *Strong Wind* by Miguel Ángel Asturias," I contextualize Asturias's *The Banana Trilogy* and analyze *Strong Wind* (1950) from a gastrocritical perspective. In this trilogy, roles related to food production are essential to understanding narrative dynamics. A main theme of the trilogy is the exploitation in banana plantations expropriated by the Guatemalan government in favor of the United Fruit Company.
4. Recent articles show new surprising archaeological findings in the Guatemalan jungle ("Sprawling"). The findings might question our knowledge of the importance of Maya civilization. Archeologists claim to have found more than sixty thousand ruins close to the city of Tikal in the rainforest of northern Guatemala. The magnitude of the findings will challenge many of the assumptions about Maya culture.
5. Asturias translated *Popol Vuh* (1927), originally written in K'iche' Maya, from French to Spanish together with José María González de Mendoza. This text has strongly influenced his work.
6. Emir Rodríguez Monegal talks about two different main narrators in Asturias's prose: on one hand, we find a conventional and realistic narrator in *The President*; on the other hand, there is a magical narrator who looks for other dimensions of reality in *Legends of Guatemala* and *Men of Maize* (16).
7. In Maya-Toltec language, "Guatemala" means "land of the trees."
8. It is interesting to note the early reference to Hungarian people at the very beginning of *Legends of Guatemala*: "they tell miracles and close the door when the Hungarians pass by: for they steal children, eat horses, talk to the Devil and shun God" (46). At that time, Asturias could not suspect that four decades later, and together with Pablo Neruda, he would write a book on Hungarian gastronomy: *Sentimental Journey Around the Hungarian Cuisine* (1969).
9. My translation.
10. Several dictionaries (Cirlot 292) and encyclopedias point out the symbolic characteristics of maize in those terms: "The Mayans said that the first humans were formed from maize. The *Popol Vuh* [. . .] recounts how the gods tried three times to make human beings and failed: They made them from the mud, but the rain destroyed them; they made them from the wood, but they were too stiff;

they made them from the flesh, but they were too easily corrupted. Finally, they made them from corn and declared them perfect" (Andrews 72–73).

11. On a more biographical note we know that after some problems with the dictator Manuel Estrada Cabrera, Asturias's parents: "became importers of grain and sugar: in the patio of the warehouse the young Asturias spends many hours talking with muleteers and peasants" (Asturias, *El señor presidente* 2000; 485). Thus, Asturias had direct contact with food trade, which will be very relevant to understanding his *Banana Trilogy*.

12. Detailed information on the power of the United Fruit Company in Guatemala can be found in *Guatemala: La democracia y el imperio* by Juan José Arévalo. Talking about the social reality of indigenous people in Peru, Antonio Cornejo Polar points to the same problem: "The problem of the Indian is rooted in the land tenure system of our economy" (22).

13. Asturias showed early preoccupation with poverty and hunger. In his first book *Guatemalan Sociology: The Social Problem of the Indian* (1923) he asserts: "Vegetable productions consist mainly of corn and beans. Very rudimentary indigenous crafts are found scattered throughout different parts of the Republic and some will soon be extinct. [. . .] The small landholders sometimes raise poultry and, on a more reduced scale, sheep and goats. As a result of the imbalance of the lands previously referred to, the imbalance of the distribution of vegetables is alarming. There are years when poverty and hunger are not lyrical clamor, but rather realities that astound us" (79).

14. A variant of the theme of exploitation of resources and people in Guatemala is developed in Asturias's *Banana Trilogy*. After *Men of Maize*, he wrote three novels that comprise the trilogy, where the United Fruit Company (UFCO) substitutes in the role of exploiter that Ladinos have in *The President* and *Men of Maize*. The UFCO was extremely powerful under the dictatorship of Jorge Ubico (1931–1944). Asturias denounces how some Central American governments were mere puppets in the hands of powerful US food companies.

15. *Ladino* is a complex term, in some places in Central America *ladino* is the same as *mestizo*, a person born of father and mother of different races who has adopted the costumes and clothing of white people and understands or speaks Spanish. Asturias's own parents were *mestizos* or *ladinos* (Asturias, *El señor presidente* 2000; 482).

16. Carlos Lenkersdorf offers a concise explanation of the defense of the earth by Maya-Tojolabal people in what he calls "bio-cosmic intersubjectivity" (43–47).

17. With "symbolic character," I refer to any physical food associated with religious, intellectual, or moral meanings in a given culture. Maize is a sacred plant/food in Mayan culture.

18. In *Guatemalan Sociology*, Asturias informs: "Hot peppers are used to add flavor to the monotony of the diet and are usually eaten in large quantities. In this case

they are not considered condiments, but rather form part of diet itself" (85–86).
19. By repeating it twice, the original text in Spanish emphasizes this fact: "llegan hasta a chuparse los dedos y entrar en confianza con los vecinos, porque se come con los dedos" (Asturias, *Hombres de maíz* 150). This last part, "porque se come con los dedos" ("because they eat with their fingers") is omitted in the translation, but it is relevant for my analysis. Furthermore, the lack of hygiene when preparing food, an early preoccupation for Asturias, is reflected in the last part of the next quote, when the cooks use their hands to cook and to wipe their noses. Asturias addresses the problem of hygiene in *Guatemalan Sociology* (87, 91, 99).
20. My translation. Spanish original: "Alargan la mano para tocarles las carnes" (Asturias, *Hombres de maíz* 150).
21. Asturias frequently enacts a kind of animalization of his characters in relation to food. This aspect can be linked to *nahualism*: in some Mesoamerican traditions, a *nahual* is a human being who has the capacity of being transformed into an animal. It happens in the novel, for instance, with Goyo Yic.
22. Asturias asserted that during the pre-Hispanic period "The indigenous populations enjoyed peace and abundance" (*The President* 69); somehow this passage seems to resemble that period.
23. The *pipian* was named, among other dishes, National Cultural Heritage of Guatemala in 2007.
24. In the passage, dishes like *sancocho* are mentioned. There are numerous varieties of *sancocho* in Latin America, and its origin could be related to Spanish stews like *cocido* (Gómez-Bravo 42).
25. My translation.
26. Juan Eduardo Cirlot shows how in a wide variety of cultures, water appears as a purifying element with connotations of life and genesis (54–57).
27. According to Carlos Reis and Ana Lopes, *mise en abyme* signifies when in a literary work: "the narrative itself or one of its significant aspects is observed, as if a reduced, slightly altered, or figurative representation of the current story or its conclusion was deeply represented by the discourse" (143).
28. *The President* is considered a precedent of the Spanish American dictator novel. It has been evaluated as a main influence on Spanish American masterpieces such as Augusto Roa Bastos's *I, the Supreme*, Alejo Carpentier's *Reasons of State*, García Márquez's *The Autumn of the Patriarch*, and Mario Vargas Llosa's *The Feast of the Goat*.
29. Though the physical place where the action is developed is not mentioned, it can be deduced as Guatemala. It can also be deduced that the president is the dictator Manuel Estrada Cabrera, president between 1898 and 1920.

WORKS CITED

Andrews, Tamra. *Nectar and Ambrosia: An Encyclopedia of Food in World Mythology*. ABC-CLIO, 2000.
Appadurai, Arjun. "Gastro-politics in Hindu South Asia." *American Ethnologist*, vol. 8, no. 3, 1981, pp. 494–511.
Arévalo, Juan José. *Guatemala: La democracia y el imperio*. Palestra, 1964.
Asturias, Miguel Ángel. *The Eyes of the Interred*. Translated by Gregory Rabassa, Delacorte P, 1973.
———. *The Green Pope*. Translated by Gregory Rabassa, Delacorte P, 1971.
———. *Guatemalan Sociology: The Social Problem of the Indian*. Arizona State U, Center for Latin American Studies, 1977.
———. *Hombres de maíz*, edited by José Mejía, Cátedra, 2014.
———. *Leyendas de Guatemala*, edited by Alejandro Lanöel d'Aussenac, Cátedra, 2005.
———. *Legends of Guatemala: Leyendas de Guatemala*. Bilingual English/Spanish Edition. Translated by Kelly Washbourne, Latin American Literary Review, 2011.
———. *Men of Maize*. Translated by Gerald Martin, Delacorte P / S. Lawrence, 1975.
———. *The President*. Translated by Frances Partridge, Waveland, 1997.
———. *El señor presidente*. Critical edition and edited by Gerald Martin, ALLCA XX, 2000.
———. *El señor presidente*, edited by Alejandro Lanöel d'Aussenac, Cátedra, 2017.
———. *Strong Wind*. Translated by Gregory Rabassa, Delacorte P, 1968.
Asturias, Miguel Ángel, and José María González de Mendoza, trans. *Popol-Vuh: O libro del consejo de los indios quichés*. Losada, 1965.
Asturias, Miguel Ángel, and Pablo Neruda. *Sentimental Journey Around the Hungarian Cuisine*. Translated by Barna Balogh, Corvina P, 1969.
Bellini, Giusseppe. *La narrativa de Miguel Ángel Asturias*. Losada, 1969.
Cirlot, Juan Eduardo. *Diccionario de símbolos y mitos*. Labor, 1992.
Cornejo Polar, Antonio. *Seven Interpretive Essays on Peruvian Reality*. Translated by Marjory Urquidi, U of Texas P, 1971.
Cruz Cruz, Juan. *Teoría elemental de la gastronomía*. EUNSA, 2002.
Curtin, Deane W., and Lisa M. Heldke, editors. *Cooking, Eating, Thinking: Transformative Philosophies of Food*. Indiana UP, 1992.
De Maeseneer, Rita. *Devorando a lo cubano: Una aproximación gastrocrítica a los textos relacionados con el siglo XIX y el Periodo Especial*. Iberoamericana, 2012.
———. "The Aesthetic of Hunger and the Special Period in Cuba." *Caribbean Food Cultures. Culinary Practices and Consumption in the Caribbean and its Dias-*

poras, edited by Wiebke Beushausen and Anne Brüske, Transcript, 2014, pp. 27–48.

Gómez-Bravo, Ana María. *Comida y cultura en el mundo hispánico*. Equinox, 2017.

Goody, Jack. *Cooking, Cuisine and Class: A Study of Comparative Sociology*. Cambridge UP, 1982.

Kittler, P. Goyan, and Kathryn P. Sucher. *Cultural Foods: Traditions and Trends*. Wadsworth, 2000.

Lenkersdorf, Carlos. *Cosmovisión maya*. Ce-Acatl, 1999.

Leon Hill, Eladia. *Miguel Ángel Asturias: Lo ancestral en su obra literaria*. Eliseo Torres, 1972.

Lévi-Strauss, Claude. "The Culinary Triangle." *Partisan Review*, vol. 33, 1966, pp. 586–96.

———. *The Raw and the Cooked*. Harper and Row, 1969.

Martin, Gerald. *Journeys Through the Labyrinth: Latin American Fiction in the Twentieth Century*. Verso, 1989.

Menton, Seymour. *Historia crítica de la novela guatemalteca*. Editorial Universitaria, 1960.

Reis, Carlos, and Ana Lopes. *Diccionario de narratología*. Almar, 2002.

Rodríguel Monegal, Emir. "Los dos Asturias." *Revista Iberoamericana*, vol. 67, 1969, pp. 13–20.

Santos, Boaventura de Sousa. *Toward a New Legal Common Sense: Law, Globalization, and Emancipation*. Butterworths, 2002.

Spivak, Gayatri Chakravorty. "Can the Subaltern Speak?" *Marxism and the Interpretation of Culture*, edited by Cary Nelson and Lawrence Grossberg, Macmillan, 1998, pp. 66–111.

"Sprawling Maya Network Discovered Under Guatemala Jungle." *BBC News*, 2 Feb. 2018, www.bbc.com/news/world-latin-america-42916261.

Tobin, Ronald W. "Qu'est-ce que la gastrocritique?" *Dix-septième siècle*, vol. 217, 1990, pp. 621–30.

CHAPTER 12

On Hunger and Brazilian Literature

Sabrina Sedlmayer,
Federal University of Minas Gerais

> Someday we'll slice freedom up and we'll love each other—
> hungerless—in absurd dawn.
>
> BARTOLOMEU CAMPOS DE QUEIRÓS

IN A LETTER to his friend Candido Portinari in 1946, writer Graciliano Ramos reflects upon the reasons that moved them both toward combining aesthetic praxis with political and economic denunciation, and also to addressing Brazilian social inequity. Both artists acted as interpreters of the condition of a people who fasted because they had no other choice, who wandered in forced nomadism in search of survival, and who were mainly concerned with matters of the stomach. However, their accusation was permeated by doubt and ambivalence:

Of the paintings you showed me when I last had lunch in Cosme Velho [neighborhood of Rio de Janeiro], the one that moved me the most was that of the mother holding the dead child. I left your home with a horrible thought in mind: in a society not divided by classes and with no misery, would it be possible to make something like that? It even occurs to me we could be making sketches, pink little angels, and that terrifies me. (Morais 228)

Upon conducting such self-analysis, the writer pinpoints some sort of fracture of ethics, a performative contradiction in his gestures. It would be reasonable to ask, though, to what degree the portrait of a mother holding a dead child would fit into that "temptation of realism," as defined by philosopher Gianni Vattimo, a tendency guided by objectivism, by adherence to the concrete, and one that often rules out hermeneutics and personal experience. Could it align itself with the "shapes of the false," as Walnice Galvão puts it, in order to describe literary narratives that conceal the real work with the language, insisting on the nuances of local culture, betting on the picturesque and on nativist sentiments?

Ten years after Ramos wrote that letter, Brazilian poverty had come to the forefront, as exemplified by the filmmaker Glauber Rocha's convulsive "aesthetics of hunger" in the Cinema Novo movement. As the years went by, some critics like Ivana Bentes stated that the radical torsion operated by Rocha was capitalized upon and turned into a "cosmetics of hunger," as one can conclude upon examining the voluminous iconography that proliferated in the first decades of the twenty-first century, underlined by the notion of "a weapon in hand and an idea in mind."[1]

However, important formal and ideological reflections swept the imminence of the naturalist-realist discourse starting in the late nineteenth century, and a considerable number of novels came to regard hunger not only as a theme, but also as an element that engenders enunciation itself, as I intend to explain here with the help of five Brazilian writers. On the other hand, there are numerous other works that keep insisting on the distance between the object being narrated and the gaze of the narrator, on the use of dichotomies—rural *vs* urban, good *vs* evil, inside *vs* outside, body *vs* soul, local *vs* universal, poverty *vs* wealth, tradition *vs* invention, and so on—and on the choice of characters who are famished, malnourished, and whose address invariably situates them in the outskirts, in the slums, and in the backlands, all those being places that Bentes calls "miséria consumível" or "consumable misery."

An audacious and heterogeneous literary *corpus* on the subject must be rostered beforehand: *A Fome* (*The Hunger*; 1890) by Rodolfo Teófilo; *O quinze* (*The Fifteen*; 1930) by Rachel de Queiroz; *Os ratos* (*The Rats*; 1935) by Dyonélio Machado, among other works markedly linked to the conventions of realism and naturalism in writing.[2] A large number of these are part of the second generation of Modernism (1930 to 1945), due to the highly belligerent context of the world at that time, with a predominant emphasis on the woes and the sagas of the Brazilian Northeast region and its weather adversities (the phenomenon of prolonged drought) and also on its economic and social struggles.[3]

In this first group of narratives, it is imperative to recall, *grosso modo*, two stances: one in which dehumanization, animalization, monstrosity, and insanity bring the famished individual closer to the animalistic, to instincts and madness; and a second one that Josué de Castro, influenced by his readings of Freud, named "the hunger taboo," meaning a kind of "blindness" when it comes to seeing the matter of hunger as a consequence of unequal distribution of wealth.

In this way, the matter brings into evidence multiple factors and a considerable system of variables. What interests me at this moment is to try to connect hunger to words, to the act of naming, to working with language, thus pushing it away from other representations that emphasize the question of hunger as intrinsically related to exogenous causes (natural catastrophes), endogenous causes (political regimes), or other causes exclusively related to structurally global factors, like the unfair division of capital. I intend to bring closer a group of literary works in Brazilian literature that do not adhere to a bond with referentiality and that propose a polarized relationship between hunger and language.

In order to explore the fundamental link between hunger and words, it is worth recalling that ever since the paradigmatic banquet in Plato's *Symposium* and the Last Supper of Christ, the discourses concerning this *topos* have always been restlessly developed. Hunger and words are examples of lacking (of food and of the thing itself, respectively) and, paradoxically, possibilities when it comes to creating something new. Considering that this is a complex problem, historically broad and polymorphically presented both in fictional and theoretical terms, I will first show the discursive grounds capable of producing strong statements, aiming at building a perspective that insinuates important interpretive keys to the field commonly known as "food studies." I will then try to outline something like a lineage of textualities and creative representations of works by Graciliano Ramos, Clarice Lispector, Guimarães Rosa, Raduan Nassar, and Bartolomeu Campos de Queirós, which are incitingly offered as a kind of magnifying lens able to potentiate the relationship between hunger and words.

Hell, Hell

The presence of hunger in Brazilian literature insinuates key elements for reflection not only in the field of Comparative Literature, but also for other fields of knowledge, opening itself as a sort of interface. In *História da alimentação no Brasil* (*History of Food in Brazil*), Luís da Câmara Cascudo inverts the biblical verse that had already been turned into poetry by Goethe when he states: "In the beginning was hunger."[4] After poring over the diets of Brazilian indigenous peoples, the African diet, and the Portuguese *ementa*, Câmara Cascudo proceeds to study Brazilian cuisine, offering information and weaving analogies and commentaries of sociological, historical, and folkloric nature on Brazilian eating patterns. When it comes to the topic of hunger, he admits there really is a hunger *bewusstsein* (awareness) with an extensive bibliography, but he also adds: "Hunger itself establishes a sociological, political, economic, artistic, literary, pictorial complex, with no harm to its very own status as a deficiency belonging in the realms of nutrition, ideally sufficient and rational. A system of concentric circles amplifies the projection of this 'conscience,' articulating it with all the other doctrine bodies that stem from the immediate and natural needs of man" (342).

From this excerpt, it can be inferred that Câmara Cascudo subscribes to a transdisciplinary view, amplifying the dimensions of the problem when he proposes articulated views and "concentric circles" regarding more perspectives. That is, therefore, different from the regionalist approach conducted by sociologist Gilberto Freyre, understood as the unification of races through the process of miscegenation. The constitution of the Brazilian people, according to Freyre, occurred due to the voluntary mixing among white, black, and native peoples. In this particular point of view, one can see the crystallization of the idea, still current today, that Brazilian food can be explained by examining territories delineated by the Brazilian Institute of Geography and Statistics (IBGE, in Portuguese), and, even more sinister, something that the Portuguese literary critic Eduardo Lourenço strongly highlights in his essay, "As contradições da mitologia colonialista portuguesa" ("The Contradictions of the Portuguese Colonialist Mythology"): "the ideal of miscegenation is none other than the supreme expression of Colonialism, translated under the optics of sex" (55). The violence of slavery, thus, is flattened on the figure of the mixed-blood individual; the violence of colonization is softened.

Monteiro Lobato was the first author to emphasize the gravity of hunger and malnutrition in Brazilian literature. It was also the first time that recipes were offered in a creative and didactic manner. The character Dona Benta would teach readers how to cook. At the *Sítio do Picapau Amarelo* (*Yellow Woodpecker Ranch*), racial tensions were tentatively dissolved under the camaraderie of the black cook, who would generously offer delicacies to her boss's grandchildren and other assorted acquaintances. Tia Nastácia, besides being the talented cook and maid who baked numerous cookies, also modeled Emilia, the doll, and was a gifted storyteller. The children would gather around the wooden stove, and, with a panoramic view of the orchard filled with jabuticaba trees, would connect the storytelling to the food. Whereas the kitchen in "that little white house" was a place exclusively destined for women—granddaughter Narizinho was also well versed in culinary arts—it also portrayed the social limits in relationships biased by slavery nostalgia. It is paramount to notice, though, how Lobato, in only one gesture, creates literature for children, an audience never contemplated until then, and broadens the presence of literature and food, when he deals with the problem of malnutrition in a precise fashion.

Reclaiming these writers who pioneered reflection on food and malnutrition—be it under Câmara Cascudo's ethnical and cultural approach, Freyre's regionalism, or Lobato's modernism/nationalism—aims solely to demonstrate the multidisciplinary character of the subject, which has been present ever since the beginning of the Modern Age in the reports of travelers. As is widely known, Amerindians were once described as monstrous beings with a bestial appetite for human flesh at a moment when, according to Rodrigo Labriola, textuality inaugurated a paradigm that promoted wonderment and amazement, thus creating a new discourse, which was repossessed and reused by Western culture. The Chroniclers of the Indies acted as potent discursive grounds to an immeasurable quantity of food representations in literary texts, and it was not for nothing that this cannibal *topos* was chosen as a national symbol of Brazilian Modernism. According to Oswald de Andrade, we are hungry for the other; we nourish ourselves on the culture of the other: "Only anthropophagy unites us. Socially. Economically. Philosophically."[5]

Traces of the Cannibalist Manifesto by Oswald de Andrade pervade the words of Glauber Rocha, who wants to recuperate a "gallery of the starving" and defend that "only a culture of hunger, weakening its own structures, can surpass itself qualitatively; the most noble cultural manifestation of hunger is violence." The aesthetics proposed by Rocha removes hunger from the biological and cultural sphere and presents it as something political.

This topic is more widely developed in an invigorating study titled *Sertão-mar: Glauber Rocha e a estética da fome* (*Backlands-Sea: Glauber Rocha and the Aesthetics of Hunger*) by Ismail Xavier. The critic analyzes how Rocha's original text was written for a roundtable in Italy, and, similarly to Fanon's gesture, was intended to defend a kind of cinema not attuned to the demands of "the Other," the colonizer, the international industry. Upon refusing the "civilized world," the filmmaker brings about other contexts, and through the aesthetics of hunger, he tries to achieve a new style that could be capable of singling out social and historical contradictions and paradoxes in Brazil (and South America). With an acute accent, he punctuates the importance of the expression "of hunger" when it comes to that new aesthetics: "The preposition 'of,' used instead of the preposition 'about,' marks the difference: hunger is not taken here as a theme or an object about which to speak. It is built in the very way of the enunciation, in the very texture of the works" (Xavier 13).

Also in this vein (talking *to* the famished, and not *about* the hungry ones) the aesthetics created by Graciliano Ramos is exemplary: it is lean, dry, precise. It is a "sharpened knife,"[6] able to cut away the regionalist repetition of patriarchal cycles, of familial sagas of the masters in their *casas-grandes* (in opposition to *senzalas*, where slaves lived), as precisely pointed out by Wander Melo Miranda: "That is how Graciliano Ramos contributes to the limits of the regionalist narrative, which, around 1930, begins to portray the country through the lens of an awareness of underdevelopment and a political engagement. In that group [of previously mentioned authors], the author of *Barren Lives* is, without a doubt, the one who most advances toward dismantling the structures of literary, cultural and political domination, while, at the same time, giving his texts an effectively innovative value" ("Texto introdutório" 13).

The Northeastern migrants, or "the drought victims," as described by the author of *Barren Lives* in the very first paragraph of his novel, were a small family composed of Fabiano, his wife Sinhá Vitória, an older boy, a younger boy, and the dog Baleia. The animal goes hungry just like all the others. The wandering through the backlands in search of food is tiresome, and there is a solidary narrator who interprets every gesture, maybe because Ramos believed that men and dogs, both tired and hungry, were the same: "We are all Baleias," the author wrote in 1937. In another letter, this time to his wife, Ramos clarifies that, before it was turned into a novel, the book was conceived as a short story:

> I wrote a short story on the death of a female dog, a difficult thing, as you can see: I tried to guess what goes on in the soul of a dog. Is there really a soul in a dog? I don't care. This creature of mine dies wishing she'll wake up in a world filled with guinea pigs. Just like we all do. The difference is that I want them to show up before I fall asleep, and Father Zé Leite wants them to come to us in dreams—but, in the end, we are all like my Baleia and we wish for guinea pigs. (*Cartas* 194)

Highlighted in that passage, we can see the fundamental difference that guided the author's demands: religion, in its idealistic inclination (and its pink little angels in a society not divided into classes, as he wrote in his letter to Portinari), is not compatible with the materialistic point of view in which the author believed. "We are all Baleia," we are hungry when awake, and we will not settle for dreams.

The characters in *Barren Lives* want to understand the inner workings of language and then feed on them, as if this were possible, like feeding on plain food. They do so in vain. Mid-book, the older boy (nameless, like his brother) asks himself and his mother what the word "hell" means:

> As he didn't know how to talk properly, the boy babbled complicated expressions, repeated syllables, imitated the cries of the animals, the noise of the wind, the sound of the branches creaking together out in the brush. Now the boy had thought he was going to learn a word that must be important, since it figured in old Miss Terta's conversation. He had to memorize it and pass it on to his brother and the dog. The dog wouldn't be impressed, but his brother would admire and envy him. (59)

Onomatopoeias, grunts, murmurs, no articulated speech. "Hell" becomes an acoustic image, a hollow sound with no meaning—just as we are going to see next, not in the Northeastern region, but in one of the most famous Brazilian cities, where another migrant with scarce language resources will try to survive.

She Doesn't Know How to Scream

In the novel *The Hour of the Star*, published in 1977, the way hunger is portrayed reverberates in the daily life of the poor young lady "who didn't have [anything]." If, for a long time, this book was regarded by literary critics as a cleavage point in Clarice Lispector's "intimate" and "psychological" prose (as if it was the first time that the outer portion, the thickness of reality, mattered to the author), such a reductive stance has already received innumerable critical readings that are important to us right now. Fundamental metalinguistic elements are present in this narrative: there is a substantial amount of parodic resources such as a dedication to the author and thirteen other possible titles to the novel; the book actually starts with a provocative delay of the plot and abusive interferences by Rodrigo, the narrator, throughout the whole narrative. That means *The Hour of the Star* opens by stating: this is not a pipe, or it is, if you, dear reader, prefer so.

To reinforce this ambivalence, it is worth mentioning that the protagonist ignores not only the origin of her name, Macabéa, but also how signs in general function, and that upsets her.[7] Because of that, the novel can be read as an initiatory journey into the realms of language. Is there any correspondence between things and their names? Or between names and people?

However, Macabéa doesn't have the proper language sophistication for social intercourse or for handling the relations of production around her—her work, the radio, society, men, her mates, her doctor—as we can perceive from the following excerpts: "There are those who have. And there are those who have not. It's very simple:

the girl had not. Hadn't what? Simply this: she had not."; "She had never figured out how to figure things out."; "She asked no questions. She divined that there were no answers."; "She was born with rickets, a legacy of the backlands."; "Even the fact of becoming a woman didn't seem to belong to her vocation."; "The girl possessed what is known as an inner life without knowing that she possessed it."

As the narrator adds, this is a non-place of limbic nature, a space that represents neither salvation nor perdition: "As for the girl, she exists in an impersonal limbo, untouched by what is worst or best. She merely exists, inhaling and exhaling, inhaling and exhaling. Why should there be anything more? Her existence is sparse. Certainly" (23).

The notion of lacking surrounds the story of Macabéa, and that is made clear in her diet: her only passion is guava paste with cheese, a dessert that has been forbidden to her every day, all her life. Her only luxury is having a sip of cold coffee before bed—and she pays for that luxury by having heartburn upon awaking. She has never had lunch or dinner at a restaurant, has never tried pasta or beer. On a daily basis, she eats hot dogs and drinks Coke, sometimes a bologna sandwich.

The story of this virgin typist, who cannot read or write well, who doesn't think about God—"nor did God think about her. God belongs to those who succeed in pinning him down" (26)—drifts away from the usually referential representations of hunger in Brazilian literary tradition and interweaves it with a time (contemporaneity, we might add) in which the poor eat processed, industrialized, low-quality food.

The end of the novel is clear in describing Macabéa's encounter with words (she goes looking for a fortune-teller and then believes wholeheartedly in the fate outlined by the woman) and with death. It's not without reason that the novel's last sentence is the one about how we forget that we die, as we always forget that a word is not the thing itself; but, counting on the irony of the narrator, we get to remember, right after, that, "in the meantime, this is the season for strawberries."

The *Jacuba*, a Mock-Up against Hunger

In the worldwide renowned and extraordinary work of Guimarães Rosa, there is, as pointed out by Antonio Candido, a bit of everything for those who can read, and "each can approach it their own way, according to their own craft" (78). That means hunger is also markedly there, in the daily life of the *jagunço* (a henchman) and of so many other wandering characters, the lunatics, the children, the wise, just waiting for a reader who can escape the references to regional food of the backlands in the state of Minas Gerais and pay attention to less regionalist matters.

Among many other food descriptions, one kind of meal catches our attention in the Rosean work: the *jacuba*, which shows up in several passages and is studied very little both in gastronomical terms and in literary studies.[8] In everyday Brazilian Portuguese, the word *jacuba* can be used either as a reference to a sort of recipe that changes according to regional culture and the circumstances or to name, derogatively, a simple dish, one that involves little technical difficulty and a certain amount of improvisation and is made when one is faced with a scarcity of ingredients and proper conditions for preparation. The character Riobaldo in the book *Grande sertão: Veredas* (*The Devil to Pay in the Backlands*) brings up this mushy food in several moments of his journey: "[That day,] my fast had been broken only by a drink of *jacuba*" (Rosa, *The Devil* 446). As we soon come to realize, this is not a complete meal, only something used when the situation demands so, to postpone satiety, a sort of imitation that fools hunger.

The *jacuba*, a kind of thickened broth, mush, soup, or even a refreshment, can be either hot or cold and prepared with different liquids: water, coffee, tea, *cachaça*, or, where the livelihood allows, stock. One can add corn or manioc flour. If it should be sweetened, sugar, *rapadura* (clumped brown sugar), or honey can be added. In some corners of Minas Gerais, some will add pieces of cheese. The *jacuba* can be sweet or savory. Not only in the backlands, but also at sea, it is a meal meant to fool hunger. In the Navy, more specifically, the name refers to a quite watery refreshment: it is green when made with limes, red when made with gooseberry.

In one passage of *A hora e a vez de Augusto Matraga* (*The Hour and Turn of Augusto Matraga*, borrowing the title of the movie based on the short story), Guimarães Rosa describes in minutia how it is made: "What I want is for you to prepare me a pretty hot *jacuba*, with pitch black *rapadura* and very fine flour, with some bitter-orange leaves mixed in" (Rosa, *Sagarana* 347). In their wandering, often the *jagunços* would "eat the nothing" or "eat the manioc mush cold." Abundance and lack of food coexist like God and Satan in Rosa's narrative. In a quicker telling, filled with ellipses, the narrator says that, in the crossing of the Sussuarão desert, deprived of any food, "obsessed with hunger," they shot and killed a big monkey who, they found out later, had no tail, for it was a man (Rosa, *The Devil* 44); others refused this diet and went for "a kind of dirt which they [found] fit to eat," as well as grass and leaves. The act of eating, in this case, is restricted not only to results; Rosa is interested in describing the diversity of this group's ways and customs: "Manioc and rapadura: heaps of it. Slabs of jerked beef. Even though there was no shortage of dried meat, frequently some of the men would go out and come back driving a steer, which they butchered and divided up. Many laced their manioc water [the jacuba] with brandy, pouring a finger of it into their gourd. I had never before seen anyone drink it that way. Different customs!" (141). The *jacuba* arises, in Rosa's prose, as a sort of formula that combines simultaneously the meal made with basic ingredients, capable of temporarily satiating hunger, with something that guards a resemblance with his own writing style—a daring dynamic, with no "static, musty, inert, stereotyped, commonplace forms," as he wrote in a letter to Harriet de Onís, his English translator[9]—or when he reveals himself as completely favorable to any author inventing their own lexicon.

Thus, in *Grande sertão: Veredas*, these problems reverberate, concerning hunger and the solutions created, having in sight the *jagunço*'s nutrition. If the recipe for the *jacuba* suggests a closeness to the concept of experiential (immaterial) heritage, it also brings up the importance of "customs." Lastly, we must recall that the whole of *Grande sertão: Veredas* is actually Riobaldo trying to find words to tell us about his ordeals. He tries, through speech, to encompass his whole experience. And, just like in language, Rosa shows that a shot of brandy (the Brazilian *cachaça*) or a few leaves of bitter orange are capable of changing the recipe of the *jacuba* completely, just like the arrangement of certain words is capable of changing a lot when it comes to literature.

Ana Is My Hunger

Through the round trip of André, the son who returns to his father's home after an exile of rebellion, we can arguably find in Raduan Nassar's first novel, *Lavoura arcaica* (*Ancient Tillage*; 1975), the biggest representation of the famished in Brazilian literary prose. André, the character-narrator, is a teenager who wants a new place at the table, but his father diminishes his juvenile words as excessively secular and corrupted by the mundane. The novel develops under the power of incest as an imperative in that culture: the hunger that the protagonist mentions actually corresponds to the desire—maybe love?—that he feels for his sister, Ana.

The seating arrangement around the table, though, is important to our understanding of the narrator's placement within the family constellation: "The right branch was a spontaneous growth off the trunk, starting from its roots; the left, though, bore the stigma of a scar, as if Mother, from where the left side started, were an anomaly, a morbid protuberance, a graft on the trunk, perhaps even fatal, it was so weighed down with affection; it might even be said that the places at the table—the whims of time—defined the two lines of the family" (156–57). The two lineages (left and right, maternal and paternal, respectively) are opposed. The mysterious and affective world of women and their domestic chores is located to the left. The one to the right is that of tradition. It is not just by chance that another table shows up in chapter 13 of *Ancient Tillage*, when we can see paraphrased the famous parable of the hungry man, "The Barber's Tale of His Sixth Brother," from *The Arabian Nights*, followed by a parenthetical that structurally, ideologically, interrogates the story: "How could the man who had bread on his table, salt to season, meat and wine, tell the story of a hungry man?" (86).

And bread is one of the first dishes that the rich old man offers the hungry man in chapter 13: "'What do you say of this bread?' asked the old man. 'This bread is quite white and delicious, and I've never in my life had one more to my taste,' promptly answered the hungry man, effortless in his kindness" (82). What follows are more delicacies worthy of one thousand and one nights: a rice- and almond-filled roast, fish with sesame sauce, lamb ribs, a rich walnut pomegranate pie, musky syrups, jams, fruits, dried dates, date syrup, raisins, and sublime wines. But we can also hear in Nassar another echo, coming from the rustic cuisine of Minas Gerais—a place where the phantasmagoria of Carlos Drummond de Andrade also dramatically sits—somewhat like a table on trestles where all is exposed: "Never mind: I'm your son just by being a negative way of affirming you" (83).

A version of the prodigal-son parable takes place, not with a yielding son coming back home, but with a son still unwilling to accept his father's words and intent on showing that the foundations of that home, and the places at the table, are fragile. The house is a microcosm that leads us to think of the group with the totem, like the legend of the primitive father discussed by Freud in the field of Anthropology in his famous book *Totem and Taboo*. Whereas in the parable of the prodigal son from the Bible we can acknowledge that the son yields when faced with his failings after departing his father's house, in *Ancient Tillage* the opposite happens: the actions of the son, daring to distrust the father's exhortation and rupturing the imperatives of work and union that bind the family members, show us that the narrator, concurrently to his distancing from the paternal law, also operates a radical departure from the holy scripture. There is a double break in comparison to the original model: the first is with the wording, which deviates from the parable and, contrary to what the evangelist proposes, does not portray the punishment received by the prodigal character—that of becoming destitute of subjectivity, feeding only on carob, which makes him equal to pigs, and returning home crestfallen. The second is with the enunciation, which, in tense language, tells us of a son who, upon leaving, contaminated the foundations of the house and sickened the family bonds.[10]

Food pervades their daily life, both in *Ancient Tillage* and in another book by Nassar, *Um copo de cólera* (*A Cup of Rage*; 1978). I take this novel as an example of how, as early as in the first chapter ("The Arrival"), an ingredient is pointedly eroticized:

> And the two of us sat in silence until she asked me "what's the matter?" but I, somewhere else entirely, remained distant and still, my thoughts lost in the red sunset, and it was because she repeated the question that I replied, "have you eaten yet?" and as she said, "later," I got up and wandered over to the kitchen (she followed me), took a tomato from the fridge, went over to the sink and washed it, then went to get the salt-shaker from the cupboard and sat down at the table (she followed all my movements from across the room, while I, to annoy her, pretended not to notice), and it was under her constant gaze that I began to eat the tomato, sprinkling more salt on what remained in my hand, making a show of biting into it with relish in order to reveal my teeth, strong as a horse's, knowing that she couldn't tear her eyes off my mouth, knowing that beneath her silence she was writhing with impatience, knowing above all that the more indifferent I seemed to be, the more attractive she found me. I only know that when I finished eating the tomato I left her there in the kitchen and went to get the radio that was on the shelf in the living room, and without going back to the kitchen we met again in the hall, and without a word and almost together we entered the half-light of the bedroom. (6)

The tomato, similar to what we iconographically associate with the apple, is, in this context, the link that leads the lovers to bed. The fruit (soft, juicy, red) points us to the female sexual organ. And the intense virility with which the narrator takes the tomato, and bites and chews it, foreshadows the passion of the act that the lovers are performing next.

A Cup of Rage, in a way, follows the standards of the *nouveau roman*, but the work by Raduan Nassar never adhered to avant-garde flights. This should be taken under consideration along with the author's desacralization of the literary institution, as he repeatedly stated from the 1980s on, when he abandoned the craft: "the only product that appeals to me now is chicken!" But there is something little known about the author: his curious perception of his creative process as related to recipes, as he explained to a journalist who wondered why he had stopped writing:

> I'm a better cook than you'd imagine, as I had to face some kitchen obligations a few years ago. I have a knack for it.
> It was in the kitchen where I made some important findings.
> Onions, for example, of which I became an unconditional supporter. As a child, I'd push the onions to the side of the plate, and, if it was still too visible [in the food], I'd just reject the whole dish, which led my father to get up from the head of the table and come make me swallow the whole thing, onions and all.
> After I rediscovered the onion, I also regained my dad at once, or, if you'd prefer, I made my definitive return to my father's house. Now, a more recent thing, and even stronger, was my discovery of garlic. A pure substance, deserving of a shrine. When you toss the crushed garlic on top of the golden onion that was already frying, that's when it comes up from the pan, that stunning smell, the smell of life. Actually, that's what made me suspect that the best cooks can be found anonymously stuck in the kitchen of the world, smelling of garlic and onion, writing with another language.
> A lot of literature is not worth a garlic clove. (Bonassa 5–6)

From the Tomato, Memory and Words

After visiting the lean prose of Ramos, the luminous one of Lispector, the syntax created by Rosa, and the baroque verb of Nassar, in a concluding gesture regarding the stances of hunger in five Brazilian authors, I would like to add the poetic prose of writer Bartolomeu Campos de Queirós. When he started writing his first book, *O peixe e o pássaro* (*The Fish and the Bird*; 1971), while still exiled in France, he befuddled the critics: they could not quite understand whether the book was addressed to adults or to children, or maybe to a juvenile audience, or whether those were verses or fables. With more than forty of his books published, we realize that Queirós's production lodges exactly in this intersection.

Food plays an important role especially in his autobiographical works, namely *Ciganos* (*Gypsies*; 1982), *Indez* (*Nest Egg*; 1989), *Ler, escrever e fazer conta na cabeça* (*Reading, Writing, and Math by Heart*; 1999), *Por parte de pai* (*On My Father's Side*; 1995), *Olho de vidro do meu avô* (*My Grandfather's Glass Eye*; 2004) and, mainly, one of his last texts, *Vermelho amargo* (*Bitter Red*; 2011), in which he explores the tomato as a point of convergence for a bundle of contradicting affections.

The tomato is the bitter red from the title of his last book published in life. It is the metaphor that, like *ritornello*, comes back insistently in the narrative to highlight the pain caused by the premature loss of the mother and the subsequent indifferent presence of a stepmother who is responsible for the kitchen and for satiating her many stepchildren's hunger. Her gestures when it comes to handling the fruit are attentively noticed by the child-narrator, who melancholically learns how to beat hunger and swallow tomatoes as someone who "bites the bullet" to go on living: "Eight. The stepmother shredded a tomato in slices, this thin, to be able to poison us all at once. One could see the white rice through the tomato, such was its transparency. With my yearning evaporating through my eyes, I insisted on justifying the economy with which she administered her gestures. Sharpening the knife with the cold cement edge of the sink, she would cut the red, bloody, ripe tomato as if she were beheading each one of us" (9).

The stepmother appreciated the tomato, but wouldn't taste it, because it was impossible to cut up only one fruit and still leave a bit of its color, its seeds, its skin, its aroma for eight diners. Not a lover of finesse, just like in stories with witchy stepmothers, she "decapitated," "beheaded" the fruit. The contrast between the coldness of the stepmother and the tenderness of the mother is marked exactly by that trait, that gesture, that performance as a cook. That way, through the description of frames with images, with interior scenes (both of the house and of the narrator's subjectivity), memory starts showing melancholically, quite slowly. The hunger, as we soon realize, is one of affection. Each of the orphans tries to cope with the loss of their mother (and the smell of alcohol that starts to exude from their father) in their own way: the elder brother learns how to eat glass, the sister learns how to embroider sufferingly, and the narrator learns how to read bulimically. As the family starts to come apart (the children are sent to other addresses) the tomato slices start getting thicker every day. The narrator, who also leaves, justifies his memories (and also the very writing of his narrative, performed years later) with the imperative of existence: "Forgetting is *disexisting*, it's not having been. As I question myself whether there is still tomato, I don't shut myself in silence" (65). If, as a boy, he wasn't allowed to choose his own food, in adulthood he meticulously selects his words.

Through these five works examined here, encompassing diverse times and singular ways, in whose plots there are no epidemics, fasts, anorexias, or, more dramatically, wars, hunger pushes away referentiality and takes the shape of a search for the right words that could express this lack that challenges us restlessly.

NOTES

Text and some quotations translated by Rodrigo Seabra.

1. The very well-known motto of Cinema Novo was "A camera in hand and an idea in mind." Among many other examples of movies brought up by the critics, Walter Salles's review of *City of God* can be mentioned, first as a book, *Cidade de Deus* (1997) by Paulo Lins, and later adapted to the silver screen by Fernando Meirelles (2002).
2. It is also worth mentioning the anonymous narrative *Olaia e Júlio, ou, A Periquita* (*Olaia and Júlio, or, The Parakeet*), maybe the first serially published novel in Brazilian literature, featured in the newspaper Beija Flor (Rio de Janeiro; 1830)

which is wholly interwoven with the presence and absence of food.

3. Naturalism/Realism took a new breath in three particular moments, according to the crucial work of Flora Süssekind, with the temperament studies of the late nineteenth century; after that, as emphasized in what came to be known as "the regionalism of the 1930s," meaning the second stage of Brazilian Modernism; and in the 1970s, in the ressurgence of the nonfiction-novel genre, partially covering the years of military dictatorship in Brazil and in which reporting and testimonies came front and center. It is important to notice that this study was conducted before the publication of Carolina de Jesus's and Paulo Lins's novels, like others from the twenty-first century, which regard the territorial locations of the slums with a strong sense of descriptivism.

4. The Bible says "In the beginning was the Word" (John 1:1), which Goethe paraphrased (in *Faust*) as "In the beginning was the act."

5. This sort of "formula" explains explicitely how literature exacerbates, questions, pluralizes the Western obsession with the hungry cannibal capable of offering new world views. In the widely read chapter 30 of the *Essays* by Montaigne, as early as 1580, the Indians of the Tupinambá tribe are described as "bloody and cruel" and also "anthropophagists and polygamists." The human-flesh eaters (of the guts, the head, the brains, and the tongue) are also described by Hans Staden when he references cannibalism (and inflates the people's imaginary) in his famed travel report published in 1557 in Germany, and not until 1892 in Portuguese. An interesting read specifically on this subject can be found in Lestringant. In the field of anthropology, I suggest Eduardo Viveiros de Castro.

6. An expression used by Flora Süssekind.

7. See *Why This World: A Biography of Clarice Lispector* by Benjamin Moser, a biography that builds an interesting analysis of the character's name. Among other information, the author argues that the origin of the protagonist's name is an important interpretive key to the narrative, considering that Judah Maccabee was a Jewish man (Lispector was a Jewish woman) who fought and resisted the Greeks but suffered a "good death," the one in combat. The history of his people, in two books, is continued in non-canonical volumes, apart from the Bible. He is also a pariah, on the road to canonization, like the Northeastern protagonist (Moser, Clarice, uma biografia 631–50). Finally, I also suggest the reading of the journal Cadernos de Literatura Brasileira volumes seventeen and eighteen (2004). In these volumes, works by Nádia Battella Gotlib, Benedito Nunes, Olga de Sá, Yudith Rosenbaum, and Silviano Santiago are highly recommended. They are all, together with the Moreira Salles Institute, important references to better understand and study Lispector's work.

8. In *Jacuba é gambiarra* (2017), I establish a critical relation between jacuba and gambiarra. Grosso modo, "gambiarra," a key concept in Brazilian culture, is

connected to improvisation and problem-solving. Just like the jacuba, it's a kind of survivalist makeshift solution that belongs in a precarious and hostile daily life. All the considerations of critical nature made about Guimarães Rosa in this article are more profoundly developed in that publication.

9. João Guimarães Rosa to Harriet de Onís, 2 January 1966, JGR-CT-04, 53, Box 017, Institute of Brazilian Studies, University of São Paulo.

10. Since 1995, I have conducted research on the concise and solid work of Raduan Nassar. Among other published titles and essays, it is worth mentioning Sedlmayer (1997, 1999, 2006, 2017).

WORKS CITED

Andrade, Oswald de. "O manifesto antropófago." *Vanguarda europeia e modernismo brasileiro: Apresentação e crítica dos principais manifestos vanguardistas*, edited by Gilberto Mendonça Teles. INL, 1976.

Bentes, Ivana. "Sertões e favelas no cinema brasileiro contemporâneo, estética e cosmética da fome." *Revista ALCEU*, Feb. 2018, revistaalceu.com.puc-rio.br/media/alceu_n15_bentes.pdf.

Bonassa, Elvis César. "Raduan vive a literatura como questão pessoal." *Folha de São Paulo*, 30 May 1995.

Cadernos de Literatura Brasileira vols. 17 and 18. Special Edition on Clarice Lispector. Instituto Moreira Salles, 2004.

Câmara Cascudo, Luís da. *História da alimentação no Brasil*. Global, 2004.

Candido, Antonio. "O homem dos avessos." *Ficção Completa*, vol. 1, edited by Guimarães Rosa, Nova Aguilar, 1994, pp. 78–92.

Cascudo, Luís da Câmara. *História da alimentação no Brasil*. Global, 2004.

Castro, Josué de. *Geografia da fome* (o dilema brasileiro: pão ou aço). Brasiliense, 1961.

Cidade de Deus. Directed by Fernando Meireles, Globo Filmes, 2002.

Freud, Sigmund. *Totem e tabu e outros trabalhos* [1913–1914]. Imago, 1996.

Freyre, Gilberto. *Casa-grande e senzala*. Globo, 2003.

Galvão, Walnice Nogueira. *As formas do falso*. Perspectiva, 1986.

Jesus, Carolina Maria de. *Quarto de despejo, diário de uma favelada*. Ática. 2014.

Labriola, Rodrigo. *A fome dos outros: Literatura, comida e alteridade no século XVI*. EduFF, 2008.

Lestringant, Frank. *Cannibals: The Discovery and Representation of the Cannibal from Columbus to Jules Verne*. U of California P, 1997.

Lins, Paulo. *Cidade de Deus*. Companhia das Letras, 1997.

Lispector, Clarice. *The Hour of the Star*. Translated by Giovanni Ponteiro, New Directions, 1992.
Lobato, Monteiro. *O sítio do Picapau Amarelo*. Brasiliense, 1986.
Lourenço, Eduardo. *Do colonialismo como nosso impensado*. Preface by Margarida Calafate Ribeiro and Roberto Vecchi, Gradiva, 2014.
Machado, Dyonélio. *Os ratos*. Civilização Brasileira, 1966.
Miranda, Wander Melo. *Graciliano Ramos*. PubliFolha, 2004.
———. "Texto introdutório Vidas secas." *Intérpretes do Brasil*, vol. 2, Nova Aguilar, 2000.
Montaigne, Michel de. *Ensaios*. Sergio Milliet, 2000.
Morais, Dênis de. *O velho Graça: Uma biografia de Graciliano Ramos*. José Olympio, 1992.
Moser, Benjamin. *Clarice, uma biografia*. José Geraldo Couto, 2011.
———. *Why this World: A Biography of Clarice Lispector*. Oxford UP, 2009.
Nassar, Raduan. *A Cup of Rage*. Translated by Stefan Tobler, Penguin Classics, 2016.
———. *Lavoura arcaica*. Companhia das Letras, 1989.
Olaia e Júlio, ou, A Periquita: novela nacional. Edição e notas José Américo Miranda; Norma Leles Amaral Pereira. Estudo Crítico Maria Cecilia Boechat. Faculdade de Letras da UFMG, 2012.
Plato. *Symposium*. Introduction by Alexander Nehamas, Hackett, 1989.
Queirós, Bartolomeu Campos de. *Vermelho amargo*. Cosac Naify, 2011.
Queiroz, Rachel de. *O quinze*. José Olympio, 1966.
Ramos, Graciliano. *Cartas*. Record, 1981.
———. *Barren Lives*. Translated by Ralph Edward Dimmick, U of Texas P, 1999.
Rocha, Glauber. *An Esthetic of Hunger*. 4 Mar 2010, mediaseized.wordpress.com/2010/03/04/an-esthetic-of-hunger-glauber-rocha.
Rosa, João Guimarães. *The Devil to Pay in the Backlands*. Translated by James L. Taylor and Harriet de Onís, Alfred A. Knopf, 1963.
———. *Grande sertão: Veredas. Ficção completa em dois volumes*, vol. 1, Nova Aguilar, 1994.
———. *Sagarana: Ficção completa em dois volumes*, vol. 1, Nova Aguilar, 1994.
Salles, Walter. "On a Wing and a Prayer." The Guardian. 21 Dec 2002. theguardian.com/books/2002/dec/21/featuresreviews.guardianreview22.
Sedlmayer, Sabrina. *Jacuba é gambiarra: A jacuba is a gambiarra*. English version by Rodrigo Seabra. Autêntica Editora, 2017.
———. *Ao lado esquerdo do pai*. UFMG, 1997.
———. *Lavoura arcaica: Um palimpsesto*. Nemo Collection, Fundação Memorial da América Latina, 1999.

———. "A ficção mediterrânea de Raduan Nassar." Edited by Marcílio Castro, *Ficções do Brasil: Conferências sobre literatura e identidade nacional*. ALEMG, 2006.

———. "Raduan Nassar conversa com o contemporâneo." *Cult*. 5 June 2017. revistacult.uol.com.br/home/raduan-nassar-conversa-com-o-contemporaneo.

Staden, Hans. *A verdadeira história dos selvagens, nus e ferozes devoradores de homens*. Translated by Pedro Sussekind, Dantes, 1998.

Süssekind, Flora. *Tal Brasil, qual romance? Uma ideologia estética e sua história: o Naturalismo*. Achiamé, 1984.

Thélot, Jérome. *Au commencement était la faim – traité de l'intraitable*. Encre Marine, 2005.

Vattimo, Gianni. *A tentação do Realismo*. Translated by Reginaldo Di Piero, Lacerda Ed./ Istituto Italiano di Cultura, 2001.

Viveiros de Castro, Eduardo. *Cannibal Metaphysics: for a Post-Structural Anthropology*. Translated by Peter Skafish, Univocal, 2014.

Xavier, Ismail. *Sertão Mar: Glauber Rocha e a estética da fome*. Cosac Naify, 2007.

CHAPTER 13

Food in Recent Cuban Literature (1990–2016)

From Hero in the Special Period Fiction to Almost Zero in the Generation Zero

Rita De Maeseneer, *University of Antwerp*

INTEREST IN FOOD-RELATED research began to gain importance in a cultural studies context in the 1980s. Since then, the food studies approach has become a well-established mode of analyzing literary works. It has also proven to be very productive in the Hispanic context. The aim of this essay is to focus on the connotations of culinary references in Cuban narrative prose since the 1990s (1990–2016). This "food lens" has been recurrently employed in commentaries on Cuban novels published in the nineties and the first years of the new millennium, because they are often situated in what is called the Special Period, which started in 1990 and was characterized by severe austerity. These omnipresent references to food (or its absence) were usually linked to traditional connotations concerning Cuba, particularly national identity and socio-politics, although in my view they lead in some cases to metaliterary and metaphorical considerations. In contrast, more recent Cuban texts (2006–2016) have moved away from this referential topic. For the youngest writers the few references to food are even non-identitarian, delocalized, and essentially used for metaliterary and metaphorical purposes.

To explain these findings, I will first give a brief introduction to gastrocriticism, the theoretical framework that underlies my research. I will then discuss some examples of Special Period fiction. Here, I will illustrate the obsessive longing for meat, one of the most identitarian products that expresses Cubanness in many Special Period narratives. At the same time, I will focus on food references in the work of the three most internationally established writers: Zoé Valdés (b. 1959), Pedro Juan Gutiérrez (b. 1950), and Leonardo Padura Fuentes (b. 1950). All three had their breakthrough during the Special Period, and they still dominate the international market. I will address their obsessions with food issues in their publications from the 1990s and compare them with their more recent work that contains fewer culinary references. Finally, I will focus on "generation zero" (*generación cero*). Writers such as Ahmel Echevarría (b. 1974), Orlando Luis Pardo Lazo (b. 1971), Jorge Enrique Lage (b. 1979), and Legna Rodríguez Iglesias (b. 1984) wanted to distance themselves from the food obsessions in these three successful writers and Special Period fiction. I will zoom in on two texts written by Rodríguez Iglesias, whose metaliterary interaction with food is very particular. This survey will lead to some reflections on the role of food references in relation to the image of Cuban literature, often seen from an exoticizing and/or referential point of view, and the creative process as a whole, posing essential questions concerning the literary endeavor caught between *mimesis* and *imitatio*.

A Gastrocritical Approach

A review of the theoretical grounds upon which literary critics build their food-based approach reveals that they are inspired by various disciplines in the human sciences. In the literary field, Bakhtin's ideas on food, feast, and carnival lie behind many studies, one example being Teja's article on Lezama Lima's *Paradiso*. Barthes's proposals on food as developed in "Toward a Psychosociology of Contemporary Food Consumption" are also frequently quoted, for example, in Ignizio's approach to Jesús Díaz's *Dime algo sobre Cuba*. Barthes considers food as a system of communication that functions as a mode by which we understand the world and our surroundings. Moreover, many scholars frequently rely on other areas, especially anthropology and sociology, because goods and products are part of the material culture and they define human behavior and perceptions. This is illustrated by Lévi-Strauss's reflections, in which food is a code that can express social and familiar relationships and identity—national, sexual, or otherwise. The anthropologist also emphasized the relationship between the means of preparing food and the degree of civilization or barbarism in his famous notion of the culinary triangle. On the sociological side, many researchers examining the links between status, class, and culture have drawn on Bourdieu's insights concerning food as cultural and economic capital, as well as de Certeau's ideas on the relationship between social class and food, as developed in *L'invention du quotidien*.

Taking into account the different areas involved in food studies, Ronald Tobin coined the term *gastrocriticism* as a subcategory of sociocriticism in his 1990 book *Tarte à la crème: Comedy and Gastronomy in Molière's Theater*. In the 2002 essay "Qu'est-ce que la gastrocritique?" he clarifies how the gastrocritical approach consists of detecting the multiple connotations of food and drink in relation to social, racial, geographical, identitarian, historical, sexual, anthropological, religious, philosophical, medical, cultural, psychological, ideological-political, gender, and linguistic issues. His work confirms that theories from other areas of the human sciences are indispensable. Moreover, Tobin states that a writer is like a cook, because he has a "cuisine of writing," *una cocina de la escritura,* to quote the essay by Puerto Rican writer Rosario Ferré. It implies that the gastrocritical approach must be interpreted within the broader context of the writer's poetics. It is clear that the presence of food, one of the most referential elements of fiction, points to the conflict between the text as a referential entity (*mimesis*) and the text as an autonomous and auto-referential entity (*imitatio*). In other words, *les mets ne sont pas les mots* or the word is not the world (Jeanneret). This struggle with the *effet de réel* (Barthes) will be at the core of my analysis of food references.[1]

Food Studies and the Special Period

As stated above, the frequent references to food in the 1990s can be explained partly by the historical context of the Special Period. This term is a euphemism invented by Fidel Castro to refer to the shortages in the 1990s, when the Cuban economy was plunged into a severe crisis, partly due to the loss of Soviet trade and support (Hernández-Reguant 1–18; Kapcia). The majority of Cubans faced poverty before Castro's regime, and their situation improved gradually during the Revolution, but in the 1990s the country experienced famine conditions again. While the first five years of the 1990s were the harshest of the Special Period, there is no consensus concerning its end, though many scholars seem to agree on 2005 (Sklodowska 91n6). Many literary texts published in the 1990s and in the first years of the new millennium by Cuban authors residing on the island, in exile, or in the diaspora integrated the referential context of hunger and the scarcity of food out of an apparent need to bear witness to the problems about which the Cuban press was completely silent. This testimonial angle was supposed to include elements such as "blackouts, misery, soy meat, boat people, prostitutes, the gay thing, witchcraft, Angola wars . . . you know, that stuff," in the ironic words of Ena Lucía Portela (73).[2]

Apart from this testimonial urgency, another important change occurred. After the post-Soviet collapse of Cuba's publishing industry, Cuban writers were allowed to publish abroad. The internationally bestselling books created a "Special Period Exotic": a construction of the Other, mainly by outsider perceptions, desires, and appropriations (Whitfield 20). Nonetheless, not only artists residing outside Cuba but also those living on the island sometimes employed culinary imagery that selected and privileged certain (auto)exotic topics from that period. The international market seemed to demand the *couleur locale* of Cuban reality, a folkloric aesthetics of scarcity. The books reflected a kind of "postcolonial exotic" that marketed the margins (Huggan). The official cultural spokesmen, and some authors on and off the island, criticized the fact that Cuba was "for sale" (Sánchez; Sklodowska 115–31). On a fictitious level, Karla Suárez's protagonist in *Silencios* states: "It seemed to me that in Cuba, writers were journalists. Nobody told stories. Everyone wrote about what I could see if I just looked out of my window. They talked about people who fled the island in rafts, prostitutes in the Havana night, the dollar that went up and up, the hope that went down and down. It was boring" (244).[3]

The two most frequently quoted authors in relation to Special Period fiction are Zoé Valdés and Pedro Juan Gutiérrez, both of whom are commented on extensively in Whitfield's foundational study, *Cuban Currency: The Dollar and "Special Period Fiction."* Another writer who gained renown during the Special Period, although not analyzed in detail in Whitfield's corpus, is Leonardo Padura Fuentes. Before addressing these three internationally famous authors (Valdés, Gutiérrez, Padura), I want to illustrate the "culinary turn" in Cuban literature of the 1990s, focusing on one of the most recurrent obsessions: meat. The highly carnivorous Cubans were so anxious to succeed in procuring meat that they searched for substitutes, such as *picadillo de soya* (minced soy meat) or the *bistec de frazada* (rag steak), probably an invention of urban mythology, as evoked in *El hombre, la hembra, el hambre* (1998) by Daína Chaviano. Cubans also began to rear pigs in their apartments. The domestication of a pig often resulted in "pig-o-philia." A number of authors, for example, René Vázquez Díaz in his short story "Macho Grande en el Balcón" (2009), Nancy Alonso in her short story "César" (2002), and Alberto Pedro Torriente in his play *Manteca* (1993), describe the way in which the protagonists are not able to kill the pig because they grow fond of it.

The search for meat has clearly identitarian and historical/political connotations, but it can also imply philosophical considerations, such as what is the border between an animal and a human being?[4] This is the case for Ronaldo Menéndez's *Las bestias* (2006). The rearing of a pig by a philosophy of art professor becomes a pretext to reflect not only on the border between human and animal, but also on good and evil, as well as racism. In this Quentin Tarantino-like story, the professor discovers that he is to be murdered but succeeds in capturing one of the suspected killers, nicknamed Bill. He locks up this black man, whom he calls Lo Negro (the Black Thing), and treats him as an object. Bill (Lo Negro) has to share the bathroom with the pig that the professor is rearing. The pig is often described using another reifying expression, "a machine that devours everything except its own body" (*una máquina de devorar todo lo que no sea su propio cuerpo*). In this situation, Bill is constantly threatened by the pig. In order to make Bill confess to the planned crime, the professor subjects him to sadistic torture: first, Bill has to share the pig's food, and, ultimately, due to the shortage of food, the pig devours Bill.

Menéndez thus invites the reader to reflect on evil (see De Maeseneer and Tabío Hernández) and creates an "animal community" (Redruello 241) or a *patria puerca* ("a dirty homeland"; López-Labourdette), questioning the distinction between civilization and barbarism (Díaz; Sklodowska 226–74). In another short story by Menéndez, *El río Quibú* (2008), the desperate search for meat even leads to acts of cannibalism, another potent trope in the Latin American context. These examples show that the referential starting point concerns the harsh conditions during the Special Period, but that some writers go beyond this concrete Cuban context due to the more wide-reaching questions it raised for them.

Food in Zoé Valdés, Pedro Juan Gutiérrez, and Leonardo Padura Fuentes

As mentioned above, Valdés, Gutiérrez, and Padura published novels that entered into dialogue with the Special Period to a certain extent. In this section, I propose to focus on these three authors' publications of the 1990s and to compare them to their more recent work, taking a gastrocritical approach. I argue that unlike their publications in the 1990s, over the last decade (2006–2016) the Special Period has vanished as the diegetic backdrop, and culinary contexts seem to have less weight. If these authors still integrate food references, the well-known political/social and identitarian connotations prevail in relation to the characters and are subordinated to the writers' central topics: erotic feminism and a sarcastic approach to Castro's regime (Zoé Valdés), autofiction and unabashed sexuality (Pedro Juan Gutiérrez), and crime and history with a nostalgic aura (Padura Fuentes).

Zoé Valdés, an outspoken critic of Castro's Cuba, went into exile in France in 1995. Whitfield considers *Te di la vida entera* (*I Gave You All I Had*; 1996) to be the paradigmatic example of Special Period fiction, alongside *La nada cotidiana* (*Yocandra in the Paradise of Nada: a Novel of Cuba*; 1995) (48–66). In *Te di la vida entera*, partly situated in the 1990s, Valdés proceeds to a hyperbolization of daily life situations (Faccini). One of the ways in which Valdés attacks the regime is by comparing dishes before and after the Revolution. Nostalgic gazing at alleged pre-Revolutionary abundance is contrasted with the scarcity experienced during the Revolution and, particularly, in the 1990s (Torres Caballero). For example, in the second chapter, the protagonist, Cuca, remembers delicious food from before the Revolution. In what seems to be a kind of ironic allusion to the typical strategies of feminist writers such as Laura Esquivel, Zoé Valdés devotes two pages to detailed recipes of certain identitarian dishes, such as roast pork or black beans.

In fact, Valdés literally transcribes the recipes from the pre-Revolutionary cookbook ¿*Gusta Usted?* (*Do You Like It?*; 1956) by Cuba's most renowned cook, Nitza Villapol. After 1959, Villapol became one of the principal "Maria Auxiliatrix" of the Revolution (Vázquez Montalbán 46), when she continued to publish versions of her cookbooks under the same titles, but eliminated all references to American products and a number of dishes. During the Special Period, Villapol invented recipes that did not contain meat—a shock for carnivorous Cubans—and suggested avoiding the question of "What are we going to prepare today?" in favor of "Which products are available to cook?" (Ponte).

By quoting pre-Revolutionary recipes, Zoé Valdés thus undertakes a pointed attack on the regime. Valdés even plays with the borders of abjection: when Cuca goes to a birthday party, she is so hungry that she devours the meatballs that turn out to be made of shoe soles and have nothing to do with the delicious pre-Revolutionary meatballs she had just been dreaming of. In Valdés's work, food is subordinated to a vehement political satire of the Revolution, a nostalgia for pre-Revolutionary times. Culinary pleasures are one of the forbidden desires that do not fit the ideology of the new man.

In Valdés's publications of the last ten years, sometimes located outside the Cuban context,[5] the feminine approach is at the core. In her novels related to Cuba, she goes on to combine this perspective with a pronounced anti-Castro strand. *El todo cotidiano* (*The Daily Everythingness*; 2010) was promoted as the continuation of her first novel and bestseller, *La nada cotidiana*, and a wordplay on daily bread (*el pan cotidiano*). The book drew the critics' attention due to the frenetic and sometimes raw language used to express Yocandra's search for herself, caught between two lovers, the Traitor and the Nihilist, and an impassioned political denunciation. Moreover, the sarcastic food descriptions of her struggle for her daily bread—for example, rationing the rationed products and exchanging food for goods—made it a paradigmatic example of Special Period fiction.

In contrast, *El todo cotidiano* more resembles a melodramatic *telenovela*, with plenty of stereotypes because it narrates Yocandra's ups and downs in exile, the Cuban community's exuberant life in Paris, and her reunion with the Nihilist as a surprising happy ending. In this context, food references, such as the very French duck *à l'orange* in Paris, or the nostalgic guava cakes or chicken croquettes in Miami, have no other function than to supply a *couleur locale* to the story.

In one of her latest novels, *La noche al revés: Dos historias cubanas* (*The Night Upside Down: Two Cubans stories*; 2016), the protagonists are two young single mothers who had both given birth to a child in 1970s Cuba. The two plot lines appear more like fairy tales about the brave women's struggle to protect their daughters, and here again everything finishes well. The culinary topic is not essential. The first story of Anisia, for example, is partly situated in the 1990s: Anisia's daughter is adopted by a Cuban Jewish family who was able to go to Israel thanks to Operation Cigar, which effectively took place between 1994 and 1999. After they leave, Anisia creates her own reality by means of her dreams and her telephone contact with her daughter in order to survive: the emotional context is what counts rather than the dire material situation, which is scarcely mentioned.

Concerning the second successful author in Special Period fiction, Pedro Juan Gutiérrez, his dirty realism and his visceral novels caused a commotion in the literary world. In *Trilogía sucia de La Habana* (*Dirty Havana Trilogy*; 1998), Gutiérrez describes extreme need in a crude and often immoral way. The most horrendous example is the selling of human liver as pork liver by one of Juan Pedro's neighbors, who works at a morgue. His obsession with corporeal needs (sex and hunger) make the problems caused by the Special Period visible. De Ferrari considers Gutiérrez's work as a manifestation of the degradation and the collapse of the revolutionary ideals (*Vulnerable States* 195). In my view, it is possible to go beyond this political scope, for example, in Gutiérrez's only non-autofictional novel of the 1990s, *El Rey de La Habana* (*The King of Havana*; 1999). This work depicts the life of Rey, a marginal figure who is always on the move, going from one master to another, or in his case, one mistress to another. He uses his "golden dick" in exchange for food; in other words, his hunger is substituted by sexual voracity. His life is a struggle for survival, a tropical Darwinism (Quintero Herencia). He lives like a savage and as a modern *pícaro* (rogue) (Birkenmaier). Although the Special Period context is alluded to in various fragments from the first sentences on, and Gutiérrez takes advantage of the stereotypes related to the Special Period, his novel invites the reader to go beyond this referential context, reflecting on the ontological and philosophical implications of hunger and the use of the body. It poses questions about how one can survive on the margins. It blurs the borders of good manners and good taste and questions the limits of abjection and the difference between human and animal. Hunger and lack of food are thus much more than a circumstantial issue arising from the Special Period. The intertextuality between this novel and the picaresque genre also intensifies the broader dimensions of this book.

In his novels of the last decade, Pedro Juan Gutiérrez has continued to narrate his alter ego's experiences, but within his autofictional scope he returns to the 1960s, the years of his rebellious childhood and adolescence. It is interesting to compare two books that are set in this period: *El nido de la serpiente: Memorias del hijo del heladero* (*The Snake's Nest: Memories of the Ice-Cream Man's Son*; 2006) and *Fabián y el caos* (*Fabian and the Chaos*; 2013). In *El nido de la serpiente*, Gutiérrez still incorporates, by means of certain details, the culinary changes at the beginning of the Revolutionary period: the gradual disappearance of beer and the frugal, monotonous meals that are invariably composed of the same identitarian ingredients, such as rice and beans. Meat is almost always absent, except in Pedro Juan's cannibalistic dreams and fabulations, and he goes fishing, as a source of more protein. Food is only a secondary topic that underscores the encompassing reality of scarceness and identitarian gastronomic obsessions. What really matters in this story are problems related to his coming of age and his sexual excesses.

Fabián y el caos concentrates on Pedro Juan's friendship with Fabian, a gay pianist, in the 1960s and early 1970s. In his succinct, referential style, Gutiérrez cannot avoid mentioning the penuries: "The decade of the 60s. We were starving. There was an excess of patriotism and a lack of food" (*Fabián* 69).[6] Nonetheless, food is not the principal concern; the emphasis is on the story of the two dissident characters, the exuberant and hedonistic Pedro Juan and the reserved homosexual Fabián. The few culinary references serve to emphasize Pedro

Juan's sexual obsessions, for example, when he expresses his longing for breast milk. Other references to food have a contextual or temporal function: the annual birthday cakes, sometimes made with ingredients that are hard to find, symbolize the monotonous passing of time. Moreover, when Fabian and Pedro Juan meet again after a long period of separation, both working in an export pork-meat canning plant because they have been punished for their "incorrect" behavior, the narrator does not concentrate on the food dimension. Rather, he insists on the cruel ways in which the pigs are slaughtered and the inhumanity and abjection of the workers in the plant. Culinary references do not have the same impact as in his former works.

The third author who gained renown in the 1990s is Leonardo Padura, thanks to his quartet of detective novels featuring the policeman Mario Conde: *Pasado perfecto* (1991), *Vientos de Cuaresma* (1994), *Máscaras* (1995), and *Paisaje de otoño* (1998) (*Havana Blue*; *Havana Gold*; *Havana Red*; *Havana Black*). Each novel takes place in a different season of 1989, still on the boundary of the Special Period. The year 1989 is a "year that never was," to quote the title of a chapter devoted to Padura by Eduardo González, in the sense that it is a fictive construction that condenses aspects of life from before and after that year.[7] In any case, Mario Conde is often confronted with an empty refrigerator and rationed goods. This contrasts with the sumptuous identitarian dishes, such as turkey stuffed with *congrí* rice in *Máscaras* (195) or boiled eddoes with garlic sauce, pork steak, and salad in *Pasado Perfecto* (30–31), which are prepared by Jose, the mother of Mario Conde's best friend, the no-longer-skinny "Skinny Carlos" ("el Flaco Carlos").

Adrián García proposes a political and gendered interpretation of this contrastive situation: "Hence for Conde, this mother figure, this nourishing origin, is a culinary and psychological safe haven within an austere father-figure autocracy that disallows an acceptable level of sustenance and impedes self-evaluation" (498). Unlike Zoé Valdés, Padura never calls into question the revolutionary project as such; he only attacks the excesses and the corruption and voices the disillusions, much in line with the aesthetics of disenchantment so typical of his generation (Fornet). The colorful descriptions of the gargantuan dishes have also been read from a metaliterary point of view. For Lucien, they point to the creative liberty and the triumph of the imaginary (202); Collard associates them with a new version of the Carpenterian real marvelous (348); while García sees Jose's feasts as a manifestation of the fantastic that "produces a somewhat more bearable Cuban story" (499). Apart from the highlights created by the lush meals, there is a "perpetual chase for a cup of coffee in all four novels" (Song 240) and for alcohol, Conde's drug of choice, to forget personal problems and the precarious situation. Thus, Padura combines identitarian, ontological, and metaliterary connotations of food.

In the new millennium, Padura Fuentes started writing historical novels that often included an enigma, just like his detective novels: *La novela de mi vida* (*The Story of My Life*; 2002) on Cuban poet José María Heredia and *El hombre que amaba a los perros* (*The Man Who Loved Dogs*; 2009) on Trotsky's murderer, Ramón Mercader, for example. In addition, he continued to invent fascinating detective stories with Conde as the protagonist, as in *La neblina del ayer* (*Havana Fever*; 2005) and *Herejes* (*Heretics: A Novel*; 2013). *La neblina del ayer* is set in the new millennium with its changing, more open economy, which is attempting to safeguard the gains in social provisions and national sovereignty. Conde, the ex-policeman, is now a used-book seller, which makes him money in US dollars. A clipping inserted into a precious 1956 edition of Villapol's *¿Gusta Usted?* incites him to investigate the murder of a bolero singer, Violeta del Río, which occurred in the 1950s. Although the hardest era of the Special Period—systematically referred to as "the Crisis"—belongs to the past, Conde as well as the other characters still struggle to satisfy their alimentary and alcoholic needs. The same contrastive techniques of hunger and abundance are still employed, for example, in the six long pages describing Jose's identitarian banquet, which includes a kind of chicken soup and stuffed turkey inspired by *¿Gusta Usted?*, all paid for by Conde's earnings in dollars (*La neblina del ayer* 123–29).

In *Herejes*, Mario Conde is involved in elucidating the mysteries surrounding a painting by Rembrandt that pertained to a Jewish-Polish family whose descendants lived in Cuba for some time. The novel takes place between 1939 and 2007, with analepsis to Rembrandt's epoch. In 1939, the parents and the sister of Daniel Kaminsky, a Jewish refugee in Cuba, were denied entry to the island from the ocean liner MS *Saint Louis*. In 2007, Conde helps Elías Kaminsky, Daniel's son, to investigate the fate of the painting that had been on the ship. As Vicky Unruh argues compellingly, there is a shift from Padura's predominantly Conde-centered fictional world: his nostalgia is no longer at the center of the book, and there is a little hope in the novel that the future will be different due to the heretics (of all sorts) (133). In my view, this change can also be illustrated by the fact that apart from a few identitarian or religious food references (for example, a mention of black beans or kosher food and the hybrid mix of both), only two short paragraphs evoking dishes prepared by Jose (344, 455) remind us of the former sensorial "tedious banquet scenes" (Casamayor). In contrast, Conde's ethylic dependence is still mentioned very frequently. Wilkinson characterizes Conde as an "individual whose soul is at odds with his surroundings" (162), and although Conde tries to settle himself more and to become more optimistic, his personal problems are still not resolved, so he continues to escape by means of rum. On the whole, however, food is less present and less invested with meaning in these more recent Padura Fuentes works.

Food and Generation Zero

It is not by chance that I emphasize the writings of Valdés, Gutiérrez, and Padura in the contemporary context. In 2014, ten young Cuban writers published the anthology *Malditos bastardos* with this significant subtitle: *Ten storytellers who are not Pedro Juan Gutiérrez nor Zoé Valdés nor Leonardo Padura nor*.... These "damned bastards" wanted to distance themselves from the consolidated writers, characterized by their disenchantment with respect to the Cuban Revolution. *Malditos bastardos* features the work of some members of what has been called "Generation Zero," writers born between 1971 and 1984. The term was invented by Jorge Enrique Lage, Ahmel Echevarría, and Lizabel Mónica. They share the fact that they started publishing in the new millennium and are very active in the virtual world. They adhere to a poetics that they define in the following way: "Far from this testimonial urgency, the so-called Generation Zero (raised amidst havoc) practices a less militant realism, often combined with elements of surrealism, the absurd and sci fi; it is also a much more intimate realism, more (dis)located in the I, where the characters do not seek to embody dramas and collective efforts" (Echevarría and Lage, "(De)generación").[8]

In their texts, characterized by pastiches and generic mixes, they try to eschew referential topics and present intersubjective, autofictional stories that are absurd, fantastic (often in Cortázar's vein), metaliterary, or futuristic.[9] Their search for new subjectivities and communities is very remote from the Cuban homogenizing construct (Dorta, "Olvidar a Cuba"; Timmer, "Sujeto y comunidad"). In this scope, food, as a marker of the real and its traditional connotations, does not have great relevance, and apparently the provision of food is no longer problematic. For example, in Ahmel Echevarría's highly metaliterary and autofictional novel, *Días de entrenamiento* (*Training Days*; 2012), wine, beer, or pizzas are mentioned as completely circumstantial items for the writer-protagonist Ahmel in his existential crisis in 2005/2006 after his lover Grethel's death. *Boring Home* (2009) by Orlando Luis Pardo Lazo depicts Orlando's weird sexual relations with different women in the new millennium, intertwined with other strange stories. His visit to Ipatria in Havana's Alamar quarter is introduced in the following way: "Then I bought an electric flower, food obscenely Italian, a bottle of wine half pixeled, and I took the escalator in the direction Ipatria" (15).[10] Throughout Jorge Enrique Lage's *La autopista: The Movie* (*The Highway: The Movie*; 2014) another futuristic novel about the construction of a highway that is going to eliminate Cuba in a dystopian manner, ads for the new national soda, Reguetonic, are mentioned, and one of the protagonists, El Autista, works in a fast-food restaurant serving happy meals and Coca-Cola. The delocalizing and globalizing traits of pizzas, wine, or Coca-Cola can be seen as a way of attempting to go beyond Cuba (Sández 91). Nonetheless, in other aspects, it is clear that the relationship with the Cuban context is still highly present. In this respect, I am thinking about the location: an apocalyptic Havana in Lage's novel, a city called "la Hanada" by Pardo Lazo and "Altahabana" by Ahmel Echevarría. Castro's spectral appearance in *Días de entrenamiento*, the multiple references to the Cuban context in *Boring Home*, from the title onward—a wordplay on *Boarding Home* by Guillermo Rosales—and a hilarious description of the bones of an alleged *homo cubensis* in *La autopista*, show that recent Cuban writers have difficulties moving beyond their Cubanness to "forget Cuba," "Olvidar a Cuba," to quote Dorta's title of his article on Generation Zero.

A significant example of moving away from testimonial food use is represented by Legna Rodríguez Iglesias, whose poems and novels integrate food in a surprising way. In the short story "Anti héroe" (2015), with the subtitle "Homenaje a José Martí" (*Antihero: A Hommage to José Martí*), Rodríguez Iglesias focuses on four unnamed figures. They buy the same book from the same bookstore—a book that contains aphorisms written by Cuba's Apostle, whose name is only alluded to in the text. In the short story, not only the deliberate absence of Martí's name but also the few culinary references debunk his mythical image. After having bought the book, the four people go to the same restaurant. Some identitarian dishes are listed on the menu (repeated in the four cases with some variation), but they all decide to buy *pan con tortilla* (bread with omelet) and sit on a bench to eat and read. The act of eating is as important as the act of reading a text by a Cuban hero. In the four "scenes," the same remark is repeated: "He looks at the bread and the book. He does not know what to do first. It is not necessary to do one thing before another if both can be done at the same time" (Rodríguez, "Antihéroe" 34, 36, 39, 43).[11] At the end of the short story, a brief flashback depicts Martí's arrival at the battlefield. The paragraph finishes with one last absurd sentence: "At a distance, [the soldiers] are gathered in a group that makes [Martí] hungry" (43).[12] Indeed, Martí was not a central figure in the battle for Independence because he was shot almost immediately. The laconic, repetitive style and the juxtaposition of noble purposes and basic needs are strategies to downplay the National Hero's role.[13]

Rodríguez Iglesias's *Mayonesa bien brillante: Una novela de amor* (*Very Shiny Mayonnaise: A Love Novel*; 2016) is not a simple recipe, in spite of its title (Echevarría, "Qué nos sucede"). Strange poems and absurd philosophical reflections alternate with more diegetic elements about the end of a love story between the would-be writer Teki Heromu in Havana and a musician, Lasso Rohjo, who leaves for Spain. Teki's sexual and culinary, or even cannibalistic, desires are intertwined. In a detailed description of one of Teki's dreams or hallucinations of a copious banquet, the mayonnaise makes its first appearance: "And she [Teki] spreads mayo on her knees so that she can eat her knees with her teeth, chew her bones and drink the liquid of her knees, then the mayo is mixed with the liquid" (64–65).[14] The metaliterary function of the product is illustrated by the fact that Teki does a performance, writing on the walls of her house with mayonnaise. Lasso Rohjo's mother, who comes to visit her, does not understand a word of the hermetic and incoherent poetry written with mayonnaise, and she wonders what all this is meant to "represent." In an ironic way, Legna Rodríguez Iglesias attacks the alleged referentiality, from which the new writers want to distance themselves, and expresses her metaliterary concerns.[15]

Conclusion

This panoramic culinary tour shows that a focus on food is far from trivial. Food references do not always play an ornamental and secondary role. Although the hunger-abundance axis and the identitarian scope are rather predictable associations, this essay has revealed that food references are imbued with a wider array of possibilities and extra-culinary meaning. The frequency of the references and their position in the texts are very meaningful when it comes to studying the way literature interacts with the encompassing reality and what it wants to emphasize. In this diachronic overview the decreasing presence of food can be partly explained by changes in the extra-textual circumstances and the writers' poetics. Nonetheless, the explanation is more complicated, and a series of broader questions have to be taken into account.

First, one can wonder to what extent food descriptions are related to our exotic and stereotypical visions of Cuba. Since its discovery, the island has been considered a sweet cornucopian paradise, and in 1959 it even became a "communist" tropical paradise. At the same time, however, Cuba (as well as many other Latin American "developing" countries) is associated with poverty. In addition, more than any other Latin American country, it has been transformed into a commodity. Some writers deliberately want to meet the needs of foreign consumers who see Cuba as a country of abundance or misery in this very special "communist" context. In this regard, it is telling that some publications in the US–Cuban diaspora that I could not consider in the scope of this article continue to evoke the Special Period in a stereotypical way, beyond 2006. For example, in Achy Obejas's *Ruins* (2009) and in Roberto Arellano's *Havana Lunar* (2009), the leitmotiv is the *bistec de frazada de piso* (rag steak). In Sindo Pacheco's *Mañana es Navidad* (2010), Cachirulo the pig is one of the main characters. Apparently, for Cuba, this is the kind of literature that is successful from a marketing standpoint.

Second, the emphasis on food is very much in line with the tendency to reduce Cuban literature to a referential context, be it *testimonio* or Special Period fiction (Timmer, "Resonancias"). Present reality as it is, an "exhibitionist, 'unmediated' manner . . . appears more interesting than fiction," and this can lead to what De Ferrari calls "hyperrealism" (*Community* 171). Food plays a central role in this interest in referentiality and a photographic manner of writing.

Third, on a more general level, in many literary movements there appears to be an oscillation between referential and non-referential texts, *mimesis* and *imitatio*. We all know that characters are made of paper (or bytes) and that they do not have to eat in order to exist in a paper or virtual world, but at the same time, one can wonder how strong the commitment to the real is, the tyranny of immediacy in literature, as expressed by food.

Fourth, the reflections on food in recent Cuban literature pose stylistic and metaliterary questions of how the materiality of the everyday realities of eating can be adequately expressed and how all the particularities of a dish can be described, relying on a limited vocabulary. Unfortunately, this could not be developed in a nuanced way in this article, but without doubt, it is apparent that the gastrocritical approach can contribute to our understanding of what literature is all about.

NOTES

I wish to express my gratitude to Diana Arbaiza, Susana Haug, Catalina Quesada, Ilse Logie, Elzbieta Sklodowska, and Nanne Timmer for their useful help and comments.

1. For the Hispanic area, a gastrocritical approach was used in my earlier work, *El festín de Alejo Carpentier*, and refined in *Devorando a lo cubano*. Scholars such as Hortensia Morell and Rafael Climent-Espino made very interesting contributions inspired by this theoretical framework.
2. "los apagones, la miseria, el picadillo de soya, los balseros, las jineteras, la cosa gay, la brujería, la guerra de Angola . . . tú sabes, esas cosas." All translations are mine.
3. "se me antojaba que los escritores hacían periodismo. Nadie contaba historias. Todos decían lo que yo podía ver con sólo asomar las narices fuera de mis paredes. Hablaban de gente fugándose en balsa de la isla, jineteras en las noches de La Habana, el dólar que subía y subía, la esperanza que bajaba y bajaba. Resultaba aburrido." It should be noted that in some novels of the 1990s, with very limited distribution in Cuba, the Special Period context is almost completely absent. For example, *La falacia* (1999) by Gerardo Fernández Fe and *Sibilas en Mercaderes* (1999) by Pedro de Jesús are complex and auto-referential texts whose characters are often writers.

4. See also Sklodowska's comments (266–74). In her analysis of the play *Manteca*, Patricia Tomé adds a metaliterary level to a philosophical interpretation, arguing that literary endeavors replace material insufficiency, and that the struggle for survival is physical and intellectual.

5. For example, she evokes the life of the Spanish surrealist painter Remedios Varo in *La cazadora de astros* (2007) and one of Picasso's muses, Dora Maar, in *La mujer que llora* (2013).

6. "La década de los sesenta. Pasamos mucha hambre. Sobraba patriotismo y faltaban alimentos."

7. Relying on an interview with Padura, Lavoie argues that his novels are not historical testimonials of the 1990s, although she admits that comments on food shortages can be related to the Special Period (84–85).

8. "Lejos ya de esa urgencia testimonial, la llamada Generación Cero (crecida entre esos destrozos) frecuenta un realismo menos militante, a menudo cortado con elementos surrealistas, del absurdo y de la ciencia-ficción; un realismo, también, mucho más íntimo, más (des)localizado en el Yo, donde los personajes no necesariamente pretenden encarnar dramas y desvelos colectivos."

9. To a certain extent they dialogue with former generations, such as some of the less marketed novísimos and Diáspora of the 1990s (Dorta, "Políticas de la distancia"), and they share traits that are typical of recent (Latin American) literature.

10. "Entonces yo compraba una flor eléctrica, comida obscenamente italiana, una botella de vino tinto a medio pixelar, y subía las escaleras rodantes con dirección a Ipatria."

11. "Mira el pan y mira el libro. No sabe qué quiere hacer primero. No es preciso hacer una cosa primero que otra, si las dos pueden hacerse al unísono."

12. "A distancia, ellos forman un grupo que le abre el apetito."

13. Rodríguez's demystification ties in with a trend that has been visible since the 1980s in Cuban (diasporic) literature (Simal; Esteban).

14. "Y [Teki] se unta mayonesa en las rodillas para que sus dientes se coman sus rodillas, mastiquen el hueso y se beban el líquido de las rodillas, entonces la mayonesa se mezcla con el líquido."

15. These reflections can also be applied to her cycle of poems *Chicle*. The *chicle* (chewing gum), so closely related to the tongue/language (both *lengua* in Spanish), is not seen as a flavored and sugary gum for chewing, but as an expression of poetics (Quesada Gómez). The choice of chewing gum is not that innocent in a Cuban context: it epitomizes the United States and the consumer society, and it recalls one of Fidel Castro's famous phrases, pronounced after his travel to the United States on September 28, 1960, when he praised Cuban exiles there who shouted: "¡Malanga sí, chicle no!" ("Malanga-tuber, yes, chewing gum, no!") (Montero).

WORKS CITED

Alonso, Nancy. "César." *Cerrado por reparación*, Ediciones Unión, 2002, pp. 12–20.
Arellano, Robert. *Havana Lunar*. Akashic Books, 2009.
Bakhtine, Michael. *L'oeuvre de François Rabelais et la culture populaire au Moyen Age et sous la Renaissance*. Gallimard, 1970.
Barthes, Roland. "Toward a Psychosociology of Contemporary Food Consumption." *Food and Culture: A Reader*, edited by Peggy Counihan and Van Esterik, Routledge, 1997, pp. 20–27.
Birkenmaier, Anke. "Más allá del realismo sucio: *El rey de La Habana* de Pedro Juan Gutiérrez." *Cuban Studies*, vol. 32, 2011, pp. 37–55.
Bourdieu, Pierre. *La distinction: Critique sociale du jugement*. Minuit, 1979.
Casamayor, Odette. "Tedio y banquete: 'cansancio histórico,' pre-reconciliación y cubanía en las novelas de Leonardo Padura." *A Contracorriente*, vol. 13, no. 1, 2015, pp. 81–104.
Certeau, Michel de, Luce Giard, and Pierre Mayol. *L'invention du quotidien*, vol. 2, *Habiter, cuisiner*, Folio, 1994.
Climent-Espino, Rafael. "El tratado médico-culinario como género de ficción en la narrativa hispanoamericana actual: Héctor Abad Faciolince y Mayra Santos-Febres." *Revista Canadiense de Estudios Hispánicos*, vol. 41, no. 2, 2017, pp. 437–59.
Collard, Patrick. "El conde en la cocina de Jose." *Saberes y sabores en México y el Caribe*, edited by Rita De Maeseneer and Patrick Collard, Rodopi, 2010, pp. 335–49.
Chaviano, Daína. *El hombre, la hembra, el hambre*. Planeta, 1998.
De Ferrari, Guillermina. *Community and Culture in Post-Soviet Cuba*. Routledge, 2014.
———. *Vulnerable States: Bodies of Memory in Contemporary Caribbean Fiction*. U of Virginia P, 2007.
De Jesús, Pedro. *Sibilas en Mercaderes*. Letras Cubanas, 1999.
De Maeseneer, Rita. *Devorando a lo cubano: Una aproximación gastrocrítica a textos relacionados con el siglo XIX y el Período Especial*. Vervuert-Iberoamericana, Frankfurt-Madrid, 2012.
———. *El festín de Alejo Carpentier: Una lectura culinario-intertextual*. Genève, Droz, Serie Romanica Gandensia XXXI, 2003.
De Maeseneer, Rita, and Juan Manuel Tabío Hernández. "La cerdofilia en el Período Especial y sus avatares en la obra de Ronaldo Menéndez." *Comidas bastardas: Gastronomía, tradición e identidad en América Latina*, edited by Ángeles Mateo del Pino and Nieves Pascual Soler, Editorial Cuarto Propio, 2013, pp. 107–30.

Díaz, Duanel. "Cuba: De puercos y hombres." *La Habana Elegante*, vol. 57, Nov. 2015, www.habanaelegante.com/November_2015/Notas_Diaz.html.

Dorta, Walfredo. "Olvidar a Cuba: Contra el 'lugar común.'" *Diario de Cuba*, 21 Dec 2012, pp. 115–35. www.diariodecuba.com/de-leer/1356084148_85.html.

———. "Políticas de la distancia y del agrupamiento: Narrativa cubana de las dos últimas décadas." *Istor: Revista de historia internacional*, vol. 15, no. 63, 2015, pp. 115–36.

Echevarría, Ahmel. *Días de entrenamiento*. Editions Fra, 2012.

———. "Qué nos sucede, belleza." *Diario de Cuba*, 22 Aug. 2013, www.diariodecuba.com/de-leer/1377164324_4716.html.

Echevarría, Ahmel, and Jorge Enrique Lage. "(De)Generación: Un mapa de la narrativa cubana más reciente." *Diario de Cuba*, 5 Dec. 2013, www.diariodecuba.com/de-leer/1386613604_6269.html.

Esteban, Ángel. "Pervivencia de José Martí en la novela cubana de las últimas décadas." *Literatura y cultura cubana en tiempos de cambio*, edited by Yannelis Aparicio, Verbum, 2017, pp. 111–26.

Faccini, Carmen. "El discurso político de Zoé Valdés: *La nada cotidiana* y *Te di la vida entera*." *Ciberletras*, vol. 7, 2002, www.lehman.cuny.edu/ciberletras/v07/faccini.html.

Fernández Fe, Gerardo. *La falacia*. Ediciones Unión, 1999.

Ferré, Rosario. "La cocina de la escritura." *La sartén por el mango: Encuentro de escritoras latinoamericanas*, edited by Patricia E. González and Eliana Ortega, Huracán, 1985, pp. 137–54.

Fornet, Jorge. *Los nuevos paradigmas*. Letras Cubanas, 2006.

García, Adrián. "Food and the Fantastic in Leonardo Padura's *Las cuatro estaciones*." *Modern Language Notes*, vol. 131, no. 2, 2016, pp. 481–502.

González, Eduardo. "1989: The Year That Never Was." *Cuba and the Tempest: Literature and Cinema in the Time of Diaspora*, U North Carolina P, 2006, pp. 170–207.

Gutiérrez, Pedro Juan. *Fabián y el caos*. Anagrama, 2015.

———. *El nido de la serpiente: Memorias del hijo del heladero*. Anagrama, 2006.

———. *El Rey de La Habana*. Anagrama, 1999.

———. *Trilogía sucia de La Habana*. Anagrama, 1998.

Hernández-Reguant, Ariana, editor. *Cuba in the Special Period: Culture and Ideology in the 1990s*. Palgrave-MacMillan, 2010.

Huggan, Graham. *Postcolonial Exotic: Marketing the Margins*. Routledge, 2001.

Ignizio, Graham. "Food, Memory, and a Starving Dentist: Jesús Díaz's Special Period in Times of Peace." *Studies in Latin American Popular Culture*, vol. 34, 2016, pp. 96–108.

Jeanneret, Michel. *Des mets et des mots: Banquets et propos de table à la Renaissance.* José Corti, 1987.

Kapcia, Antonio. *Cuba in Revolution: A History since the Fifties.* Reaktion Books, 2008.

Lage, Jorge Enrique. *La autopista: The Movie.* Editorial Caja China, 2014.

Lavoie, Sophie M. "Trafficking History: Leonardo Padura Fuentes' *Neblina del ayer.*" *Revista de Estudios Hispánicos*, vol. 38, no. 1, 2013, pp. 79–100.

Lévi-Strauss, Claude. "The Culinary Triangle." *Food and Culture*, edited by Peggy Counihan and Van Esterik, Routledge, 1997, pp. 28–35.

López Labourdette, Adriana. "La patria puerca: Discursos y contradiscursos de la especie en la Cuba postsocialista." *Boletín Hispánico Helvético*, vol. 27, 2016, pp. 211–36.

Lucien, Renée Clémentine. *Résistance et cubanité: Trois écrivains nés avec la Révolution cubaine.* L'Harmattan, 2006.

Malditos bastardos. Antología: Diez narradores que no son Pedro Juan Gutiérrez, ni Zoé Valdés ni Leonardo Padura ni...., by Echevarría, Ahmel, et al., Colección G, 2014.

Menéndez, Ronaldo. *Las bestias.* Lengua de Trapo, 2006.

———. *El Río Quibú.* Lengua de Trapo, 2008.

Montero, Rebeca. "Malanga sí, chicle no." *Cubaencuentro*, 25 Sept. 2012, www.cubaencuentro.com/cuba/articulos/malanga-si-chicle-no-280341.

Morell, Hortensia. "Ficción gastronómica y gastronomía de la ficción en 'Cinco boleros aún por melodiarse' de *La importancia de llamarse Daniel Santos.*" *Revista Iberoamericana*, vol. 215–216, 2006, pp. 619–32.

Obejas, Achy. *Ruins.* Akashic, 2009.

Pacheco, Sindo. *Mañana es Navidad.* Iduna, 2010.

Padura Fuentes, Leonardo. *Herejes.* Tusquets, 2013.

———. *El hombre que amaba a los perros.* Tusquets, 2010.

———. *Máscaras.* Tusquets, 2001.

———. *La neblina del ayer.* Tusquets, 2005.

———. *La novela de mi vida.* Tusquets, 2002.

———. *Paisaje de otoño.* Tusquets, 2006.

———. *Pasado perfecto.* Tusquets, 2000.

———. *Vientos de cuaresma.* Tusquets, 2007.

Pardo Lazo, Orlando L. *Boring Home.* Bibliotecas Independientes de Cuba, 2009.

Pedro Torriente, Alberto. *Mar nuestro: Manteca.* Fragmento Imán, 2005.

Ponte, Antonio José. "¿Quién va a comerse lo que esta mujer cocina?" *Diario de Cuba*, 2 March 2012, www.diariodecuba.com/cultura/1330677346_1206.html.

Portela, Ena L. "Literatura versus lechuguitas." *Voces para cerrar un siglo*, vol. 1, edited by René Vázquez Díaz, Skogs Grafiska, 1999, pp. 70–79.

Quesada Gómez, Catalina. "Arqueologías globales en la literatura cubana: De las ruinas al chicle." *Cuadernos de Literatura*, vol. 20, no. 40, 2016, pp. 301–12.

Quintero Herencia, Juan Carlos. "No es lo mismo llamar al cimarrón, que verlo huir." *La Torre*, vol. 10, no. 35, 2005, pp. 1–28.

Redruello, Laura. "Touring Havana in the Work of Ronaldo Menéndez." *Havana Beyond the Ruins: Cultural Mappings After 1989*, edited by Anke Birkenmaier and Esther Whitfield, Duke UP, 2011, pp. 229–45.

Rodríguez Iglesias, Legna. "Anti héroe." *No sabe, no contesta*, Ediciones Cajachina, 2015, pp. 31–43.

———. *Chicle (Ahora es cuando)*. Colección Limón Partido, 2013.

———. *Mayonesa bien brillante: Una novela de amor*. Hypermedia Ediciones, 2016.

Sánchez, Yvette. "'Esta isla se vende': Proyecciones desde el exilio de una generación ¿desilusionada?" *Todas las islas la isla: Nuevas y novísimas tendencias en la literatura y la cultura de Cuba*, edited by Ottmar Ette and Janet Reinstädler, Iberomericana-Vervuert, 2000, pp. 183–76.

Sández, Laura V. "Generación Cero: pasado, presente y pecado: Emociones/tiempo/espacio en la narrativa de un grupo de escritores cubanos." *Letral*, vol. 18, 2017, pp. 85–100.

Simal, Mónica. "Lecturas suicidas para repensar a José Martí: Carlos Vitoria y la Generación del Mariel." *Literatura y cultura cubanas en tiempos de cambio*, edited by Yannelis Aparicio, Verbum, 2017, pp. 85–109.

Sklodowska, Elzbieta. *Invento, luego resisto: El Período Especial en Cuba como experiencia y metáfora (1990–2015)*. Editorial Cuarto Propio, 2016.

Song, H. Rosi. "Hard-Boiled for Hard Times in Leonardo Padura Fuentes's Detective Fiction." *Hispania*, vol. 92, no. 2, 2009, pp. 234–43.

Suárez, Karla. *Silencios*. Santillana Ediciones, 2008.

Teja, Ada María. "Bajtín y los banquetes de Lezama." *Revista de Literatura Cubana*, vol. 11, no. 21, 1993, pp. 78–99.

Timmer, Nanne. "Sujeto y comunidad; voz, isla y muerte en la narrativa cubana del siglo XXI." *Mitologías hoy*, vol. 12, 2015, pp. 71–82.

———. "Resonancias Sarduyanas: Deseo barroco y referencialidad en la narrativa cubana de los noventa." *Revista Laboratorio*, vol. 15, 2016, revistalaboratorio.udp.cl/wp-content/uploads/2016/12/Nanne-Timmer-Sarduyanas-deseo-barroco-y-referencialidad-en-la-%C3%BAltima-literatura-cubana.pdf.

Tobin, Ronald W. "Qu'est-ce que la gastrocritique?" *XVIIe siècle*, vol. 217, no. 4, 2002, pp. 621–30.

———. *Tarte à la crème: Comedy and Gastronomie in Molière's Theater*. Ohio State

UP, 1990.
Tomé, Patricia, "La contingencia intelectual y gastronómica según Alberto Pedro Torriente: *Manteca* y otras necesidades alimenticias en la Cuba de los noventa." *Latin American Theatre Review*, vol. 49, no. 1, 2015, pp. 115–30.
Torres Caballero, Benjamín. "Imágenes de escasez y abundancia: La función de la comida en la literatura cubana." *La Torre*, vol. 14, no. 51–52, 2009, pp. 317–32.
Unruh, Vicky. "Heretics, Heritage, Possession: Leonardo Padura's *Herejes.*" *A contracorriente*, vol. 13, no. 1, 2015, pp. 128–49.
Valdés, Zoé. *Te di la vida entera*. Planeta, 1997.
———. *La nada cotidiana*. Emecé, 1995.
———. *La noche al revés: Dos historias cubanas*. Stella Maris, 2016
———. *El todo cotidiano*. Planeta, 2010.
———. *La cazadora de astros*. Plaza and Janés, 2007.
———. *La mujer que llora*. Planeta, 2013.
Vázquez Díaz, René. "Macho grande en el balcón." *El pez sabe que la lombriz oculta un anzuelo*, Icaria, 2009, pp. 25–41.
Vázquez Montalbán, Manuel. "Las comidas profundas." *El País Semanal*, 23 Mar. 2008, pp. 46–48.
Villapol, Nitza. *¿Gusta Usted?* 1956. Ediciones Universal, 1999.
Whitfield, Esther. *Cuban Currency: The Dollar and "Special Period Fiction.*" U of Minnesota P, 2008.
Wilkinson, Stephen. *Detective Fiction in Cuban Society and Culture*. Peter Lang, 2006.

INDEX

Page numbers in *italic* refer to figures.

acorns, 42, 82, 84
Acosta, José de, 76–78, 83, 87
adafina, 44, 48–49, 58, 65n9, 66n16
Africans, 26, 85, 274–75, 283
agave, 245, 256
agriculture, 12, 23, 82, 169, 239, 278, 303
ajiaco, 12, 13, 28n3, 93, 100, 276
alborayque, 47–48
alcohol, 6, 289, 298, 335, 351
Altamiras, Juan de, 24, 146n11, 203, 207–9, 216
Amado, Jorge, 6, 28n1
Andrade, Oswald de, 16, 323
animals
   classification of, 80
   husbandry, 60
   sacrifice, 58, 69n35
   treatment of, 15, 292, 307–8
   use of, 79, 82–87, 134, 233–35, 244, 278, 283, 304
   See also specific animals
annatto, 280, 283, 287, 289

Anthropocene, 8
anthropophagy, 323
Antilles, 77, 81–82, 88
Appadurai, Arjun, 5, 15, 27, 296–97, 302–3, 310
appetite, 172, 223, 227, 247, 305
Archimboldo, Giuseppe, 104, 106
atole, 243, 259–60, 273, 280, 306
Aviñón, Juan de, 50–51, 53, 63, 66n19, 67nn23–24, 70nn48–51
avocado, 18, 90, 273, 286
Aztec, 26, 244–45, 247, 249, 254, 274

banana
   cooking of, 274–80, 252, 261, 286–87, 306
   crop, 12, 312–14
   leaves, 249–50, 303
   skin, 18
banquet
   for elites, 155, 180–81, 195, 247
   menu, 197, 210

banquet (*continued*)
   and social practices, 102–4, 112n7, 187, 304, 321, 351–52, 355
   traditions, 253, 306–8
   for weddings, 105, 165–67, 171
baptism, 40, 45–47, 56, 65n8, 311
baroque
   art, 105, 107, 112, 113n8, 276
   period, 106, 111, 168
   style, 103, 110, 277, 283, 307, 333
   See also neo-baroque
Barthes, Roland, 14, 342–43
bean
   cooking of, 249–50, 261, 273, 280, 285–88, 293, 303
   crop, 239, 291, 314n13
   in diet, 252–53, 259, 282, 305, 346, 349, 352
beef (cow)
   cooking of, 12, 223, 233, 239, 249, 255, 265–66, 329
   diet, 183, 275–76, 278, 280–81, 283, 285, 288–89
   and gastronomic abundance, 158, 171
Bernáldez, Andrés, 43–47, 49
birds
   cooking of, 128, 137–38, 233
   diet, 44, 84, 101, 252, 260
   and gastronomic abundance, 171, 246–47
   as symbols, 309–10
black people, 12, 82, 84–85, 87, 91, 278, 322
blood
   body and, 336n5
   food and, 235, 289, 300, 303–4
   purity, 21, 322
   witchcraft and, 259
bodegón, 22, 102, 107, 110–12, 182
body
   conceptions, 18–19, 21
   converso, 44–45, 47–48, 56–58
   food and, 50–54, 91, 153–54, 254, 259, 345
   hunger and, 8–9, 349

body (*continued*)
   politic, 39–41
   raza and, 62–64
Brazil
   country, 16–17
   cuisine, 282
   literature, 27
bread
   cooking of, 134, 173–74, 180, 260–61, 279, 281, 293
   crumbs, 126, 158
   diet, 17, 53–56, 83, 207, 252, 259, 273, 284
   hunger and, 89, 91–92, 152, 156
   oven, 124, 139
   religion and, 42, 44, 63
   and social practices, 67n24, 160–61, 168–71, 215, 242, 330–31, 347, 354
Buenos Aires, 222, 224, 227–28

cacao, 6, 151, 273, 284, 286, 293n2
café, 6, 160, 182, 185–87, 189–90
Calderón de la Barca, Frances Erskine Inglis, 14, 252, 263
Campos de Queirós, Bartolomeu, 27, 318, 321, 333
cannibal
   Cannibalist Manifesto, 16, 323
   practice of cannibalism, 5, 254, 336, 345, 349, 355
Cárdenas, Juan de, 6, 87–89, 91
Caribbean, 5, 26, 112n7, 253, 274–78, 280, 282
Carpentier, Alejo, 13, 100–104, 112n5, 315n28, 357n1
cassava, 276–81, 285, 287
Castile, 43, 188, 261
Cei, Galeotto, 81–82, 86–90
Central America, 277, 282, 285, 298, 302, 314nn14–15
cheese
   cheesecloths, 116, 136, 144
   cooking of, 134–35, 172, 240, 266–67, 277–78, 293n4

cheese (continued)
  in diet, 180, 207, 281–82, 287, 306, 327–28
chicken
  cooking of, 93, 130, 136–38, 191, 233, 282–86
  in diet, 180, 183, 249–50, 255, 259, 266, 275, 279
  and gastronomic abundance, 84, 155–58, 171, 246
  and social practices, 133–34, 206, 303–4, 314n13, 348, 351
Chile, 9, 11
chile, chili (pepper)
  crop, 12, 209, 273
  cooking of, 252–55, 282
  in diet, 91, 259–62, 265–68, 286, 289, 303–6
  and social practices, 239, 241–42, 245
chileatole, 243
chocolate
  Como agua para chocolate (Esquivel), 265, 267
  cooking of, 235
  in diet, 208–9, 252, 259–61
  hunger and, 245
  and social practices, 5–6, 14, 160, 162–63, 239, 288, 311
Christianity, 39, 55, 64n5
Cieza de León, Pedro de, 92
Clavijo y Fajardo, José, 23, 151, 161–65, 167, 175
cocido, 186, 191, 198n4, 211, 254, 281, 315n24
coconut, 275, 280, 291
coffee
  diet, 180, 285, 287–88
  for elites, 151, 169–70
  and social practices, 5–6, 160, 190, 327–28, 351
Colombia, 250, 291
colonialism, 8, 16, 21, 260
colonial period, 22, 26, 258, 304
Columbus, Christopher, 83, 100
commensality, 10, 55–56, 160
communist, 356

Como agua para chocolate (Esquivel), 265, 267
conquest, 22, 26, 77, 104, 108, 241–42, 245–46, 263
consumption
  classification, 84–86, 88–93, 145n4, 154–55, 231
  conspicuous, 161–62, 164–67, 174, 175n2
  food production and, 6, 15–16, 284, 296, 298, 304
  politics of, 1–2, 77, 150–51, 158, 179, 306
  religious, 44–45, 63
converso, 21, 39–44, 46–49, 56–59, 62–63, 64n2, 66n18, 68n28, 70n46
cookbook
  as historical source, 19–22, 24–25, 115, 256–58, 263–64, 267, 346–47
  politics, 220–22, 224, 226, 229–35, 240, 297
  writing, 10, 198, 307
  See also Martínez Montiño, Francisco
cooking
  as analytical tool, 3, 11–14, 158–59, 178, 216, 291–92, 305
  historical context of, 186, 203–10, 212–14, 251, 273–74, 279, 283
  literacy and, 18–20, 221–23, 229, 231–35
  material culture, 116, 118, 120, 122, 124, 128–30, 134, 139
  politics and, 44, 90, 92–93, 226
  practical applications, 23, 67n23, 259, 267, 281
  equipment, *120, 123, 127, 131, 132, 137*
corn
  cooking of, 243–46, 254–55, 267, 276, 284–86, 289–90, 292, 328
  crop, 110, 241
  in diet, 93, 259–64, 273, 278, 280–81
  identity and, 12, 104, 248–51, 299–300, 305, 314n10
  politics and, 238–39, 302
Cortés, Hernán, 109, 245–46, 262
Costa Rica, 276, 284
Cruz, Ramón de la, 23, 151, 155–60

Cuba, 5, 12–13, 27–28, 100, 282, 284
cuisine
    as analytical tool, 11–13, 20, 203–4, 229–34, 321, 331
    national, 7–8, 15, 23–26, 100, 105, 279–82, 284–86, 291–92
    popular, 207–10
    as a status symbol, 156–58, 161, 166, 288–89
    traditional, 225, 274–77, 307
    of writing, 19, 343
culinary
    capital, 15, 21, 24, 205–6, 212–13, 216–17
    context, 13, 100, 203, 346
    history, 10, 210–11
    triangle, 3, 342
Cullen de Aldao, Mercedes (*Marta*), 220, 222–23, 225, 229, 232–35
Cuneo, Michele da, 82–83

Darwinism, 348
deer, 244, 246, 249, 283, 286–87, 289, 292
diet
    historical context of, 203, 209, 231, 260
    identity and, 245, 285, 305, 314n18, 321, 329
    politics of, 87–89, 91, 93, 256, 263, 297
    religion and, 42, 47, 49, 53–54, 63, 154
    as status symbol, 82–85, 171, 287, 327
dietary laws, 41, 56
distinction
    in cooking, 126, 207, 244
    social, 23, 151, 158–59, 161–62, 165, 167, 174, 175n2
    symbols, 93, 345
Doménech, Ignacio, 24, 198, 203, 213–17
Dominican Republic, 277–78
drink
    identity and, 56, 154, 187, 249, 255, 290, 306–7
    politics and, 17, 157, 240, 296, 342
    types, 260, 263, 278–80
    See also specific drinks

eating
    disorders, 2, 8
    economic class and, 208, 234, 245, 309–11
    establishments, 181, 183, 185, 192, 195
    historical context of, 24, 89, 179, 329, 332, 354, 357
    identity and, 246, 273–74, 283, 287–88, 292, 304–5, 307, 321
    politics and, 9, 17–18, 20, 157, 159, 175n3, 296, 298
    religion and, 42, 48, 55, 63, 173
environment, 1, 2, 8, 11, 77, 178, 194, 291
Esquivel, Laura, 6, 9, 257, 265, 267, 346
ethnicity, 12, 27, 296, 304, 306

fat studies, 8–9
Feijoo, Benito Jerónimo, 23, 150–55
Fernández de Moratín, Leandro, 6, 189
Fernández de Oviedo, Gonzalo, 77–78, 86–87, 90, 92, 277, 285, 289
figón, figoneros, 181–82, 185
fish
    classification of, 84, 232–33
    cooking of, 131, 135, 263, 279, 280, 283
    historical context of, 242–43, 245–47
    identity and, 14, 49, 155–56, 171, 191, 215, 331
    in diet, 275, 285–87, 289, 291
fishing, 82, 228, 241, 349
flavor
    cooking and, 265–66, 282, 285, 289–90, 314n18
    historical context of, 242, 252
    identity and, 12, 85–86, 280
    literature and, 80–81
fonda, 160, 181, 183, 189–90, 192–94, 196
Fonda de San Sebastián, 186, 189
Fonda Española, 191–92
food studies, 296–97, 321, 340, 342
France
    cultural context, 11, 209, 227
    historical context, 179–81, 184, 189, 198, 267, 333, 346

frijoles, 14, 239, 241, 245, 252, 282
fruit
　classification of, 85–89, 242
　cooking of, 134–35, 235, 253, 281–82
　in diet, 273, 286, 290–92
　historical context of, 94n7, 105, 107, 171–73, 227, 257, 278, 334
　identity and, 91, 156, 244–47, 261, 300, 312, 331–32
　politics and, 14, 56, 81–83
fusion, 26, 77, 241, 258, 274

gastrocriticism, 5, 27, 296–97, 341–42
gastronomes, 23, 116, 239
gastronomy
　field of, 4, 10–11, 221, 227, 240–42
　molecular, 20
　national, 25, 247, 266
gastro-politics, 5, 15, 27, 296–98
gender
　differentials, 11, 159, 216, 221
　roles, 14, 303–5
　studies, 5, 19, 21, 27, 201–2, 296–98, 342, 350
Generation Zero, 5, 28
gluttony, 90, 156, 168, 170, 305
Golden Age, 16, 107–8, 179, 181, 202
Gregorio de Salas, Francisco, 23, 151, 172–74
Guimarães Rosa, João, 17, 321, 328–29, 337nn8–9
Gutiérrez, Pedro Juan, 28, 341, 344, 346, 348–49, 352

herbs
　classification of, 80–81
　cooking with, 134, 276
　historical context of, 240–44, 246–47, 307
　identity and, 85–86, 89, 260
Hernández, Francisco, 79–81, 94n2, 241
Honduras, 276
hotel, 185–86, 188–89, 192–98
Huarte de San Juan, Juan, 9, 53

humoral theory (humors), 40, 49–53, 66n21, 81, 83, 88, 154, 175n6
hunger
　historical context of, 108, 348–49
　identity and, 8, 16–17, 23, 27, 243–45
　literature and, 111, 151–52, 155–56, 167, 172, 214–15, 343, 351
　politics of, 14, 159, 170, 175n9, 309, 311–12, 314n13, 355
hunting, 16, 228, 241, 303
hybridization, 25, 258
hygiene, 287, 310, 315n19

Iberian Peninsula, 88, 208, 272–73, 283–84
identity
　food and, 15, 17, 54–55, 64, 90, 151, 238–39, 241
　historical context of, 245, 296, 341–42
　literature and, 202, 204, 216, 221, 225–26, 229, 306
　national, 12–13, 23, 27, 102, 156, 158, 162, 209–10
　politics, 21, 49, 298, 304
　religious, 42, 48, 58–59
immigration, 21, 274–75, 284, 291
indigenist, 262
indigenous
　cooking, 104, 243, 258–64, 280, 283, 289
　diet, 82–87, 89–91, 252, 286
　history, 79, 299
　peoples, 26, 93, 94n10, 272–77, 304, 314n12, 315n22
Inquisition (inquisitorial), 7, 11, 13, 40–41, 43, 58–59
insect, 244–45, 255–56
Italy, 116, 178, 180, 188, 196, 209, 324

Jews, 39–49, 55–63, 65–66, 68n29, 69nn35–37, 336, 348, 352
Jovellanos, Gaspar Melchor de, 151, 168
Juana Inés de la Cruz, 241, 257
Judaism, 39, 48, 55, 58, 69nn35–36

kitchens, *119, 120, 127*
  as analytical tool, 19, 77, 265, 323
  cultural context of, 12, 157, 198, 226–28, 231, 239, 282–85
  historical context of, 107, 258–59, 272, 276, 290–91
  literature and, 100, 103–4, 110, 205–6, 208, 224, 235, 332–34
  royal, 22–24, 179–81, 183

Ladino, 5, 26, 298, 301–2, 304, 308, 312, 314n14
Larra, Mariano José de, 183, 186
Lezama Lima, José, 104–5, 342
Lispector, Clarice, 17, 27, 321, 326, 336n7

Madrid, 24, 161, 170, 211, 213, 250
maize, 21, 94n10, 244, 249, 273, 279–80, 283, 286
markets
  cultural context of, 245–46, 248, 255–56
  historical context of, 197, 260, 262, 287–88
  politics of, 49, 55, 272, 309
Martínez Montiño, Francisco, 115–18, 120, 122–26, 128–31, 133–42, 203–7, 216–17
Mata, Juan de la, 175n7, 209
material culture, 17, 19–20, 23, 25, 116, 139, 231, 342
Maya, 26, 301–2, 304, 308, 313nn4–10
meat
  cooking, 122, 128, 146n8, 175n10, 198n4, 211–12, 235
  in diet, 12, 92, 154, 207, 267, 274, 279–81, 341
  literature and, 15, 28, 330, 343, 347, 349
  religion and, 44, 48, 100
  See also specific animals
medicine
  field of, 2, 9, 19, 81, 94n2, 175n6
  food and, 50, 154, 259, 266, 297
  historical context of, 55, 195

Meléndez Valdés, Juan, 23, 151, 168–70
memento mori, 99, 106, 111, 112n2
memory
  books, 43, 221
  cooking and, 7, 10, 205, 277
  cultural, 102, 213, 231, 260
  writing and, 78, 335
Mesoamerica, 108, 247–48, 273, 279, 315n21
Mesonero Romano, Ramón de, 182, 184, 190
Mestayer de Echagüe, María, 24, 203, 210–13, 216, 218n8
mestizaje, 12, 240, 242, 265
metate, 244, 249, 253, 259, 286
Mexico, 13–14, 29n5, 109, 288
miscegenation, 102, 240, 258, 322
mole, 25, 280, 286
Montoro, Antón de, 41–43, 64n6, 70n46
Muslim, 39–41, 49, 55, 60–63, 208

Nahuatl, 26, 79, 248, 256, 274, 276
Nassar, Raduan, 17, 27, 321, 330–32
Native American, 13, 26, 77, 82, 85, 108, 241, 285–86
nature
  food and, 5, 51, 63, 76, 89, 299
  theories on, 26, 78–79, 82–83, 174, 301, 304, 307–8
nature morte, 105–7, 111
neo-baroque, 10, 22, 99, 104
Neruda, Pablo, 9–11, 313n8
New Kingdom of Granada, 77, 87–88
New Spain, 77, 79–80, 87, 108, 241, 246, 252
New World, 8, 21–22, 77, 82, 89, 110, 208–9
nostalgia, 7, 15, 213, 291, 323

Old World, 21, 84, 110
olive oil, 209, 284–85
Ortega, Julio, 107–8, 110–11, 113n9
Ortiz, Fernando, 4, 11–13, 100, 102, 112

Padura Fuentes, Leonardo, 28, 341, 346, 350–52, 358
partridge, 45, 49, 156, 171, 246
Paso, Fernando del, 254, 256–57
Pérez Galdós, Benito, 6, 24, 180–81, 184, 186–87, 189, 191–92
Peru, 77, 109, 276, 278, 314n12
picaresque, 16, 157, 273, 349
pigeon, 206, 233, 246
pineapple
    classification of, 83, 86, 90
    diet, 245, 247, 273, 276, 281, 284, 290–91
pinole, 244, 280, 286, 292
plantain, 12, 14, 274–85, 287, 289, 291, 292
plants
    classification of, 79–81, 85, 87–89
    cooking of, 259, 268
    cultural context of, 13, 241–44, 246, 256, 300, 314n17
    historical context of, 248, 308
pork (pig)
    cooking of, 249–50, 265–66
    in diet, 253–55, 258–59, 273, 275–78, 282–89, 344–46
    historical context of, 206, 239, 309, 331, 348, 350
    identity and, 12, 42–43, 49, 63, 174
Portugal, 88, 135
postcolonial, 16, 344
potatoes
    in diet, 12, 93, 273, 281, 284–85
    historical context of, 109, 208, 239, 311
    identity and, 11, 303, 306
pre-Columbian, 13, 25–26, 282–83, 289
Puerto Rico, 277
pulque, 239, 245, 252, 260–63, 268

quesadillas, 243, 260
Quito, 77, 87

rabbit, 49, 171, 242, 246, 268
race
    food and, 39–75, 258, 263, 297

race (*continued*)
    identity and, 62, 314, 322
    theory, 21, 41, 60, 64, 201
racism, 40–41, 64, 245, 345
Ramos, Graciliano, 16–17, 27, 318–19, 321, 324–25, 333
Recchi, Nardo Antonio, 79–81
refresco, 161–67, 175n7
Reyes, Alfonso, 10, 112, 244, 246, 252, 257, 259
Rocha, Glauber, 16, 27, 319, 323–24
Román, Diego, 41, 64n6
roots, 81–83, 85–89, 246, 307–8, 330
royal kitchen, 22–24, 179–80

Sahagún, Bernardino de, 7, 241, 253
scala naturae, 8, 78
scarcity, 175n3, 274, 298, 308, 310, 328, 344, 346. See also hunger
Spain
    cuisine, 88, 178–81, 183–85, 208–13, 275, 277, 281, 285
    history, 10–11, 15, 17, 22–24, 107, 215, 289
    literature, 206, 355
Spaniard
    cuisine, 26, 82, 84–87, 89–93, 94nn1–10, 209, 273
    history, 193, 195, 198, 214, 245, 258, 285
Special Period, 5, 27–28
spices
    cooking with, 146n14, 175n10, 252, 289
    historical context of, 123–24, 169, 206, 208
    identity and, 12, 56, 239, 273, 286
starvation, 8, 18, 309–10
street food, 286–87
sugar
    cooking with, 93, 126, 134, 146n8, 223, 233, 252, 328
    identity and, 163, 244, 273–74, 280–82, 305–6
    importation, 4–6, 151, 284, 314n11
sugarcane, 246, 278–79, 289–92

sweet potato, 12, 86, 91–92, 273, 290–91

taco, 243, 255, 258, 260
tamal, 232, 275, 279–80, 282–83, 303–6, 311
taste
    as analytical tool, 4, 9, 14, 25, 151, 161, 334, 349
    economic class and, 23, 153–56, 166–67, 192, 233
    of food, 111, 235, 258–61, 274, 278–79, 281, 289–92, 306
    literature and, 158–59, 172, 227–28, 242, 283, 287, 303, 331
tianguis, 248, 255, 260, 272
tomatoes
    cooking of, 223, 245, 265, 268, 280–81, 303
    in diet, 208–9, 252–53, 273, 276, 286–87, 290–91, 293n4, 306
    historical context of, 158, 239, 242, 283–84, 332–35
Torres de Castex, Susana (Teófila Benavento), 220, 224–30, 232–35
tortilla, 125, 147n18, 285, 293n4, 303, 305–6, 354
tree, 49, 249, 260, 277, 279, 309, 313n7, 322. *See also* fruit; nature; plants
turkey, 262, 283, 305–6, 310, 350. *See also* birds; chicken
turnips, 12, 82–84, 171

United Fruit Company, 277, 301, 313n3, 314nn12–14
ut pictura poesis, 103–4

Valdés, Zoé, 28, 341, 344, 346–47, 350
Venezuela, 88, 250, 276, 280

water
    access, 23, 53–54, 116, 120–22, *120*, *121*, 192
    cooking with, 122, 130, 136, 234, 253, 268, 293n3, 328–29
    drinking of, 18, 92, 101, 163, 198n5, 280, 288
    element of, 78, 84, 308, 315n26
    geographical, 245, 247
    literary references to, 12, 45, 171, 180, 286, 301, 311
wheat
    flour, 136, 284–85
    identity and, 17, 53–54, 104, 169–70, 239, 259, 263, 273
wine
    historical context of, 151, 179–80, 182–83, 186, 191, 207, 239
    identity and, 14, 42, 63, 82, 156–57, 160–61, 284, 289
    literary references to, 171–74, 193, 330–31, 353–54

Ximénez de Cisneros, Francisco, 80–81, 87, 90–92

yucca, 12, 83, 91–93, 277–80, 306

www.ingramcontent.com/pod-product-compliance
Lightning Source LLC
Chambersburg PA
CBHW030518230426
43665CB00010B/663